D1478350

IDEAS IN CONTEXT

POLITICAL INNOVATION AND CONCEPTUAL CHANGE

IDEAS IN CONTEXT

Edited by Wolf Lepenies, Richard Rorty, J.B. Schneewind and Quentin Skinner

The books in this series will discuss the emergence of intellectual traditions and of related new disciplines. The procedures, aims and vocabularies that were generated will be set in the context of the alternatives available within the contemporary frameworks of ideas and institutions. Through detailed studies of the evolution of such traditions, and their modification by different audiences, it is hoped that a new picture will form in the development of ideas in their concrete contexts. By this means, artificial distinctions between the history of philosophy, of the various sciences, of society and politics, and of literature may be seen to dissolve.

Titles published in the series:

Richard Rorty, J.B. Schneewind and Quentin Skinner (eds.), *Philosophy in History*
J.G.A. Pocock, *Virtue, Commerce and History*
M.M. Goldsmith, *Private Vices, Public Benefits: Bernard Mandeville's Social and Political Thought*
A. Pagden (ed.), *The Languages of Political Theory in Early-Modern Europe*
D. Summers, *The Judgment of Sense*
L. Dickey, *Hegel: Religion, Economics and the Politics of Spirit, 1770–1807*
Margo Todd, *Christian Humanism and the Puritan Social Order*
Edmund Leites (ed.), *Conscience and Casuistry in Early Modern Europe*
Lynn S. Joy, *Gassendi the Atomist: Advocate of History in an Age of Science*
Gerd Gigerenzer *et al., The Empire of Chance: How Probability Changed Science and Everyday Life*
Wolf Lepenies, *Between Literature and Science: The Rise of Sociology*
Peter Novick, *That Noble Dream: The 'Objectivity Question' and the American Historical Profession*

This series is published with the support of the Exxon Education Foundation.

POLITICAL INNOVATION AND CONCEPTUAL CHANGE

EDITED BY

TERENCE BALL
JAMES FARR
RUSSELL L. HANSON

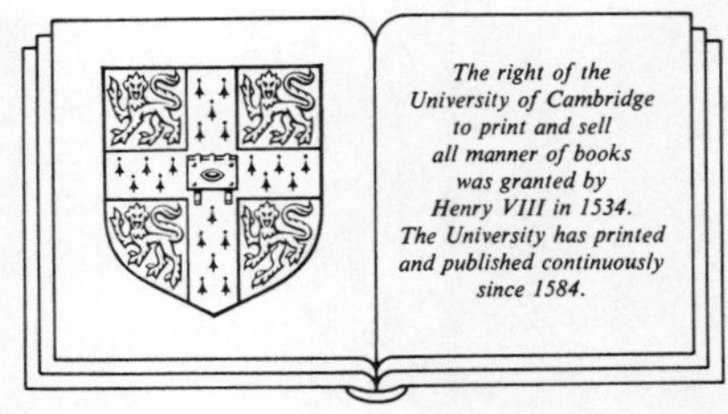
The right of the
University of Cambridge
to print and sell
all manner of books
was granted by
Henry VIII in 1534.
The University has printed
and published continuously
since 1584.

CAMBRIDGE UNIVERSITY PRESS

CAMBRIDGE
NEW YORK NEW ROCHELLE MELBOURNE SYDNEY

Published by the Press Syndicate of the University of Cambridge
The Pitt Building, Trumpington Street, Cambridge CB2 1RP
32 East 57th Street, New York, NY 10022, USA
10 Stamford Road, Oakleigh, Melbourne 3166, Australia

First published 1989

Printed in Great Britain at the Bath Press, Avon

British Library cataloguing in publication data

Political innovation and conceptual change. – (Ideas in context).
1. Politics. Linguistic aspects
I. Ball, Terence II Farr, James
III. Hanson, Russell L., *1953–*
IV. Series 320'.014

Library of Congress cataloguing in publication data

Political innovation and conceptual change
edited by Terence Ball, James Farr, Russell L. Hanson
p. cm. – (Ideas in context)
Includes index
ISBN 0 521 35190 1
ISBN 0 521 35978 3
1. Political science – Terminology – History.
2. Political science – History.
I. Ball, Terence. II. Farr, James. III. Hanson, Russell L., 1953–
IV. Series
JA61.P65 1988
320–dc19 88–10211 CIP

ISBN 0 521 35190 1 hard covers
ISBN 0 521 35978 3 paperback

CONTENTS

CONTRIBUTORS

Terence Ball is Professor of Political Science at the University of Minnesota. He is the author of *Transforming Political Discourse* (1988), editor of *Idioms of Inquiry* (1987), coeditor (with James Farr) of *After Marx* (1984) and *Conceptual Change and the Constitution* (with J.G.A. Pocock), and the author of several essays in political theory and the history of political thought.

Richard Dagger is Associate Professor of Political Science at Arizona State University. His essays on rights, political obligation, and other topics in political and legal philosophy have appeared in several professional journals and books. At present he is engaged on a study to be entitled *Politics and the Pursuit of Autonomy*.

Mary G. Dietz is Associate Professor of Political Science at the University of Minnesota. She is the author of *Between the Human and the Divine: The Political Thought of Simone Weil* (1988) and a variety of articles on the history of ideas and feminist political thought. She is currently at work on a longer study of patriotism and conceptual change.

John Dunn is Professor of Political Theory at the University of Cambridge and a Fellow of King's College. His books include *The Political Thought of John Locke* (1969); *Modern Revolutions* (1972); *Western Political Theory in the Face of the Future* (1979); *Political Obligation in its Historical Context* (1980); *Locke* (1984); *The Politics of Socialism* (1984); and *Rethinking Modern Political Theory* (1985). He is the editor of *The Economic Limits to Modern Politics* (forthcoming 1988).

J. Peter Euben is a member of the Committee on Classics and Professor of Politics and the History of Consciousness at the University of California-Santa Cruz. He is the editor of *Greek Tragedy and Political Theory* (1987). His book *The Road Not Taken* will be published in 1989. He is currently working on a book on political education and democratic politics.

James Farr is Associate Professor of Political Science at the University of Minnesota. He is coeditor of *After Marx* (1984) and author of a number of articles in the history and philosophy of the social sciences. He is currently studying the science of politics in the early American republic.

Mark Goldie is Fellow, Lecturer, and Director of Studies in History at Churchill College, Cambridge. He has published several articles on the political and intellectual history of later Stuart England, and has a book, *The Tory Ideology: Politics, Religion and Ideas in Restoration England*, forthcoming from Cambridge University Press.

J.A.W. Gunn is Professor of Political Studies at Queen's University, Kingston, Canada, and was Head of the Department of Political Studies from 1975 to 1983. He has published *Politics and the Public Interest in the Seventeenth Century* (1969), *Factions No More* (1972), *Beyond Liberty and Property* (1983), and, with J.P. Matthews and D.M. Schurman, has edited *Benjamin Disraeli, Letters* (1982). He is now writing a book on the idea of "public opinion" in French thought of the eighteenth century.

Russell L. Hanson is Associate Professor of Political Science at Indiana University, Bloomington. He is the author of *The Democratic Imagination in America: Conversations With Our Past* (1985) and articles on American politics and political thought. He is currently studying the political underpinnings of welfare policy in the United States.

Graham Maddox is Associate Professor of Politics at the University of New England, New South Wales. He is author of *Australian Democracy in Theory and Practice* (1985) and articles on constitutionalism and constitutional history.

Hanna Fenichel Pitkin is Professor of Political Science at the University of California-Berkeley. She is the author of *The Concept of Representation, Wittgenstein and Justice*, and *Fortune is a Woman: Gender and Politics in the Thought of Niccolò Machiavelli.*

Alan Ryan is Professor of Politics at Princeton University and was until recently Reader in Politics and Fellow of New College, Oxford. He is the author of *The Philosophy of John Stuart Mill* (1970 and 1987), *The Philosophy of the Social Sciences* (1970), *J.S. Mill* (1975), *Property and Political Theory* (1984), *Property* (1987), and *Russell: A Political Life* (1988).

Quentin Skinner is Professor of Political Science in the University of Cambridge and a Fellow of Christ's College. His books include a study of Machiavelli and a two-volume work, *The Foundations of Modern Political Thought*. His most recent book is *Meaning and Context*, a collection of his papers on interpretation, edited by Professor J.H. Tully.

Michael Walzer is Professor of Social Science at the Institute for Advanced Study, Princeton, New Jersey. His books include *Obligations*, *Just and Unjust Wars*, and *Spheres of Justice*.

PREFACE

The present volume has a dual purpose. The first is to re-emphasize the by now familiar claim that politics is a linguistically constituted activity. Our Editors' Introduction and the two essays that follow spell out this claim and develop a number of implications following from it. Not the least of these is that this claim, which has been more often asserted than defended, requires detailed and in-depth exploration within the context of actual political discourses. This takes us to our second and more pervasive purpose, which is to show that the concepts constitutive of political beliefs and behavior have historically mutable meanings. To trace the changing meanings of specific concepts is the task undertaken by our other contributors. Their conceptual histories reveal the mutations of meaning that attend all our political concepts.

Since there is no one right way to construct a conceptual history, the editors have not attempted to impose any orthodoxy of method or approach. We have, to be sure, selected a particular set of concepts for study and arranged them in a specific order. Our selection of concepts is hardly comprehensive. Some unquestionably important ones – equality, liberty, authority, and power among them – are altogether absent. However, our aim here is to show, in a fairly selective way, how we might begin to think about the political dimension of conceptual change and the conceptual dimension of political innovation, both being different sides of the same coin of communication. To have aimed at anything more comprehensive would have required greater ambition and more erudition than the editors possess. While we greatly admire such recent editorial undertakings as Professors Brunner, Conze, and Koselleck's *Geschichtliche Grundbegriffe* and Reichardt and Schmitt's *Handbuch politisch-sozialer Grundbegriffe in Frankreich*, we have not sought to duplicate their encyclopedic efforts. What we do share with them, however, is the common conviction that speaking a language involves taking on a world, and altering the concepts constitutive of that language involves nothing less than remaking the world. Insofar as the political world is linguistically and communicatively constituted, then, conceptual change must be understood politically, and political change conceptually.

In ordering the chapters we sought to balance two considerations. We wanted to present these conceptual histories roughly in the order in which the concepts came to be historically important. Hence, those concepts which early on became significant in Western political discourse appear first in the following pages. Other concepts follow more or less in the order they rose to special prominence in politics, though some of them actually entered discourse much earlier. We departed from this rule of thumb where it seemed important to group concepts that dealt with closely related themes. Concepts referring mainly to the institutions of government are followed by those which have to do with popular participation in government, and these in turn are followed by concepts bearing on the popular reconstitution of government – a thematic ordering that is fairly consistent with the historical appearance of particular concepts.

In commissioning and assembling these essays the editors have incurred numerous debts, more of them of a moral than a financial nature. We are especially grateful to our contributors for being so patient through numerous delays and requests for revision. To Quentin Skinner we owe a special debt for the various ways in which he contributed to the present volume. His services as series editor, contributor, critic, and advisor have proved invaluable. Each of the editors also thanks the others for having remained relatively good humored through a rather long and sometimes arduous journey.

Finally, we would like to express our appreciation to Roberta Scott and Barbara Hopkins, who typed the manuscript, and Steven Flinn, who provided technical assistance. David Sharp helped prepare the final manuscript, ably attending to matters of style and format. Lawrence Biskowski read proofs and prepared the index. Dr. Jeremy Mynott, Joanna Rainbow, Richard Fisher, and Ann Rex of Cambridge University Press expeditiously handled matters of production with care. For all this help we are most grateful.

Terence Ball

James Farr

Russell L. Hanson

Editors' Introduction

"Language," Locke wrote, "is the great bond and common tie of society" (1961, bk.III, i: 1). By this he meant that language enables us to engage in the practices that make us the moral and political creatures that we are. It is by virtue of possessing a common stock of concepts that we constitute the communities in which we live. And yet the common tie of language is apt to become worn and frayed. There is a real and recurrent fear that our conceptually constituted communities are, after all, among the most fragile and least durable of all human creations. Not surprisingly, then, the fear is often aired in the form of a cautionary tale in which communicative entropy ends in individual isolation and mute violence. It is a tale told most memorably, perhaps, in the biblical story of Babel, but there are more recognizably political variations on the theme in Thucydides' account of the revolution at Corcyra and in Hobbes's imaginary state of nature. They are tales with a common moral: the loss of a common language is the loss of community and the destruction of a common world.

In speaking of losing the language out of which our common world is constituted we do not refer to the entity analyzed by modern linguists. A moral or political language is not, that is, reducible without remainder to the vocabulary, grammatical structure, and syntax of this or that natural language – Attic Greek, say, or Latin, or modern English. Rather, a moral or political language is a medium of shared understanding and an arena of action because the concepts embedded in it inform the beliefs and practices of political agents. The social and political world is conceptually and communicatively constituted, or, more precisely, preconstituted. According to this constitutive view of language, who and what we are, how we arrange and classify and think about our world – and how we act in it – are deeply delimited by the argumentative and rhetorical resources of our language. The limits of one's language mark the limits of one's world. Our moral language maps political possibilities and impossibilities; it enables us to do certain things even as it discourages or disables us from doing others. But although our language maps moral and political possibilities, it is not a map depicting an independently existing topography. On the contrary, the political landscape is partially constituted by that which locates and marks its main features. Far from being fixed or stable, these features change over time. Thus map and terrain vary together.

As our language goes, so goes our society. "Even as people belong to the same culture by the use of the same language," writes Bertrand De Jouvenel, "so they belong to the same society by the understanding of the same moral language. As this common moral language extends, so does society; as it breaks up, so does society" (De Jouvenel 1957: 304). Many of the major works of political philosophy can be read as responses to, reflections upon, and antidotes for conceptual chaos and communicative breakdown (White 1984). These usually take the form of a critique in which the political philosopher attempts to undermine an existing moral or political language that he takes to be incoherent or contradictory, often in preparation for proposing particular conceptual innovations of his own. Such conceptual changes are therefore never without political import. For, as Alasdair MacIntyre (1966: 2–3) observes,

> since to possess a concept involves behaving or being able to behave in certain ways in certain circumstances, to alter concepts, whether by modifying existing concepts or by making new concepts available or by destroying old ones, is to alter behavior.

Conceptual change is therefore itself a species of political innovation. To link political and conceptual change in this way leads us to view the world in ways that might at first sight seem disturbing. There are at least two sources of unease. The first is that this perspective undermines the so-called contingency thesis, which holds that linguistic entities like political (or moral, or economic, or scientific) theories are one thing and (empirical) reality another; from which it follows that political (or moral, or economic, or scientific) change is one thing and conceptual change another. On this view conceptual change is an altogether secondary matter, perhaps even an effect or a reflection or an epiphenomenon. The contingency view has had far-reaching consequences, not least for the thinking of those who believe themselves immune to philosophical influences. Something like the contingency view undergirds the conception of the role of political ideas shared by Namierites and Marxists alike (thereby proving nothing, save perhaps that it is not only politics that makes strange bedfellows). Yet to accept this view, as the first two essays attempt to show, is to subscribe to a distorted and misleading account of the relation between thought and action, theory and practice. An alternative "constitutive" view of language yields an altogether different and arguably more accurate account of that relation.

A second and closely connected source of unease is that the constitutive view appears to entail relativistic implications of a rather radical sort. For if politics is an activity partially constituted via concepts whose meanings are historically mutable, it then follows that there are no objective or transhistorical truths – no political givens, no grounds, no rock-bottom bases upon which arguments can be founded and against which truths can be tested. And if moral codes are historically mutable, nihilism necessarily follows. The conceptual chaos of the Corcyrean Revolution and Hobbes's state of nature become the norm, not the exception. Several of the essays address this sense of unease, and others try to show in some detail why the constitutive idea of "conceptual history," although arguably relativistic, is anything but nihilistic. For conceptual histories tell stories of change within continuity and of continuity within change. Concepts, or more precisely the criteria for their correct application, cannot be changed at will or by whim.

Conceptual-cum-political change is at once critical, creative, and conservative. It is critical, inasmuch as it stems from a sense that, in Lamartine's famous phrase, the world has jumbled its catalog or has somehow become deranged. To expose and to criticize contradictions or incoherences in one's moral language is to begin to remake and rearrange one's moral and political world. This process is itself a creative one, in as much as it may require argumentative and rhetorical skills of a fairly high order. Although critical and creative, conceptual change has a profoundly conservative aspect as well. For it never occurs *de novo* or *ex nihilo*. Almost always occurring with reference to relatively settled and stable linguistic conventions, conceptual change tends to be piecemeal and gradual, sometimes proceeding at an almost glacial pace. Paraphrasing what Burke says about the state, we might say that a language that is without the means of change is without the means of its own preservation. And what is preserved and periodically enhanced is nothing less than the possibility of communication and, hence, of community itself.

To construct a conceptual history is to show in some detail how this process works in specific historical settings. It is also to trace the thread of life and language that connects past and present. Far from being purely academic or antiquarian, our aim in conducting these conversations with our past is a political one. It stems from an uneasy sense that our own culture is in the throes of a deepening crisis, a crisis characterized in no small part by the breakdown and corruption of a common moral and political language. The crisis afflicting our culture bears an uncanny resemblance to the earlier one narrated by Thucydides. And as words lost their meaning and the measured eloquence of Pericles gave way to the verbal and physical violence of Cleon, so do we live in an age of one-dimensional discourse, of Newspeak and psychobabble and bureaucratese spoken by communicators great and small who communicate little save violence and threats of violence.

The construction of conceptual histories can have the emancipatory effect of opening up the unidimensional discourse in whose terms our political and cultural conversations have for too long been conducted. Consider, for example, the concept of corruption. A conceptual history suggests that our present understanding of corruption might itself be impoverished if not corrupt. To retrace the history of "corruption" is to show how our use of the concept is in certain respects contradictory if not incoherent. Or consider the concept of patriotism. To be a patriot or to be patriotic, we are told nowadays, is to be uncritically supportive of one's government, whoever its leaders and whatever their policies. And since "patriot" has considerable commendatory force, would-be patriots are unlikely to be outspokenly critical of their government. A conceptual history, however, calls this present-day understanding into question by showing that to be a patriot or to be patriotic was once to have the courage to take a principled stand against one's government.

This is not to say, however, that conceptual histories are romantic, or still less reactionary, attempts to return to or to restore earlier meanings. Quite the contrary. The aim is not to restore the past but to remember it and to retrace the path to the present (O'Neill 1976). Novelists as different as Dos Passos and Proust and Orwell and Kundera have shown how remembering our past enables us to have a clearer – and perchance a more critical – perspective on our present. Little wonder, then, that the modern state, East and West, attempts to control the past by rewriting history or, failing that, by obliterating memory altogether. Citizens adrift in the present and cut off from their past become more manipulable and pliable subjects. If we are not to remain lost in the present we have little choice save to retrace our steps. By uncovering and recovering lost meanings conceptual histories enable us to escape the politically stultifying confines of a parochial and increasingly dangerous present.

REFERENCES

De Jouvenel, Bertrand. 1957. *Sovereignty: An Inquiry Into the Political Good*, translated by J.F. Huntingdon. Chicago, IL: University of Chicago Press.

Locke, John. 1961. *An Essay Concerning Human Understanding*, 2 vols., edited by J.W. Yolton. London: Oxford University Press.

MacIntyre, Alasdair. 1966. *A Short History of Ethics*. New York: Macmillan.

O'Neill, John. 1976. "Critique and Remembrance." In O'Neill (ed.), *On Critical Theory*. New York: Seabury Press, pp.1–11.

White, James Boyd. 1984. *When Words Lose their Meaning: Constitutions and Reconstitutions of Language, Character, and Community*. Chicago, IL: University of Chicago Press.

1

Language and political change

QUENTIN SKINNER

I

This volume is concerned principally with the relations between our changing political world and the changing language we use to describe and appraise it. While individual chapters trace these interconnections in a series of conceptual histories, in this opening essay I shall attempt in a more general way to consider what can be learned about the processes of political innovation by examining the changing meanings of words. This is of course a vast question, and in order to make it manageable I shall concentrate on one recent and highly influential study which has focused on the links between linguistic and political change. The work I have in mind – which I shall use as a stalking-horse in what follows – is Raymond Williams's *Keywords*.[1] It is Williams's central contention that a study of "variations and confusions of meaning" may help us to improve our understanding of matters of "historical and contemporary substance" (1976: 21; 1983: 24). If we take "certain words at the level at which they are generally used," he suggests, and scrutinize their developing structures of meaning "in and through historical time," we may be able "to contribute certain kinds of awareness" to current social and

[1] Raymond Williams, *Keywords: A Vocabulary of Culture and Society* (London: Fontana, paperback, 1976), reissued in a revised and expanded form by Fontana in 1983. My critique of the book originally appeared (under the title "The Idea of a Cultural Lexicon") in *Essays in Criticism*, July, 1979. For help with that version I remain greatly indebted to John Dunn, Susan James, Jonathan Lear, Christopher Ricks, and Richard Rorty. The present essay is a revision and extension of the (slightly altered) reprint of the 1979 article which appeared in *The State of the Language*, ed. L. Michaels and C. Ricks, Berkeley: University of California Press, 1980, pp. 562–78. I gratefully acknowledge their permission to publish it here in its revised form. Most of the claims in Williams which I criticized in 1979 and 1980 have been revised or deleted in Williams's 1983 edition. I have therefore given page references to both editions of his book.

political debates, and in particular an "extra edge of consciousness" (Williams 1976: 20–1; 1983: 23–4). But what precise kinds of awareness can we hope to attain from studying the histories of keywords? And how should we conduct our studies in order to ensure that this awareness is duly attained? These are the questions I should like to examine at somewhat greater length.

II

Before proceeding, however, we need if possible to neutralize one serious doubt. It might be objected that, in singling out "a shared body of words," we are focusing on the wrong unit of analysis altogether (Williams 1976: 13; 1983: 15). Williams's aim, he tells us, is to illuminate "ways not only of discussing but at another level of seeing many of our central experiences" (1976: 12–13; 1983: 15). But if we wish to grasp how someone sees the world – what distinctions he[2] draws, what classifications he accepts – what we need to know is not what words he uses but rather what concepts he possesses.

It is true that this objection may appear a purely verbal one. For it might be replied – and the claim has often been made – that possessing a concept is equivalently a matter of knowing the meaning of a word. This certainly seems to be Williams's own view, for in discussing the term *nature* he equates "the word and the concept," and in speaking of *democracy* he explains how the "concept" is "embodied" in the word.[3]

However, to argue for any such equivalence is undoubtedly a mistake. First of all, it cannot be a necessary condition of my possessing a concept that I need to understand the correct application of a corresponding term. Suppose, for example, that I am studying Milton's thought, and want to know whether Milton considered it important that a poet should display a high degree of originality. The answer seems to be that he felt it to be of the greatest importance. When he spoke of his own aspirations at the beginning of *Paradise Lost*, what he particularly emphasized was his decision to deal with "things unattempted yet in prose or rhyme." But I could

[2] Or she, of course. But in what follows I shall often allow myself the convenience of treating "he," "his," etc., as abbreviations, where appropriate, for "he and she," "his and her," etc.

[3] Williams (1976: 84, 189). But in the later edition (1983: 95, 224), these claims are deleted, and in the new Introduction Williams (1983: 21) explicitly acknowledges "the difficult relations between words and concepts."

never have arrived at this conclusion by examining Milton's use of the word *originality*. For while the concept is clearly central to his thought, the word did not enter the language until a century or more after his death. Although a history of the word *originality* and its various uses could undoubtedly be written, such a survey would by no means be the same as a history of the concept of originality – a consideration often ignored in practice by historians of ideas.

Moreover, it cannot be a sufficient condition of my possessing a concept that I understand the correct application of a corresponding term. There is still the possibility (explored by Wittgenstein as well as Kant) that I may believe myself to be in possession of a concept when this belief is in fact mistaken. Consider for example the difficulties raised by certain highly general terms such as *being* or *infinity*. A whole community of language users may be capable of applying these terms with perfect consistency. Yet it might be possible to show that there is simply no concept which answers to any of their agreed usages.

What then is the relationship between concepts and words? We can scarcely hope to capture the answer in a single formula, but I think we can at least say this: the surest sign that a group or society has entered into the self-conscious possession of a new concept is that a corresponding vocabulary will be developed, a vocabulary which can then be used to pick out and discuss the concept with consistency. This suggests that, while we certainly need to exercise more caution than Williams does in making inferences from the use of words to the understanding of concepts and back again, there is nevertheless a systematic relationship between words and concepts to be explored. The possession of a concept will at least *standardly* be signalled by the employment of a corresponding term. As long as we bear in mind that "standardly" means neither necessarily nor sufficiently, I think we may legitimately proceed.

III

If our aim is to illuminate ideological disputes through the study of linguistic disagreements, the first issue we need to clarify – as Williams acknowledges – is obviously this: what exactly are we debating about a word when we find ourselves debating whether or not it ought to be applied as a description of a particular action or state of affairs?

Unfortunately, Williams's answer is confusingly vague. "What is really happening in such encounters," he claims, is a "process" whereby "meanings are offered" and are then "confirmed, asserted, qualified, changed" (Williams 1976: 9; 1983: 11–12). All such debates are thus taken to be about "meanings"; about the "historical origins and developments" which have issued in the "present meanings" of the terms involved (Williams 1976: 13, 19–20; 1983: 15, 22–23).

This question-begging tendency to speak without further explication about "changes of meaning" is due, I believe, to the fact that Williams at no point tries to isolate and describe the class of terms in which he is chiefly interested – the class of what he calls the "strong" or "persuasive" words, the words which "involve ideas and values" (Williams 1976: 12, 15; 1983: 14, 17). No consistent account of how certain words come to "involve values" is ever presented. But it seems clear that, if any further progress is to be made in discussing the phenomenon of meaning change in ideological debates, the provision of such an analysis will have to be treated as a crucial preliminary step. As it happens, this is a less Herculean task than might be feared. A great deal of attention has lately been paid by theorists of language as well as moral philosophers to isolating and commenting on precisely these terms.[4] Drawing on their accounts, we may say, I think, that three main requirements need to be met if such terms are to be understood and correctly applied.

First, it is necessary to know the nature and range of the criteria in virtue of which the word or expression is standardly employed. Suppose, for example, that I am unaware of the meaning of the appraisive term *courageous*, and ask someone to explain to me how to use the word properly. He (or she) will most naturally reply by mentioning various criteria that serve to mark off the word from similar and contrasting adjectives, and so provide it with its distinctive role in our language of social description and appraisal. When listing these criteria, he will surely have to include at least the following: that the word can be used only in the context of voluntary actions; that the actor involved must have faced some danger; that he must have faced it with some consciousness of its nature; and he must have faced it heedfully, with some sense of the probable consequences of the action involved. Summarizing these criteria (in what is only apparently a tautology), we may say that the conditions

[4] Among moral philosophers I am most indebted to Foot (1958); Murdoch (1970); and the very illuminating comments in Hampshire (1959), especially pp. 195–222. Among philosophers of language, my approach owes most to the writings of Austin (1975); Wittgenstein (1959); and the analysis of Gottlob Frege's views presented in Dummett (1973a), especially pp. 81–109.

under which the term *courageous* can be applied are such that the action involved must have been a courageous one.

Next, to apply an appraisive term correctly I also need to know its range of reference. I need, that is, to have a clear sense of the nature of the circumstances in which the word can properly be used to designate particular actions or states of affairs. The concept of reference has often been taken to be an aspect or feature of the meaning of a word. But it is perhaps more helpful to treat the understanding of the reference of a word as a consequence of understanding the criteria for applying it correctly. To grasp these criteria is to understand the sense of the word, its role in the language, and thus its correct use. Once I have acquired this understanding, I may expect in consequence to be able to exercise the further and more mysterious skill of relating the word to the world. I may expect, for example, to be able to pick out just those actions which are properly to be called courageous, and to discuss the sort of circumstances in which we might wish to apply that particular description, or might wonder whether we ought to apply it rather than another one. For instance, someone might call it courageous if I faced a painful death with cheerfulness. However, it might be objected that strictly speaking no danger is involved in such circumstances, and thus that we ought not to speak of courage but rather of fortitude. Or again, someone might call it courageous if I stepped up from the circus audience to deputize for the lion tamer. But it might be countered that this is such a heedless action that it ought not to be viewed as courage but rather as sheer recklessness. Both these arguments are about the reference (but not the meaning) of *courageous*: both are concerned with whether a given set of circumstances – what a lawyer would call the facts of the case – are such as to yield the agreed criteria for the application of the given appraisive term.

To apply any word to the world, we need to have a clear grasp of both its sense and its reference. But in the case of appraisive terms a further element of understanding is also required. We need in addition to know what exact range of attitudes the term can standardly be used to express. (To adopt J. L. Austin's jargon: it is necessary to know what type of speech acts the word can be used to perform.) For example, no one can he said to have grasped the correct application of the adjective *courageous* if they remain unaware that it is standardly used to commend, to express approval, and especially to express (and solicit) admiration for any action it is used to describe. To call an action courageous is at once to describe it and to place it in a specific moral light. Thus I can praise or rejoice at an action by calling it courageous, but I cannot condemn or sneer at it by describing it in this way.

If these are the three main things we need to know in order to isolate the class of appraisive terms and apply them correctly, we can now return to the question raised at the beginning of this section. I asked what we might be debating about a keyword if we found ourselves asking whether or not it ought to be applied in a particular case. As we have seen, Williams's answer is that such arguments must be about the senses or meanings of the words involved. As I have sought to show, however, we might be disagreeing about one of at least three different things, not all of which are self-evidently disagreements about meaning: about the criteria for applying the word; about whether the agreed criteria are present in a given set of circumstances; or about what range of speech acts the word can be used to perform.

IV

So far I have tried to isolate the main debates that arise over the application of our appraisive vocabulary to our social world. I turn now to what I take to be the crucial question: in what sense are these linguistic disagreements also disagreements about our social world itself?

I have suggested that one type of argument over appraisive terms centres on the criteria for applying them. Now this is certainly a substantive social debate as well as a linguistic one. For it can equally well be characterized as an argument between two rival social theories and their attendant methods of classifying social reality.

As an illustration of such a dispute, recall the way in which Marcel Duchamp liked to designate certain familiar objects (coat-pegs, lavatory bowls) as works of art, thereby causing them to be framed and hung on the walls of galleries. Some critics have accepted that these are indeed significant works of art, on the grounds that they help us to sharpen and extend our awareness of everyday things. Others have insisted that they are not works of art at all, on the grounds that we cannot simply *call* something a work of art, since works of art have to be deliberately created.

This disagreement arises at the linguistic level. It centres on whether or not a certain criterion (the exercise of skill) should or should not be regarded as a necessary condition for the correct application of a particular appraisive term (*a work of art*). But this is certainly a substantive social dispute as well. What is at issue is whether or not a certain range of objects ought or ought not to be treated as having a rather elevated status and significance. And it is obvious that a great deal may depend on how this question is answered.

A number of the arguments in *Keywords* are primarily of this character. For example, the essays on "literature" and "science" largely fit this analysis, as does the useful discussion of "the unconscious," where Williams actually points out that "different theories" have generated "confusions between different senses" of the term (1976: 272; 1983: 322). Moreover, Williams is surely right to claim that in these cases the argument is in fact about the senses or meanings of the words involved. It is true that powerful voices have lately been raised against the contention that, if we introduce a new theory relating to a given subject matter (for example, what constitutes a work of art) this will inevitably give rise to changes in the meanings of the constitutive terms.[5] And there is little doubt that Paul Feyerabend and other post-empiricists have tended to employ this assumption with an altogether excessive enthusiasm. Certainly we cannot readily say that every change of theory brings about a change in the meaning of all the words involved (if only because nouns and adjectives shift in meaning so much more readily than, say, conjunctions). Moreover, it seems unduly anarchistic to claim that the meaning of a word must have changed if we simply change our beliefs about whatever the word is customarily used to denote (although it is admittedly very hard to think of clear cases in which meanings have in fact remained constant in the face of changing beliefs).[6] However, it does seem that if someone is mistaken about the criteria for applying a term, then he cannot be said to know its current meaning. And since I have argued that the question of whether Duchamp's coat-peg is a work of art is (at one level) an argument about the criteria for applying the term *a work of art*, I agree with Williams that in this type of argument about keywords the disagreement really is about the meaning of the word concerned.

What Williams misses, however, in his account of these disputes is

[5] For an attack on this line of thought, see Putnam (1975).

[6] Even Putnam's examples are unconvincing. In "How Not to Talk about Meaning," he takes the case of *gold*, and argues that the meaning of the word would not be affected if we found gold rusting, and were thus obliged to change our beliefs about the substance. This seems dogmatic. Would we really go on saying things like "as good as gold"? And if not, would we not have to concede that the meaning of *gold* had changed? (See Putnam 1975: 127–8.)

their almost paralyzingly radical character. He remains content to suppose that in all discussions about "meaning" we can "pick out certain words, of an especially problematical kind" and consider only "their own internal developments and structures."[7] This fails to recognize the implications of the fact that a term such as *art* gains its meaning from the place it occupies within an entire conceptual scheme. To change the criteria for applying it will thus be to change a vast deal else besides. Traditionally, the concept of art has been connected with an ideal of workmanship, has been opposed to the "merely useful," has been employed as an antonym for *nature* and so on. If we now endorse the suggestion that an *objet trouvé* or a manufactured article can count as a work of art, we at once sever all these and many other conceptual links. So an argument over the application of the term *art* is potentially nothing less than an argument over two rival (though not of course incommensurable)[8] ways of approaching and dividing up a large tract of our cultural experience. Williams appears in short to have overlooked the strongly holistic implications of the fact that, when a word changes its meaning, it also changes its relationship to an entire vocabulary.[9] What this tells us about such changes is that we must be prepared to focus not on the "internal structure" of particular words, but rather on their role in upholding complete social philosophies.

V

Even if we agree about the criteria for applying an appraisive term, I have suggested that a second type of dispute can arise over its use: a dispute about whether a given set of circumstances can be claimed to yield the criteria in virtue of which the term is normally employed. Again, such a disagreement will certainly be a substantive social one, not merely linguistic in character. For what is being contended in effect is that a refusal to apply the term in a certain situation may constitute an act of social insensitivity or a failure of social awareness.

As an illustration of this second type of argument, consider the

[7] Williams (1983: 22–3), slightly revised from the earlier version (1976: 20). Williams (1983: 23) protests at the kind of reader who, in criticizing this approach, is "content to reassert the facts of connection and interaction from which this whole inquiry began." Williams's new Introduction is thus explicit about the problems posed by a holistic (and in that sense a skeptical) approach to "meanings." But I cannot see that the implications of this skepticism have been accommodated even in the revised version of his text.

[8] Otherwise it is hard to see how the disputants could be *arguing*.

[9] On this point see Dummett (1973b).

contention that wives in ordinary middle-class families at the present time can properly be described as suffering exploitation, as being an exploited class. The social argument underlying this linguistic move might be characterized as follows. It ought to be evident to all persons of goodwill that the circumstances of contemporary family life are such that this strongly condemnatory term does indeed (if you think about it) fit the facts of the case. Conversely, if we fail to acknowledge that the application of the term *exploitation* – in virtue of its agreed criteria – is indeed appropriate in the circumstances, then we are willfully refusing to perceive the institution of the family in its true and baleful light.

This is clearly a dispute of an entirely different character from the first type of argument I singled out. Nevertheless, there has been a persistent tendency among moral and political philosophers to conflate the two. Consider, for example, the analysis Stuart Hampshire offers in *Thought and Action* (1959: 197) of an imagined debate between a Marxist and a liberal in which the latter is "startled to find that actions of his, to which he has never thought to attach a political significance, in his sense of 'political,' are given a political significance" by his Marxist opponent. As the above quotation already indicates, Hampshire (1959: 196) classifies this kind of disagreement as one about the "sense" of the word "political"; as "a disagreement about the criteria of application" of the term. If this is a genuine argument, however, it is obviously crucial that the Marxist should be able to claim with some plausibility that he is employing the term in virtue of its *agreed* sense. It is not clear that he can even be said to be arguing with the liberal if he is simply content to point out that, as Hampshire (1959: 197) puts it, he has a different concept of "the political," with the result that he and the liberal are both confined to "the largely separated worlds of their thought." It is even less clear, if this is all that he wishes to point out, why the liberal should feel in the least affected by the argument, given that it amounts to nothing more than a declaration of an intention to use a certain appraisive term in an idiosyncratic way. If the Marxist is genuinely seeking to persuade the liberal to share or at least acknowledge some political insight, he needs in effect to make two points. One is of course that the term *political* can appropriately be applied to a range of actions where the liberal has never thought of applying it. But the other, which his application of the term challenges the liberal to admit, is that this is due not to a disagreement about the meaning of the term, but rather to the fact that the liberal is a person of blinkered political sensitivity and awareness.

The same confusion appears to afflict many of Williams's discussions about keywords. He gives historical examples of debates about, for example, whether a certain procedure can be appraised as *empirical*, whether a particular kind of household can be called a *family*, whether someone can be said to have an *interest* in a particular state of affairs, and so on (Williams 1976: 99, 109, 143; 1983: 115, 131, 171). In each case he classifies the dispute as one about the "sense" of the term involved. Again, however, it seems essential to the success of the social argument underlying such linguistic debates that the appraisive words in question should be offered in virtue of their accepted meanings as an apt way of describing situations which have not hitherto been described in such terms.

It is true that, as a consequence of such arguments, new meanings are often generated. But the process by which this happens is the opposite of the one Williams describes. When an argument of this nature is successful, the outcome will hardly be the emergence of new meanings, save that the application of a term with a new range of reference may eventually put pressure on the criteria for applying it. The outcome will rather be the acceptance of new social perceptions, as a result of which the relevant appraisive terms will then be applied with unchanged meanings to new circumstances. It is only when such arguments fail that new meanings tend to arise.

This contention can readily be supported if we consider some of the ways in which a failure in this type of argument is capable of leaving its traces on the language. It may be that, when a social group seeks to insist that the ordinary criteria for applying a particular appraisive term are present in a wider range of circumstances than has commonly been allowed, the other users of the language – not sharing the underlying social perceptions of the first group – may simply assume in good faith that a "new meaning" has indeed been "offered," and may then accept it. The history of our culture (and in consequence our language) has been punctuated with many such misunderstandings. One fruitful source has been the continuing efforts of the proponents of commercial society to legitimate their undertakings by reference to the most highly approved moral and spiritual values. Consider, for example, the special use of the term *religious* that first emerged in the later sixteenth century as a way of commending punctual, strict, and conscientious forms of behaviour.[10] The aim was clearly to suggest that the ordinary criteria for applying the strongly commendatory term *religious* could be found in such actions, and thus that the actions themselves should be seen

[10] Here I offer what I take to be a corrected account of an example I originally mentioned in an earlier article (Skinner 1974a, at pp. 298–9).

essentially as acts of piety and not merely as instances of administrative competence. The failure of this move was quickly reflected in the emergence of a new meaning for the term *religious* in the course of the seventeenth century – the meaning we still invoke when we say things like "I attend the meetings of my department religiously." It seems clear that the need for this new lexical entry originally arose out of the incapacity of most language users to see that the ordinary criteria for *religious* (including the notion of piety) were in fact present in all the circumstances in which the term was by then beginning to be used.

There are many recent instances of the same phenomenon, some of which are cited in *Keywords*. For example, many industrial firms like to claim – with reference to their own business strategies – that they have a certain *philosophy*; and firms regularly promise to send their *literature* (meaning only their advertising brochures) to prospective customers. Again a crude attempt is clearly being made to link the activities of commercial society with a range of "higher" values. And again the failure of such efforts often gives rise to genuine polysemy. Hearing that a firm has a certain philosophy, most language users have assumed that a new meaning must be involved, and have gone on to use the term accordingly; they have not in general come to feel that corporations can indeed be said to have philosophies in the traditional sense of the term.

The language also supplies us with evidence of such ideological failures in a second and more decisive way. After a period of confusion about the criteria for applying a disputed term, the final outcome may be not polysemy, but rather a reversion to the employment of the original criteria, together with a corresponding obsolescence of the newer usages. This can be observed, for example, in the history of the word *patriot*. During the eighteenth century, the enemies of the ruling oligarchy in England sought to legitimate their attacks on the government by insisting that they were motivated entirely by their reverence for the constitution, and thus that their actions deserved to be commended as patriotic rather than condemned as factious. This at first bred such extreme uncertainty that the word *patriot* eventually came to *mean* (according to one of Dr. Johnson's definitions) "a factious disturber of the government." With the gradual acceptance of party politics, however, this condemnatory usage gradually atrophied, and the word reverted to its original meaning and its standard application as a term of praise.[11]

[11] For a fuller discussion of this example, see my article (Skinner 1974b).

Finally, the same form of argument can also have a more equivocal outcome, one which the language will again disclose. It may be that, after a similar period of semantic confusion, the original rather than the newer usage becomes obsolete. At first sight this may seem to indicate a success in the underlying campaign to change people's social perceptions. For this certainly makes it harder to invoke the primitive meaning of the word in order to insist that its new applications may be nothing more than a deformation of its basic sense. But in fact such changes again tend to be indexes of ideological failure. For the standardization of a new set of criteria will inevitably carry with it an alteration of the term's appraisive force. Sometimes the power of the word to evaluate what it is used to describe may be retained in a different (and usually weaker) form, as in the well known case of the word *naughty*. But often the process of acquiring a new meaning goes with a total loss of appraisive force. A good example is provided by the history of the word *commodity*. Before the advent of commercial society, to speak of something as a commodity was to praise it, and in particular to affirm that it answered to one's desires, and could thus be seen as beneficial, convenient, a source of advantage. Later an attempt was made to suggest that an article produced for sale ought to be seen as a source of benefit or advantage to its purchaser, and ought in consequence to be described and commended as a commodity. For a time the outcome of this further effort by the earliest English capitalists to legitimate their activities was that *commodity* became a polysemic word. But eventually the original applications withered away, leaving us with nothing more than the current and purely descriptive meaning of *commodity* as an object of trade. Although the capitalists inherited the earth, and with it much of the English language, they were unable in this case to persuade their fellow language users to endorse their attempted eulogy of their own commercial practices.

VI

Even if we agree about the criteria for applying an appraisive term, and also agree that a given set of circumstances can properly be said to answer to those criteria, I have suggested that still a third type of dispute can arise: a dispute about the direction of the term's evaluative force – a dispute, that is, about the nature and range of the speech acts it can be used to perform. Once again this can certainly be characterized as a substantive social dispute and not merely a linguistic one. For in this case what is at issue is the possibility that a group of language users may be open to the charge of having a mistaken or an undesirable social attitude.

We can distinguish two main routes by which an argument of this kind will be likely to issue in a contentious use of evaluative language. First, we may dissent from an orthodox social attitude by employing an appraisive term in such a way that its standard speech-act potential is weakened or even abolished. This can in turn be achieved in one of two ways. If we do not share the accepted evaluation of some particular action or state of affairs, we may indicate our dissent simply by dropping the corresponding term from our vocabulary altogether. There are many instances of this move in current social debate. Among terms which have hitherto been used to commend what they describe, this seems to be happening in the case of *gentleman*. Among terms previously used to express an element of condescension or patronage, this already seems to have happened with *native*, at least when used as a noun.

The other method of registering the same form of protest is more challenging. While continuing to employ an accepted term of social description and appraisal, we may make it contextually clear that we are using it merely to describe, and not at the same time to evaluate what is thereby described. Again, there are many contemporary instances of this move. Among terms previously used to evince condescension or even hatred, the classic example is provided by the word *black* (used as the description of a person), whether employed as an adjective or a noun. Among terms previously used to commend, we may note the new and carefully neutral applications of such words as *culture* and *civilization*. As Williams himself observes, these latter usages appear to have originated within the discipline of social anthropology, but have now come to be very generally accepted by those who wish to disavow any suggestion that one particular civilization may be more deserving of study than another (1976: 50, 80; 1983: 59, 91).

The other main way in which we can use our evaluative language to signal our social attitudes is more dramatic in its implications. It is possible to indicate, simply through our use of appraisive terms, not that we dissent from the idea of evaluating what they describe, but rather that we disagree with the direction of the evaluation and wish to see it reversed.

Again there are obviously two possibilities here. We may use a term normally employed to condemn what it describes in such a way as to make it contextually clear that, in our view, the relevant action or state of affairs ought in fact to be commended. As Williams points out, one interesting example of this reversal can be seen in the history of the word *myth* (1976:176–8; 1983: 210–12). In a more confidently rationalist age, to describe an explanation as mythological was to dismiss it. But in recent discussions the term has often been used to extol the mythological "version of reality" as "truer" and "deeper" than more mundane accounts. Conversely, we may dislike a form of behavior now regarded as praiseworthy, and indicate our disapproval by making it contextually clear that, although the term we are using is standardly employed to commend, we are employing it to condemn what is being described. Once again, there are many instances of this kind of struggle in current ideological debates. One only has to think of those politicians who are regularly praised by one group of commentators as *liberal* while others employ the same term in order to denounce them.

Williams surveys a large number of disagreements that fall within this third general category, and in many cases his comments on them are extremely interesting and shrewd. But his discussion suffers throughout from a failure to distinguish this type of argument from the first type we considered, in which the primary point at issue was the proper sense or meaning of the terms involved. Indeed Williams not only fails but refuses to distinguish between these two types of argument. For example, he insists that the change involved in the move from condemning myths to commending them must be construed as a change in the "sense" of the word *myth* (Williams 1976: 177; 1983: 211).

It would be perfectly possible, however, for both the sense and the reference of *myth* to remain stable in the face of the sort of changes in the use of the word that Williams is concerned to point out. It may be that all (and only) those theories and explanations which used to be called mythological are still called mythological, and that the *only* change involved in the use of the term derives from the shift from condemning myths to commending them. It is true that such a variation of speech-act potential will be very likely in due course to affect the sense (and in consequence the reference) of the word. But it is a mistake to suppose that this type of argument is primarily (or even necessarily) concerned with sense. What is changing – at least initially – is nothing to do with sense; what is changing is simply a social or intellectual attitude on the part of those who use the language.[12]

[12] In this paragraph I draw on Searle (1962). However, Searle does not, I think, succeed in showing that meaning and speech acts are wholly separate. All he shows is that sense and reference are capable of remaining stable while speech-act potential is undergoing a change. Depending on one's view of meaning, one might still want to insist that speech-act potential is a part of meaning, even if it is distinct from both sense and reference.

VII

I have now tried to furnish at least a preliminary response to the very large question I raised at the outset. I asked what kinds of knowledge and awareness we can hope to acquire about our social world through studying the vocabulary we use to describe and appraise it. I have answered that there are three main types of insight we can hope to gain: insights into changing social beliefs and theories; into changing social perceptions and awareness; and into changing social values and attitudes. I have thus attempted to supply at least a sketch of what seems to me most seriously lacking in Williams's book: an account of the sort of methodology we need to develop in order to use the evidence of our social vocabulary as a clue to the improved understanding of our social world.

This in turn suggests a further and even more vertiginous question: are we now in a position to say anything about the nature of the role played by our appraisive vocabulary in the process (and hence in the explanation) of social change?

Williams clearly thinks that we are, and conveys this sense by alluding repeatedly to the image of language as a mirror of social reality. The process of social change is treated as the primary cause of developments in our vocabulary; conversely, such developments are treated as reflections of the process of social change.[13] Describing the emergence of capitalism as "a distinct economic system," for example, Williams remarks that this gave rise to "interesting consequent uses of language."[14] And in commenting more specifically on "the economic changes of the Industrial Revolution," he notes that these produced a "greatly sharpened" and extended "vocabulary of class" (Williams 1976: 53; 1983: 62).

There is no doubt that this image serves to remind us of an important point. Where we encounter a wide measure of agreement about the application of key social terms, we must be dealing with a strikingly homogeneous social and moral world; where there is no such agreement, we can expect chaos. But it is arguable that the metaphor is also misleading in one crucial respect. It encourages us to assume that we are dealing with two distinct and contingently related domains: that of the social world itself, and that of the language we then apply in an attempt to delineate its character. This certainly seems to be the assumption underlying Williams's account.

[13] Note, however, that Williams (1983: 22) now counters this criticism.
[14] Williams (1976: 43). But in Williams (1983) this claim is deleted.

He sees a complete disjunction between "the words" he discusses and "the real issues" in the social world. And he sometimes speaks as if the gap between the two is one we can barely hope to bridge. "However complete the analysis" we offer at the linguistic level, he maintains, we cannot expect that "the real issues" will be fundamentally affected.[15]

To speak in this way is to forget something that Williams emphasizes at other points in *Keywords* with striking force: the fact that one of the most important uses of evaluative language is that of legitimating as well as describing the activities and attitudes of dominant social groups. The significance of this consideration can be brought out if we revert for a moment to an example already cited – the entrepreneurs of Elizabethan England who were anxious to persuade their contemporaries that, although their commercial enterprises might appear to be morally doubtful, they were in fact deserving of respect. One device they adopted was to argue, as we have seen, that their characteristically punctual and conscientious behavior could properly be seen as religious in character, and hence as motivated by pious and not merely self-seeking principles. Their underlying purpose was of course to legitimate their apparently untoward behavior by insisting on the propriety of describing it in these highly commendatory terms.

Now it may seem – and this is evidently Williams's view – that this sort of example precisely fits the metaphor of language as a mirror of a more basic reality. The merchant is perceived to be engaged in a more or less dubious way of life which he has a strong motive for wishing to exhibit as legitimate. So he professes just those principles, and offers just those descriptions, that serve to present what he is doing in a morally acceptable light. Since the selection of the principles and their accompanying descriptions both relate to his behavior in an obviously *ex post facto* way, it hardly seems that an explanation of his behavior need depend in the least on studying the moral language he may elect to use. For his choice of vocabulary appears to be entirely determined by his prior social needs.

As I have tried to hint, however, this is to misunderstand the role of the normative vocabulary which any society employs for the description and appraisal of its social life. The merchant cannot hope to describe *any* action he may choose to perform as being "religious" in character, but only those which can be claimed with some show of plausibility to meet such agreed criteria as there may be for the application of the term. It follows that if he is anxious to

[15] Williams (1976: 13–14). But in Williams (1983: 16) this claim is modified.

have his conduct appraised as that of a genuinely religious man, he will find himself restricted to the performance of only a certain range of actions. Thus the problem facing the merchant who wishes to be seen as pious rather than self-interested cannot simply be the instrumental one of tailoring his account of his principles in order to fit his projects; it must in part be the problem of tailoring his projects in order to make them answer to the pre-existing language of moral principles.[16]

The story of the merchant suggests two morals. One is that it must be a mistake to portray the relationship between our social vocabulary and our social world as a purely external and contingent one. It is true that our social practices help to bestow meaning on our social vocabulary. But it is equally true that our social vocabulary helps to constitute the character of those practices. To see the role of our evaluative language in helping to legitimate social action is to see the point at which our social vocabulary and our social fabric mutually prop each other up. As Charles Taylor (1971: 24) has remarked, "we can speak of mutual dependence if we like, but what this really points up is the artificiality of the distinction between social reality and the language of description of that social reality."

The other moral is that, if there are indeed causal linkages between social language and social reality, to speak of the one as mirroring the other may be to envisage the causal arrows pointing in the wrong direction. As the example of the Elizabethan merchant suggests, to recover the nature of the normative vocabulary available to an agent for the description and appraisal of his conduct is at the same time to indicate one of the constraints on his conduct itself. This in turn suggests that, if we wish to explain why our merchant chose to concentrate on certain courses of action while avoiding others, we are bound to make some reference to the prevailing moral language of the society in which he was acting. For this, it now appears, must have figured not as an epiphenomenon of his projects, but as one of the determinants of his actions.

To conclude with these morals is to issue a warning to literary critics and social historians alike to avoid a prevalent but impoverishing form of reductionism. But it is also to suggest that the special techniques of the literary critic have – or ought to have – a central place in the business of cultural criticism which a book like Williams's *Keywords* has scarcely begun to recognize.

[16] Here I draw heavily on the preface to my book (Skinner 1978).

REFERENCES

Austin, J.L. 1975. *How to do Things with Words*, edited by J. Urmson and M. Sbisa, 2nd edn. Oxford: Oxford University Press.

Dummett, Michael. 1973a. *Frege: Philosophy of Language*. London: Duckworth.

1973b. "The Justification of Deduction." *The Proceedings of the British Academy* 59: 201–32.

Foot, Philippa. 1958. "Moral Arguments." *Mind* 67: 502–13.

Hampshire, Stuart. 1959. *Thought and Action*. London: Chatto and Windus.

Murdoch, I. 1970. *The Sovereignty of Good*. London: Routledge and Kegan Paul.

Putnam, Hilary. 1975. "How Not to Talk about Meaning." In *Mind, Language and Reality, Philosophical Papers*, vol. II. Cambridge: Cambridge University Press, pp. 117–31.

Searle, John R. 1962. "Meaning and Speech Acts." *The Philosophical Review* 71: 423–32.

Skinner, Quentin. 1974a. "Some Problems in the Analysis of Political Thought and Action." *Political Theory* 2: 277–303.

1974b. "The Principles and Practice of Opposition: The Case of Bolingbroke versus Walpole." In Neil McKendrick (ed.), *Historical Perspectives: Studies in English Thought and Society in Honour of J.H. Plumb*. London: Europa Publications, pp. 93–128.

1978. *The Foundations of Modern Political Thought*, 2 vols. Cambridge: Cambridge University Press.

Taylor, Charles. 1971. "Interpretation and the Sciences of Man." *The Review of Metaphysics* 25: 3–51.

Williams, Raymond. 1976. *Keywords: A Vocabulary of Culture and Society*. London: Fontana (revised and expanded, 1983).

Wittgenstein, Ludwig. 1959. *Philosophical Investigations*. Oxford: Blackwell.

2

Understanding conceptual change politically

JAMES FARR

The concept of a "festivity." We connect it with merrymaking; in another age it may have been connected with fear and dread. What we call "wit" and "humour" doubtless did not exist in other ages. And both are constantly changing.

Wittgenstein 1980: 78

Had Wittgenstein's imagination taken a political turn, how much more emphatically and dramatically might he have made his point. "The concept of 'revolution'," he might have begun. "We connect it with radical novelty; in another age it was definitely connected with restoration and return. What we call 'patriotism' and 'public opinion' doubtless did not exist in other ages. And both are constantly changing."

Constant change appears to be the only truly constant thing about our political concepts. The concepts which these days give meaning to political life, facilitate communication, and arm us with the weapons of criticism did not always do so, or did so in very different ways. There are continuities, to be sure; but our "continuously evolving grammar" (Wolin 1960: 27) bears witness to the sort of continuities these are.[1] The evolution of grammar is not a narrowly linguistic or conceptual matter either, but a political one too. For our concepts and beliefs and actions and practices go together and change together. To understand conceptual change is in large part

For comments and criticisms, I m indebted to Charles Anderson, Terence Ball, Terrell Carver, Murray Edelman, J.A.W. Gunn, and Robert Goodin. I owe a special debt of thanks to Mary G. Dietz and Russell L. Hanson for many discussions and readings.

[1] For similar sentiments on "the continuum of discourse called political philosophy," see Pocock (1980: 147).

to understand political change, and vice versa. And such understanding must of necessity be historical.

This essay hopes to contribute to a political theory of conceptual change. But theories being what they are – and hopes what they are – this essay here advances only an idealized sketch of a basic explanatory mechanism of conceptual change. Conceptual change is one imaginative consequence of political actors criticizing and attempting to resolve the contradictions which they discover or generate in the complex web of their beliefs, actions, and practices as they try to understand and change the world around them. A general model of political problem-solving – a model which upholds both the centrality and limits of human intentionality and rationality – lies behind this basic mechanism of conceptual change.

Elucidating these claims frames the task of the second section below. The first section prepares ground by offering some general reflections on politics and language. The third section begins by acknowledging some limits and goes on to consider the narrative form appropriate to understanding conceptual change, namely, conceptual histories. The final section offers two brief conceptual histories which hope to illustrate conceptual change in action. However theoretical are the hopes of this essay, its moral is a historical one. For understanding conceptual change requires and underscores the need for historical understanding. Given the demands of temporal scope and imaginative detail, this can be provided only by histories of our key political concepts. In this way, this essay may be read as a defense of the conceptual histories we already have, and a call for more.

I

Politics as we know it would not only be indescribable without language, it would be impossible. Emerging nations could not declare independence, leaders instruct partisans, citizens protest war, or courts sentence criminals. Neither could we criticize, plead, promise, argue, exhort, demand, negotiate, bargain, compromise, counsel, brief, debrief, advise nor consent. To imagine politics without these actions would be to imagine no recognizable politics at all. At best, there would be silence; at worst, a politics rather like Hobbes's war of all against all, missing only its gibes, taunts, and insults.

No one, I suspect, would challenge this minimal characterization of the impossibility of politics without language. Hobbes certainly would not, for without language, he once observed, there would be "amongst men, neither Commonwealth, nor Society, nor contract, nor Peace, no more than amongst Lyons, Bears, and Wolves" (1968: 100). Yet Hobbes did not even begin to draw the appropriate moral from his own observation. For in the very same breath he identifies language not with political action or the bonds of community, but only and wrongly with "Names . . . and their connexions" whose "general use is to transferre our Mental Discourse, into Verbal" (1968: 100–1).

Although the thinker is three hundred years and more dead, his ideas in these domains surely are not. The fear of the *bellum omnium contra omnes* lives on in our worst fears about nuclear holocaust; and, less ominously, his view of language has these days an underground but lively existence in much of political life and in most of contemporary political science. It may be found flourishing in all those views which consider only the descriptive function of language; or in those which describe the activity of language as "verbal behavior" whose general use is to express "attitudes" and "opinions" subjectively formed independently of language.

Such views radically underestimate the politics of language. Only in the rarest of circumstances – or language-games, as Wittgenstein would say – does language function apolitically as a neutral medium for expressing ideas or describing things. Rather, language generally functions in overtly and covertly political ways by playing (or preying) upon the needs, interests, and powers of those individuals or groups who use it. And use it they do for strategic or partisan ends of one kind or another. Most of language, in short, is politically constituted by the ends to which it is intentionally put or by the consequences which it is subsequently seen to entail. Understanding what we might call, then, the "political constitution of language" is crucial for understanding conceptual change politically. This directs our attention to the political designs of individuals or groups who change their concepts in order to solve problems and remove contradictions in theory and practice. Before turning to this, however, we must understand how language could be even a relevant arena for political actors such as these. What, to give it a name, is the "linguistic constitution of politics"?

The notion of the linguistic constitution of politics embodies two general claims, (1) an enormous number of political actions are carried out (and can only be carried out) in and through language; and (2) political beliefs, actions, and practices are partly constituted by the concepts[2] which political actors hold about those beliefs, actions, and practices. Since these two general claims lie behind an adequate understanding of conceptual change, let us develop them a bit.

Political acts are often carried on *in* language, and expressly articulated as such. Consider for starters the brief list which opens this section. But political acts are also carried on *through* language, either in speech or texts, even when these acts are not expressly articulated. In his budget speech, for example, the President proposes a budget, as he says, and so sets in motion the yearly spectacle of the dismal science in all its bureaucratic manifestation. But through his speech he may also criticize his predecessor, mobilize constituent support, or warn foreign adversaries by recommending alarmingly high levels of "defense" spending. Or take an earlier and more dramatic example. The authors of the *Declaration of Independence* declared independence, to be sure; but through their document they also warned Britain of armed resistance and sought to inspire American colonists to change their very identities and so forge "one people."[3]

Political actions of this linguistic sort presuppose shared understandings among political actors, understandings which are deeply embedded in social and political practices.[4] Among other things, this presupposes shared agreements – when, of course, there *are* agreements – about (the use of) political concepts. This means

[2] Throughout I will speak of concepts, not of words, unless the distinction needs to be drawn. The distinction frequently need not be drawn because our language is so richly developed that most of our concepts – especially our political concepts – express themselves with matching words which name them explicitly and uniquely. This is not always so, of course, for someone may possess a concept without (yet) possessing the matching word ("I love my country" says the young girl before "patriotism" enters her vocabulary); some words express different concepts (as when we "bear" arms to fend off the menacing grizzly "bear"); and some concepts may be expressed in different words (perhaps "liberty" and "freedom" in modern political discourse, though I am very reluctant to forward this as my own view, precisely because of their different histories). However, our ability to identify with any confidence our own much less others' political concepts wholly depends upon the range of (other) words at our or their disposal (as in the above example of "patriotism"). That is, no concepts without language. Thus *political concepts are linguistically constructed* even when matching words are missing. Most assuredly political concepts do not exist "in the head," as Hume put it, much less are they laid up in some Platonic world of Forms.

[3] For an intriguing discussion of the inspirational act and intent of the *Declaration*, see White (1984, chap. 9) and Wills (1979).

[4] The sort of understandings characterized as "shared meanings" by Michael Walzer (1983), or as "social self-knowledge" by Samuel Beer (1970); or as social "self-recognition" by J.A.W. Gunn (1983).

agreement about (1) the criteria for applying political concepts; (2) the range of things to which these concepts refer in the political world; and (3) the range of attitudes which these concepts express.[5] For the *Declaration* to realize the intentions behind its actions, for example, there had to be a large measure of agreement between authors and readers that certain usurpations and abuses amounted to calling some policies "tyrannical"; that George III's policies were indeed "tyrannical"; and that calling them "tyrannical" was to condemn them, and to commend actions resisting them.

That actions might be commended in and through language points to the second general claim about the political life of language: political concepts partly constitute the beliefs which inform action and practice.[6] How revolutionaries, for example, will respond to the government's decree will depend upon their shared beliefs about what actions and practices the revolution requires. And these beliefs are partly constituted by the concept of "revolution" which these revolutionaries hold. Some actions and practices will be believed to be "revolutionary," others "reformist," still others "counterrevolutionary." Of course, different revolutionaries at the same, much less another, time may have fundamentally different beliefs about these actions and practices (compare Mensheviks with Bolsheviks; Patriots of '76 with Communists on the Long March). But the general point remains the same, for these differences generally express themselves as differences over the concept of "revolution" itself.[7] In this way, conceptual conflict may express political conflict.[8]

In qualifying practices as being *partly* constituted by concepts, we remind ourselves of some important political realities – especially amidst the turbulence inevitably called up by a concept like "revolution" or by acts like "declaring independence." First, concepts never fully constitute political practices because political practices usually have unintended and even unconceptualized consequences. Over the long term, these consequences may even come to be seen as contradicting the practice, and this will generally

[5] Here I am following the distinctions which Quentin Skinner makes in his essay "Language and Social Change" (1980), as modified in this volume. Behind this lies J.L. Austin (1962).

[6] Charles Taylor and Alasdair MacIntyre have done the most in our times to articulate what is at stake with the constitutive function of concepts and beliefs. See MacIntyre (1971 and 1973b) and Taylor (1985).

[7] For development of these points about the concept of "revolution," see Farr (1982: 699–702) and Dunn (1982).

[8] This is not always so, of course. Conceptual agreement may well lead to political conflict, as when all agree "war" or a "strike" is under way.

lead to its *re*conceptualization. This is an important source of conceptual change and political innovation, as we shall see below. Second, practices may influence concepts in yet another way. For example, an army is indeed partly constituted by the concept of "army" which informs the beliefs of a nation's soldiers and civilians; but army life – especially in a society (increasingly) dominated by the army – may in turn (come to) shape other concepts, like "order," "authority," and "loyalty." Wittgenstein once made the anarchistic converse of this point in his usual interrogatory way. "Orders are sometimes not obeyed. But what would it be like if no orders were *ever* obeyed? The concept 'order' would have lost its purpose" (1958, §345). Finally, political practices obviously require a material basis in our bodies, and in the productive mechanisms which sustain us; and they sometimes express deep psychological processes about fear, domination, or self-deception. These things happen "below language," as it were, and are surely important for making the political world what it is.

But whatever the qualification "partly" imparts, when we acknowledge that practices are *constituted* by concepts, we remind ourselves how very much of language is "in" the political world and how decisive this is for our understanding of it. This, too, is an important political reality, for where there are different concepts, there are different beliefs, and so different actions and practices. This entails some epistemological obligations for the student of politics. For the study of political concepts now becomes an essential not an incidental task of the study of politics. Actors' concepts will figure necessarily in the identification and description of political beliefs, actions, and practices.[9] Beyond this, they may figure in the very explanations of political phenomena (and sometimes these explanations will be those which political actors themselves offer). How often this proves to be so is an empirical matter, loosely speaking, for no abstract rule is available here.

[9] In hopes of forestalling the usual sorts of misunderstandings which arise on this score, nothing stated here about linguisitic action and conceptual constitution underwrites the utterly naive and impolitic strategy of believing literally everything actors *say* about themselves. Disentangling what actors say from what they actually believe, enact, or practice is a problem of considerable importance and difficulty. But the general point remains the same, for to identify beliefs, actions, and practices is to identify the concepts which constitute them (whatever actors say). Note, further, that this must be done even if we come to the study of politics armed with skeptical explanatory theories of one kind or another. To say, for example, that a political actor's beliefs and concepts are products of false consciousness – especially in the hopes of changing them through criticism – is to know what those false beliefs and concepts actually are. Marx himself says as much, and his critical social science shows it in practice.

Without abstract rules, students of politics must engage their judgments. But just because of this, they cannot exclude, as a matter of principle or convenience, the explanatory role of ordinary political concepts, or the explanations which political actors themselves give.

Nothing like this obtains in the natural sciences (however many other similarities obtain). Whatever the complex connections between language and the natural world – and it was never so simple as words naming things – the natural sciences do not face the special problems (or opportunities) of a subject matter consisting of political actors whose beliefs, actions, and practices are partly constituted by their concepts and for whom language is an arena of political action. Nothing, accordingly, exists ready-made in the philosophy of the natural sciences for helping us understand conceptual change politically.[10]

II

Conceptual change attends any *re*constitution of the political world. Revolutionary eras, say, or great awakenings, reveal this in a most dramatic way. As beliefs, actions, and practices face crises of the most profound sort, older concepts expire and others are born. Even our vocabulary changes. We may feel, as Thucydides did during the Peloponnesian War, that words lose their meaning (1951: 189). Other words gain radically new meanings. Some emerge for the first time. Consider, for example, how our words today still bear witness to the great transformation in the concepts (and so the beliefs, actions, and practices) which emerged or gained their modern meaning during "the age of revolutions," which E.J. Hobsbawm dates from 1789 to 1848.

> They include such words as "industry," "industrialist," "factory," "middle class," "capitalism," and "socialism." They include "aristocracy" as well as "railway," "liberal" and "conservative" as political terms, "nationality," "scientist," and "engineer," "proletariat," and (economic)

[10] There is, of course, much to be learned from debates over conceptual change in the philosophy of the natural sciences, and my debts will be obvious below. The most sustained and helpful analysis of conceptual change in the natural sciences may be found in Toulmin (1972). For the classic statement of conceptual relativism in our times, see Kuhn (1970, chap. 10) (though see the qualifications registered in the Postscript, pp. 192–8). For discussion of concepts from a realist perspective, see a number of essays in Putnam (1975). Also see Shapere (1966); Pearce and Maynard (1973); Katz (1979); and Davidson (1984). For a discussion more attuned to history and the social sciences, see Dunn (1978).

> "crisis." "Utilitarian" and "statistics," "sociology" and several names of modern sciences, "journalism" and "ideology" are all coinages or adaptations of this period. So are "strike" and "pauperism."
>
> 1962: 17

Faced with such a list, we can almost feel what Wittgenstein once called "the labor pains at the birth of new concepts" (1980: 62).

But conceptual change need not always be so painful or so dramatic. Nor need it be heralded by such wordy or worldly turbulence. We find conceptual change *whenever* we find changes in any of the interrelated features of a concept as outlined above, in its criteria of application, its range of reference, or its attitudinal expressiveness. Conceptual change, accordingly, varies from wholesale changes across an entire constellation of concepts (as in Hobsbawm's tally) to more localized changes in, say, the reference or attitudinal expressiveness of a single concept. Consider, as an example of the latter, change in the concept of "patriotism" (and its cognates) at the hands of eighteenth-century Tories. By about the 1730s the Tories, following Bolingbroke, turned conceptual coat. They abandoned their previous rhetoric of denigrating "patriotism" and of allowing republican martyrs or Whig policies to be advertised as uniquely "patriotic." Tories now too were to be "patriots," and this was a rhetorical shift of considerable moment.[11] But their aristocratic policies, not to mention British party politics as a whole, were hardly turned upside down.

Whether or not the world is turned upside down, there is a general temptation – especially when faced with examples like those above – to understand conceptual change as a *reflection* of political change. It should be clear by now, I hope, why this temptation must be avoided at all costs. Besides the metaphorical (if not metaphysical) howler involved in reflection imagery – as if the world does it with mirrors – political change cannot be isolated in a conceptually uncontaminated way so that conceptual change could then be said to be its reflection. To understand political change is in large part to understand conceptual change, and vice versa. To think otherwise would be to fail to draw the appropriate moral from our discussion of the linguistic constitution of politics.

Given popular conceptions we might call reflection theories Marx*ish* theories, but by this we must understand a number of

[11] For discussion of the details and the methodological importance of this case, see Skinner (1974b). Also see Mary G. Dietz's conceptual history of "patriotism" in this volume.

Marxist and non-Marxist theories of political change. Marxish theories, of varying degrees of vulgarity, not only frequently fail to draw the above moral, but make a virtue of temptation. Frequently "consciousness" or "ideas" or "opinions" substitute for "concepts" or "language," but the point remains much the same. As a class, these related notions are said to be reflections of the world, and change because (and so after) the world changes. How far Marx himself was in the grip of, or helped create, this temptation is a matter of some debate. If taken out of their polemical and anti-idealist contexts, some of his remarks about the "phantoms . . . in the human brain" might appear to incline in that direction, as might his gibes against those idealist historians who think "each principle has had its own century in which to manifest itself" (1970: 47; 1963: 115). But a more complex and interesting – and arguably more representative – picture emerges in Marx's discussion in the *Grundrisse* of the historical concept of "labor," not to mention his nonreflectionist remarks about the concept of art (1973: 103–11). Moreover, it is certainly true that many modern theories inspired by Marx are not "reflection" theories; and many of Marx's notions (especially contradiction and critique) should further inform the study of conceptual change.

Not much help in understanding conceptual (amidst political) change comes from opposing quarters, either. Theories of historical semantics frequently proceed as if conceptual change is a linguistic process largely independent of political change. "The development of language follows its own laws," as Gustaf Stern put it in his classic work on semantic change. Stern did allude to "general cultural factors," at least for explaining why the referential aspect of a concept like "ship" changes "as new types of ships are built." But these changes, he adds, "lie altogether outside language" (1956: 176, 191, 166). Thus we are left either with purely internal linguistic changes, or with purely external political changes. But never the twain do meet.

A political theory of conceptual change must avoid such stark alternatives. It must take its point of departure from the political constitution of language and the linguistic constitution of politics. That is to say, its premises must acknowledge that in acting politically actors do things for strategic and partisan purposes in and through language; and that they can do such things because the concepts in language partly constitute political beliefs, actions, and practices. Consequently, political change and conceptual change must be understood as one complex and interrelated process.

The attempt to develop a political theory of conceptual change faces a number of difficulties, to be sure, not the least of which is the enormity of the subject matter. Moreover – like any *political* theory – it must be humble about its predictive prowess;[12] and – like *any* theory – it will face an "ocean of anomalies" even when developed (Lakatos 1978: 48).

To take some first steps towards such a theory, conceptual change might be understood as one rather strikingly imaginative outcome of the process of political actors attempting to solve the problems they encounter as they try to understand and change the world around them. To see this, we may draw attention to an obvious feature of language intimated above: concepts are never held or used in isolation, but in constellations which make up entire schemes or belief systems. These schemes or belief systems are theories, and those who hold them are theorists – of varying degrees of articulation and sophistication, of course. Theories, in turn, may be understood as intentional and rational attempts to solve practical and speculative problems generated in or between political beliefs, actions, and practices.[13] In attempting to solve particular problems which continue to arise, theories may undergo change. As theorists struggle to explain or to reconstitute the world, they may propose that some of the concepts in their theories be abandoned, others conceived, or still others changed, whether in terms of their criteria of application, their reference, or their attitudinal expressiveness.

[12] Besides the numerous practical difficulties associated with prediction in the social sciences, conceptual change cannot be predicted in principle. This is especially the case with those concepts connected with the growth of knowledge. Karl Popper's version of this argument contends that "if there is such a thing as growing human knowledge, then we cannot anticipate today what we shall know only tomorrow . . . No scientific predictor can possibly predict, by scientific methods, its own future results. Attempts to do so can attain their result only after the event, when it is too late for a prediction; they can attain their result only after the prediction has turned into a retrodiction" (1960: xii). More generally, however, the argument holds for all social and political beliefs, actions, and practices which are influenced by the growth of knowledge – which is to say, almost all of them. (See MacIntyre [1973a: 331; and 1981: 89–91]; and Farr [1982: 703–5].) The skepticism about prediction involved here could be waived only if we had good reasons to believe that there would be no more conceptual change in the future. Though this is a logical possibility, I wouldn't bet on it. Nor should students of political change.

[13] In this I follow Popper (1972) and Laudan (1977) who discuss scientific contexts, but also MacIntyre (1966: 92f.), who discusses ethical and political contexts. For further discussion of the rationality and progressiveness of conceptual change, as well as the connections and distinctions between speculative and practical problems, see Hanson (1985, chaps. 1, 12). The sustained conceptual history of "democracy" in America which Hanson narrates provides the best context for general discussions of this nature.

These conceptual changes brought about amidst theoretical development may be wholesale and happen all of a sudden. But generally they will proceed incrementally, slowly, even glacially, and always against a backdrop provided by those concepts which are not at that moment in the process of change. Theories may be judged successful – and so rational and progressive – to the extent that they solve their problems. This judgment does not belong uniquely to the theorist who proposes change, any more than a private language is possible. A community of speakers and theorists, however grand or humble, must be convinced of the rationality and progressiveness of the proposed changes. Their being convinced shows itself in their subsequent use of the concept in the proposed way.

Problems never rest. Not only may theorists change their concepts in attempting to solve problems, but they may discover *new* problems or *reconceptualize* old ones. Thus both theories and problems undergo conceptual change, and this is enough to disabuse us of any notions that problems, much less their solutions, are timeless or universal. Once reconceptualized, problems call forth new theories, and new theories reconceptualize those problems, and so on. This scene of palpable restlessness is thus not only historical, but dialectical in that it revives the ancient conception of the reconciling of arguments to the problems which oppose them in such a way as to change both the argument and their problems – and often the speakers themselves. In this way, the general schema of problem-solving intimates a rudimentary model of the classical dialectic.

A dialectical understanding of conceptual change may be deepened by considering contradictions. Contradictions form a special class of problems (thus reducing the range of the problem-solving schema, while increasing the likelihood of interesting exceptions emerging). Whereas "problem" covers an enormous range of solvable difficulties or removable obstacles which a belief system might face, a contradiction implies manifestly *inconsistent* beliefs *within* a system, such that holding or asserting one implies the denial or negation of another. Hence contradictions imply more than mere conflicts, and they are logically (and perhaps psychologically) less easily shelved than are many other kinds of problems.[14] Indeed if Hume is right, "the Heart of Man is made to reconcile Contradictions" (1748: 98).

[14] Leon Festinger's work on the psychology of cognitive dissonance (1957; 1964) is relevant to the problem of contradictions. Lakatos (1978) and Feyerabend (1975), among others, discuss the shelving of problems in scientific contexts.

In the advanced sciences, contradictory beliefs (as embedded in theoretical propositions) require resolution usually by the elimination of one belief or another, or more generally by the elimination of erroneous belief. Karl Popper has elevated this insight into a wholly general and expressly dialectical principle about scientific change. "Without contradictions," Popper once said, "there would be no rational motive for changing our theories" (1965: 316). Criticism forms the mediating rational link here between contradiction and change, including conceptual change, for, as Popper sees it, "concepts are partly means for formulating theories . . . and may always be replaced by other concepts" (1972: 123–4).

Criticism plays an altogether more *political* role in the kinds of contexts which interest us, since they are theoretical, ideological, and practical at the same time. Criticism – itself a political action undertaken in and through language – will not be directed just against abstract propositions, as in science, but against beliefs, actions, and practices in the political domain. For political problems generally lie in the contradictions in or between beliefs, actions, and practices – all of which are conceptually constituted features of political life. These contradictions may therefore be understood as *real* contradictions, not just as logical ones.[15] That is, they are embedded not only in the propositions which actors advance, but in the complex realities of political life. Real contradictions may be generated in any number of concrete ways, but contradictory *beliefs* are central to most of these ways. Contradictions are generally found not so much in the simultaneous profession of two directly and glaringly incompatible or negating beliefs. Rather they emerge in the extended implications or unintended consequences of two or more beliefs; or they emerge in the confrontation between (consequences of) actions or practices and the beliefs which inform them. Criticism brings these contradictions to the surface – when of course there is a critical attitude. Contradictions may subsequently be resolved – when or if they are resolved – by changes in belief or action or practice. As these change, so do their constitutive concepts.

Innovating ideologists – to use Quentin Skinner's apt term (1974a: 293) – generally change concepts in this way, more or less dramatically. Faced with contradictions or incoherencies between prevailing beliefs and newly proposed beliefs, actions, or practices,

[15] On the reality of contradictions and their epistemological importance (after Hegel and Marx) see Elster (1978, chaps. 3 and 4); Ball (1983); and Feyerabend (1985, chap. 4).

ideologists may propose innovations of a conceptual nature in order to realize their political designs. Mid-eighteenth-century Tories change reference to become "patriots"; late-sixteenth-century Protestant investors introduce "frugality" as the new virtue of their practice; American "blacks" in the 1960s and 1970s dramatically overturn the expression of attitudes by adopting as their own a previously denigrated term of color; "behavioral" scientists in the late 1940s emerge to avoid the socialist implications feared to be latent in "social" science. In short, in order to gain popular support for party policy, or to gain religious acceptance of new economic practices, or to mobilize the political power of ethnic pride, or to gain federal funding for the sciences of social phenomena, all in the face of contradictions thrown up by prevailing beliefs about partisanship or usury or ethnicity or ideology, concepts may be changed. In these and a myriad other cases, conceptual change may be explained in terms of the attempt by political actors to solve speculative or practical problems and to resolve contradictions which their criticism has exposed in their beliefs, actions, and practices.

III

Here then is a sketch of a paradigmatic mechanism which we need in order to understand conceptual change politically. In the subsequent section, changes in two concepts – "fourth estate" and "hegemony" – provide the occasion to illustrate, at least briefly, the explanatory intent of this mechanism. But before turning to such illustration, two further tasks should concern us. The first and briefer task requires us to acknowledge some limits faced by the mechanism sketched above, especially if one hopes for an exhaustive account of conceptual change.

Other mechanisms may well be at work simultaneously or independently in the overall dynamics of conceptual change. For example, simple adaptation may be at work, especially in the relatively straightforward cases of new reference (as in Gustaf Stern's above-mentioned example of new ships being referred to as "ships"). In those cases where words do name things, established words come to name new things often without much pressure from contradictions. We should also hardly discount the sheer playfulness of the human imagination when it comes to what can be said or conceptualized anew. In short, play without problems or contradictions may trigger conceptual change.

Moreover, not all contradictions or problems generate corresponding efforts to criticize, solve, or resolve them. Indeed it appears to be a fact about the human condition that all of us some of the time, and some of us all of the time, live with contradictions, or allow problems to go without solution, or even so much as an attempted solution. In such cases, of course, our concern shifts from explaining why concepts do in fact change, to why they do *not* change in the face of problems or contradictions. There are still other limits, too. Many problems or contradictions emerge, when and if they emerge, in a *post hoc* manner. That is, changes in theory or in political practice often bring in their wake a belated acknowledgment of previously unrecognized problems or contradictions which are now solved or removed. In such cases, change may precede the very recognition of some problems or contradictions – those, that is, that did not motivate change in the first place.

Limits such as these need not amount to refutations of the mechanism sketched above, though surely any subsequent theoretical development will have to integrate them. A political theory of conceptual change should also recognize what might at first sight be a paradox, at least when judged by the usual promises or aspirations to generality which attend theories. Its value does not reside in generality as such, but in the historical understanding which it makes possible, indeed demands. This is so because contradictions and problems must be identified in terms of the concepts of those whose contradictions and problems they were – or in some cases still are. Of necessity, this requires that we locate them in their particular historical contexts, and, over time, in the changing historical contexts which follow from their criticism and attempted solution. Thus *conceptual histories* will be the vehicles for the sort of historical understanding which the study of conceptual and political change demands. They promise to bring out the political importance of conceptual change, and the conceptual importance of political change. Saying something about the nature of conceptual histories and about their connection to political theory in our day forms, then, the second and longer task alluded to above.

Conceptual histories tell the tales of conceptual change and political innovation. They narrate some stretch of human imagination – in belief, action, or practice – by tracing the emergence, transformation, and sometimes the demise of key political concepts. Thus conceptual histories contribute to genuinely historical thinking about politics (as opposed to steeping oneself in one or another historical period, a method which too has its virtues, especially when the period is not just or always one's own). They also contribute to the activity of political theorizing.

Conceptual histories form a genre in the sister disciplines of political theory and the history of discourse. Their domain is the political life of language in general, though their particular subjects are the concepts which constitute political beliefs, actions, and practices. Since concepts are linguistic constructs, conceptual histories will be linguistic (even word) histories, for such is our only access to the conceptually constituted world of political actors, past or present. As Quentin Skinner remarks of the emergence of a new political concept, "The surest sign that a society has entered into the secure possession of a new concept is that a new vocabulary will be developed, in terms of which the concept can then be publicly articulated and discussed" (1978, vol. II: 352). And criticized, we should add.

Conceptual histories, however, cannot be mere etymological lifelines, especially of a single word. There are at least three reasons for this. First, for a conceptual history to be a genuine history, the concept's genesis must be told; and this requires an understanding of its pre-history. (Take the obvious connections between "patria" and "patriotism," and the less obvious connections between "priestcraft" and "ideology.") How concepts (and words) emerge – sometimes explosively, usually rather more glacially – out of earlier conceptual material is itself an essential part of the story.

Second, since concepts figure in theoretical constellations or conceptual schemes, a single concept can hardly be traced without reference, however briefly, to other concepts. Only in this way can we grasp the life of a concept in the overall structure of political argument which governs and unites a political community. In this way, too, conceptual histories avoid the charge of being histories of "unit ideas" (Laudan 1977: chap. 6).

Finally, since concepts are not subjects – except in the trivial sense of being subject matter – conceptual histories must *explain* the emergence and transformation of concepts as outcomes of actors using them for political purposes. That is, political concepts do not have any agency or life apart from the political actors who use and change them; and conceptual histories have a commensurate project to explain why these actors used and changed them as they did. This utterly general commitment should be narrowed, as I have indicated above, by understanding conceptual change as one sort of imaginative consequence of actors attempting to solve their problems and to resolve the contradictions they criticize.

These three reasons express methodological commitments whose concrete mobilization will depend upon at least three further practical considerations. A first consideration will be the sources which the conceptual historian will be forced to consult for his or her particular concept. Here we discover something of a spectrum. Some political concepts (like "freedom" or "justice") make frequent appearances in what we loosely call (in some intuitive and historically mutable sense) the Great Political Theories, like those of Aristotle or Hobbes or Hegel. These concepts, of course, also play in the scenes of more ordinary political discourse and rhetoric, scenes in which other concepts play almost exclusively (like "fourth estate" or "patriotism"). From the Great Texts, and lesser ones too, to pamphlets, speeches, and letters, concepts will have their various sites. Different sites require different skills from the conceptual historian – from the (usually sympathetic) reconstruction of a concept within an imposing edifice of meaning, to the (often skeptical) archaeology of uncovering layers of meaning amidst pamphlet warfare or the manipulative rhetoric of partisan speech-making.

Second, varying degrees of detail – about any or all episodes of a particular concept's life, about the constellation of which the concept is a part, or about the problems and contradictions which exercise those who invent or change their concepts – will be dictated by the chosen form and length of the conceptual history. This is always a practical matter, as is the audience to whom the history is directed. Along a sliding scale, one may compare the scholarly and detailed conceptual history of the "state" as performed by Quentin Skinner across the Renaissance and the Reformation (1978), with the more popular and fast-paced conceptual history of "sex" as penned by Lawrence Stone across the whole of recorded history – and then some (1985; cf. 1977). That we learn from both is important and obvious. In form and length, then, conceptual histories may vary from cribs to tomes.

Finally, conceptual histories are never finished. Not only is there a future history (yet) to tell, but the past is hardly as fixed as it (sometimes) seems. There are scores of hermeneutic worries about all this. But I have in mind a humbler, even if similarly intractable, concern. The explanatory project embedded in telling a concept's story – what problems its invocation attempted to solve, what contradictions when criticized paved the way for its metamorphosis – must allow for the tentative and promissory character of conceptual histories. Why complex conceptual transitions occurred is not always transparent. Thus conceptual histories will often be forced merely to record some conceptual change, and at best intimate the rough outlines of some particular explanation for it. These explanations will be open to criticism. And so may ensue contests over explanations of concepts; and many of the concepts in question will themselves be open to contest.[16] These various contests all but ensure that conceptual histories will never be fixed or final. And then there is the next generation – or so we hope.

When we marvel at the specter of new generations writing anew their conceptual histories, we are confronted with the dizzying prospect of conceptual histories of conceptual histories, and of conceptual change in "conceptual change." No timeless consolation is to be found here; but perhaps some lessening of the vertigo may be had by reflecting on how the conceptual historians of any age are also some of its theorists.

Conceptual historians theorize *with* past political theorists by sympathetically and imaginatively entering their structure of political argument. Attempting to understand past episodes of conceptual change requires much more than merely recording etymological shifts. Rather, it requires rediscovering and rethinking problems; tracing out lines of inquiry not recorded; grappling with ideas that seem irrelevant when judged by contemporary standards; even criticizing contradictions or posing counterfactuals which originally went unnoticed. These tasks are essential if we are ever to pretend that we understand past political ideas – or to avoid being guilty of "the enormous condescension of posterity" (Collini, Winch, and Burrow 1983: 377). But in performing these tasks the conceptual historian opens up the prospect that things may have been different – in concept or belief or action or practice. In short, alternative pasts existed; and if alternative pasts, then alternative presents and alternative futures. In this way conceptual histories may help stimulate the critical, creative, and even utopian impulse which characterizes political theory of any age.

Conceptual historians also theorize *across* the conceptual, argumentative, and political transformations which they record. In this way they engage in genuinely historical thinking. Historical thinking of this sort is especially evident when the conceptual changes and political innovations being narrated are stark, profound, or radical, and when our temporal distance has as its sole reward some inklings of the unintended and unconceptualized outcomes

[16] For beginnings, on the literature on the contestability of concepts, see Gallie (1968), MacIntyre (1973b), Lukes (1975), Gray (1977), and Connolly (1983).

which past actors and theorists could not in principle have had. This in turn encourages thinking about the emergence – and eventually the passing away – of our own concepts and beliefs and actions and practices. This is an evident task of contemporary political theory, one which occasions debates. Conceptual historians cannot but take sides in these debates.

Conceptual historians, furthermore, theorize *how* to do conceptual history at all. Theory here may be understood as methodology or historiography. I have already played my hand for a theory whose principal categories are contradictions, problems, and criticism. But whether this is accepted or not, plenty of other issues or debates may be seen to emerge. For example, why certain conceptual connections are identified as important – and especially how these connections are established – is a question which issues from some theory. Even something as threadbare as saying that within a particular past political theory a certain concept was more important to later theorists than another concept because we may count more later theorists citing the one over the other, presupposes a rudimentary method that more citations means more important. Though this appears simple enough, it is a simplicity not universally shared. Many historians of ideas who share or follow Leo Strauss's (1952) theory about the historical transmission of important concepts and meaningful teachings will not count in the above way.

Conceptual historians, in sum, are theoretical and methodological partisans. The way in which I have structured the discussion suggests what sort of partisanship informs my own views about the ways in which conceptual histories should proceed. The emphasis on actors' criticisms of contradictions and their attempts to solve problems, as well as on the constellations of concepts which help comprise their own structure of political argument, inclines towards a fairly strong contextualism. The meaning of political concepts is to be understood in terms of the contexts within which actors put them to use; and tracing conceptual change over time will require studying changes of contexts and use. Relevant contexts are always both linguistic and political at the same time; and conceptual historians must attend to speakers and hearers, writers and readers. Intentions are, accordingly, of enormous importance, but they alone never exhaust the meaning of political concepts or the structure of political argument at any point in time.

Such partisanship informs not so much a party as a United Front. In my counting, the Front includes all those who take political theory to be a political activity or performance, perhaps especially those who are associated with the so-called new history of political thought.[17] It includes many cultural Marxists, at least those for whom superstructures do not readily collapse into bases.[18] It may also be seen to include a certain mobilization of critical rationalism, especially given the dialectical emphasis on contradictions and criticism.[19] To be sure, this is a broad United Front, but not so broad as to unite all – and, of course, deep distinctions and divisions remain here amidst unity. Many voices we hear these days would gladly resist joining it, I suspect. Among them might be counted Straussians, Namierites, Whig historians, dialectical materialists, a number of post-structuralists, and all those who claim to catalog the allegedly timeless questions of political theory. In principle, absolute idealists of Hegel's stripe would surely resist, as well. But there are no more of them around to join any resistance or to do battle of any sort.

IV

General reflections must prove themselves in practice. Although nothing can substitute for detailed conceptual histories, let me here in this final section look briefly at two concepts not discussed elsewhere in this volume. These two concepts cover different periods and political contexts; they draw on different linguistic and theoretical sources; and they constitute different sorts of beliefs, actions, and practices. But when documenting their changes, both concepts reveal the explanatory importance of the criticism of contradictions.

Consider, first, the changes in the "fourth estate," a concept whose life was parasitic on the tripartite formula of king, lords, and commons which were said to be the only estates legitimated by the English constitution after the Revolution Settlement of 1689–90. "Here lay the frontiers of eighteenth century political understanding," as J.A.W. Gunn puts it in his intriguing conceptual history of the fourth estate, appropriately subtitled "the language of political innovation" (1983: 43). At first, anything labeled the "fourth estate" was to be criticized and condemned because it lay beyond the

[17] Here one would include the works of Quentin Skinner, John Dunn, their students and colleagues. For some sympathetic qualifications, see Ashcraft (1975); Gunn (1983: 3–6); and especially Pocock (1985, chap. 1). Also see the fine collection of essays edited by Rorty, Schneewind, and Skinner (1984).

[18] See Gramsci's (1971) remarks on "hegemony," which I use below. Also see the sentiments expressed in Christopher Hill's history of "anti-Christ" (1971: vi).

[19] Here I include Popper, especially his *Objective Knowledge* (1972). Also see Agassi (1963) and Jarvie (1972). MacIntyre's methodological ideas (1966 and 1981) often fit this general description, as well.

frontier. Accordingly, it marked out the borders of partisan conflict. But it became quite clear over time to the various partisans involved that there was a contradiction between believing that king–lords–commons exhausted the estates of the constitution and believing that other corporate entities had increasing legitimate claims on citizens' constitutional loyalties. This contradiction led to change. As Gunn points out,

> Indeed, when much the greater part of informed opinion came to accept the estates as King, Lords, and Commons, the history of the fourth estate was only beginning. Not only did allusions to such a body grow in number as the century advances, but their tone became more moderate with growing appreciation that the formal theory of the constitution was incapable of doing justice to the richness and variety of day-to-day politics. Through all the dreary bickering of the first two Hanoverian reigns there was at least some recognition that the nation was experiencing innovations in the machinery and processes of government. 1983: 57

Conceptual change in the "fourth estate," in short, registered and in part carried political changes in the beliefs and practices of eighteenth-century Englishmen. The change was thoroughgoing. Not only did the increasing moderation of tone mark a shift in attitude (or attitudinal expressiveness, as called above), but the range of reference expanded – from the army to the opposition to the ministry to the people and to other "estates" as well. Because of these changes over the course of the century, even greater change was wrought in the very criteria for applying the term at all. For the contradiction between having so many "fourth" estates only showed up the more fundamental contradiction in believing that the constitution could be expressed in the language of "estates" at all. The "fourth estate" lingered on – where it still lingers as an anachronistic reminder of politics past – as a synonym for the press. But the criteria for applying the "fourth estate" these days as a mere name have been utterly severed from the criteria (and thus the theory and practice) which originally gave it coherence. (That it persists is quaint, and perhaps the standing contradiction between having a fourth estate without the first three will be the cause of its eventual demise.)

Whatever its future, its past is marked. In terms evocative of the language of contradictions, Gunn summarizes the sense and importance of the political and conceptual changes involved here:

> When the cabinet had won acceptance, despite its failure to conform to the three estates, and both the loyal Opposition and the people found respectability as estates by courtesy, the fetters imposed by eighteenth century language were broken . . . The fact that the century witnessed a series of fourth estates testifies to the nature of the prevailing political assumptions. It is not surprising that the tradition specified no mode of responding to new features of politics; rather, the logic of the political culture simply led to common responses to different phenomena. On that happy regularity hangs the tale of political innovation and its acceptance in the eighteenth century. 1983: 95

Criticism of contradictions is also evident in the political and conceptual changes associated with "hegemony." Though "hegemony" has an ancient history, the idea of general political predominance, usually of one state over another, is not older than the nineteenth century (see entry in Williams 1983: 144–6). But decisive changes have come about with developments in twentieth-century Marxism, largely under Gramsci's inspiration. Gramsci articulated a number of contradictions he found associated with "economism." As an historiographical principle, "economism" holds that all political developments could be explained directly by the economic interests of the ruling class. But this led to contradictions with partisan political practice which went well beyond economic struggle (rightly, in Gramsci's mind) to make possible the creation of a new consciousness among workers of what was to be a politically aspirant class. Without articulating this clearly, however, the working class would fail to achieve the consciousness required for state rule because it would fail to understand the degree of bourgeois control over its very ideas and ideals, even as it achieved localized victories in the economic sphere. Gramsci insisted, therefore, that the political struggle to change beliefs and practices required conceptual change. "It is therefore necessary," Gramsci wrote from a Fascist prison, "to combat economism not only in the theory of historiography, but also and especially in the theory and practice of politics. In this field, the struggle can and must be carried on by developing the concept of hegemony" (1971: 165).

With an audience of workers and socialist theorists subsequently willing to follow Gramsci's lead, "hegemony" thus changed its criteria of application. From "the predominance of one state over another," it came to mean "the predominance of one class over another," including the mechanisms for the control of consciousness. Its reference changed accordingly. The range of attitudes it could express now depended on how "hegemony" was modified: condemned if bourgeois, commended if proletarian. The commendation carried a political message: the battle for hegemony was to be fought in part by changing and advancing the concept of "hegemony" itself. Whatever one's partisanship or one's particular judgment of Gramsci's political strategies, the general point is not to be gainsaid. Language may indeed be a material force amidst political struggle.

If these two examples help us understand conceptual change, then they do so by connecting conceptual and political change in a direct and intimate way. They may also serve as promissory notes for a political theory of conceptual change based on problem-solving and the criticism of contradictions. How far other examples would help to increase or decrease the value of these notes remains to be seen. A number of conceptual histories must be consulted – and in many cases written or rewritten – to see this matter through. I suspect that many concepts would fit quite handily, and that telling their story in this way would increase our understanding of them as *political* realities: the coining of "boycott";[20] the change in the meaning of "nobility";[21] the obsolescence of the concept of "honor";[22] the expansion of "gentleman";[23] the manifold changes in "slavery" along its tortuous history;[24] the change in New World "enthusiasm" from heresy to conspiracy;[25] the dramatic shift in the meaning of "revolution" in the late seventeenth century;[26] the changes in many legal concepts and principles;[27] the metamorphoses of the "science of politics" and many of the concepts associated with it;[28] the feminist transformation of "patriarchy"; the coining of the "helping" professions and other less-than-benign manipulations of the symbolic

[20] The materials for such a reading can be found in the story as recounted in Connolly (1983: 185). More generally, see Connolly's discussion of conceptual revision and political reform.

[21] See the observations on the contradictions in the feudal concept of "nobility" in Gellner (1968).

[22] For beginnings see the remarkable essay by Berger (1984).

[23] Tocqueville (1955: 82–3) ends his brief discussion of "gentleman" with the observation that "its history is the history of democracy itself." See similar remarks on "individualism," p. 96.

[24] For the history of discourse about slavery, see Davis (1966); and for a particular study of the contradictions which "slavery" generates for Locke's political thought, see Farr (1986).

[25] For this neglected aspect of early American history, see Lovejoy (1985).

[26] See Hatto (1949) and Snow (1962) for the materials for such a reading. Also see Kosseleck (1985: 39–54).

[27] See James Boyd White's discussion of our "controlled change of language" in the law as generated by the dialectical tensions between one version of events and another (1984: 273).

[28] Collini, Winch, and Burrow (1983: 107–8).

aspects of politics.[29] Many others suggest themselves, as well, including many of those concepts whose histories are narrated in this volume.

[29] For these manipulations, and their contradictions, see Edelman (1977 and 1984).

REFERENCES

Agassi, Joseph. 1983. "Towards an Historiography of Science." *History and Theory*, Beiheft 2: 1–117.

Ashcraft, Richard. 1975. "On the Problem of Methodology and the Nature of Political Theory." *Political Theory* 3: 5–25.

Austin, J.L. 1962. *How to Do Things With Words*. Oxford: Oxford University Press.

Ball, Terence. 1983. "Contradiction and Critique in Political Theory." In John S. Nelson (ed.), *What Should Political Theory be Now?* Albany, NY: State University of New York Press, pp. 127–68.

Beer, Samuel H. 1970. "Political Science and History." In Melvin Richter (ed.), *Essays in Theory and History*. Cambridge, MA: Harvard University Press, pp. 41–73.

Berger, Peter. 1984. "On the Obsolescence of the Concept of Honour." In Michael Sandel (ed.), *Liberalism and Its Critics*. New York: New York University Press, pp. 149–58.

Collini, Stefan, Donald Winch, and John Burrow. 1983. *The Noble Science of Politics*. Cambridge: Cambridge University Press.

Connolly, William E. 1983. *The Terms of Political Discourse*, 2nd edn. Princeton, NJ: Princeton University Press.

Davidson, Donald. 1984. *Inquiries into Truth and Interpretation*. Oxford: Oxford University Press.

Davis, David Byron. 1966. *The Problem of Slavery in Western Culture*. Ithaca, NY: Cornell University Press.

Dunn, John. 1978. "Practicing History and Social Science on 'Realist' Assumptions." In Christopher Hookway and Philip Pettit (eds.), *Action and Interpretation*. Cambridge: Cambridge University Press, pp. 145–74.

1982. "Understanding Revolutions." *Ethics* 92: 299–315.

Edelman, Murray. 1977. *Political Language*. New York: Academic Press.

1984. *The Symbolic Aspects of Politics*, 2nd edn. Champaign, IL: University of Illinois Press.

Elster, Jon. 1978. *Logic and Society*. New York: John Wiley and Sons.

Farr, James. 1982. "Historical Concepts in Political Science: The Case of 'Revolution.' " *American Journal of Political Science* 26: 688–708.

1986. " 'So Vile and Miserable an Estate': The Problem of Slavery in Locke's Political Thought." *Political Theory* 14: 263–89.

Festinger, Leon. 1957. *A Theory of Cognitive Dissonance*. Stanford, CA: Stanford University Press.

1964. *Conflict, Decision, and Dissonance*. London: Tavistock.
Feyerabend, Paul K. 1975. *Against Method*. London: New Left Books.
1985. *Problems of Empiricism*. Cambridge: Cambridge University Press.
Gallie, W.B. 1968. *Philosophy and the Historical Understanding*, revised edn. New York: Schocken.
Gellner, Ernest. 1968. "The New Idealism." In Imre Lakatos and Alan Musgrave (eds.), *Problems in the Philosophy of Science*. Amsterdam: North Holland, pp. 377–406.
Gramsci, Antonio. 1971. *Prison Notebooks*. New York: International.
Gray, John. 1977. "On the Contestability of Social and Political Concepts." *Political Theory* 5: 333–48.
Gunn, J.A.W. 1983. *Beyond Liberty and Property: The Process of Self-Recognition in Eighteenth Century Political Thought*. Kingston and Montreal: McGill-Queen's University Press.
Hanson, Russell L. 1985. *The Democratic Imagination in America*. Princeton, NJ: Princeton University Press.
Hatto, Arthur. 1949. "Revolution: An Enquiry into the Usefulness of an Historical Term." *Mind* 58: 495–517.
Hill, Christopher. 1971. *Anti-Christ in Seventeenth Century England*. Oxford: Oxford University Press.
Hobbes, Thomas. 1968. *Leviathan*, edited by C.B. MacPherson. Harmondsworth: Penguin.
Hobsbawm, E.J. 1962. *The Age of Revolutions*. New York: New American Library.
Hume, David. 1748. *Essays, Moral and Political*. London: A. Millar.
Jarvie, Ian. 1972. *Concepts and Society*. London: Routledge and Kegan Paul.
Katz, Jerold J. 1979. "Semantics and Conceptual Change." *Philosophical Review* 88: 327-65.
Kosseleck, Reinhardt. 1985. *Futures Past: On the Semantics of Time*. Cambridge, MA: MIT Press.
Kuhn, Thomas. 1970. *The Structure of Scientific Revolutions*, 2nd edn. Chicago, IL: University of Chicago Press.
Lakatos, Imre. 1978. *The Methodology of Scientific Research Programmes*. Cambridge: Cambridge University Press.
Laudan, Larry. 1977. *Progress and Its Problems*. Berkeley, CA: University of California Press.
Lovejoy, David S. 1985. *Religious Enthusiasm in the New World: Heresy to Revolution*. Cambridge, MA: Harvard University Press.
Lukes, Steven. 1975. *Power: A Radical View*. Atlantic Highlands, NJ: Humanities Press.
MacIntyre, Alasdair. 1966. *A Short History of Ethics*. New York: Macmillan.
1971. *Against the Self Images of the Age*. New York: Schocken.
1973a. "Ideology, Social Science, and Revolution." *Comparative Politics* 5: 321–42.
1973b. "The Essential Contestability of Some Social Concepts." *Ethics* 84: 1–9.
1981. *After Virtue*. Notre Dame, IN: University of Notre Dame Press.

Marx, Karl. 1963. *The Poverty of Philosophy*. New York: International.
1970. *The German Ideology*. New York: International.
1973. *Grundrisse*. New York: Vintage.
Pearce, G. and P. Maynard (eds.). 1973. *Conceptual Change*. Dordrecht: Reidl.
Pocock, J.G.A. 1980. "Political Ideas as Political Events: Political Philosophers as Historical Actors." In Melvin Richter (ed.), *Political Theory and Political Education*. Princeton, NJ: Princeton University Press, pp. 139–58.
1985. *Virtue, Commerce, and History*. Cambridge: Cambridge University Press.
Popper, Karl. 1960. *The Poverty of Historicism*. New York: Harper and Row.
1965. *Conjectures and Refutations*. New York: Harper and Row.
1972. *Objective Knowledge*. Oxford: Oxford University Press.
Putnam, Hilary. 1975. *Mind, Language and Reality, Philosophical Papers*, vol. II. Cambridge: Cambridge University Press.
Rorty, Richard, J.B.Schneewind, and Quentin Skinner (eds.). 1984. *Philosophy in History*. Cambridge: Cambridge University Press.
Searle, John. 1969. *Speech Acts*. Cambridge: Cambridge University Press.
Shapere, Dudley. 1966. "Meaning and Scientific Change." In R. Colodny (ed.), *Mind and Cosmos*. Pittsburgh, PA: University of Pittsburgh Press, pp. 41–85.
Skinner, Quentin. 1974a. "Some Problems in the Analysis of Political Thought and Action." *Political Theory* 2: 277–303.
1974b. "The Principles and Practice of Opposition: The Case of Bolingbroke versus Walpole." In Neil McKendrick (ed.), *Historical Perspectives: Studies in English Thought and Society in Honour of J.H. Plumb*. London: Europa Publications, pp. 93–128.
1978. *The Foundations of Modern Political Thought*, 2 vols. Cambridge: Cambridge University Press.
1980. "Language and Social Change." In Leonard Michaels and Christopher Ricks (eds.), *The State of the Language*. Berkeley, CA: University of California Press, pp. 562–78.
Snow, Vernon. 1962. "The Concept of Revolution in Seventeenth Century England." *Historical Journal* 5: 167–74.
Stern, Gustaf. 1965. *Meaning and Change of Meaning*. Bloomington, IN: Indiana Unversity Press.
Stone, Lawrence. 1977. *The Family, Sex, and Marriage in England, 1500–1800*. New York: Harper and Row.
1985. "Sex in the West." *The New Republic* (July 8): 25–37.
Strauss, Leo. 1952. *Persecution and the Art of Writing*. Glencoe: Free Press.
Taylor, Charles. 1985. *Human Agency and Language*. Cambridge: Cambridge University Press.
Thucydides. 1951. *The Peloponnesian Wars*. New York: Vintage.
Tocqueville, Alexis de. 1955. *The Old Regime and the French Revolution*, translated by Stuart Gilbert. Garden City, NY: Doubleday.
Toulmin, Stephen. 1972. *Human Understanding*. Princeton, NJ: Princeton University Press.

Walzer, Michael. 1983. *Spheres of Justice*. New York: Basic Books.
White, James Boyd. 1984. *When Words Lose Their Meaning: Constitutions and Reconstitutions of Language, Character, and Community*. Chicago, IL: University of Chicago Press.
Williams, Raymond. 1983. *Keywords*, revised edn. New York: Oxford University Press.
Wills, Garry. 1979. *Inventing America: Jefferson's Declaration of Independence*. New York: Vintage.
Wittgenstein, Ludwig. 1958. *Philosophical Investigations*. New York: Macmillan.
1980. *Culture and Value*. Chicago, IL: University of Chicago Press.
Wolin, Sheldon. 1960. *Politics and Vision*. New York: Little, Brown.

3

Constitution

GRAHAM MADDOX

I

When Thomas Paine declared that the American colonial constitutions "were to liberty what a grammar is to language" (Paine 1969: 117), he was referring explicitly to written documents. In his view, "A constitution is a thing antecedent to a government," being the act "of the people constituting a government" (Paine 1969: 93). Standing at the foundation of politics – as its etymology implies – it anticipates a new era of constitutional government (Wolf-Phillips 1972: 7–9; Schochet 1979: 1–15). Yet the constitutional threshold opens both ways; it draws lessons from previous experience, declaiming the grievances of the past in clauses designed to block their recurrence. An "antecedent" constitution, however, also celebrates past discoveries of liberty, and while Paine's polemic against the English monarchical system led him into accusations that there was no constitution at all in England, it was to a large extent English liberties that instructed the American constitution writers. Paine would not accept that "constitutional" governments could be forged by a people's experience, and that a conspectus of that experience could be incorporated into the conceptual apparatus transmitted by its language. Constitutional government was well established before the term "constitution" was first employed, but its appearance signalled a new sophistication about the relationship between public powers and private aspirations, and a new concern to promote the value of holding them in the right balance. Limited government was emblazoned upon the political consciousness of the West as "constitution" long before there were written constitutions.

Nevertheless, the term "constitution" itself has had a mottled history, and does not always coincide with various communities' understanding of limited government. As a political concept *constitutio* appeared in the time of the Roman statesman, Cicero, and may well have been coined by him. Its chief function was to gather up past experience. Cicero is well known as a conservator and transmitter of Greek political thought, and first used the term in a passage of the *De re publica* in which he had been paraphrasing Plato's discussion of democracy.[1] *Constitutio* was very likely his approximation to the Greek *politeia*, a descriptive term for the political community "as it actually is" (McIlwain 1947: 26; Morris-Jones 1965: 439–40). Adding the Latin connotation of "establishment" to the *polis*-ness of *politeia*, Cicero appeared to offer, in a piece describing a "moderate and balanced form of government" (Cicero, *Rep.*, 1.69), a new conception of the deployment of institutions and powers in a political community.

As Professor Sartori has suggested, Cicero's *constitutio* was "republican specific" (Sartori 1984: 497–9), referring to institutional arrangements that would ensure stability, freedom, and above all justice. Though never fully conceptualized in quite the same way, such arrangements had been explored in Greek political experience and reflected upon by the great philosophers. We are therefore justified in seeking the origins of a constitutional tradition of limited government, cushioned by an ethos of inner restraint and mutual obligation on the part of citizens, in the Greek polis. Moreover, since it is our purpose to reaffirm that the ancient world perceived with clarity principles of limited but creative government which subsequent experience, especially since the rise of the modern "sovereign state," has only clouded, we shall dwell for a little on the ancient polity. We may then light upon some analytical moments in the story of limited government, namely the modern elaboration of the political contract, the movement for written constitutions, and modern controversies about the nature and purpose of the constitution.

This eclectic approach is not meant to be idiosyncratic, but merely to acknowledge the impossibility of following the vicissitudes of constitutionalism through its long history. Cicero's *constitutio* is not always of help. Being "republican specific," it enjoyed only a brief currency in the Roman world, the republic itself scarcely surviving Cicero's death. The term was then appropriated by the emperors for their edicts and decrees, and continued so to be used throughout medieval times. The constitutional tradition was therefore carried

[1] Cicero, *De re publica*, 1.69; cf. Plato, *Republic*, bk. VIII. In later generations "constitutio" was certainly used as a direct translation of "politeia." See e.g. Apuleius, *De Platone et eius dogmate*, 2.24.1.

forward in other terms until "constitution" was redeployed in the sixteenth or seventeenth century in something like the sense Cicero had intended. We first meet it, however, as Cicero's version of *politeia*.

II

The Greek *politeia* covered perverted forms of government as well as the good; a polity could be mob rule, oligarchy or, worst of all, tyranny. None of these could be called "constitutional" in our sense, and yet, in all the comparison and classification of polities undertaken by the philosophers, there was an urgent quest for the "good" form that would produce "the good life." In the end, Aristotle simply called his best feasible system – a moderate, "constitutional" form (as modern translators call it) – "polity" (Aristotle, *Politics*, 4.6.1).

Polities preferred by philosophers in the Socratic tradition were identified either with the rule of law or the rule of right, and we may with justification speak of embryonic constitutional principles opposing the rule of force as early as the eighth century BC when, in his *Theogony*, Hesiod praised Zeus for "laying down Good Order, Right and Peace as principles of human society" (Sinclair 1967: 19). Set so early in a religious and philosophical framework, precepts of right and peace were directed at people's inner nature, suggesting to them a mode of restrained behavior conforming with unwritten laws. The sophist, Hippias of Elis, was said to have believed that such laws were universal, and therefore natural (Plato, *Hippias major*, 291). In the famous Funeral Speech, Thucydides has Pericles boasting of the respect his countrymen had for the laws, "especially those which are for the protection of the oppressed, and those unwritten laws which it is an acknowledged shame to break" (Thucydides, 1943: 117). According to Aristotle, while written laws are important, the laws of unwritten custom "are more sovereign and deal with more sovereign matters than written laws" (Aristotle, *Politics*, 3.11.6). Barker interprets Aristotle to mean that "Greater than the writing of excellent laws on paper, is the writing of them into the spiritual fibre of a people, law abidingness is more than law . . . the essence of law is the will of the citizen to abide by the law" (Barker 1959: 323).

Such a disposition was of little consolation to people ruled by oppressors who interpreted the will of the gods according to their own arbitrary judgments. While the spirit of "law abidingness" would always be essential to constitutionalism, it was nevertheless also necessary that a community should know in explicit terms where it stood in relation to its rulers and the laws they administered. The early efforts of the Greek *thesmothetai*, or law-givers, were therefore of immense importance. *Thesmos* denoted the law, supplied by the gods, but at last written down for public reference. The Athenians regarded Solon, whose legal code of 594–593 BC superseded the unwarrantedly infamous code of Draco, as the founder of their polity. His laws, inscribed on rotating wooden tablets, embodied social reforms that established an order designed to protect the poor against abuses by the rich and powerful (Murray 1980: 174–6, 180–91). The social and political arrangements produced by this code were one of the earliest expressions of popular sovereignty, since his "people's court," in the view of Aristotle or one of his collaborators, "made the people sovereign of the verdict," and "the sovereign of the verdict is sovereign of the constitution [i.e. polity]" (*Ath. Pol.*, 9.1, in Barker 1960: 50).

The impulses toward democracy set free by Solon's legislation culminated in the democratic arrangements of Cleisthenes and his successors. The emergence of the democracy is a complex history, but for our purposes popular sovereignty – and the belief that what a community's government can do is held within limits set by the people – was transferred into the law itself. According to the careful studies of Martin Ostwald, at some time at or about the end of the sixth century BC, *thesmos*, the word for law as set down for the people's benefit by the law-giver, was replaced by *nomos*, the law as approved and enacted by the people itself. *Nomos*, of course, was also the word for "custom," a usage derived from its earlier meaning as "the normal way of acting under given sets of circumstances or for a particular kind of individual" (Ostwald 1969: 24–5). However indirectly, the new word for the written law, promulgated in the people's assembly, was connected both with the custom of a people and the inner direction of the individual person's behavior.

When, after a century of self-confident operation, the democracy had given way to brief periods of oligarchic rule, its restored form provided for the passage or the revision of laws by *nomothetai*, "law-fixers," who were also the jurors of the people's courts. We may assume that their work included adjusting the ancient fundamental laws to accommodate changing circumstances without violating time-honored democratic principles. The resolutions of the assembly were themselves binding laws, but Aristotle found it instructive to distinguish between these "assembly" laws (*psephismata*) and fundamental laws (*nomoi*), for "where the *nomoi* do not govern there is no constitution (*politeia*)" (Aristotle, *Politics*, 4.4.7). This distinction seems to suggest that even over the (sovereign) assembly "stood a higher instance, 'the law,' of which all single laws were parts and reflexes" (Ehrenberg 1965: 57). Certainly the democracy evolved a fascinating procedure, the *graphe paranomon*, whereby laws passed by the assembly could be invalidated as repugnant to the existing *nomoi*, an implication that new laws should conform with the spirit of law itself, and should not offend general and universal principles of humanity (Hansen 1974: 55).

The oath sworn by the jurors who, acting as *nomothetai*, heard cases concerning the *graphe paranomon*, placed their activities under the supervision of heaven, as did their sacred duty to protect the *nomoi*. In some sense the *nomoi* were collective discoveries of the will of the gods for moral human behavior, and the prophetic utterance of Heraclitus at the beginning of the democratic era, that "All human laws are fed by one divine law" (quoted in Bowra 1957: 79; cf. Kitto 1961: 131), was congenial to the democratic temperament. The notion of a higher law which might even adjure disobedience to particular human laws found its noblest expression in the defiant speech of Antigone, who did not think the king's edicts "strong enough to overrule the unwritten unalterable laws of God and heaven" (Sophocles, *Antigone* [1947]: 453).

It was the Greeks, of course, who imported notions of a higher law, expressed in explicit terms by the Hellenistic Stoics, to Rome. A more receptive host could scarcely have been found, since republican institutions had almost obsessively denied power to individuals after the expulsion of tyrannical kings at the end of the sixth century BC. These institutions were shot through with checks and balances, since the "regal power" inherited from the kings was shared by colleges of magistrates who could veto each other's initiatives and whose tenure was limited to one year in office (Crawford 1978: 30). Moreover, the official magistrates were opposed by tribunes, unofficial representatives of the *plebs*, originally an oppressed caste entirely excluded from political privilege, but at all times more numerous and containing the many poor. The tribunes also could veto nearly all official acts of state.

Rome was very experienced at limited government – at least insofar as individual rulers or potential rulers were concerned – when the Stoic philosophers, teaching at Rome from the middle of the second century BC, further "emancipated mankind from its subjection to despotic rule" (Lord Acton, quoted by McIlwain 1947: 155–6). The Greek Stoics had developed old ideas of a higher law into a full-blown theory of the law of nature which, while not explicitly political, had eased the path of those alienated by the imperial conquest of the city-states towards membership of the "world state." Stoic virtues of constancy, dignity, gravity, magnanimity, and endurance had been the practical virtues of the Roman aristocracy all along (Clarke 1968: 32). So while the Roman ruling classes could welcome this philosophic reinforcement of civic virtues, they also imbibed a universal law of nature of which every living being partook through its power of reason. Teaching of this kind gave the eclectic Cicero a revolutionary notion that wherever the laws of states did not conform with true law – eternal, unchangeable reason – then these particular laws would be invalid, for nothing can free us from our obligation to obey the higher law (Cicero, *Rep.*, 3.33). His *constitutio* was ruled by true law.

According to McIlwain, duty to the higher law compelled jurists of the Roman empire to invent the political fiction that, even under an absolutist imperial regime, laws should be administered according to principles of equity whatever the strict letter of the law. Equity was defined by reason and the law of nature, with which the popular sovereignty inherited from the republican era undoubtedly conformed. Furthermore, equity implied an individual's right to be treated with fairness, and preferred to him an area of autonomy enshrined in a *private law* clearly distinguished from the *public law*. In this distinction we mark the beginnings of a separation between state and society which would imply for later generations the confinement of government activity to a sphere of competence delimited by the function of the political realm. Yet the most valuable political bequest of the Romans to Western society was probably the rule of reason, further to be elaborated by St. Thomas Aquinas and later jurists who would find cause to insist on the separation of the sacred from the secular. The foundation of Western constitutionalism, therefore, was popular sovereignty, rooted in the *nomos* of the Greeks, and hallowed in the jurisprudence of the Romans as the rule of right reason deriving from the universal law of nature.

III

Since the Roman emperors had annexed *constitutio* to their own purpose, the term itself naturally took on authoritarian overtones not to be shaken off until the sixteenth or seventeenth century. Some Latin writers continued to translate the Greek *politeia* as *constitutio*, or to mention the "constitution" of the world or of the church. The idea of political institutions arranged in such a way as to limit government and to secure liberty to subjects remained, however, and was embodied, for example, in Marsiglio's term *forma*, as in the later English terms "form" or "model" or "instrument" of government. The constitution of the Romans itself was embodied in laws that were "common engagements" of the people (Papinian, *Digest*, 1.3.1). The rule of reason did not particularly depend on a political or social contract, but the idea was quite well known in the ancient world,[2] and in the Christian era could be accommodated alongside the law of nature. Yet the contract entered modern constitutional thought mainly as the inheritance of readers of the Old Testament. The Mosaic and Joshuanic covenants had founded a religious community, but it was also a self-governing, egalitarian federation of tribes which, for the best part of two centuries, brooked no earthly ruler (Mendenhall 1954: 50–76; Bright 1972: 164–6).

The covenant would be revived by Calvin and the Puritans (Skinner 1978, vol. II: 236–8), and find a powerful secular expression in the works of Hobbes and Locke. Contract theories would strike a special resonance among those whose public institutions had developed directly from feudal law, a tradition which many writers believe to be at the core of modern constitutionalism. For "the essential feature of medieval feudalism was its contractual nature" (Ullmann 1978: 151–2). Contract was evident in all formal relationships, but at the highest level the contract between the king and his tenants-in-chief seriously modified the prerogatives of the crown, since two barely compatible functions jostled together within the person of the monarch. McIlwain characterized the feudal regime as a balance between *gubernaculum* and *jurisdictio*, a separation of functions "far sharper than we make in our modern times between government and law" (McIlwain 1947: 77–8). *Gubernaculum* was exercised to provide security and impose the king's heavy peace. In this aspect the king's power was absolute. Ruling by the grace of God and receiving in trust the tutelary care of his subjects, he discharged what Ullmann has called a "theocratic" function (Ullmann 1969: 45; Schramm 1937: 25). On the other hand, the king was also the fountain of justice, and his *jurisdictio* implied protection for his subjects, even against possible abuse of his own autocratic power, "For in *jurisdictio* . . . there are bounds to the king's discretion

[2] See e.g. Plato, *Protagoras*, 322–3; *Republic*, 2. 259; Aristotle, *Politics*, 3.5.11; Cicero, *Rep.*, 3. 33; Lucretius, *De rerum natura*, 5.

established by a law that is positive and coercive, and a royal act beyond these bounds is *ultra vires*" (McIlwain 1947: 85; cf. Jolliffe 1963: 24). McIlwain draws a parallel between the independence of the medieval jurists of England and the *praetores peregrini* of Rome; issues were tried according to the principles of equity upheld in each tradition, often in defiance of the express wishes of the monarch. Yet the feudal monarch's "absolutism" was much more explicitly modified by the limited lease of power he acquired under the feudal law. The compact between the king and his magnates, just as much as between any lord and his vassals, was entered on both sides by autonomous parties, and both were bound under the law.

Although the feudal relationship was essentially legal, the system was supported by an ethos which came close to the "inner restraint" by which alone modern constitutionalism can persist. We should not exaggerate this restraint, since medieval life was in general violent and uncertain, but that very uncertainty taught the urgent necessity of moderation, which, even if at times it took the form of myth, was nevertheless a fruitful source for subsequent political thinking. The mutual obligations of the contract embraced good faith, trust, and a respect of persons on both sides (Ullmann 1967: 65–6; Painter 1961: 267–72). The vassal owed his lord an obligation of honor, but "fealty, as distinct from obedience, is reciprocal in character, and contains the implicit condition that one party owes it to the other only so long as the other keeps faith" (Kern 1939: 87). Fealty also entailed the duty of *consilium*, offering advice to the lord before any action affecting the estate, or the realm in the case of the liege lord, was taken. This primitive rule by consent presumed that the vassal's opinion was to be valued, his person respected. Consultation was a special characteristic of medieval times, and "according to the code of good government universally accepted at the time, no chief, whatever his rank, could make any serious decision without first taking counsel."[3]

Contracts freely entered could be repudiated on either side. Just as any lord who failed to keep faith with his vassals could lose his rights over them, so too "if the king breaks the law, he automatically forfeits any claim to the obedience of his subjects" (Kern 1939: 87; Van Caenegem 1973: 34–5). The underlying threat of "defiance" (*diffidatio*) imposed restrictions on the crown's prerogatives, and in the famous rebellion resulting in the Magna Carta the provisions of

[3] Bloch (1962, vol. II: 410). When the king took counsel with his magnates this was sometimes represented as tantamount to consulting with his entire people. See e.g. *Monumenta Germaniae historica, constitutiones et publica*, vol. I, p. 28.

the law were enforced upon the king. Regarded by many as the foundation of the British constitution (Wolf-Phillips 1968: 182–4), this document not only censured the king's conduct but also underlined the requirement that the king consult with his magnates and obtain consent for actions affecting his subjects.

The feudal law of medieval Europe evolved to meet the needs of local circumstances, but impulses toward limiting government power and asserting the liberties of subjects appeared to some medieval jurists to be universal. In England they civilized and canonized their common law by supplying a theoretical support borrowed from Roman jurisprudence. The common law toughened inside the armour of right reason. Conceptual weapons in Bracton's commentaries came from the citadel of Rome's imperial *Digest* (Rathbone 1967). The immediate good sense of the common law was assimilated to the constitutional tradition of the West, itself adding along the way a highly practical method of dealing with rulers who break the law.

When in later times monarchs tried to exercise an absolutist rule, the much re-enacted Magna Carta was cited with the assertion that the liberties it proclaimed extended to all subjects of the realm (McIlwain 1939: 128). Chief Justice Coke quoted to his monarch, James I, Bracton's dictum that while the king is subject to no person, he is under God and the law. Although dismissed from the bench, Coke subsequently applied his faith in the common law to parliamentary debates, contributing at the forefront to a bill of liberties, accepted by the crown as the Petition of Right, which condemned as illegal arbitrary acts of government (Keir 1966: 192). Although the basis of his reasoning is in dispute, Coke even asserted the common law over against acts of parliament, contending that it could "sometimes adjudge them to be void."[4]

Being framed in an ancient tradition of right reason, the common law was sometimes regarded as a collective discovery of a whole people. Richard Hooker had written in the late sixteenth century, "the general and perpetual voice of men is as the assent of God himself" (quoted by Friedrich [1964: 52]). The consent of the people made laws reasonable, and "laws they are not therefore which public approbation hath not made so" (quoted in Friedrich [1964: 54]). The most famous of all contract theories, that of John Locke,

[4] Coke's Reports, pt. XII, 65, quoted in Sabine and Thorson (1973: 419); cf. Thorne (1968: 15–24). Coke was not, however, in the feudal tradition of argument, since he claimed that the Magna Carta was the product of common law born of time immemorial, and certainly time beyond the Norman Conquest. See Pocock (1973: 214–15).

argued that society was formed by the assent of the people given to protect their "natural rights" to life, liberty, and estate. Governments are constituted over society as a trust, but "*are dissolved* . . . when the Legislative, or the Prince, either of them act contrary to their trust" (Locke 1965: 460).

Both the compact and common law traditions were assimilated to the term "constitution" when it began to gain currency in English. Although Cicero's usages were of course known, we cannot be certain that the new employment of "constitution" as the arrangement providing for limited government was a conscious revival of his approach. We can observe the transition in English of "constitution" as mere "establishment" to something more like "the composition of the political community." This new meaning had to wrestle with medieval survivals of "constitution" as "edict." In the "constitutionalist" tradition, the establishment that was being spoken of was an establishment of *good faith* or of *justice*, connotations which resonate with Cicero's intentions for the term. As early as 1531 Sir Thomas Elyot was writing, "Since faith [i.e., 'fidelity to contract and to law' – Allen] is the foundation of justice, which is the chief constitution and maker of a public weal, faith is the conservator of the same" (quoted by Allen [1957: 248]). Hobbes referred to the "Constitution of a Civil Power" in the sense of "the erection of a Common-wealth," but this "constitution" was also clearly connected with the incorporation of justice (*Leviathan*, pt. I, chap. 15). By 1703 Locke was referring comfortably to the "English constitution" in the fully modern sense (Laslett 1965: 475), and the term was in wide use in succeeding decades (Foord 1964: 104–5).

In Bolingbroke's famous definition of 1738 the constitution was "that Assemblage of Laws, Institutions and Customs *derived from certain fix'd principles of Reason* that compose the general System, *according to which the Community hath agreed to be governed*" (Bolingbroke 1809, vol. III: 157; emphasis added). This, of course, was too loose for Paine, who insisted that a constitution must have "a real existence; and wherever it cannot be produced in visible form, there is none" (Paine 1969: 93). The revolutionary causes to which Paine bent his energies set up irresistible demands for the "visible" constitutions which have since become almost universal.

IV

Those in the American colonies who pressed for the adoption of written constitutions were not inclined to stress the radical nature of their invention. They were familiar with something like written constitutions in the form of company charters; their easy acceptance of a public life regulated by charters and the "fundamental orders" that succeeded them, together with a growing disaffection for the British parliament in the 1760s, led many to reject the British notion of constitution altogether and to seek a new legitimacy for self-government.

The company charters of the early colonists were, of course, no more constitutions than were other charters, letters patent and writs issued by the crown. From the colonists' point of view, however, they were seen to relate to the whole of their life in the new territory, and to assume for them, if not for the British government, a fundamental importance. They certainly enunciated constitutional principles, the charter of Maryland, for example, insisting that all laws of the colony "be constant to Reason" (quoted by Perry [1964: 108]). More significant, however, was the charter granted by Charles I to the governor and company of the Massachusetts Bay in 1628–9, which the colonists took with them and treated, to all intents and purposes, as a commission to found a community with independent political institutions (McIlwain 1939: 231–43). In 1639 migrants from Massachusetts enacted the Fundamental Orders of Connecticut, "the first written constitution of modern democracy" (Charles Borgeaud, quoted by McIlwain 1939: 241). By the second half of the seventeenth century the colonists would have known of the Levellers' *Agreement of the People* (Woodhouse 1974: 443–5); they had observed Cromwell's attempt to govern England under an *Instrument of Government* (1653) and had read Harrington's suggestion, in *Oceana*, that the "Lord Archon" should call a council of legislators to promulgate a "Model of the Commonwealth" (Harrington 1955: 114). In 1682 William Penn was writing of "frames" and "models" of government that might "secure the people from the abuse of power" (quoted by Perry [1964: 211–12]). Although Penn did indeed speak vaguely of "that which makes a good constitution," we do not find the colonists explicitly identifying "frames" or "models" or "instruments" or "fundamental orders" with "constitution" in an age that had not yet given up the idea of a constitution as an "assemblage" of laws, customs, and institutions (Bailyn 1967: 176).

In the revolutionary era, however, the amorphous constitution of the British was rejected by the colonials, partly because, as they believed, under it a tyrannical parliament had treated them unjustly, and because it was seen in general to provide no enforceable limit to an omnicompetent legislature. A form of government and a constitution were not the same thing, it was argued, and in any case England had neither. Only a written constitution, setting down the limits to government authority and guaranteeing justiciable rights to citizens, would henceforth be acceptable (Bailyn 1967: 182–3). The new state constitutions that emerged from this climate of opinion "were built by Americans on the solid foundation of colonial experience, with the timber of English practice, using Montesquieu as consulting architect" (Morison and Commager 1962, vol. I: 236–7).

Montesquieu's quest for liberty was taken up energetically in the colonies (Madison, *Federalist*, 47 in Hamilton *et al.* 1961; cf. Lutz 1984: 189–97). The constitutional principles explored in *The Spirit of the Laws* were of great interest to the Americans, in particular four allied theories (Richter 1977: 84–97): the first, that a mixed constitution could combine the peculiar virtues of monarchic, aristocratic, and republican government; the second, that the separation of powers earlier taught by Locke would produce liberty by ensuring that the executive, legislative, and judicial powers would not accumulate in the hands of one person or group of persons; thirdly, that these separated powers would check and balance each other by exercising "the mutual privilege of rejecting," a power something akin to the veto powers of the Roman magistracies that Montesquieu had studied so closely (Montesquieu 1949: 160; and 1965: 26–7); and fourthly, perhaps his most original contribution, that liberty is to be found within the institutionalized clash of class interest (Merry 1970: 155–239).

Although the Founding Fathers of the United States were of oligarchic temperament, they imparted no intrinsic class bias to the constitution of 1787. They were, however, greatly concerned to blunt the passions of faction, to raise obstacles in the way of would-be tyrants, to avoid "the moral diseases under which popular governments everywhere have perished" (Madison, *Federalist*, 10 in Hamilton *et al.* 1961) and to shun "the evils . . . from the excess of democracy" (Gerry, quoted by Merriam [1903: 99]). There was no precedent for the federal system of government which, entrenched in the written constitution, either vested sovereignty in the entire people or ignored it altogether (MacIver 1968: 60–1). Defending popular sovereignty from other pretenders to the title, they overlaid the system with checks and balances hitherto unheard of in any government or theory of government, Adams later claiming that the constitution set up no fewer than eight levels of balance.[5] Modern constitutionalists like McIlwain were to complain that the Founding Fathers, "in their fear of the government's doing harm ... incapacitated it for doing much good" (McIlwain 1939: 246).

V

In the opinion of Paine's arch-rival, Edmund Burke, written constitutions were no more than the political manifestos of the ruling groups at the time they were promulgated (cited by Zurcher [1951: 1]). Such disdain, however, did not prevent countries all over Europe adopting written constitutions during the nineteenth century. Burke's view, of course, was overstated, since a drafted constitution does not necessarily have to favor one party or another. There are, nevertheless, intrinsic problems in the example of a "rigid" constitution that the American Founders gave the world (Bryce 1901, vol. I: 145–254; cf. Friedrich 1967). It was not that constitutions, once written down, could never be amended or replaced – the French managed to adopt a dozen between 1791 and 1875. The difficulty is that while neither a "rigid" nor any other sort of constitution will block the path of those determined to wrest power by violent means, it may nevertheless prevent law-abiding, self-restrained reformers from carrying out policies that the electoral majority might legitimately have entrusted to them.

Entrenched constitutions, embodying a "higher law," are necessarily placed beyond the power of legislatures to amend, and are often made extraordinarily difficult to change. Amendment procedures in some federal countries, for example, make it possible for the voters of the small states of the federation to place the constitution beyond the reach of a substantial majority of the population taken as a whole. Difficult procedures are necessary, it is said, to immunize the "higher law" from manipulation by fickle and transient majority opinion, yet such arguments forget that a constitution was first approved and established by a majority that may well have been transient, and may well have numbered only a fraction of the present-day voters now bound by it.

The tendency of the constitutionalism of the previous two centuries was to diminish the possibility of tyrannical government,

[5] In Merriam (1903: 139–40). For the view that "separation of powers" has never been a satisfactory interpretation of American constitutionalism, see e.g. Spiro (1959: 11–13).

and at the same time greatly to reduce the opportunities for decisive government intervention in economic and social affairs. Giovanni Sartori has argued that the defining *telos* of constitution is *garantisme*, the guarantee of limited government consisting in part of prescriptions for the allocation of power, a bill of rights, the rule of law, and judicial review (Sartori 1962: 853–64). Sartori recognizes the requirement for government power to be held in balance with *garantisme*. With the "parliamentary sovereignty" of the British constitution – restricted only by custom, tradition, and "convention" (Marshall 1984) – clearly in his sights, however, he advocates an individualist approach that narrowly constricts the area in which governments can engage the populace in collective enterprise. Yet in the open competition of the individualist society some individuals or groups fall victim to the power of the successful, and for them government intervention is the only hope of protection. In this case government power itself is the *garantisme* against possible tyranny from private powers.

The existence of private sources of tyranny seems scarcely to have been recognized by the written constitutions of the nineteenth century. According to Karl Loewenstein they demonstrated that "Constitutions function well so long as the competition for power is confined to different groups of the same social class; but they are strained to the limit, and often break, when their rules become insufficient to accommodate the power ambitions of a class excluded by its very rules" (Loewenstein 1951: 197; cf. 1965: 153–63). Loewenstein implied that the written constitution was an invention of the bourgeoisie designed both to entrench its values and to strengthen its claim to power. Writers in the tradition of libertarian individualism like Benjamin Constant, and more recently Sartori and Harvey Wheeler (1975), while not necessarily vesting constitutionalism in the written constitution alone, maintain that "constitution" did not exist before the rise of the modern sovereign state, since constitutionalism was a specific response to the problems of sovereignty. As Constant, whose writing was influential on the nineteenth-century constitutions of Europe, believed, "We can no longer enjoy the freedom of the ancients, which consisted in taking an active and constant part in the collective government . . . This is why our individual independence must be much more dear to us than it was to the ancients" (quoted by Sartori [1965: 277]; cf. Lerner 1968: 191–207; Berger 1977).

From the point of view of those who were excluded from both economic and political power, however, a guaranteed preserve of individual independence was of little value, and Loewenstein found no cause for increased optimism in the constitutional experience of this century. "Liberty the constitutions could and did promise, but not bread and the modicum of economic security the little man yearns for. To him it is the plain and unadorned truth that the political decisions which are vital for the well-being of all no longer occur within the frame of the constitution" (Loewenstein 1965: 200). If constitutional processes are to be open to all, government power must be accessible in a way not always provided for by "rigid" constitutions. We need a constitutionalism, as McIlwain repeatedly affirmed, that keeps a balance between government power and its control without dissipating that power so far as to make for weak and unresponsive government. For this reason we are justified in reaching back beyond the era of the written constitution, beyond the epoch of the sovereign state, to find a more even balance between *gubernaculum*, government power exercised on behalf of the people, and *jurisdictio*, control of that power in the name of a higher law. Only thus can we tap a deep tradition that unites the discovery and enhancement of an inner self with a faith in what a people can do acting collectively through its political association. In this case "constitution" is legitimately a "frame" of political association so ordered as to contain government power within a precise competence while yet permitting it to exist in sufficient measure to protect, and where possible, to uplift the horizons of, the people. Such a constitution establishes and defines a political community which, to give Aristotle the last word, "comes into being to secure life itself, but remains for the sake of the good life" (Aristotle, *Politics*, 1.1.8; cf. Ridley 1966: 312–23).

REFERENCES

Allen, J.W. 1957. *A History of Political Thought in the Sixteenth Century*, revised edn. London: Methuen.

Aristotle. 1977. *Politics*, translated by H. Rackham, Loeb Classical Library. Cambridge, MA: Harvard University Press.

Bailyn, B. 1967. *The Ideological Origins of the American Revolution*. Cambridge, MA: Belknap Press.

Barker, E. 1959. *The Political Thought of Plato and Aristotle*, new edn. New York: Dover Publications.

1960. *Greek Political Theory*, 5th edn. London: Methuen.

Berger, R. 1977. *Government by Judiciary*. Cambridge, MA: Harvard University Press.

Bloch, M. 1962. *Feudal Society*, 2 vols., translated by L.A. Manyon, 2nd edn. London: Routledge and Kegan Paul.
Bolingbroke, Viscount (Henry St. John). 1809. *Works*, 8 vols., new edn. London: J. Johnson *et al.*
Bowra, C.M. 1957. *The Greek Experience*. New York: Mentor Books.
Bright, J. 1972. *A History of Israel*, revised edn. London: SCM Press.
Bryce, J. 1901. *Studies in History and Jurisprudence*, 2 vols. Oxford: Oxford University Press.
Cicero. 1928. *De re publica*, translated by C.W. Keyes, Loeb Classical Library. New York: Heinemann.
Clarke, M.L. 1968. *The Roman Mind*. New York: Norton.
Crawford, M. 1978. *The Roman Republic*. Glasgow: Fontana Books.
Ehrenberg, V. 1965. *The Greek State*, 2nd edn. London: Methuen.
Foord, A.S. 1964. *His Majesty's Opposition 1714–1830*. Oxford: Clarendon.
Friedrich, C.J. 1964. *Transcendent Justice: The Religious Dimension of Constitutionalism*. Durham, NC: Duke University Press.
1967. *The Impact of American Constitutionalism Abroad*. Boston, MA: Boston University Press.
Hamilton, Alexander, James Madison, and John Jay, 1961. *The Federalist Papers*, edited by Clinton S. Rossiter. New York: New American Library.
Hansen, M.H. 1974. *The Sovereignty of the People's Court in Athens in the Fourth Century BC and the Public Action against Unconstitutional Proposals*. Odense: Odense University Press.
Harrington, J.L. 1955. *The Political Writings of James Harrington*, edited by C. Blitzer. New York: Liberal Arts Press.
Jolliffe, J.E.A. 1963. *Angevin Kingship*, 2nd edn. London: Black.
Keir, D.L. 1966. *The Constitutional History of Modern Britain since 1485*, 8th edn. London: Black.
Kern, F. 1939. *Kingship and Law in the Middle Ages*, translated by S.B. Chrimes. Oxford: Oxford University Press.
Kitto, H.D.F. 1961. *Greek Tragedy*, 3rd edn. London: Methuen.
Laslett, P. 1965. [Commentary on Locke. 1965.]
Lerner, M. 1968. "Minority Rule and the Constitutional Tradition." In C. Read (ed.), *The Constitution Reconsidered*, revised edn. New York: Harper Torchbooks, pp. 191–207.
Locke, J. 1965 [1689–90]. *Two Treatises of Government*, edited by P. Laslett, revised edn. New York: Mentor Books.
Loewenstein, K. 1951. "Reflections on the Value of Constitutions in our Revolutionary Age." In A. Zurcher (ed.), *Constitutions and Constitutional Trends since World War II*. New York: New York University Press, pp. 191–224.
1965. *Political Power and the Governmental Process*, 2nd edn. Chicago, IL: Phoenix Books.
Lutz, D.S. 1984. "The Relative Influence of European Writers on Late Eighteenth-century American Political Thought." *American Political Science Review* 78 (March): 189–97.

McIlwain, C.H. 1939. *Constitutionalism and the Changing World*. Cambridge: Cambridge University Press.
1947. *Constitutionalism Ancient and Modern*, revised edn. Ithaca, NY: Cornell University Press.
MacIver, R.M. 1968. "European Doctrines and the Constitution." In C. Read (ed.), *The Constitution Reconsidered*, revised edn. New York: Harper Torchbooks, pp. 51–61.
Marshall, G. 1984. *Constitutional Conventions: The Rules and Forms of Political Accountability*. Oxford: Clarendon.
Mendenhall, G.E. 1954. "Covenant Forms in Israelite Tradition." *Biblical Archaeologist* 17 (3).
Merriam, C.E. 1903. *A History of American Political Theories*. New York: Macmillan.
Merry, H.J. 1970. *Montesquieu's System of Natural Government*. West Lafayette, IN: Purdue University Studies.
Montesquieu. 1949 [1748]. *The Spirit of the Laws*, translated by T. Nugent. New York: Hafner.
1965 [1734]. *Considerations on the Causes of the Greatness of the Romans and Their Decline*, translated by D. Lowenthal. New York: The Free Press.
Morison, S.E. and Commager, H.S. 1962. *The Growth of the American Republic*, 2 vols. New York: Oxford University Press.
Morris-Jones, W.H. 1965. "On Constitutionalism." *American Political Science Review* 59 (June): 439–40.
Murray, O. 1980. *Early Greece*. Glasgow: Fontana Books.
Ostwald, M. 1969. *Nomos and the Beginnings of the Athenian Democracy*. Oxford: Clarendon.
Paine, T. 1969 [1791]. *Rights of Man*, edited by H. Collins. Harmondsworth: Penguin Books.
Painter, S. 1961. *Feudalism and Liberty*. Baltimore, MD: Johns Hopkins University Press.
Perry, R.L. (ed.). 1964. *Sources of Our Liberties*. New York: McGraw-Hill.
Pocock, J.G.A. 1973. *Politics, Language and Time*. New York: Athenaeum.
Rathbone, E. 1967. "Roman Law in the Anglo-Norman Realm." *Studia Gratiana* 11: 255–71.
Richter, M. 1977. *The Political Theory of Montesquieu*. Cambridge: Cambridge University Press.
Ridley, F.F. 1966. "The Importance of Constitutions." *Parliamentary Affairs* 19 (3).
Sabine, G.H. and Thorson, T.L. 1973. *A History of Political Theory*, 4th edn. Hinsdale, IL: Dryden Press.
Sartori, G. 1962. "Constitutionalism: a Preliminary Discussion." *American Political Science Review* 56 (December): 853–64.
1965. *Democratic Theory*. New York: Praeger.
1984. "Reply." *American Political Science Review* 78 (June): 497–9.
Schochet, G.J. 1979. "Introduction: Constitutionalism, Liberalism and the Study of Politics." In J.R. Pennock and J.W. Chapman (eds.), *Constitutionalism. Nomos XX*. New York: New York University Press, pp. 1–15.

Schramm, P.E. 1937. *A History of the English Coronation*, translated by L.G. Wickham Legg. Oxford: Oxford University Press.
Sinclair, T.A. 1967. *A History of Greek Political Thought*, 2nd edn. London: Routledge and Kegan Paul.
Skinner, Q. 1978. *The Foundations of Modern Political Thought*, 2 vols. Cambridge: Cambridge University Press.
Sophocles. 1947. *Antigone*, translated by E.F. Watling. Harmondsworth: Penguin Books.
Spiro, H.J. 1959. *Government by Constitution*. New York: Random House.
Thorne, S.E. 1968. "The Constitution and the Courts: a Reexamination of the Famous Case of Dr. Bonham." In C. Read (ed.), *The Constitution Reconsidered*, revised edn. New York: Harper Torchbooks, pp. 15–24.
Thucydides. 1943. *The History of the Peloponnesian War*, translated by R. Warner. Harmondsworth: Penguin Books.
Ullmann, W. 1967. *The Individual and Society in the Middle Ages*. Baltimore, MD: Johns Hopkins University Press.
1969. *The Carolingian Renaissance and the Idea of Kingship*. London: Methuen.
1978. *Principles of Government and Politics in the Middle Ages*, 4th edn. London: Methuen.
Van Caenegem, R.C. 1973. *The Birth of the English Common Law*. Cambridge: Cambridge University Press.
Wheeler, H. 1975. "Constitutionalism." In F.I. Greenstein and N.W. Polsby (eds.), *Handbook of Political Science*, vol. V: *Governmental Institutions and Processes*. Reading, MA: Addison-Wesley, pp.1–91.
Wolf-Phillips, L.A. 1968. *Constitutions of Modern States*. London: Pall Mall Press.
1972. *Comparative Constitutions*. London: Macmillan.
Woodhouse, A.S.P. 1974. *Puritanism and Liberty*, 2nd edn. London: Dent.
Zurcher, A. (ed.). 1951. *Constitutions and Constitutional Trends since World War II*. New York: New York University Press.

4

Democracy

RUSSELL L. HANSON

I

We live in a world that agrees on the importance and desirability of democracy. This hegemony of the democratic ideal was noted as early as 1951, amidst the Cold War and the emergence of the Third World, by a UNESCO report on *Democracy in a World of Tensions*:

> For the first time in the history of the world, no doctrines are advanced as antidemocratic. The accusation of antidemocratic action or attitude is frequently directed against others, but practical politicians and political theorists agree in stressing the democratic element in institutions they defend and theories they advocate. This acceptance of democracy as the highest form of political or social organization is a sign of a basic agreement in the ultimate aims of modern social and political institutions – an agreement that the participation of the people and the interests of the people are essential elements in government and in the social relations which make good government possible.
>
> McKeon 1951: 522–3

It was not always so. Until the middle of the nineteenth century, or perhaps even later, democracy was regarded as a dangerous and unstable form of politics. Since then, the odious connotations of democracy have gradually receded. They have been replaced by new, and quite positive, associations with popular sovereignty and political equality (themselves concepts with interesting histories). In the process democracy became a concept without peer in modern politics. Now even the natural enemies of democracy, the aristocracy and its political representatives, agree with Churchill[1] that "democ-

I am very grateful to Terence Ball and James Farr for their helpful comments and suggestions on this essay.

[1] Winston Churchill, speech before the House of Commons on the Parliament Bill, November 11, 1947. Ironically, Churchill, as leader of the Conservative opposition, was instructing the Labour party members of parliament on the virtues of democracy, and admonishing them to be good democrats.

racy is the worst form of government, except for all the rest that have been tried from time to time."

The popularization of democracy, as we might call it, in which a form of politics once roundly condemned came to be highly commended, has no parallel in the history of Western politics. It is a story worth telling, and in the second section of this essay I describe the rising esteem in which democracy came to be held. I do this by referring to mass political movements that valued democracy and struggled to achieve what they took to be "democracy." Thus, as "the people" sought and gained power and influence in the name of democracy, the meaning of democracy changed, and so, too, did its respectability.

By emphasizing the constitution and reconstitution of meaning in politics I want to call attention to another, equally significant, aspect of the history of democracy, and that is the present confusion over its meaning. As the *value* of democracy became transcendent, its *meaning* was lost in the cacophony of competing interpretations of democracy. In fact, this is the starting point of most contemporary treatments of democracy, which begin rather despairingly with the observation that democracy is everywhere approved, though its true meaning is almost nowhere understood. The tremendous popularity of democracy has invited appropriation by movements of every stripe. In the process, we are told by some that democracy has been transformed into nothing more than a "hurrah" word with very little meaning of its own. It is as if the anarchic results once expected from democratic politics have manifested themselves in language instead.

Such accounts often conclude with the recommendation that "democracy" ought to be abandoned in favor of more precise concepts, e.g. polyarchy, or at the very least refined into a more scientific concept (Dahl 1956; Oppenheim 1971). This sort of linguistic legerdemain is unlikely to end our confusion over the meaning of democracy, since the alleged confusion stems more from political struggles to define a key word, than from any regrettable semantic variability that afflicts ordinary language. That is, the popularization of democracy and the alleged degradation of its meaning are part of the same process by which our language is constituted in political action.

I try to demonstrate this in the third section of my essay, where I consider the historical development of "democracy" in America. I show how ideas about democracy found practical expression in the course of arguments over the desirability of particular political institutions and practices. Similarly, the beliefs that informed and partially constituted those institutions and practices were made explicit during the course of debates over their standing within particular political communities. Hence, the conceptual link between ideas about democracy and the practices implied by them was forged in and through political rhetoric.

The same argument might as well be made with respect to other countries. But the United States of America is a particularly important case, not only because it is the nation with the longest continuous experience with "democracy," but also because it is heavily involved in the business of exporting its political traditions and institutions to other members of the international community. However, the appeal of American practices in the real world of democracy is limited by Americans' own uncertainty concerning the meaning of "democracy" – an uncertainty that is the result of the extreme popularization of this form of politics in America.[2] I conclude with some remarks about the political importance of understanding the historical roots of this aspect of "democracy" in America.

II

For two millennia politicians and philosophers regarded democracy as an inferior form of politics. Few among the elite doubted the accuracy of Plato's characterization of democracy as "a state in which the poor, gaining the upper hand, kill some and banish others, and then divide the offices among the remaining citizens, usually by lot."[3]

A fear of class rule underlay this opinion. The unchecked exercise of power by a single class of society without regard for the interests of other classes signified corruption in the body politic, the proper health of which depended upon an appropriate balance of class power. Unbalanced regimes were, by definition, unjust, and unstable for that reason. Indeed Plato's *Politeia*, an inquiry into the proper constitution of the virtues in a just city, was translated by Cicero as *Res publica*, capitalizing on the Roman understanding of the importance of mixed regimes involving a balance of power.

However, democracy was not only a form of class rule. It was rule

[2] See Macpherson (1966) for a comparison of the relative moral appeal of liberal and nonliberal varieties of democracy.

[3] Plato, *Republic*, bk. VIII, 557a. But cf. Vlastos's (1983) claim that Socrates, or rather Plato's Socrates, preferred Athenian democracy to oligarchy, even though he was extremely critical of the Athenians' failure to abide by their own democratically constituted laws. Thus, Vlastos argues that Socrates was no "crypto-oligarch," and that his thought was *demotikos*, or in English "demophilic," and hence "democratic" in some extended sense. Note, however, that the term democracy does not figure in any of the key texts Vlastos examines.

by the worst class, and therefore doubly reprehensible. Significantly, we commonly translate *demokratia* as "rule by the people," without making distinctions among "the people," whereas *demos* originally referred also and quite specifically to "common people" with little or no economic independence.[4] These people were not slaves, but rather politically untutored citizens who had neither breeding nor education that might have prepared them for participating in affairs of state. They were therefore inclined to pursue their own interests in politics at the expense of the commonweal, or at least what was understood to be the commonweal by upper-class politicians and philosophers.[5]

During the fifth and fourth centuries before Christ, these citizens had forced their way into city politics. The rhetoric of this transformation has apparently not been fully investigated (Raaflaub 1983, esp. nn. 12 and 21). But Raaflaub avers that the concept of freedom was crucially important, as it was exclusively associated with the democrats' cause. In turn this concept was linked to an inclusive understanding of membership in the political community, a notion that did not advance in the name of democracy, but under the banner of *isonomia*, which referred both to equality before the law and, in a more directly political sense, equality through the law (Vlastos 1964). That is, democracy was not the object, but rather the result (as we understand it) of popular insurgency aimed at achieving greater equality. Among other things, this entailed *isegoria*, or the right of every citizen to address the assembly and urge the adoption of proposals by it. This was, of course, moderated by the fact that men who made "illegal" proposals, as determined by the *graphe paranomon* (a large jury selected by lot from the *demos* and charged

[4] It was apparently William of Moerbeke who, in the thirteenth century, translated Aristotle's δημοκρατία into the Latin word "democratia." According to the *Oxford English Dictionary*, the earliest mention of "democratia" in English was in 1531 by Elyot, who noted that "An other publique weale was amonge the Atheniensis, where equalitie was of astate amonge the people . . . This maner of gouernance was called in greke *Democratia*, in latine *Populis potentia*, in englisshe the rule of the comminaltie."

[5] Ochlocracy, or "mob rule," was often held up as the extreme form of democracy. Aristotle occasionally used "ochlos" to refer to the oarsmen of Athenian triremes, who congregated in great numbers in the Piraeus, and who were widely regarded as the most radical "democrats" of the time. He was willing to disenfranchise them, for such "landless" people were even less restrained in their pursuit of self-interest than the *demos*, who at least lived in the *demes*, or parishes, that were the basic geographical unit of Cleisthenes' tribal reorganization of 509 BC. According to Sir Ernest Barker (1975: lxv), the reorganization of the *demes* coincided with a broader interpretation of *demos* as referring to the whole community assembled for domestic policy-making, whereas it was previously construed more narrowly to refer to the dwellers of the countryside. That is, *demos* came to include both city dwellers, the people of *asty*, and country dwellers, the people of *agros*, under the new tribal regime.

with powers of judicial review), could be penalized, even if their proposals had won the assent of the assembly.

Later generations also expressed their resentments against governing elites without invoking the notion of democracy at all. Indeed it was not until the latter part of the eighteenth century that "democracy" and its cognates, "democrat" and "democratic," became important in western European political rhetoric. Not coincidentally, this is also when "aristocracy," "aristocrat," and "aristocratic" came into common use, the two sets of terms designating the main lines of cleavage in the Age of Revolution.

Before that conflict surfaced, however, both commoners and lords rebelled against the crown, sometimes jointly, and sometimes not. Few of the early uprisings were directed against monarchy *per se*. Rather, they opposed individual monarchs whose actions were deemed tyrannical, and they asserted the role of the people, not to choose new kings, but to depose unjust rulers. Later rebellions were often "revolutions of the saints" carried out in God's name against those who would subvert His will, whether through pride, ambition, or avarice, or because of an inability to divine that will through right reason (Walzer 1965). As such, the rights of man were not directly at issue, at least in any recognizably modern sense, though the political implications of Calvinism were no less radical for that. As Wolin (1960) notes, the Calvinist conception of church–state relations was quite conducive to more general discussions of liberty and equality. For the same reason, Gooch (1898: 9) claims that "the principles of modern democracy, however mutilated by a theocratic bias, advanced under the wing of the Reformation . . . For without the fighting power, if the phrase be allowed, which they derived from their patron and ally, they would have failed to make any progress in an age where the struggle of creed was the dominant factor of national life. And with the decline of the theocratic spirit, the popular basis came ever more clearly into view."

Not surprisingly, this occurred first in the most dissenting of the dissenting English colonies. The 1641 constitution of Rhode Island established a "Democratical or Popular Government; that is to say, It is in the Power of the Body of Freemen, orderly assembled, or the major part of them, to make or constitute Just Lawes, by which they will be regulated, and to depute from among themselves such Ministers as shall see them fairly executed between Man and Man."[6] The 1647 constitution of Rhode Island declared that "the forme of Government established in Providence Plantations is Democraticall;

[6] Arnold 1899: 148.

that is to say, a Government held by ye free and voluntary consent of all, or the greater parte of the free inhabitants."[7] And Roger Williams, who played a leading role in gaining and renewing the original patent on which this constitution depended, has been designated the "irrepressible democrat" for his unsuccessful efforts to expand the number of freeholders entitled to give or withhold their consent to government.[8] Similarly, his commitment to the separation of church and state, religious toleration, and, to a more limited extent, civil liberties is often taken as evidence of the early appearance of democracy in America.[9]

But Williams never developed a general philosophy of political rights, nor did he draw upon contemporaries, e.g. the Levellers, who espoused a more radical conception of liberty and popular sovereignty.[10] Whereas Williams was content to let suffrage depend on freeholding, and countenanced strict regulation of nonreligious action by the state, the Levellers insisted on a broader range of civil liberties. For them consent was not merely an expedient way of protecting soul liberty, as it was for Williams. It was a matter of birthright, as Colonel Rainsborough argued in the Putney Debates:

> for really I think that the poorest he that is in England hath a life to live as the greatest he; and therefore truly, sir, I think it's clear, that every man that is to live under a government ought first by his own consent to

[7] Barlett 1856: 156.

[8] Cf. Brockunier (1940). As he explains, both land and suffrage had to be granted by a vote in a town meeting, which gave original settlers the power to decide who enjoyed the privileges of citizenship. Against this "patriarchal democracy" Williams urged greater access to land and suffrage.

[9] This may be an anachronistic reading, however. Simpson (1955) claims that Williams was never committed to an equal distribution of land and influence in Providence Plantations, and that his support of a popular faction against the proprietary faction in control of politics stemmed from his belief that the latter had betrayed the public trust. Furthermore, Simpson, Miller (1953), and Morgan (1967) all demonstrate the centrality of Williams's religious thought in his political writings. His preference for government by consent was not based on concern about the rights of man; for him, men were sinners, and liable to do great evil, especially when they employed the powers of the state in the name of God. The liberty of conscience, or what he called "soul liberty," was always endangered where religion was established, and so the separation of church and state was necessary, as were those civil liberties, e.g. freedom of expression, vital to religious life. In this view, then, establishing government on consent was a way of preserving "soul liberty."

[10] He was surely familiar with these ideas; upon his first return to England in 1643, he published several pamphlets (most notably *Bloudy Tenent Of Persecution For Cause of Conscience discussed in A Conference between Truth and Peace*) that won him friends in the War party and among the Independents in the Long Parliament. And he followed with great interest the political scene in England, and supported Cromwell, with whom he was on good terms, apparently because he believed that the achievement of religious liberty was vastly more important than the promise of civil liberty offered by the English Revolution (Simpson 1955; Garret 1969).

> put himself under that government; and I do think that the poorest man in England is not at all bound in a strict sense to that government that he hath not had a voice to put himself under.[11]

This concern over the political rights of common men is reflected in the three versions of the Levellers' *Agreement of the People*, which gave successively more details on the meaning of consent and the conditions under which it was to be given by the people. According to the third *Agreement of the People*, the monarch and House of Lords were to be abolished. Legislative, executive, and judicial powers were to be separated and limited. Parliament was prohibited from legislating matters of religion. It could not grant monopolies, tax food, nor conscript men against their will. No one could be compelled to incriminate themself; prisoners would be allowed counsel; and all cases were to be settled within six months (Aylmer 1975: 159–68).

Furthermore, the Levellers proposed a nearly universal male suffrage, excluding only criminals, servants, and the recipients of relief, all of whom had "voluntarily" surrendered their birthright.[12] This, in combination with a reapportionment of parliament according to population and provision for annual elections, as well as limited tenure in office, gave full force to the consent of the governed by collecting that consent at regular intervals from a very broad segment of citizens.

The divine origins of these political rights gave them a distinctive political caste in Leveller writings. According to these, men who hold such rights are bound to exercise them, or else fail in their duty to God. Just as surely, those who deny or abridge the rights of others not only commit injustice against men, but they also afront God by their actions. Thus, in 1646 Overton defended the idea of popular consent by asserting that "as we are delivered of God by the hand of nature into this world, every one with a naturall, innate freedome and propriety (as it were writ in the table of every mans heart, never to be obliterated) even so are we to live, every one equally and alike to enjoy his Birthright and priviledge; even all whereof God by nature hath made him free" (Aylmer 1975: 69). And John Lilburne

[11] Excerpt from Clarke's notes on the Putney Debates, in Aylmer (1975: 100). Rainsborough was arguing against Ireton and Cromwell, who would have restricted suffrage to those with a "permanent and local" interest in the affairs of the realm, i.e. property holders and members of trading corporations. As Rainsborough and Sexby noted, this would have excluded many members of the New Model Army who had neglected their smallholdings and risked their lives for a liberty they would not enjoy under the Independents' Heads of Proposals.

[12] For an account of the Putney Debates on suffrage, see C.B. Macpherson (1960), as well as Hill (1970), and of course Gooch (1898).

noted that the deprivation of such natural rights by tyrants was an abomination to the Lord, citing God's revenge on Cain for subjecting Abel (Aylmer 1975: 70–1).

Religious invocations did not save the Levellers from being denounced as radicals – or from being imprisoned, either. Both their opponents and their sometime collaborators denounced the Levellers as "democrats," i.e. anarchists.[13] Radicals vigorously resisted that allegation, and found an alternative language of innovation, to borrow a phrase of J.A.W. Gunn's (1983), in the republican tradition so well explicated by Pocock (1975; 1985) and Skinner (1978). That tradition was sufficiently broad-minded to include both the radicals and the Independents, and some royalists who believed in the possibility and desirability of monarchical republic.[14] Moreover, the tradition extended beyond England to much of Europe.

Within this context, "democracy" was sometimes interpreted favorably, especially where it referred to the version of republicanism preferred by radicals. Palmer (1954) reports that this was true in Italy, perhaps because its long familiarity with republics provided few other linguistic resources for innovation, by contrast to nations with no such heritage. The Swiss also used the term favorably to refer to the self-governing practices of the rural cantons, and so did some citizens of "free" German cities of this period. And democracy was explicitly endorsed by some of the "Patriots" of the Dutch Revolution of 1784–7 and the Belgian Revolution of 1789–91, both of which were suppressed with the aid of foreign intervention. In England and Scotland, on the other hand, "antidemocrats seem to have monopolized the word," associating it with the excesses of the Reign of Terror in France. There Robespierre and his allies in the Jacobin Club and on the Committee of Public Safety confirmed the worst fears of royalists and moderates alike as they used "democracy" as a rallying cry for mobilizing the *sans-culottes*.

The French Revolution signalled the emergence of a radical tradition of democracy that was quite distinct from the tradition of liberal democracy in England. The connections between this new, or at least newly articulated, conception of democracy and latter-day Marxism, on the one hand, and independence movements, on the

[13] In fact, the Levellers were not levellers at all, at least as far as property rights were concerned. That distinction belonged to the Diggers, whose chief spokesman, Gerard Winstanley, described a truly classless society in his *The Law of Freedom*, published in 1652.

[14] Even Gooch, the title of whose book refers to the history of English *democratic* ideas, reverts to the language of republicanism in his account of the politics of this period, suggesting that few, if any, radicals were self-styled "democrats." See also Fink (1945), and Pocock (1975).

other, have been explored by C.B. Macpherson (1966), who relates them all to Rousseau's notion of the general will. However, the first democratic republic of France proved short-lived and, with the rise of Bonaparte and the eventual restoration of the Bourbon monarchy, "democracy" understandably fell into disuse in Europe, at least until 1848.

That was the year in which Louis-Philippe was forced to abdicate, the second French republic was established, and revolutions broke out in several European countries. Amidst this turmoil Tocqueville (1969: 19) reminded the readers of the twelfth edition of his *Democracy in America* that he had foreseen these events. Convinced as he was that the rise of democracy in the West was irresistible, Tocqueville earlier looked to the United States because "I saw in America more than America; it was the shape of democracy itself which I sought, its inclinations, character, prejudices and passions; I wanted to understand it so as at least to know what we have to fear or hope therefrom."

If Tocqueville was right about the quintessentially democratic character of American society, it is there that we ought to see the popularization of democracy best illustrated. It is in the United States that the concomitant rise of "democracy" as a rallying cry and the degradation of its meaning ought to be most visible. I will now examine that process more closely, exploring the political constitution of language in a concrete setting.[15]

III

At the time of the American Founding, democracy was held in low regard by most Americans, as it was by most Europeans, for reasons previously mentioned. For example, Madison, in his duly famous paper on the mischief of faction, observed that "democracies have ever been spectacles of turbulence and contention; have ever been found incompatible with personal security or the rights of property; and have in general been as short in their lives as they have been violent in their deaths." Only "theoretic politicians" who failed to appreciate the danger of majoritarian tyranny recommended its adoption.[16]

[15] I have elsewhere done this at much greater length and with numerous bibliographic references: Hanson (1985). Here I simply present a summary account of this historical evolution of "democracy" in America.

[16] Madison, in Hamilton, Madison, and Jay (1961: 81). The reference is apparently to Rousseau.

A properly constituted republican government, on the other hand, was widely valued, insofar as it stood for the commonweal or "public good" (which was a common rendering of *res publica* at the time). Whereas a democracy represented rule *by* the "commons" or *demos*, a republic was ruled *in* common *for* the commonweal. Of course, the United States was bound to be a democratic republic because it lacked both monarchical and aristocratic orders, but a republic nonetheless. The democracy, or people, variously apportioned, would be represented in republican councils, and the interests expressed in the "compound republic" would be balanced in the same way as were multiple classes or orders in other societies.[17]

The Federalists, whose constitutional proposals were intended to remedy the chief defect of democratic republics, namely, the absence of virtue among the citizenry and the correspondingly high incidence of majoritarian factionalism, were especially hostile toward democracy, and used the appellation "democrat" to excoriate their opponents. Indeed, the Federalists' new science of politics made little provision for popular participation in affairs of state, just because they feared the influence of "the democracy," unrefined by mechanisms of representation.[18] As Noah Webster (1953: 207–8) explained in a famous letter to Joseph Priestly,

> By democracy is intended a government where the legislative powers are exercised directly by all the citizens, as formerly in Athens and Rome. In our country this power is not in the hands of the people but of their representatives. The powers of the people are principally restricted to the direct exercise of the rights of suffrage. Hence a material distinction between our form of government and those of the ancient democracies. Our form of government has acquired the appellation of a *Republic*, by way of distinction, or rather of a *representative Republic*.
>
> Hence the word *Democrat* has been used as synonymous with the word *Jacobin* in France; and by an additional idea, which arose from the

[17] To be sure, a certain structure of deference was assumed to form the constitutional underpinning of republican rule, and when that structure was upset, politics became unbalanced, factions ruled in their own interest, and the republic was undone. See J.R. Pole (1966) and Pocock (1975).

[18] By limiting popular participation to the selection of leaders, the Federalists consigned the population to a state of civic lethargy, in which citizens failed to develop a sense of moral and political responsibility that, according to classical republican theories, accompanied civic involvement. Citizens failed to learn to love liberty, i.e. to love and pursue the public good in politics. Thus, the Federalists' "realistic" assessment of the decline of virtue and deference in America turned out to be a "gigantic self-fulfilling prophecy" once it found institutional expression in constitutional arrangements that made scant provision for participation. See Ball (1983) and Jacobson (1963).

attempt to control our government by private popular associations, the word has come to signify a person who attempts an undue opposition to or influence over government by means of private clubs, secret intrigues, or by public popular meetings which are extraneous to the constitution. By *Republicans* we understand the friends of our Representative Governments, who believe that no influence whatever should be exercised in a state which is not directly authorized by the Constitution and laws.

The Jeffersonian Republicans, and especially the Democratic–Republican societies, responded with criticisms of the "aristocratic" prejudices of their opponents, and in the process began to forge rhetorical links between democracy and popular sovereignty and political equality (Morantz 1971). This chain of ideas was tempered in the heat of partisan struggles to control the Republican party itself, after it vanquished the unpopular Federalists. The deeply personal factions and deferential politics of the Founding Period were overthrown in the name of majority rule in these struggles and those over the extension of the franchise, and new, professional politicians, e.g. Martin Van Buren, came to the fore on the strength of their ability to mobilize mass support (Williamson 1960). In the process, parties, as distinct from factions, began to form, and the legitimacy of a party system that acknowledged differences of interest and opinion in the body politic began to replace traditional republican fears of the mischief of faction (Wallace 1968; Hofstadter 1969).

Indeed, during the Jacksonian era the Democratic party (originally the Republican Supporters of General Jackson) pitted itself against the interests of a monied faction whose domination of politics symbolized the corruption of the republic. The Jacksonians understood this as a contest between classes over the destiny of the nation. The Democracy presented itself as the organized expression of the will of common men, i.e. the producers of wealth who, as Jackson put it, were "the bone and sinew" of the body politic.[19] They characterized their Whig opponents as the defenders of an old, deferential style of politics in which an unproductive class of bankers, speculators, and their ilk lived luxuriously by reason of its privileged position in a complex politico-economic system symbolized by the Monster Bank.

The Whigs, for their part, offered an American system of internal improvements as an alternative to the Jacksonian advocacy of *laissez faire* and manifest destiny. This system would ostensibly dissolve

[19] Andrew Jackson, "Farewell Address" of March 4, 1837.

class differences by calling forth economic prosperity, the benefits of which would redound to all. At the same time, they conceded the popularity of the Democratic label, and emulated the mobilizing tactics of the Jacksonians. They even pioneered new techniques of "democracy," thereby institutionalizing a party system and channeling popular participation into electoral politics.[20]

The advance of the Democracy and "democratic" methods of electioneering by parties with at least nominally distinct class bases made men like John C. Calhoun fearful of majoritarian democracy. To be sure, Calhoun's fears were quite specific: Northern majorities, organized under the auspices of a political party, seemed on the verge of uniting the powers so carefully separated by the Founders. They might then use them to compel the South to abolish slavery, or, in the case of Whig industrialists, expropriate Southern wealth by means of a tariff (Schlesinger 1945). Against such possibilities Calhoun formulated his scheme of concurrent majorities, which he defended on Madisonian grounds. A majority, for him, was no less a faction than a minority. It did not stand for the people, but only a part of them, and so democracy, conceived as majority rule, was something to be nullified by constitutional safeguards designed to protect minority interests.[21]

If the Monster Bank symbolized the exploitation of producer classes in the North, the "Southern Slave Power" stood for an even more extreme form of exploitation. Northerners were frustrated by the South, which, by reason of its influence over national policy-making institutions, was able to defend itself from political attacks on slavery. They sought to abolish the peculiar institution in the South itself, extending the area of freedom in a fashion Jackson never imagined. Of these abolitionists, a few are willing to confer political rights, including suffrage, on freed slaves. Most, however, merely opposed the extension of slavery to the western territories for fear of mingling the races and undermining the position of white labor. Northern sentiment in this regard was well expressed by Lincoln, who averred

> I will say then that I am not, nor have ever been in favor of bringing about in any way the social and political equality of the black and white

[20] By 1839 the Whigs convened under the label of "Democratic Whig National Convention," and Calvin Colton, a noted Whig author, later published an anonymous tract in which he cynically argued that any American party, regardless of whether its principles were radical or conservative, was well advised to use the rhetoric of democracy to sell its cause to voters. See Schlesinger (1945).

[21] Calhoun never defended minority *rights*, as he did not subscribe to doctrines of natural right. He insisted on the protection of minority *interests*, however. See Calhoun (1883).

> races – that I am not nor ever have been in favour of making voters or jurors of Negroes, nor of qualifying them to hold office, nor to intermarry with white people; and I will say in addition that there is a physical difference between the white and black races which I believe will forever forbid the two races living together in terms of social and political equality.[22]

After the Civil War, of course, the Fifteenth Amendment enfranchized black males over the age of twenty-one, though Southern state legislatures soon discovered effective devices for nullifying this – for example white primaries, literacy tests, and the like. They thus refused blacks admission to the ranks of the democracy, despite the fact that blacks had been elevated from slave to wage labor by the war.

The reconstruction of labor relations was not confined to the South. During the Gilded Age that followed the Civil War, increasingly sharp divisions arose between those who owned the means of production and a burgeoning class of workers with no economic independence of their own. In the industrial centers of the nation unions began to form. The older free-labor ideology – in which the independent proprietor was a central figure – gave way to the ideology of wage labor in which the laborer was the common man. This transition from free labor to trade unionism represented a decisive shift in the ideology of labor – and in the meaning of "democracy" – transforming a resentment of capitalism and the displacement of workers into a tacit acceptance of the maturing economic order and labor's place within it (Grob 1961).

Among the nation's farmers, however, resentment of the robber barons ran high, and efforts were made to mobilize the political power of the producers of wealth against them. In order to break the stranglehold of "plutocrats" – bankers, railroaders, and land speculators – "the democracy" were exhorted to undertake cooperative experiments in purchasing supplies and marketing produce on terms more favorable to farmers (Goodwyn 1976). At the same time, the Populists proposed a much-expanded role for government in regulating the money supply and providing the necessary infrastructure for agricultural exchange. As one Populist explained, "We favor a democracy and stand by the principle that governments are organized to perform for the whole people at cost, that service which the citizen and family cannot best perform for themselves" (Pollack 1967: 214; see also Tindall 1966).

The Populists failed in their efforts "to restore the government of

[22] See Abraham Lincoln (1965: 102). See also Foner (1970).

the Republic to the hands of 'the plain people,' with which class it originated," as Ignatius Donnelly put it in the preamble to the Omaha Platform. Consequently, they also failed in their effort to exert control over the economy by political means. However, many of their proposals for political change were subsequently enacted by the Progressives, who pursued reforms, like primary elections and Australian ballots, that broke the monopoly held by business and party interests over the instrumentalities of popular control.

At the same time, many middle-class Progressives were wary of reforms that might expand the influence of untutored citizens. The mass of illiterate immigrants were, after all, the principal constituency of machine politicians. At-large and nonpartisan elections, as well as other reform proposals, were calculated to neutralize this group of citizens. When coupled with the expansion of the civil service and other measures intended to promote efficiency in government, these reforms reduced the role of the populace in governance. As Haber puts it, "the progressives who greeted efficiency with such enthusiasm were often those who proposed to let the people rule through a program in which the bulk of the people, most of the time, ruled hardly at all."[23]

Other Progressives, like Herbet Croly and Walter Weyl of the *New Republic*, believed that with proper leadership and tutelage "the democracy" might become the moving force for true progress in America. The goal of true progress was to establish *The New Democracy*, to use the title of Weyl's manifesto, in which the *laissez faire* ethos of "live and let live" was replaced by a new ethic of "live and help live." "The new democracy," suitably educated and led by men like Theodore Roosevelt, was to move America to a new and higher level of civilization, wherein the *social* rights of "life, leisure, a share in our natural resources, and a dignified existence in society" were to gain precedence over the narrow and exclusive claims of property (Weyl 1912: 161). In other words, substantive democracy was to replace the merely formal democracy of *laissez faire*, as industry, society, and government were organized along more equitable lines.

The obdurate refusal of the common men to heed exhortations to realize the promise of American life led to the disillusionment of true Progressives, some of whom then expressed a preference for what might be called "expert democracy." After all, Walter

[23] Haber (1964: xii). The ultimately successful defense of women's suffrage drew heavily on the possibility that the inclusion of large numbers of educated, middle-class women might improve the intellectual quotient of the electorate, offsetting the impact of illiterate immigrants.

Lippmann argued, the purpose of modern government was not to burden a citizen with difficult issues and problems that were beyond his or her interest and comprehension, "but to push that burden away from him towards the responsible administrator." Truly virtuous citizens, in fact, would refuse the responsibility to decide these issues, reserving their opinion until after the effects of decisions on them were known, whereupon they might pass judgment on those who made the decisions in the first place.[24]

From expert democracy and scientific management it was but a short step to the program of "enlightened administration" of social life advocated by Franklin Delano Roosevelt and his fellow New Dealers. The New Dealers rejected the regulatory approach of the Progressives, which was designed to prevent abuses of power by big business, in favor of a complex system of "interest group liberalism" in which the role of government was radically transformed. From a coercive instrument of regulation, government was to become an arbiter of disputes between interests, some of them, e.g. farmers and laborers, newly incorporated in policy-making roles. Indeed, even this may be too strong, for Rexford Tugwell (1935: 20) argued that government would act only as the "senior and controlling partner" in negotiations among interests, representing the general interest of all in establishing a "concert of interests."

This abstract conception of unity was given material underpinning by greatly expanding the range of goods and services provided by the newly invigorated political system (Mollenkopf 1983). The Great Society further enlarged the bounds of democratic consumption by enlarging the sphere of distributive politics. But this later democratization of consumption was carried out from above, without benefit of substantial grass-roots involvement, except where that involvement was itself induced by policies of "maximum feasible participation."

This "technocratic takeover" of policy-making was a hallmark of the Great Society (Beer 1978). In effect, the "enlightened administration" of FDR gave way to a more analytical approach to policy-

[24] According to Lippmann, the enlightened public in which the Progressives had placed their trust was a "phantom." He insisted that "no reform, however sensational, is truly radical, which does not consciously provide a way of overcoming the subjectivism of human opinion based on the limitation of indiviudal experience." Most citizens never escaped the parochialism of outlook that prevented them from viewing public affairs with disinterest; only those trained in the sciences had the inclination to take a global point of view. Hence, political decision-making ought to incorporate a greater reliance on "intelligence work" by experts whose "interests reach beyond locality." See Lippmann (1922: 397–410; 1925).

making, one that no longer drew its energy and inspiration from popular pressures, but instead from the accumulated wisdom of the behavioral revolution in the social sciences. The professionalization of reform, as Daniel Moynihan described it, was made possible by the "end of ideology" announced by Daniel Bell in 1962. With the alleged end of ideology, more rational, scientific approaches to problems of poverty, unemployment, and discrimination might come to fruition; by bringing knowledge to bear on social problems, the Great Society might "put an end to the 'animal miseries' and stupid controversies" that afflicted people under the influence of utopian ideologies (Moynihan 1967: 474).

Against this understanding of politics and its reduction of citizens to consumers of goods and services the idea of "participatory democracy" was raised by the Students for a Democratic Society (SDS), and in different ways by advocates of Black Power and women's liberation. The SDS, in its famous Port Huron Statement, insisted that

> the search for truly democratic alternatives to the present, and a commitment to social experimentation with them, is a worthy and fulfilling human enterprise, one which moves us and, we hope, others today. On such a basis we offer this document of our convictions and analysis: as an effort in understanding and changing the conditions of humanity in the late twentieth century, an effort rooted in the ancient, still unfulfilled conception of man [*sic*] attaining determining influence over his circumstances of life. Goldwin 1971: 3–4

The SDS insisted, against all evidence known to mainstream social science, on the capacity of human beings for reason, freedom, and love. They attributed the frustration of these capacities to the patently undemocratic organization of American society, especially its failure to provide meaningful opportunities for participation in political and economic decision-making. Consequently, the SDS sought the establishment "of a democracy of individual participation, governed by two central aims: that the individual share in those social decisions determining the quality and direction of his [*sic*] life; that society be organized to encourage independence in men and provide the media for their common participation" (Goldwin 1971: 3–4).

"Participatory democracy" became the rallying point for a New Left that eschewed the Old Left's insistence on making the working class the focal point of democratic movement building. In this the New Left was joined by advocates of Black Power, who demanded racial autonomy, and the supporters of women's liberation, for whom sisterhood was the basis of political power. However, all three groups eventually returned to the importance of class in America, and the relationship between class and democracy, as their efforts to move the system failed to alter the distribution of power and influence in America.[25]

Nevertheless, the dominant culture never regained an interest in the relationship between class and democracy, perhaps because democratic consumerism was easy to practice in the affluent society. The Great Society delivered the goods to most of its members, most of the time, and was for that reason "democratic." This conclusion was underpinned by the widely held conviction that the US had entered an era of "post-scarcity" politics in which the benefits to be distributed would grow exponentially, while the costs to be borne would decline rapidly as more efficient and less destructive technologies of production were discovered.

Economic growth was particularly important after the commencement of the War on Poverty and the expansion of social spending during the Johnson Administration. Entitlement programs multiplied and an increasing number of people joined the ranks of consumer democrats. But slowing rates of growth during the 1970s made it increasingly difficult to satisfy the demands of consumers accustomed to the entitlements of democratic citizenship. Indeed, neoconservatives began to discuss openly the problems of governability confronting regimes that were "overloaded" with demands by citizens for more participation and greater equality, and to seek collective immunization against the "democratic distemper" associated with rising expectations among the masses (Huntington 1975). Out of this grew the "Reagan Revolution" or, as some call it, the "new class war," of the 1980s, amidst the fiscal crisis of the welfare state.

IV

The history of "democracy" in America clearly shows the rhetorical ascendance of "democracy" and the subsequent proliferation of its interpretations. It also reveals the extent to which democracy has lost its connotations of *class* rule, as "the people" came to be understood as an undifferentiated mass of political consumers. Throughout its history democracy always referred to a specific class in society and the form of government in which that class

[25] For an account of male chauvinism in the New Left and the subsequent emergence of women's liberation, see Evans (1978).

predominated. In the United States, "the democracy" were members or the productive class in society, while their opponents – the "aristocrats" or "plutocrats" – were wealthy members of the parasitic or nonproductive class.

This explicit reference to the underlying class structure of society informed virtually all American conceptions of democracy until well into the twentieth century. Even as late as the New Deal, the notion of democracy as a class concept prevailed among all of the major competing usages of "democracy" *except* for that of the New Dealers themselves. Hence, politics was widely understood to entail some sort of compromise between classes in which the democracy and the plutocracy lived in uneasy peace, if not harmony. Naturally, this involved a recognition that the proper relationship between classes *was* problematic, and this recognition provided a context in which rhetorical arguments about the true meaning of democracy made sense.

However, beginning with the Progressive era, extending through the New Deal, and culminating in the Great Society, the class connotations of democracy were gradually eliminated in favor of a more "universal" conception of democracy founded on an all-inclusive social group – consumers. As class came to be understood in terms of consumption rather than with reference to the relations of production, the image of a class-divided society began to fade from American political rhetoric. So, too, did the partisan interpretations of democracy that were grounded in class divisions. The *rhetorical* transcendance of class conflict emptied democracy of its traditional meaning and import.[26]

The fact that democracy is no longer understood in class terms does not mean that classes have disappeared from American society, or that class conflict has dissipated. However, it does mean that we no longer understand the relationship between political power and social class as a central problem of democracy, and therein lies the political significance of our confusion about the meaning of democracy. We now lack meaningful political concepts for describing, criticizing, and defending our political institutions and practices. As a result, our political discourse is confused, for our language of politics no longer seems to provide us with the resources we need to understand our situation and conduct our affairs.

This confusion reaches the very core of our community. When keywords such as democracy lose their meaning, our *identity* is necessarily called into question; if we are confused about the

[26] Compare Thompson (1978: 151).

meaning of democracy, then we are also uncertain about whether *we* are democratic (Williams 1976). That uncertainty may not be admitted, and may even be denied in ever-more strident criticisms of the "undemocratic" tendencies of other societies. But this uncertainty cannot be dispelled without re-creating a meaningful vocabulary of democratic politics, and that requires an appreciation of what has been lost, and how. In short, the re-creation of meaning depends on a political community's ability to recall its past, how it came to be confused about democracy, and its own standing *vis-á-vis* democracy. Only then will our political community remember what it means to conduct itself democratically.

This sort of collective remembrance of things past most assuredly does not by itself remove confusion, but neither does it leave things unchanged (Hanson 1986). When we understand the meaning of our confusion by placing it within a historical context, we also come to understand our place in the story, and what we must do to make history. Retelling our history points us toward the future, a future that we must invest with meaning during the course of our struggle to understand democracy, and to discover, in the words of Heinrich Böll, "a habitable language in a habitable land."

REFERENCES

Arnold, Samuel Green. 1899. *History of the State of Rhode Island and Providence Plantations*, vol. I: 1636–1700. Providence, RI: Preston and Rounds.

Aylmer,G.E. (ed.). 1975. *The Levellers in the English Revolution*. Ithaca, NY: Cornell University Press.

Ball, Terence W. 1983. "The Ontological Presuppositions and Political Consequences of a Social Science." In Daniel R. Sabia and Jerald Wallulis (eds.), *Changing Social Science: Critical Theory and Other Critical Perspectives*. Albany, NY: State University of New York Press, pp. 31–52.

Barker, Sir Ernest (ed. and trans.). 1975. *The Politics of Aristotle*. New York: Oxford University Press.

Barlett, John Russell (ed.). 1856. *Records of the Colony of Rhode Island and Providence Plantations in New England*, vol. I: 1636–1663. Providence, RI: A. Crawford Greene and Brother.

Beer, Samuel. 1978. "In Search of a New Public Philosophy." In *The New American Political System*, edited by Anthony King. Washington, DC: American Enterprise Institute for Public Policy Research, pp. 5–44.

Bell, Daniel. 1962. *The End of Ideology: On the Exhaustion of Political Ideas in the 'Fifties*. New York: Crowell-Collier Publishing.

Brockunier, Samuel H. 1940. *The Irrepressible Democrat: Roger Williams*. New York: Ronald Press Co.

Calhoun, John C. 1883. [1853]. "A Disquisition on Government" [1850] and "Discourse on Government" [1850]. In *Works*, 6 vols., vol. I, edited by R.K. Crallé. New York: D. Appleton and Co.

Dahl, Robert A. 1956. *A Preface to Democratic Theory*. Chicago, IL: University of Chicago Press.

Evans, Sara. 1978. *Personal Politics: The Roots of Women's Liberation in the Civil Rights Movement and the New Left*. New York: A.A. Knopf.

Fink, Z.S. 1945. *The Classical Republicans: An Essay in the Recovery of a Pattern of Thought in Seventeenth Century England*. Evanston, IL: Northwestern University Press.

Foner, Eric. 1970. *Free Soil, Free Labor, Free Men: The Ideology of the Republican Party before the Civil War*. New York: Oxford University Press.

Garret, John. 1969. *Roger Williams: Witness Beyond Christendom, 1603–1683*. New York: Macmillan.

Goldwin, Robert (ed.). 1971. *How Democratic is America? Responses to the New Left Challenge*. Chicago, IL: Rand McNally.

Gooch, G.P. 1898. *History of English Democratic Ideas in the Seventeenth Century*. Cambridge: Cambridge University Press.

Goodwyn, Lawrence. 1976. *Democratic Promise: The Populist Moment in America*. New York: Oxford University Press.

Grob, Gerald N. 1961. *Workers and Utopia: A Study of Ideological Conflict in the American Labor Movement, 1865–1900*. New York: New York Times Book Co.

Gunn, J.A.W. 1983. *Beyond Liberty and Property: The Process of Self-Recognition in Eighteenth-Century Political Thought*. Kingston and Montreal: McGill-Queen's University Press.

Haber, Samuel. 1964. *Efficiency and Uplift: Scientific Management in the Progressive Era*. Chicago, IL: University of Chicago Press.

Hamilton, Alexander, James Madison, and John Jay. 1961. *The Federalist Papers*, edited by Clinton S. Rossiter. New York: New American Library.

Hanson, Russell L. 1985. *The Democratic Imagination in America: Conversations with our Past*. Princeton, NJ: Princeton University Press.

1986. "Remembrance of Times Lost: On the Recoverability of Political Traditions." In *Tradition, Interpretation, and Science: Political Theory in the American Academy*, edited by John S. Nelson. Albany, NY: State University of New York Press, pp. 156–91.

Hill, Christopher. 1970. *God's Englishman: Oliver Cromwell and the English Revolution*. New York: Harper and Row.

Hofstadter, Richard. 1969. *The Idea of a Party System: The Rise of Legitimate Opposition in the United States, 1780–1840*. Berkeley, CA, and Los Angeles, CA: University of California Press.

Huntington, Samuel. 1975. "United States." In *The Crisis of Democracy: Report on the Governability of Democracies to the Trilateral Commission*, edited by Michel Crozier. New York: New York University Press, pp. 59–118.

Jacobson, Norman. 1963. "Political Science and Political Education." *American Political Science Review* 57 (September): 561–9.

Lincoln, Abraham. 1965. *The Lincoln–Douglass Debates of 1858*, edited by Robert W. Johannsen. New York: Oxford University Press.

Lippmann, Walter. 1922. *Public Opinion.* New York: Macmillan.

1925. *The Phantom Public*. New York: Macmillan.

McKeon, Richard (ed.). 1951. *Democracy in a World of Tensions*. Paris: UNESCO.

Macpherson, C.B. 1960. *The Political Theory of Possessive Individualism*. Oxford: Oxford University Press.

1966. *The Real World of Democracy*. Oxford: Oxford University Press.

Miller, Perry. 1953. *Roger Williams: His Contribution to the American Tradition*. Indianapolis, IN: Bobbs-Merrill.

Mollenkopf, John. 1983. *The Contested City*. Princeton, NJ: Princeton University Press.

Morantz, Regina Ann Markel. 1971. "'Democracy' and 'Republic' in American Ideology, 1787–1840." Unpublished PhD. Dissertation, Columbia University.

Morgan, Edmund S. 1967. *Roger Williams: The Church and State*. New York: Harcourt, Brace, and World.

Moynihan, Daniel. 1967. "The Professionalization of Reform." In Marvin Gettleman and David Mermelstein (eds.), *The Great Society Reader: The Failure of American Liberalism*. New York: Random House, pp. 461–75.

Oppenheim, Felix. 1971. "Democracy – Characteristics Included and Excluded." *The Monist* 55: 29–50.

Palmer, R.R. 1954. "Notes on the Use of the Word 'Democracy.' " *Political Science Quarterly* 68 (June): 203–26.

Pocock, J.G.A. 1975. *The Machiavellian Moment: Florentine Political Thought and the Atlantic Republican Tradition*. Princeton, NJ: Princeton University Press.

1985. *Virtue, Commerce, and History*. Cambridge: Cambridge University Press.

Pole, J.R. 1966. *Political Representation in England and the Origins of the American Revolution.* New York: St. Martin's Press.

Pollack, Norman (ed.). 1967. *The Populist Mind*. Indianapolis, IN: Bobbs-Merrill.

Raaflaub, Kurt. 1983. "Democracy, Oligarchy, and the Concept of the 'Free Citizen' in the late Fifth-century Athens." *Political Theory* 11 (4) (November): 517–44.

Schlesinger, Arthur, Jr. 1945. *The Age of Jackson*. Boston, MA: Little, Brown.

Simpson, Alan. 1955. "How Democratic Was Roger Williams?" *William and Mary Quarterly*, 3rd series, 13 (January): 53–67.

Skinner, Quentin. 1978. *The Foundations of Modern Political Thought*, 2 vols. Cambridge: Cambridge University Press.

Thompson, E.P. 1978. "Eighteenth Century English Society: Class Struggle without Class?" *Social History* 3 (May).

Tindall, George B. (ed.). 1966. *A Populist Reader: Selections from the Works of American Populist Leaders*. New York: Harper and Row.

Tocqueville, Alexis de. 1969. *Democracy in America*, translated by George Lawrence and edited by J.P. Mayer. New York: Doubleday, Anchor Books.

Tugwell, Rexford. 1935. *The Battle for Democracy*. New York: Columbia University Press.

Vlastos, Gregory. 1964. "Isonomia politike." In *Isonomia*, edited by J. Mau and E.G. Schmidt. Berlin: Akademie Verlag, pp. 1–35.

1983. "The Historical Socrates and Athenian Democracy," *Political Theory* 11 (4) (November): 495–516.

Wallace, Michael. 1968. "Changing Concepts of Party in the United States: New York, 1815–1828." *American Historical Review* 74 (December): 453–91.

Walzer, Michael. 1965. *The Revolution of the Saints: A Study in the Origins of Radical Politics*. Cambridge, MA: Harvard University Press.

Webster, Noah. 1953. *The Letters of Noah Webster*, edited by Harry R. Warfel. New York: Library Publishers.

Weyl, Walter. 1912. *The New Democracy: An Essay on Certain Political and Economic Tendencies in the United States*. New York: Macmillan.

Williams, Raymond. 1976. *Keywords: A Vocabulary of Culture and Society*. New York: Oxford University Press.

Williamson, Chilton. 1960. *American Suffrage: From Property to Democracy, 1760–1860*. Princeton, NJ: Princeton University Press.

Wolin, Sheldon S. 1960. *Politics and Vision: Continuity and Innovation in Western Political Thought*. Boston, MA: Little Brown.

5

The state

QUENTIN SKINNER

I

In the Preface to *De cive*, his first published work on government, Hobbes describes his own project as that of undertaking "a more curious search into the rights of states and duties of subjects."[1] Since that time, the idea that the confrontation between individuals and states furnishes the central topic of political theory has come to be almost universally accepted. This makes it easy to overlook the fact that, when Hobbes issued his declaration, he was self-consciously setting a new agenda for the discipline he claimed to have invented, the discipline of political science. His suggestion that the duties of subjects are owed to the state, rather than to the person of a ruler, was still a relatively new and highly contentious one. So was his implied assumption that our duties are owed exclusively to the state, rather than to a multiplicity of jurisdictional authorities, local as well as national, ecclesiastical as well as civil in character. So, above all, was his use of the term "state" to denote this highest form of authority in matters of civil government.

Hobbes's declaration can thus be viewed as marking the end of one distinct phase in the history of political theory as well as the beginning of another and more familiar one. It announces the end of an era in which the concept of public power had been treated in far more personal and charismatic terms. It points to a simpler and altogether more abstract vision, one that has remained with us ever since and has come to be embodied in the use of such terms as *état*,

[1] Hobbes (1983: 32). *De cive* was first published in Latin in 1642, in English in 1651. See Warrender (1983: 1). Warrender argues that the translation is at least mainly Hobbes's own work (1983: 4–8). But this is disputed by Tuck (1985: 310–12). Note that, in this as in most other quotations from primary sources, I have modernized spelling and punctuation.

stato, *staat*, and state.[2] My aim in what follows will be to sketch the historical circumstances out of which these linguistic and conceptual transformations first arose.

II

As early as the fourteenth century, the Latin term *status* – together with such vernacular equivalents as *estat*, *stato*, and state – can already be found in general use in a variety of political contexts. During this formative period these terms appear to have been employed predominantly to refer to the state or standing of rulers themselves.[3] One important source of this usage was undoubtedly the rubric *De statu hominum* from the opening of Justinian's *Digest*. There the authority of Hermogenianus had been adduced for the fundamental claim that, "since all law is established for the sake of human beings, we first need to consider the *status* of such persons, before we consider anything else."[4] Following the revival of Roman Law studies in twelfth-century Italy, the word *status* came in consequence to designate the legal standing of all sorts and conditions of men, with rulers being described as enjoying a distinctive "estate royal," *estat du roi*, or *status regis*.[5]

When the question of a ruler's *status* was raised, this was generally in order to emphasize that it ought to be viewed as a state of majesty, a high estate, a condition of stateliness. Within the well-established monarchies of France and England, we encounter this formula in chronicles and official documents throughout the latter half of the fourteenth century. Froissart, for example, recalls in book I of his *Chroniques* that when the young king of England held court to entertain visiting dignitaries in 1327, "the queen was to be seen there in an *estat* of great nobility."[6] The same usage recurs poignantly in the speech made by William Thirnyng to Richard II in 1399, in which he reminds his former sovereign "in what presence you renounced and ceased of the state of King, and of lordship and of all the dignity and worship that [be]longed thereto" (Topham *et al.* 1783: 424, col. 1).

[2] On "the state as an abstract entity," and the political transformations that underlay the emergence of the concept, see further in Shennan (1974); and cf. Maravall (1961).

[3] See Hexter (1973: 155) on "the first of its medieval political meanings."

[4] Mommsen (1970, I.5.2: 35): "Cum igitur hominum causa omne ius constitutum sit, primo de personarum statu ac post de ceteris . . . dicemus."

[5] For example, see Post (1964: 333–67, 368–414).

[6] Froissart (1972: 116): "La [sc. the queen] peut on veoir de l'estat grand noblece."

Underlying the suggestion that a distinctive quality of stateliness "belongs" to kings was the prevailing belief that sovereignty is intimately connected with display, that the presence of majesty serves in itself as an ordering force. This was to prove the most enduring of the many features of charismatic leadership eventually subverted by the emergence of the modern concept of an impersonal state.[7] As late as the end of the seventeenth century, it is still common to find political writers using the word "state" to point to a conceptual connection between the stateliness of rulers and the efficacy of their rule. As one might expect, exponents of divine-right monarchy such as Bossuet continue to speak of the *état* of *majesté* in just such terms (Bossuet 1967: 69, 72). But the same assumptions also survived even among the enemies of kingship. When Milton, for example, describes in his *History of Britain* the famous scene where Canute orders the ocean to "come no further upon my land," he observes that the king sought to give force to his extraordinary command by speaking "with all the state that royalty could put into his countenance" (Milton 1971: 365).

By the end of the fourteenth century, the term *status* had also come to be regularly used to refer to the state or condition of a realm or commonwealth.[8] This conception of the *status reipublicae* was of course classical in origin, appearing frequently in the histories of Livy and Sallust, as well as in Cicero's orations and political works.[9] It can also be found in the *Digest*, most notably under the rubric *De iustitia et iure*, where the analysis opens with Ulpian's contention that law is concerned with two areas, the public and the private, and that "public law is that which pertains to the *status rei Romanae*."[10]

With the revival of Roman Law, this further piece of legal terminology also passed into general currency. It became common in the fourteenth century, both in France and England, to discuss "the state of the realm" or *estat du roilme* (Post 1964: 310–22). Speaking of the year 1389, for example, Froissart remarks that the king decided at that point "to reform the country *en bon état*, so that

[7] For a comparison between those systems of state power in which "the ordering force of display" is proclaimed, and those in which (as in the modern West) it is deliberately obscured, see Geertz (1980: 121–3), whose formulation I have adopted.

[8] See Ercole (1926: 67–8). Hexter (1973: 115) similarly notes that *status* acquired this "second political meaning during the middle ages." Cf. Rubinstein (1971: 314–15), who begins his analysis by discussing this stage.

[9] See for example Livy (1962, 30.2.8: 372; 1966, 23.24.2: 78); Sallust (1921, 40.2: 68); Cicero (1913, 2.1.3: 170).

[10] Mommsen (1970, I.1.2: 29): "publicum ius est quod ad statum rei Romani spectat." Ercole (1926: 69) emphasizes the importance of this passage.

everyone would be contented."[11] The idea of linking the good state of a king and his kingdom soon became a commonplace. By the middle of the fifteenth century, petitioners to the English parliament regularly ended their pleas by promising the king that they would "tenderly pray God for the good estate and prosperity of your most noble person of this your noble realm."[12]

If we turn from northern Europe to the Italian city-states, we encounter the same terminology at an even earlier date. The first known advice-books addressed to *podestá* and other city-magistrates in the early years of the thirteenth century already indicate that their main concern is with the *status civitatum*, the state or condition of cities as independent political entities.[13] The anonymous *Oculus pastoralis*, perhaps written as early as the 1220s,[14] repeatedly employs the phrase,[15] as does Giovanni da Viterbo in his treatise *De regimine civitatum*,[16] completed around the year 1250.[17] By the early fourteenth century we find the same concept widely expressed in the vernacular, with writers of *Dictamina* such as Filippo Ceffi offering extensive instruction to magistrates, in the form of model speeches, on how to maintain the *stato* of the city given into their charge (Giannardi 1942: 27, 47, 48, etc.).

Discussing the state or standing of such communities, the point these writers generally wish to stress is that chief magistrates have a duty to maintain their cities in a good, happy, or prosperous state.[18] This ideal of aspiring to uphold the *bonus* or even the *optimus status reipublicae* was again Roman in origin, and was largely taken over from Cicero and Seneca by the thirteenth-century writers of advice-books.[19] The author of the *Oculus pastoralis* frequently speaks of the need to uphold the happy, advantageous, honorable and prosperous *status* of one's *civitas*.[20] Giovanni da Viterbo likewise insists on the

[11] Froissart (1824–6, vol. XII: 93): "Le roi . . . réforma le pays en bon état tant que tous s'en contentèrent."

[12] Petition from the abbey of Syon in Shadwell (1912, vol. I: 64). Cf. also vol. I: 66; I: 82, etc.

[13] For a survey of this literature see Hertter (1910).

[14] Sorbelli (1944) discusses this claim, originally put forward by Muratori; Sorbelli prefers a date in the 1240s.

[15] See Franceschi (1966: 26, 27, 28, etc.).

[16] Giovanni da Viterbo (1901: 230–2, etc.).

[17] For a discussion of the date of composition see Sorbelli (1944).

[18] See Ercole (1926: 67–8) and the similar discussions in Post (1964: 18–24, 310–32, 377–81), Rubinstein (1971: 314–16), and Mansfield (1983: 851–2).

[19] There are references to the *optimus status reipublicae* in Cicero (1914, 5.4.11: 402 and 1927, 2.11.27: 174), and to the *optimus civitatis status* in Seneca (1964, 2.20.2: 92).

[20] See Franceschi (1966: 26) on the need to act "ad . . . comodum ac felicem statum civitatis" and p. 28: "ad honorabilem et prosperum statum huius comunitatis."

desirability of maintaining the *bonus status* of one's community,[21] while Filippo Ceffi writes with equal confidence in the vernacular of the obligation to preserve a city "in a good and peaceful *stato*," in a good *stato* and complete peace" (Giannardi 1942: 28).

These writers also provide the first complete restatement of the classical view of what it means for a *civitas* or *respublica* to attain its best state.[22] This requires, they all agree, that our magistrates should follow the dictates of justice in all their public acts, as a result of which the common good will be promoted, the cause of peace upheld, and the general happiness of the people assured. This line of reasoning was later taken up by Aquinas and his numerous Italian disciples at the end of the thirteenth century. Aquinas himself presents the argument at several points in his *Summa*, as well as in his commentary on Aristotle's *Politics*. A judge or magistrate, he declares, "has charge of the common good, which is justice," and ought therefore to act in such a way "as to exhibit a good aspect from the point of view of the *status* of the community as a whole."[23] But the same line of reasoning can already be found a generation earlier in advice-books for city-magistrates. Giovanni da Viterbo, for example, develops precisely the same theory of the *optimus status* in his treatise *De regimine civitatum*, while Brunetto Latini reiterates and enlarges on Giovanni's arguments in his chapter "Dou gouvernement des cités" at the end of his encyclopedic *Livres dou trésor* of 1266.[24]

This vision of the *optimus status reipublicae* later became central to *quattrocento* humanist accounts of the well-ordered political life. When Giovanni Campano (1427–77)[25] analyzes the dangers of faction in his tract *De regendo magistratu*, he declares that "there is nothing I count more unfavourable than this to the *status* and safety

[21] See Giovanni da Viterbo (1901: 230) on the "bonus status totius communis huius civitatis."

[22] Note that they begin to discuss this issue nearly a century earlier than such chroniclers as Giovanni Villani, one of the earliest sources usually cited in this context. See Ercole (1926: 67–8), Hexter (1973: 155), and Rubinstein (1971: 314–16). For Villani on the "buono et pacifico stato" see Villani (1802–3, vol. III: 159; vol. IV: 3, etc.).

[23] Aquinas (1963, I.II.19.10: 104): "Nam iudex habet curam boni communis, quod est iustitia, et ideo vult occisionem latronis, quae habet rationem boni secundum relationem ad statum commune."

[24] See Giovanni da Viterbo (1901: 220–2) on the attributes and policies to be demanded of an elected *rector*, and cf. Latini (1948: 402–5), paraphrasing Giovanni's account.

[25] Note that, in providing dates for the more obscure humanists, I have taken my information from Consenza (1962).

of a *respublica*."[26] If the good *status* of a community is to be preserved, he goes on, all individual or factional advantage must be subordinated to the pursuit of justice and "the common good of the city as a whole" (Campano 1502, fo. xxxxvii^{r-v}). Filippo Beroaldo (1453–1505) endorses the same conclusions in a treatise to which he actually gave the title *De optimo statu*. The best state, he argues, can be attained only if our ruler or leading magistrate "remains oblivious of his own good, and ensures that he acts in everything he does in such a way as to promote the public benefit."[27]

Finally, the Erasmian humanists imported precisely the same values and vocabulary into northern Europe in the early years of the sixteenth century. Erasmus (1974: 162) himself contrasts the *optimus* with the *pessimus reipublicae status* in his *Institutio* of 1516, and argues that "the happiest *status* is reached when there is a prince whom everyone obeys, when the prince obeys the laws and when the laws answer to our ideals of honesty and equity."[28] His younger contemporary Thomas Starkey (1948: 63; also 65, 66–7) offers a very similar account in his *Dialogue* of what constitutes "the most prosperous and perfect state that in any country, city or town, by policy and wisdom may be established and set." And in More's *Utopia* the figure of Hythloday, the traveller to "the new island of Utopia," likewise insists that because the Utopians live in a society where the laws embody the principles of justice, seriously aim at the common good, and in consequence enable the citizens to live "as happily as possible," we are justified in saying that the Utopians have in fact attained the *optimus status reipublicae* – which is of course the title of More's famous book (More 1965: 244).

III

I now turn to consider the process by which the above usages – all of them common throughout late-medieval Europe – eventually gave rise to recognizably modern discussions of the concept of the state. I shall argue that, if we wish to trace both the acquisition of this concept and at the same time its expression by means of such terms

26 Campano (1502, fo. xxxxvii^{r}): "nihil existimem a statu et salute reipublicae alienius."

27 Beroaldo (1508, fo. xv^{v}): "oblitis suorum ipsius commodorum ad utilitatem publicam quicquid agit debet referre."

28 Erasmus (1974: 194): "felicissimus est status, cum principi paretur ab omnibus atque ipse princeps paret legibus, leges autem ad archetypum aequi et honesti respondent."

as *status*, *stato* or state, we ought not to focus our main attention – as medieval historians have commonly done – on the evolution of legal theories about the *status* of kings in the fourteenth and fifteenth centuries.[29] It was rare even among civil lawyers of that period to use the Latin word *status* without qualification,[30] and virtually unheard of for political writers to employ such a barbarism at all. Even when we find *status* being used in such contexts, moreover, it is almost always evident that what is at issue is simply the state or standing of the king or his kingdom, not in the least the modern idea of the state as a separate apparatus of government.

I shall instead suggest that, in order to investigate the process by which the term *status* and its vernacular equivalents first came to acquire their modern range of reference, we need to keep our main attention fixed on the early histories and advice-books for magistrates I have already singled out, as well as on the later mirror-for-princes literature to which they eventually gave rise. It was within these traditions of practical political reasoning, I shall argue, that the terms *status* and *stato* were first consistently used in new and significantly extended ways.[31]

These genres of political literature were in turn a product of the new and distinctive forms of political organization that arose within late-medieval Italy. Beginning in the early years of the twelfth century, a growing number of cities throughout the *Regnum Italicum* succeeded in acquiring for themselves the status of autonomous and self-governing republics.[32] It is true that these communities later proved unstable, and were widely reorganized in the course of the next century under the stronger and more centralized regimes of hereditary princes (Waley 1978: 128–40). But even in this later period, the great city-republics of Florence and Venice managed to preserve their traditional hostility to the idea of hereditary

[29] Cf. Kantorowicz (1957, esp. pp. 207–32, 268–72), Post (1964, esp. pp. 247–53, 302–9), Strayer (1970, esp. pp. 57–9), and Wahl (1977: 80). By contrast, see Ullmann (1968–9, esp. pp. 43–4) on traditional legal concepts as an obstacle to the emergence of the concept of the state.

[30] Note how loftily Hotman still speaks of such usages in his *Francogallia* as late as the 1570s. Writing about the Public Council, he observes that its powers extend "to all those matters which the common people in vulgar parlance nowadays call Affairs of State" ("de iis rebus omnibus, quae vulgus etiam nunc Negotia Statuum populari verbo appellat") (1972: 332).

[31] For the thesis that "*stato*, meaning a State, derives in the main . . . from *lo stato del principe*, meaning the status or estate of an effectively sovereign prince," see Dowdall (1923: 102). Cf. also Skinner (1978, vol. II: 352–8).

[32] On this development see Waley (1978: 83–330).

monarchy, and thereby carried the ideals of participatory republican government into the era of the high Renaissance.[33]

The development of these new political formations posed a new series of questions about the concept of political authority. One of the most pressing concerned the type of regime best suited to ensuring that an independent *civitas* or *respublica* is able to remain in its *optimus status* or best state. Is it wisest to opt for the rule of an hereditary *signore*, or ought one to retain an elective system of government based on a *podestá* or other such magistrate?

Although this question remained in contention throughout the history of Renaissance Italy, it is possible to distinguish two main phases of the debate. The earliest treatises intended for city-magistrates invariably assumed – in line with their Roman authorities – that the best state of a *civitas* can be attained only under an elective form of republican government. After the widespread usurpation of these regimes, however, by the rise of hereditary *signori* in the fourteenth century, this commitment increasingly gave way to the claim that the best means of ensuring the good standing of any political community must be to institute the rule of a wise prince, a *pater patriae*, whose actions will be governed by a desire to foster the common good and hence the general happiness of all his subjects.[34]

Building on this assumption, the writers of mirror-for-princes treatises in the Renaissance generally devoted themselves to considering two related points. Their loftiest aim was to explain how a good ruler can hope to reach the characteristically princely goals of honour and glory for himself while at the same time managing to promote the happiness of his subjects.[35] But their main concern was with a far more basic and urgent question of statecraft: how to advise the new *signori* of Italy, often in highly unsettled circumstances, on how to hold on to their *status principis* or *stato del principe*, their political state or standing as effectively governing rulers of their existing territories.

As a result, the use of the term *stato* to denote the political standing of rulers, together with the discussion of how such rulers should behave if they are to manage *mantenere lo stato*, began to resound through the chronicles and political literature of fourteenth-century

[33] On this "moment" see Pocock (1975: 83–330). Cf. also Skinner (1978, vol. I: 139–89).

[34] On the *pater patriae*, see for example Beroaldo (1508, fos. xiv^r and xv^r) and Scala (1940: 256–8, 273).

[35] Petrarch already states these twin ideals (1554: 420–1, 428). They become standard during the *quattrocento*, even recurring in Machiavelli's *Il principe* (1960: 102).

Italy. When Giovanni Villani, for example, speaks in his *Istorie Fiorentine* of the civic dissensions that marked the city during the 1290s, he observes that they were largely directed against *il popolo in suo stato e signoria* – against the people in their positions of political power.[36] When Ranieri Sardo in his *Cronaca Pisana* describes the accession of Gherardo d'Appiano as leader of the city in 1399, he remarks that the new *capitano* continued to enjoy the same *stato e governo* – the same political standing and governmental authority – as his father had enjoyed before him (Sardo 1845: 240–1). By the time we reach such late contributions to the mirror-for-princes literature as Machiavelli's *Il principe* of 1513, the question of what a ruler must do if he wishes to maintain his political standing had become the chief topic of debate. Machiavelli's advice is almost entirely directed at new princes who wish *tenere* or *mantenere lo stato* – who wish to maintain their positions as rulers over whatever territories they may have managed to inherit or acquire.[37]

If such a ruler is to prevent the state in which he finds himself from being altered to his disadvantage, he must clearly be able to fulfil a number of preconditions of effective government. If we now turn to consider the ways in which these preconditions were formulated and discussed in the traditions of thought I am considering, we shall find the terms *status* and *stato* employed in an increasingly extended manner to refer to these various aspects of political power.[38] As an outcome of this process, we shall eventually find these writers deploying at least some elements of a recognizably modern conception of the state.

One precondition of maintaining one's standing as a ruler is obviously that one should be able to preserve the character of one's existing regime. We accordingly find the terms *status* and *stato* being used from an early period to refer not merely to the state or condition of princes, but also to the presence of particular regimes or systems of government.

This usage in turn appears to have arisen out of the habit of employing the term *status* to classify the various forms of rule described by Aristotle. Aquinas has sometimes been credited with popularizing this development, since there are versions of his *Expositio* of Aristotle's *Politics* in which oligarchies are described as *status paucorum* and the rule of the people is identified as the *status*

36 Villani (1802–3, vol. IV: 24). Cf. also vol. IV: 190–4.

37 For these phrases see Machiavelli (1960: 16, 19, 22, 25–6, 27, 28, 35, etc.).

38 Rubinstein (1971) similarly analyzes some of these extended usages. While I have avoided duplicating his examples, I am much indebted to his account.

popularis.[39] Such usages later became widespread in humanist political thought. Filippo Beroaldo begins his *De optimo statu* with a typology of legitimate regimes, speaking of the *status popularis*, the *status paucorum* and even the *status unius* when referring to monarchy (1508, fos. xi^r and xii^v). Francesco Patrizi (1412–94) opens his *De regno* with a similar typology, one in which monarchy, aristocracy, and democracy are all characterized as types of *civilium status* or states of civil society (Patrizi 1594b: 16–17, 19, and esp. 21). Writing in the vernacular at the same period, Vespasiano da Bisticci (1421–98) likewise contrasts the rule of *signori* with the *stato populare*, while Guicciardini later invokes the same distinction in his *Discorsi* on the government of Florence (Vespasiano 1970–6, vol. I: 406; Guicciardini 1932: 274). Finally, Machiavelli used *stato* in just this fashion at a number of places in *Il principe*,[40] most notably in the opening sentence of the entire work, in which he informs us that "All the *stati*, all the dominions that have had or now have power over men either have been or are republics or principalities."[41]

By this stage, the term *stato* was also in widespread use as a way of referring simply to prevailing regimes. When Giovanni Villani, for example, notes that in 1308 "it was the members of the *parte Nera* who held control" in Florence, he speaks of the government they established as *lo stato de'Neri*.[42] When Ranieri Sardo (1845: 125) writes about the fall of the Nove in Siena in 1355, he describes the change of regime as the loss of *lo stato de'Nove*. When Vespasiano (1970–6, vol. II: 171, 173) relates how the enemies of Cosimo de'Medici succeeded in setting up a new government in 1434, he expresses the point by saying that "they were able to change *lo stato*." By the time we reach a theorist such as Machiavelli's friend Francesco Vettori, writing in the early part of the sixteenth century, both these usages of *stato* were firmly established. Vettori employs the term not only to refer to different forms of government, but also to describe the prevailing regime in Florence that he wished to see defended.[43]

[39] See Aquinas (1966: 136–7, 139–40, 310–11, 319–21, 328–30). Rubinstein (1971: 322) credits Aquinas with popularizing these usages. But they were largely the product of the humanist revision of his text issued in 1492. See Mansfield (1983: 851), and cf. Cranz (1978: 169–73) for a full account.

[40] See for example Machiavelli (1960: 28 and 29) on the *stato di pochi*.

[41] Machiavelli (1960: 15): "Tutti li stati, tutti e'dominii che hanno avuto et hanno imperio sopra li uomini sono stati e sono o republiche o principati."

[42] Villani (1802–3, vol. IV: 190–1). Cf. also vol. IV: 25; vol. VIII: 186.

[43] Vettori (1842: 432, 436). Rubinstein (1971: 318) notes that these were already standard usages in late *quattrocento* Florence.

A second precondition of maintaining one's existing state as a ruler is obviously that one should suffer no loss or alteration in the range of territories given into one's charge. As a result of this further preoccupation we find the terms *status* and *stato* pressed into early service as a way of referring to the general area over which a ruler or chief magistrate needs to exercise control. When the author of the *Oculus pastoralis*, for example, wishes to describe the duty of chief magistrates to look after their cities and localities, he already speaks of it as a duty to promote *suos status* (Franceschi 1966: 24). When the authors of the *Gratulatio* sent to the people of Padua in 1310 wish to express the hope that the entire province may be able to live in peace, they say that they are hoping for the *tranquillitas vestri status* (Muratori 1741: 131). Similarly, when Ambrogio Lorenzetti tells us, in the verses that accompany his celebrated frescoes of 1337–9 on the theme of good government, that a *signore* must cultivate the virtues if he is to succeed in levying taxes from the areas under his command, he expresses his point by saying that this is how he must act *per governare lo stato*.[44]

These early and isolated usages first begin to proliferate in the chronicles and political treatises of the high Renaissance. When Sardo (1845: 91), for example, wants to describe how the Pisans made peace throughout their territories in 1290, what he says is that the truce extended throughout *stato suo*. When Guicciardini (1933: 298) remarks in his *Ricordi* that the French revolutionized warfare in Italy after 1494, producing a situation in which the loss of a single campaign brought with it the forfeiture of all one's lands, he describes such defeats as bringing with them the loss of *lo stato*. So too with Machiavelli, who frequently uses the term *stato* in *Il principe* in order to denote the lands or territories of a prince. He clearly has this usage in mind when he talks at length in chapter 3 about the means a wise prince must adopt if he wishes to acquire new *stati*; and he evidently has in mind the same usage when he asks in chapter 24 why so many of the princes of Italy have lost their *stati* during his own lifetime (Machiavelli 1960: 18, 22, 24, 97).

Finally, due in large measure to these Italian influences, the same usage can be found in northern Europe by the early years of the sixteenth century. Guillaume Budé, for example, in his *L'Institution du prince* of 1519, equates the range of *les pays* commanded by Caesar after his victory over Antony with the extent of *son estat*.[45] Similarly,

[44] The verses are reproduced in Rowley (1958, vol. I: 127).
[45] Budé (1966: 140). Although Budé's *Institution* was not published until 1547, it was completed by the start of 1519. See Delaruelle (1907: 201).

when Thomas Starkey (1948: 167) argues in his *Dialogue* of the early 1530s that everyone living in England should be represented by a Council, he remarks that such a body "should represent the whole state." And when Lawrence Humphrey warns in his tract *The Nobles* of 1563 that evil conduct on the part of a ruler can easily set a bad example throughout an entire community, he expresses his point by saying that the vices of a ruler can easily "spread the same into the whole state" (1973, sig. Q. 8^{r}).

As the writers of advice-books always emphasized, however, by far the most important precondition of maintaining one's state as a prince must be to keep one's hold over the existing power structure and institutions of government within one's *regnum* or *civitas*. This in turn gave rise to the most important linguistic innovation that can be traced to the chronicles and political writings of Renaissance Italy. This took the form of an extension of the term *stato* not merely to denote the idea of a prevailing regime, but also, and more specifically, to refer to the institutions of government and means of coercive control that serve to organize and preserve order within political communities.

Vespasiano speaks on several occasions in his *Vite* of *lo stato* as just such an apparatus of political authority. In his life of Alessandro Sforza, for example, he describes how Alessandro conducted himself "in his government of *lo stato*" (Vespasiano 1970–6, vol. I: 426). In his life of Cosimo de'Medici he speaks of "those who hold positions of power in *stati*," and praises Cosimo for recognizing the difficulties of holding on to power in *uno stato* when faced by opposition from influential citizens.[46] Guicciardini in his *Ricordi* similarly asks why the Medici "lost control of *lo stato* in 1527," and later observes that they found it much harder than Cosimo had done "to maintain their hold over *lo stato di Firenze*," the institutions of Florentine government.[47] Finally, Castiglione in *Il cortegiano* likewise makes it clear that he thinks of *lo stato* as a distinct power structure which a prince needs to be able to control and dominate. He begins by remarking that the Italians "have greatly contributed to discussions about the government of *stati*," and later advises courtiers that "when it comes to

[46] Vespasiano (1970–6, vol. I: 177, 192). On the latter passage see also Rubinstein (1971: 318).

[47] Guicciardini (1933: 287, 293). Note that Guicciardini – though not Machiavelli – also speaks explicitly of *ragione di stato*. See Maffei (1964, esp. pp. 712–20). For the subsequent history of that concept in *cinquecento* Italy, see Meinecke (1957, esp. pp. 65–145).

questions about *stati*, it is necessary to be prudent and wise" in order to counsel one's rule about the best way to behave.[48]

Of all the writers of advice-books, however, it is Machiavelli in *Il principe* who shows the most consistent willingness to distinguish the institutions of *lo stato* from those who have charge of them. He thinks of *stati* as having their own foundations, and speaks in particular of each *stato* as having its own particular laws, customs, and ordinances (Machiavelli 1960: 53; 76, 84). He is willing in consequence to speak of *lo stato* as an agent, describing it as capable, among other things, of choosing particular courses of action and of calling in times of crisis upon the loyalty of its citizens (Machiavelli 1960: 48, 92). This means, as Machiavelli makes clear at several points, that what he takes himself to be discussing in *Il principe* is not simply how princes ought to behave; he also sees himself as writing more abstractly about statecraft (*dello stato*) and about *cose di stato* or affairs of state (Machiavelli 1960: 21, 25).

IV

It has often been argued that, by the time we reach the usages I have just been examining, we are already dealing with a recognizably modern conception of the state as an apparatus of power whose existence remains independent of those who may happen to have control of it at any given time. Gaines Post and others have even suggested that this conception is already present in a number of allusions to the *status regni* in the fourteenth century.[49] A similar claim has been advanced with even greater confidence about the employment of the term *stato* by Machiavelli and some of his contemporaries. As Chiappelli puts it, for example, "the word bears the meaning of 'State' in its full maturity" in a majority of the places where Machiavelli uses it.[50]

These claims, however, are I think greatly exaggerated. It is usually clear – except in the small number of deeply ambiguous cases I have cited[51] – that even when *status* and *stato* are employed by these writers to denote an apparatus of government, the power structure

[48] Castiglione (1960: 10, 117–18). For other *cinquecento* uses see Chabod (1962, esp. pp. 153–73).

[49] See Post (1964, esp. pp. viii, 247–53, 302–9, 494–8 and pp. 269, 333) for alleged "anticipations" of Machiavelli's thought. Cf. also Kantorowicz (1957, esp. pp. 207–32) on "polity-centered kingship."

[50] Chiappelli (1952: 68). Cf. also Cassirer (1946: 133–7), Chabod (1962: 146–55), D'Entrèves (1967: 30–2).

[51] It is important to emphasize, however, that in the cases cited in nn. 46 to 48, as in the case of Machiavelli, it would arguably be no less of an overstatement to insist

in question is not in fact viewed as independent of those who have charge of it. As Post himself concedes, the usual aim in early legal discussions of the *status regni* was to insist on a far more personal view of political power,[52] a view that was later to be revived by the proponents of absolute monarchy in the seventeenth century.[53] According to this argument, the ruler or chief magistrate, so far from being distinguishable from the institutions of the state, is said to possess and even embody those institutions himself. The same point can in most cases be made about Machiavelli's invocations of *lo stato* in *Il principe*. When he uses the term to refer to an apparatus of government, he is usually at pains to emphasize that it needs to remain in the hands of the prince: that *lo stato*, as he often puts it, remains equivalent to *il suo stato*, the prince's own state or condition of rulership.[54]

Even after the reception of humanist ideas about *lo stato* in northern Europe, the belief that the powers of government should be treated as essentially personal in character was to die hard. It is clearly this assumption, for example, which underlies many of the quarrels between kings and parliaments over the issue of taxation in the course of the sixteenth century. The basis of the parliamentary case was generally an assertion of the form that, except in times of dire necessity, kings should be able "to live of their own."[55] They should be able, that is, to ensure that their personal revenues remain sufficient to uphold both their own kingly state and the good state of their government.

that these are all unequivocally traditional usages. In the retreat from the type of overstatements cited in n. 50, this point seems in danger of being lost. Hexter in particular irons out a number of ambiguities that ought to be admitted (1973, esp. pp. 164–7 and cf. the corrective in Gilbert [1965, 329–30]). Mansfield (1983: 853) similarly concludes that we do not find anywhere in Machiavelli's writings "an instance of the impersonal modern state among his uses of *stato*." If by this he means that Machiavelli cannot unambiguously be said to express that concept, this is undoubtedly correct. My only objection is that there are several ambiguous passages; the history of the acquisition of the concept cannot be divided into such watertight compartments.

[52] See Post (1964: 334), on *status* being used to stress that the king "was not only the indispensable ruler but also the essence of the territorial State which he ruled."

[53] For this revival, see below, n. 94. Post claims that the medieval sources he discusses "anticipated the idea" of "l'état, c'est moi" (1964: 269; and cf. also pp. 333–5). But when this remark was uttered in seventeenth-century France (if it ever was) it was by then blankly paradoxical, and this would have been the point of uttering it. On this point see Mansfield (1983: 849) and cf. Rowen (1961) on Louis XIV as "proprietor of the state."

[54] See Machiavelli (1960: 16, 47, 87, 95). Cf. on this point Mansfield (1983: 852).

[55] In England this demand (and this phrase) can be found as late as early-Stuart arguments over royal revenues. See for example the parliamentary debate of 1610 quoted in Tanner (1930: 359).

I conclude that, for all the importance of the writers I have been considering, they cannot in general be said to articulate a recognizable concept of the state with anything like complete self-consciousness. It would not perhaps be too bold to assert, indeed, that in all the discussions about the state and government of princes in the first half of the sixteenth century, there will be found scarcely any instance in which the *état*, *staat* or state in question is unequivocally separated from the status or standing of the prince himself.[56]

This is not to deny, however, that the crystallizing of a recognizable concept of the state was one of the legacies of Renaissance political thought. It is merely to suggest that, if we wish to follow the process by which this development took place, we need to focus not merely on the mirror-for-princes literature on which I have so far concentrated, but also on the other strand of thought about the *optimus status reipublicae* that I began by singling out. We need, that is, to turn our attention to the rival tradition of Renaissance republicanism, the tradition centring on the claim that, if there is to be any prospect of attaining the *optimus status reipublicae*, we must always institute a self-governing form of republican regime.

Among the republican theorists of Renaissance Italy, the main reason given for this basic commitment was that all power is liable to corrupt. All individuals or groups, once granted sovereignty over a community, will tend to promote their own interest at the expense of the community as a whole. It follows that the only way to ensure that the laws promote the common good must be to leave the whole body of citizens in charge of their own public affairs. If their government is instead controlled by an authority external to the community itself, that authority will be sure to subordinate the good of the community to its own purposes, thereby interfering with the liberty of individual citizens to attain their chosen goals. The same outcome will be no less likely under the rule of an hereditary prince. Since he will generally seek his own ends rather than the common good, the community will again forfeit its liberty to act in pursuit of whatever goals it may wish to set itself.

This basic insight was followed up within the republican tradition in two distinct ways. It was used in the first place to justify an

[56] Even in France, the country in which, after Italy, traditional assumptions about the *status* of princes first changed, this arguably remains true until the 1570s. On this point see below, section V, and cf. Lloyd (1983: 146–53). In Spain the old assumptions appear to have survived until at least the middle of the seventeenth century, *pace* Maravall (1961). See Elliot (1984: 42–5, 121–2). In Germany a purely patrimonial concept of government appears to have survived even longer. See the comments in Shennan (1974: 113–14).

assertion of civic autonomy and independence, and so to defend the *libertas* of the Italian cities against external interference. This demand was initially directed against the Empire and its claims of feudal suzerainty over the *Regnum Italicum*. It was first developed by such jurists as Azo, and later by Bartolus and his followers,[57] seeking to vindicate what Bartolus described as "the *de facto* refusal of the cities of Tuscany to recognize any superior in temporal affairs."[58] But the same demand for *libertas* was also directed against all potential rivals as sources of coercive jurisdiction within the cities themselves. It was claimed on the one hand against local feudatories, who continued to be viewed, as late as Machiavelli's *Discorsi*, as the most dangerous enemies of free government (Machiavelli 1960, I.55: 254–8). And it was even more vehemently directed against the jurisdictional pretensions of the church. The most radical response, embodied for example in Marsilius's *Defensor pacis* of 1324, took the form of insisting that all coercive power is secular by definition, and thus that the church has no right to exercise civil jurisdictions at all (Marsilius 1956, esp. II.4: 113–26). But even in the more orthodox treatises on city government, such as that of Giovanni da Viterbo, the church is still refused any say in civic affairs. The reason, as Giovanni expresses it, is that the ends of temporal and ecclesiastical authority are completely distinct (Giovanni da Viterbo 1901: 266–7). The implication is that, if the church tries to insist on any jurisdiction in temporal matters, it will simply be "putting its sickle into another man's harvest."[59]

The other way in which the basic insight of the republican tradition was developed was in the form of a positive claim about the precise type of regime we need to institute if we are to retain our *libertas* to pursue our chosen goals. The essence of the republican case was that the only form of government under which a city can hope to remain "in a free state" will be a *res publica* in the strictest sense. The community as a whole must retain the ultimate sovereign authority, assigning its rulers or chief magistrates a status no higher than that of elected officials. Such magistrates must in turn be treated not as rulers in the full sense, but merely as agents of *ministri* of justice, charged with the duty of ensuring that the laws established by the community for the promotion of its own good are properly enforced.

[57] See Calasso (1957: 83–123), and Wahl (1977). For analogous reinterpretations of the Decretals, see Mochi Onory (1951). For a survey see Tierney (1982).

[58] See Bartolus (1562, 47.22: 779) on the "civitates Tusciae, quae non recognoscunt de facto in temporalibus superiorem."

[59] Giovanni da Viterbo (1901: 266): "in alterius messem falcem suam mittere."

This contrast between the freedom of republican regimes and the servitude implied by any form of monarchical government has often been viewed as a distinctive contribution of *quattrocento* Florentine thought.[60] But the underlying assumption that liberty can be guaranteed only within a republic can already be found in many Florentine writers of the previous century.[61] Dante speaks in the *Inferno* of the move from seigneurial to republican rule as a move from tyrany to a *stato franco*, a state or condition of civic liberty (1966, xxvii. 54: 459). Ceffi repeatedly emphasizes in his *Dicerie* that the only means of guaranteeing civic *libertá* is to ensure that one's city remains under the guidance of an elected magistrate (Giannardi 1942: 32, 35, 41, 44). And Villani in his *Istorie Florentine* likewise contrasts the free *stato* of the Florentine republic with the tyranny imposed by the Duke of Athens as *signore* in 1342 (1802–3, vol. VIII: 11).

It is certainly true, however, that the equation between living in a republic and living "in a free state" was worked out with the greatest assurance by the leading republican theorists of Venice and Florence in the course of the high Renaissance. Among the Venetian writers, Gasparo Contarini furnished the classic statement of the argument in his *De republica Venetorum* of 1543. Owing to the city's elective system of government, he declares, in which "a mixture of the *status* of the nobility and of the people" is maintained, "there is nothing less to be feared in the city of Venice than that the head of the republic will interefere with the *libertas* or the activities of any of the citizens."[62] Among Florentine theorists, it was of course Machiavelli in his *Discorsi* who provided the most famous version of the same argument. "It is easy to understand," as he explains at the start of book II, "whence the love of living under a free constitution springs up in peoples. For experience shows that no cities have ever increased in dominion or in riches except when they have been established in liberty."[63] The reason, he goes on, "is easy to perceive, for it is not the pursuit of individual advantage but of the common good that makes cities great, and there is no doubt that it is only

[60] This is, for example, the main thesis of Baron (1966).

[61] For this assumption in *trecento* Florentine diplomacy, see Rubinstein (1952).

[62] Contarini (1626: 22 and 56): "temperandam . . . ex optimatum et populari statu . . . nihil minus urbi Venetae timendum sit, quam principem reipublicae libertati ullum unquam negocium facessere posse." On Contarini see Pocock (1975: 320–8).

[63] Machiavelli (1960, II.2: 280): "E facil cosa è conoscere donde nasca ne' popoli questa affezione del vivere libero: perché si vede per esperienza le cittadi non avere mai ampliato né di dominio né di ricchezza se non mentre sono state in libertà."

under republican regimes that this ideal of the common good is followed out."[64]

From the point of view of my present argument, these commitments can now be seen to be crucial in two different ways. It is within this tradition of thought that we encounter, for the first time, a vindication of the idea that there is a distinct form of "civil" or "political" authority which is wholly autonomous, which exists to regulate the public affairs of an independent community, and which brooks no rivals as a source of coercive power within its own *civitas* or *respublica*. It is here, in short, that we first encounter the familiar understanding of the state as a monopolist of legitimate force.

This view of "civil government" was of course taken up in France and England at an early stage in their constitutional development. It underlies their hostility to the jurisdictional power of the church, culminating in France in the "Gallican" Concordat of 1516, in England in the Marsiglian assumptions underpinning the Act of Appeals in 1533. It also underlies their repudiation of the Holy Roman Empire's claim to exercise any jursidictions within their territories, a repudiation founded on a reworking of Azo's and later Bartolus's theories of *imperium* into the celebrated dictum that *Rex in regno suo est Imperator*.

For the origins of this view of civil government, however, we need to turn back to thirteenth-century Italy, and specifically to the political literature engendered by the self-governing city-republics of that period. Writing in the 1250s, Giovanni da Viterbo already takes his theme to be the analysis of civil power, that form of power which upholds the *civium libertas* or liberty of those who live together as citizens (Giovanni da Viterbo 1901: 218). Writing only a decade later, Brunetto Latini goes on to add that those who study the use of such power in the government of cities are studying "politics," "the noblest and the highest of all the sciences."[65] It is this neoclassical tradition to which later theorists of popular sovereignty are ultimately alluding when they speak of an autonomous area of "civil" or "political" authority, and offer to explicate what Locke (1967: 283) was to call "the true original, extent and end of civil government."

The other way in which the republican tradition contributed to

[64] Machiavelli (1960, II.11: 280): "La ragione è facile a intendere: perché non il bene particulare ma il bene comune è quello che fa grandi le città. E sanza dubbio questo bene comune non è osservato se non nelle republiche."

[65] See Latini (1948: 391) on "politique . . . la plus noble et la plus haute science."

crystallizing a recognizable concept of the state is of even greater importance. According to the writers I have been considering, a city can never hope to remain in a free state unless it succeeds in imposing strict conditions on its rulers and magistrates. They must always be elected; they must always remain subject to the laws and institutions of the city which elects them; they must always act to promote the common good – and hence the peace and happiness – of the sovereign body of its citizens. As a result, the republican theorists no longer equate the idea of governmental authority with the powers of particular rulers or magistrates. Rather they think of the powers of civil government as embodied in a structure of laws and institutions which our rulers and magistrates are entrusted to administer in the name of the common good. They cease in consequence to speak of rulers "maintaining their state" in the sense of maintaining their personal ascendancy over the apparatus of government. Rather they begin to speak of the *status* or *stato* as the name of that apparatus of government which our rulers may be said to have a duty to maintain.

There are already some hints of this momentous transition in the earliest treatises and *dictamina* intended for chief magistrates of city-republics. Brunetto Latini insists in his *Trésor* of 1266 that cities must always be ruled by elected officials if the *bien commun* is to be promoted. He further insists that these *sires* must follow the laws and customs of the city in all their public acts (Latini 1948, esp. pp. 392, 408, 415; 402, 412). And he concludes that such a system is indispensable not merely to maintaining such officials in a good *estat*, but also to maintaining "the *estat* of the city itself."[66] A similar hint can be found in Giovanni da Vignano's *Flore de parlare* of the 1270s. In one of his model letters, designed for the use of city ambassadors when seeking military help, he describes the government of such communities as their *stato*, and accordingly appeals for support "in order that our good *stato* can remain in wealth, honor, greatness and peace."[67] Finally, the same hint recurs soon afterwards in Matteo dei Libri's *Arringa* on the identical theme. He sets out a very similar model speech for ambassadors to deliver, advising them to appeal for help "in order that our good *stato* may be able to remain in peace."[68]

It is only with the final flowering of Renaissance republicanism,

[66] Latini (1948: 403) on "l'estat de vous et de cette ville." Cf. p. 411 on the idea of remaining "en bon estat."

[67] Giovanni da Vignano (1974: 247): "che il nostro bom stato porà remanere in largheça, honore, grandeça e reponso."

[68] Matteo dei Libri (1974: 12): "ke 'l nostro bon stato potrà romanire in reposo."

however, that we find such usages occurring with their unequivocally modern sense. Even here, moreover, this development is largely confined to the vernacular literature. Consider, by contrast, a work such as Alamanno Rinuccini's Latin dialogue of 1479, *De libertate* (1957). This includes a classic statement of the claim that individual as well as civic liberty is possible only under the laws and institutions of a republic. But Rinuccini never stoops to using the barbarous term *status* to describe the laws and institutions involved; he always prefers to speak of the *civitas* or *respublica* itself as the locus of political authority. So too with such classic Venetian writers as Contarini in his *De republica Venetorum*. Although Contarini has a clear conception of the apparatus of government as a set of institutions independent of those who control them, he never uses the term *status* to describe them, but always prefers in a similar way to speak of their authority as embodied in the *respublica* itself.[69]

If we turn, however, to the rather less pure latinity of Francesco Patrizi's *De institutione reipublicae*, we encounter a significant development in his chapter on the duties of magistrates. He lays it down that their basic duty is to act "in such a way as to promote the common good," and argues that this above all requires them to uphold "the established laws" of the community.[70] He then summarizes his advice by saying that this is how magistrates must act "if they are to prevent the *status* of their city from being overturned."[71]

It is in the vernacular writers on republicanism of the next generation, however, that we find the term *stato* being used with something approaching full self-consciousness to express a recognizable concept of the state. Guicciardini's *Discorso* on how the Medici should act to improve their control over Florence provides a suggestive example. He advises them to gather around themselves a group of advisers who are loyal to the *stato* and willing to act on its behalf. The reason is that "every *stato*, every form of sovereign power, needs dependents" who are willing "to serve the *stato* and benefit it in everything."[72] If the Medici can manage to base their regime on such a group, they can hope to establish "the most

[69] See Contarini (1626, at pp. 28 and 46), two cases where, in Lewkenor (1969), *respublica* is rendered as "state." On Lewkenor's translation see Fink (1962: 41–2).

[70] Patrizi (1594: 281) on the duty to uphold "veteres leges" and act "pro communi utilitate."

[71] Patrizi (1594a: 292 and 279) on how to act "ne civitatis status evertatur" and "statum reipublicae everterunt."

[72] Guicciardini (1932: 271–2): "ogni stato ed ogni potenzia eminente ha bisogno delle dependenzie . . . che tutti servirebbono a beneficio dello stato." Cf. also pp. 276, 279.

powerful foundation for the defence of the *stato*" that anyone could aspire to set up.[73]

Finally, if we turn to Machiavelli's *Discorsi*, we find the term *stato* being used with even greater confidence to denote the same apparatus of political authority. It is of course true that Machiavelli continues largely to employ the term in the most traditional way to refer to the state or condition of a city and its way of life (Machiavelli 1960: 135, 142, 153, 192, 194, etc.). And even when he mentions *stati* in the context of describing systems of government, these usages are again largely traditional: he is generally speaking either about a species of regime,[74] or about the general area or territory over which a prince or republic holds sway.[75]

There are several occasions, however, especially in the analysis of constitutions at the start of book I, where he appears to go further. The first is when he writes in chapter 2 about the founding of Sparta. He emphasizes that the system of laws promulgated by Lycurgus remained distinct from, and served to control, the kings and magistrates entrusted with upholding the laws themselves. And he characterizes Lycurgus's achievement in creating this system by saying that "he established *uno stato* which then endured for more than eight hundred years."[76] The next instance occurs in chapter 6, where he considers whether the institutions of government in republican Rome could have been set up in such a way as to avoid the "tumults" which marked that city's political life. He puts the question in the form of asking "whether it might have been possible to establish *uno stato* in Rome" without that distinctive weakness.[77] That last and most revealing case occurs in chapter 18, where he considers the difficulty of maintaining *uno stato libero* within a corrupt city. He not only makes an explicit distinction between the authority of the magistrates under the ancient Roman republic and the authority of the laws "by means of which, together with the magistrates, the citizens were kept under control."[78] He adds in the same passage that the latter set of institutions and practices can best be described as "the order of the government or, indeed, of *lo stato*."[79]

[73] Guicciardini (1932: 273): "uno barbacane e fondamento potentissimo a difesa dello stato."

[74] See for example Machiavelli (1960, I.2: 130–2, and also pp. 182, 272, 357, etc.).

[75] See in particular Machiavelli (1960, II.24: 351–3).

[76] Machiavelli (1960, I.2: 133): "Licurgo . . . fece uno stato che durò più che ottocento anni."

[77] Machiavelli (1960, I.6: 141): "se in Roma si poteva ordinare uno stato . . ."

[78] Machiavelli (1960, I.18: 180): "le leggi dipoi che con i magistrati frenavano i cittadini."

[79] Ibid.: "l'ordine del governo o vero dello stato."

It has often been noted that, with the reception of Renaissance republicanism in northern Europe, we begin to encounter similar assumptions among Dutch and English protagonists of "free states" in the middle of the seventeenth century.[80] It has less often been recognized that the same assumptions, couched in the same vocabulary, can already be found more than a century earlier among the first writers who attempted to introduce the ideals of civic humanism into English political thought. Thomas Starkey, for example,[81] distinguishes at several points in his *Dialogue* between the state itself and "they which have authority and rule of the state" (Starkey 1948: 61; cf. also 57, 63). It is the "office and duty" of such rulers, he goes on, to "maintain the state established in the country" over which they hold sway, "ever looking to the profit of the whole body" rather than to their own good (Starkey 1948: 64). The only method, he concludes, of "setting forward the very and true commonweal" is for everyone to recognize, rulers and ruled alike, that they are "under the same governance and state" (Starkey 1948: 71).

The same assumptions can be found soon afterwards in John Ponet's *Short Treatise of Politic Power* of 1556. He too speaks of rulers simply as the holders of a particular kind of office, and describes the duty attaching to their office as that of upholding the state. He is thus prompted to contrast the case of "an evil person coming to the government of any state" with a good ruler who will recognize that he has been "to such office called for his virtue, to see the whole state well governed and the people defended from injuries" (Ponet 1942: 98).

Finally, and perhaps most significantly, we find the same phraseology in Tudor translations of the classic Italian treatises on republican government. When Lewes Lewkenor, for example, issued his English version of Contarini's *De republica Venetorum* in 1599, he found himself in need of an English term to render Contarini's basic assumption that the authority of the Venetian government remains inherent at all times in the *civitas* or *respublica* itself, with the Doge and Council serving merely as representatives of the citizen-body as a whole. Following standard humanist usage, he generally expresses this concept by the term "commonwealth." But in speaking of the relationship between a commonwealth and its

[80] See Fink (1962: 10–20, 56–68); Raab (1964: 185–217); Pocock (1975: 333–422); Haitsma Mulier (1980: 26–76).

[81] I see no justification for the claim that Starkey merely "dressed up" his *Dialogue* in civic humanist terms. See Mayer (1985: 25) and cf. Skinner (1978, vol. I: 213–42) for an attempt to place Starkey's ideas in a humanist context.

own citizens, he sometimes prefers instead to render *respublica* as "state." When he mentions the possibility of enfranchizing additional citizens in Venice, he explains that this can take place in special circumstances when someone can be shown to have been especially "dutiful towards the state." And when he discusses the Venetian ideal of citizenship, he feels able to allude in even more general terms to "the citizens, by whom the state of the city is maintained" (Lewkenor 1969: 18, 33).

V

For all the undoubted importance of these classical republican theorists, however, it would still be misleading to conclude that their use of the term *stato* and its equivalents may be said to express our modern concept of the state. That concept has come to embody a doubly impersonal character.[82] We distinguish the state's authority from that of the rulers or magistrates entrusted with the exercise of its powers for the time being. But we also distinguish its authority from that of the whole society or community over which its powers are exercised. As Burke (1910: 93) remarks in his *Reflections* – articulating a view already well entrenched by that time – "society is indeed a contract," but "the state ought not to be considered as nothing better than a partnership agreement" of a similar nature. Rather the state must be acknowledged to be an entity with a life of its own; an entity which is at once distinct from both rulers and ruled and is able in consequence to call upon the allegiances of both parties.

The republican theorists embrace only one half of this doubly abstract notion of the state. On the one hand there is, I think, no doubt that they constitute the earliest group of political writers who insist with full self-consciousness on a categorical distinction between the state and those who have control of it, and at the same time express that distinction as a claim about the *status*, *stato* or state. But on the other hand they make no comparable distinction between the powers of the state and those of its citizens. On the contrary, the whole thrust of classical republican theory is directed towards an ultimate equation between the two. Although this undoubtedly yields a recognizable concept of the state – one that many Marxists and exponents of direct democracy continue to

[82] A point emphasized by Shennan (1974: 9, 113–14) and Mansfield (1983: 849–50).

espouse – it is far from being the concept we have inherited from the more conservative mainstream of early-modern political thought.

The differences can be traced most clearly in the literature in praise of "free states." Consider again, for example, one of the earliest English works of this character, John Ponet's *Short Treatise of Politic Power*. As we have seen, Ponet makes a firm distinction between the office and person of a ruler, and even uses the term "state" to describe the form of civil authority our rulers have a duty to uphold. But he makes no analogous distinction between the powers of the state and those of the people. Not only does he maintain that "kings, princes and governors have their authority of the people"; he also insists that ultimate political authority continues to reside at all times in "the body or state of the realm or commonwealth" (Ponet 1942: 106, 105). If kings or princes are found to be "abusing their office," it is for the body of the people to remove them, since the ultimate powers of sovereignty must always remain lodged within "the body of every state" (Ponet 1942: 105; cf. also pp. 111, 124).

The same commitment is upheld even by the most sophisticated defenders of "free states" in the seventeenth century. A good example is furnished by Milton's *Ready and Easy Way to Establish a Free Commonwealth*. If we are to maintain "our freedom and flourishing condition," he argues, and establish a government "for preservation of the common peace and liberty," it is indispensable that the sovereignty of the people should never be "transferred." It should be "delegated only" to a governing Council of State (Milton 1980: 432–3, 456). The institutions of the state are thus conceived as nothing more than a means of expressing the powers of the people in an administratively more convenient form. As Milton had earlier emphasized in *The Tenure of Kings and Magistrates*, whatever authority our rulers may possess is merely "committed to them in trust from the people, to the common good of them all, in whom the power yet remains fundamentally" at all times (Milton 1962: 202). As a result, Milton, Harrington, and other defenders of "free states" hardly ever use the term "state" when speaking of the institutions of civil government. Believing as they do that such institutions must remain under the control of the whole community if its members are to preserve their birthright of liberty, they almost always prefer the term "commonwealth" as a means of referring not merely to bodies of citizens, but also to the forms of political authority by which they must be governed if they are to remain "in a free state."[83]

The same is no less true of the "monarchomachs" and other contractarian opponents of early-modern absolutism who first rose to prominence in the later sixteenth century, especially in Holland and France. Deriving their arguments mainly from scholastic rather than classical republican sources, these writers are not generally republican in the strict sense of believing that the common good of a community can never be satisfactorily assured under a monarchical form of government. Usually they are quite explicit in claiming that (to cite Marsilius of Padua's terminology) as long as the ultimate powers of a *legislator humanus* within a *civitas* or *respublica* remain in the hands of the *populus*, there is no reason to doubt that – as Aristotle had taught – a variety of different constitutional forms may be equally capable of promoting the common good, and hence the peace and happiness of the community as a whole. Some writers within this tradition, such as Marsilius himself, in consequence exhibit little interest in whether a republican or a monarchical regime is established, save only for insisting that if the latter type is chosen, the *pars principans* must always be elected.[84] Others, including François Hotman and other French monarchomachs who followed his lead in the 1570s, remain content to assume that the body of the commonwealth will normally have a monarchical head, and similarly concentrate on hedging the institution of monarchy in such a way as to make it compatible with the liberty and ultimate sovereignty of the people.[85] Still others, such as Locke in his attack on Filmer's absolutism in the *Two Treatises of Government*, suppose there to be good reasons for preferring a monarchical form of government with a liberal allowance of personal prerogative, if only to mitigate the rigours of an undiluted theory of distributive justice by allowing a "power to act according to discretion for the public good."[86]

In common with the defenders of "free states," however, these writers still assume that the apparatus of government in a *civitas* or *respublica* amounts to nothing more than a reflection of, and a device

[83] See Harrington (1977: 173) for the claim that "the interest of the commonwealth is in the whole body of the people," and his invariable preference, in the "Preliminaries" to *Oceana*, for speaking of "the city" or "commonwealth" as the locus of political authority. See also pp. 161, 170, 171–2, 182–3.

[84] Marsilius of Padua (1956, I.8 and 9: 27–34). For the special significance of Marsilius within this tradition of thought see Condren (1985: 262–9).

[85] See esp. Hotman (1972: 287–321), where he lays out his view of the French constitution as a mixed monarchy.

[86] Locke (1967: 393). On Locke's *Two Treatises* essentially as an attack on Filmerian absolutism, see Laslett (1967: 50–2, 67–78) and cf. Dunn (1969: 47–57, 58–76, 87–95). On the place of this concept in Locke's theory see Dunn (1969: 148–56).

for upholding, the sovereignty of the people. Even in a theory such as Locke's, government is still viewed simply as a trust established by the members of a community for the more effective promotion of their own good, "the peace, safety and public good of the people" (Locke 1967: 371).

The effect of this commitment, in this tradition no less than in classical republicanism, is that no effective contrast is drawn between the power of the people and the powers of the state.[87] These writers do distinguish, of course, between the apparatus of government and the authority of those who may happen to have control of it at any one time. Just as strongly as the republican theorists, they insist on a complete separation between a ruler's person and his office, and argue that – as Locke puts it – even a supreme magistrate is merely a "public person" who is "vested with the power of the law" and charged with directing the legislative toward the attainment of the common good.[88] They still assume, however, that the range of powers a community establishes over itself when its members consent to become subjects of a civil government must ultimately be identified with its own powers as a community. As Locke (1967: 369, 385) insists, we never "deliver up" our fundamental liberties in establishing a commonwealth, but merely depute or delegate a known and indifferent judge to safeguard them more effectively on our own behalf. Although this means that we commit ourselves to setting up a complex apparatus of government, it also means that the powers of such a government can never amount to anything more than "the joint power of every member of the society." This is how it comes about, as Locke concludes, that "the community perpetually retains a supreme power" over its prince or legislative, "and must, by having deputed him, have still a power to discard him when he fails in his trust" (Locke 1967: 375, 385, 445).

As a result, these writers never find themselves tempted to use the terms *status* or state when describing the powers of civil government. When they envisage the members of a *civitas* or community instituting what Locke (1967: 434) calls a form of umpirage for the settlement of their controversies, they conceive of them not as

[87] Howell (1983: 155), while agreeing that this is true of Hotman, argues that two other "monarchomach" theorists – Beza and the author of the *Vindiciae contra tyrannos* – "implied the existence of the secular state as an entity distinct from ruler and people." I cannot see that either writer distinguished the powers of the state from those of the people. Cf. Skinner (1978, vol. II: 318–48).

[88] Locke (1967: 386). Cf. also pp. 301, 360–1, 371, 381 for the idea of rulers as mere trustees. See also Hotman (1972: 154 and 402–4) on kings as magistrates "tied" by the duties of their office.

entering a new state, but simply as setting up a new form of society–a civil or political society within which the wealth or welfare of the community can be better secured. So they continue to invoke the terms *civitas* or *respublica* to refer to the apparatus of civil government, usually translating these terms as "city" or "commonwealth." As Locke (1967: 373) explicitly states, "by commonwealth I must be understood all along" to mean "any independent community which the Latins signified by the word *civitas*, to which the word which best answers in our language is commonwealth."

If we wish, therefore, to trace the process by which the powers of the state finally came to be described as such, and seen at the same time as distinct from both the powers of the people and of their magistrates, we need at this juncture to turn to a strongly contrasting tradition of early-modern political thought. We need to turn to those writers who addressed themselves critically to the thesis of popular sovereignty we have just been considering, whether in its republican guise as a claim about "free states," or in its neoscholastic form as a claim about the inalienable rights of communities. We need to turn, that is, to those theorists whose aspirations included a desire to legitimize the more absolutist forms of government that began to develop in western Europe in the early part of the seventeenth century. It was as a by-product of their arguments, and in particular of their efforts to insist that the powers of government must be something other than a mere expression of the powers of the governed, that the concept of the state as we have inherited it was first articulated with complete self-consciousness.

Some of these counter-revolutionary theorists were mainly concerned with the radical scholastic thesis – associated in particular with Marsilius and his successors – to the effect that the *populus* and the *legislator humanus* can be equated. The repudiation of this doctrine became one of the chief polemical aims of later sixteenth-century Thomism, with Suarez's *De legibus* of 1612 containing the fullest and most influential summary of the alleged counter arguments.[89] Others were more disturbed by the monarchomach theories of popular soveignty thrown up by the religious wars in the latter part of the sixteenth century. Bodin in particular seeks in his *Six livres de la république* of 1576 to refute the arguments of those who were claiming that, as Knolles's translation of 1606 puts it, "princes sent

[89] On this school of thought see Hamilton (1963) and Fernandez–Santamaria (1977). On the character of their natural-law (as opposed to divine-right) theories of absolutism see Sommerville (1982 and 1986: 59–80). For a contrast with later theories of popular sovereignty see Tully (1980: 64–8 and 111–16).

by providence to the human race must be thrust out of their kingdoms under a pretence of tyranny."[90] Still others were no less perturbed by the implications of the republican allegation that, as Hobbes (1968: 369) scornfully paraphrases it in *Leviathan*, "the subjects in a popular commonwealth enjoy liberty," while "in a monarchy they are all slaves." Hobbes himself, like Grotius before him, engages with this as well as with the neoscholastic thesis of popular sovereignty, and undoubtedly offers the most systematic attempt to answer the question that preoccupies all these theorists: how to vindicate an account of civil government which at once concedes the original sovereignty of the people and is at the same time absolutist in its political allegiances.

If there is one thesis by which these writers are all especially agitated, it is the suggestion that the powers of civil government constitute nothing more than a reflection of the powers of the people. They concede, of course, that coercive authority must be justified by its capacity to ensure the common good, and in consequence the peace and happiness of the citizen-body as a whole. Hobbes believes no less firmly than Marsilius that, as he repeatedly declares in *Leviathan*, all governments must be judged by their "aptitude to produce the peace and security of the people, for which end they were instituted."[91] What none of these writers can accept, however, is the idea that the form of authority required to produce such benefits can appropriately be envisaged as nothing more than a trustee, a type of official to whom the people delegate the exercise of their own authority purely as a matter of administrative convenience. Political power, they all admit, is originally instituted by the people, but never in the form of a trust. It is instituted by means of what Suarez calls "absolute transfer" of the people's sovereignty, one that takes the form of "a kind of alienation, not a delegation at all."[92] To set up a mere "depository" or "guardian" of sovereign power, as Bodin agrees, is not to set up a genuine "possessor" of sovereignty at all.[93] For the people to perform that particular act, as Hobbes similarly stresses at several points in *Leviathan*, it is essential for them to recognize that they are "renouncing and transferring" their own original sovereignty, with

[90] See Bodin (1962: A71). For Bodin's concern to refute the "monarchomachs" see Franklin (1973, esp. pp. vii. 50, 93) and Salmon (1973, esp. pp. 361, 364).

[91] Hobbes (1968: 241). Cf. also pp. 192, 223, 237, etc.

[92] Suarez (1612: 210): "Quocirca translatio huius potestatis a republica in principem non est delegatio, sed quasi alienatio . . . simpliciter illi conceditur."

[93] Bodin (1576: 125) distinguishes between "possesseurs" of sovereignty and those who "ne sont que depositaires et gardes de cette puissance."

the implication that it is totally "abandoned or granted away" to someone else (Hobbes 1968: 190, 192).

Civil government, they insist, cannot therefore be seen as the powers of citizens under another guise. It must be seen as a distinct form of power, for reasons that Hobbes enunciates with complete assurance in *De cive* almost a decade before giving them classic expression in *Leviathan*. "Though a government," he declares, "be constituted by the contracts of particular men with particulars, yet its right depends not on that obligation only" (Hobbes 1983: 105). By constituting such a government, "that right which every man had before to use his faculties to his own advantages is now wholly translated on some certain man or council for the common benefit" (Hobbes 1983: 105). It follows that whatever power is thereby installed in authority must be recognized "as having its own rights and properties, insomuch as neither any one citizen, nor all of them together" can now be accounted its equivalent (Hobbes 1983: 89). This, as he was later to put it, "is the generation of that great Leviathan, or rather (to speak more reverently) of that mortal God, to which we owe, under the immortal God, our peace and defence. For by this authority, given him by every particular man in the commonwealth, he hath the use of so much power and strength conferred on him, that by terror thereof, he is enabled to form the wills of them all to peace at home and mutual aid against their enemies abroad" (Hobbes 1968: 227).

It is important, however, not to conflate this form of absolutism with that of the divine-right theorists who rose to such prominence during the same period. A writer like Bossuet, for example, deliberately sets out to obliterate the distinction between the office and person of a king. Echoing the celebrated remark attributed to Louis XIV, he insists that the figure of a ruler "embodies in himself the whole of the state": *tout l'état est en lui*.[94] By contrast, even Hobbes declares as unambiguously as possible that the powers of a ruler are never personal powers at all. They are owed entirely to his standing as holder of "the office of the sovereign," the principal duty of which, as Hobbes never tires of repeating, "consisteth in the end for which he was trusted with the sovereign power, namely the procuration of the safety of the people" (Hobbes 1968: 376).

With Hobbes no less than with Bodin, Suarez, Grotius, and the whole developing tradition of natural-law absolutism, we accordingly arrive at the view that the ends of civil or political association

[94] Bossuet (1967: 177). On this variety of absolutism see Keohane (1980: 241–61) and Sommerville (1986: 9–50).

make it indispensable to establish a single and supreme sovereign authority whose power remains distinct not merely from the people who orginally instituted it, but also from whatever office-holders may be said to have the right to wield its power at any particular time. What, then, is this form of political authority to be called?

Not surprisingly, these writers at first respond by reaching for traditional names. One suggestion, much canvassed by Bodin and later adopted by Hobbes in *De cive*, was that we should think of the authority in question as embodied in the *civitas*, the *ville* or the city as opposed to either its citizens or its magistrates.[95] But the most usual proposal was that we should think of it as that form of authority which inheres in the *respublica*, the *république* or the commonwealth. Suarez and Grotius, writing in Latin, both speak of the *respublica*.[96] Bodin, writing originally in French, speaks analogously of *la république*; translating his treatise into Latin in 1586, he rendered this as *respublica*; and when Knolles issued his English version in 1606, he in turn called the work *The Six Bookes of a Commonweale*.[97] Finally, Hobbes largely comes round to this terminology in *Leviathan*, speaking far less frequently of the city, and instead describing his work on its title-page as an enquiry into "the matter, form and power of a commonwealth" (Hobbes 1968: 73).

As these writers increasingly recognized, however, none of these traditional terms really served to render their meaning adequately. One obvious difficulty with "commonwealth" was the fact that, as Raleigh (1661: 3,8) complains in his *Maxims of State*, it had come to be used "by an usurped nickname" to refer to "the government of the whole multitude." To invoke it was thus to risk confusion with one of the theories of popular sovereignty they were most anxious to repudiate. Nor was it altogether satisfactory to speak instead of the city or *civitas*. It is true that Hobbes (1983: 89) consistently does so in *De cive*, declaring that "a city therefore (that we may define it) is one person whose will, by the compact of many men, is to be received for the will of them all." But the obvious difficulty here – in the face of which even Hobbes's confidence seems to have evaporated – was the need to insist on such a purely stipulative definition so strangely at variance with the ordinary meaning of the term.

It was at this juncture, within this tradition of thought, that a

[95] See Bodin (1576: 9 *et passim*) on the "ville" and "cité." Cf. Hobbes (1983: 89–90 *et passim*) for the concept of "a city or civil society."

[96] See Suarez (1612: 351–60) on the relations between the *princeps*, *leges* and *respublica*, and cf. Grotius (1625: 65) on *civitas* and *respublica* and p. 84 on the *romana respublica*.

[97] Cf. the full titles of Bodin (1576), Bodin (1586), and Bodin (1962).

number of these theorists began to resolve their difficulties by speaking instead of the *state*, while making it clear at the same time that they were consciously using the term to express their master concept of an impersonal form of political authority distinct from both rulers and ruled.

Bodin already hints at this final crystallizing of the concept at several points in his *République*.[98] Although he continues to write in traditional terms about rulers "who maintain their *estats*," he also uses the word *estat* on several occasions as a synonym for *république*.[99] Most significantly of all, he feels able to speak of "the state in itself" (*l'estat en soi*), describing it both as a form of authority independent of particular types of government, and as the locus of "indivisible and incommunicable sovereignty."[100] It is striking, moreover, that when Knolles came to translate these passages in 1606, he not only used the word "state" in all these instances, but also in a number of other places where Bodin himself had continued to speak in a more familiar vein of the authority of the *cité* or *république*.[101]

If we turn to English writers of the next generation, and above all to those "politic" humanists who were critical of classical republicanism, we find the same terminology used with increasing confidence. Raleigh, for example, not only speaks freely of the state in his *Maxims*, but makes it clear that he thinks of the state as an impersonal form of political authority, defining it as "the frame or set order of a commonwealth" (Raleigh 1661: 2). Bacon (1972: 89) writes in the final version of his *Essays* in a way that often suggests a similar understanding of political authority. He describes rulers as well as their councillors as having a duty to consider "the weal and advancement of the state which they serve." And he writes in a

[98] See Lloyd (1983: 156–62). Fell (1983, esp. pp. 92–107, 175–205) lays all his emphasis on Bodin's contemporary Corasius, though without investigating the extent to which he used the term *status* to express his concept of "the legislative state." But by the next generation the use of the vernacular term *état* (or *estat*) to express such a concept had become well entrenched in France. See Church (1972: 13–80) and Keohane (1980: 54–82, 119–82). Dowdall (1923: 118) singles out Loyseau's discussion in his *Traité des seigneuries* (1608) of the relationship between "seigneuries souveraines" and "estats" as being of particular importance, and this point has been much developed. See Church (1972: 33–4) and Lloyd (1981 and 1983: 162–8).

[99] Bodin (1576, e.g. at pp. 219, 438).

[100] Bodin (1576: 282–3): "Et combien que le gouvernement d'une Republique soit plus ou moins populaire, ou Aristocratique, ou Royale, si est-que l'estat en soi ne reçoit compairison de plus ni de moins: car toujours la souverainté indivisible et incommunicable est à un seul." Note also Bodin's use of the phrase 'en matière d'estat" (576: 281, 414).

[101] See Bodin (1962: 184, 250, 451) and cf. pp. 10, 38, 409, 700 for some additional uses of "state."

number of other passages about the state and its rulers, the state and its subjects, the "founders of states" and the "subversion of states and governments" (Bacon 1972: 11, 42, 160, 165).

It is above all in Hobbes, however, and in other theorists of *de facto* sovereignty in the English revolution, that we find this new understanding of the state being articulated with complete assurance. It is true, as we have seen, that if we turn to the body of Hobbes's texts, we still find him exhibiting a preference for the traditional terminology of "city" and "commonwealth." But if we turn instead to his Prefaces, in the course of which he stands back from his own arguments and reviews their structure, we find him self-consciously presenting himself as a theorist of the state.

This transition can already be observed in the Preface to *De cive*, in the course of which he describes his project as that of explaining "what the quality of human nature is, in what matters it is, in what not, fit to make up a civil government, and how men must be agreed among themselves, that intend to grow up into a well-grounded state" (Hobbes 1983: 22). But it is in the Introduction to *Leviathan* that he proclaims most unequivocally that the subject matter of his entire investigation has been "that great Leviathan, called a Commonwealth or State (in Latin Civitas)" (Hobbes 1968: 81). Hobbes's ambition as a political theorist had always been to demonstrate that, if there is to be any prospect of attaining civil peace, the fullest powers of sovereignty must be vested neither in the people nor in their rulers, but always in the figure of an "artificial man."[102] Surveying this final redaction of his political philosophy, he at last felt able to add that, in speaking about the need for such an impersonal form of sovereignty, what he had been speaking about all along could best be described as the state.

VI

As the above account suggests, the idea that the supreme authority within a body politic should be identified as the authority of the state was originally the outcome of one particular theory of politics, a theory at once absolutist and secular-minded in its ideological allegiances. That theory was in turn the product of the earliest major counter-revolutionary movement within modern European history, the movement of reaction against the ideologies of popular sovereignty developed in the course of the French religious wars,

[102] Hobbes (1968: 82) states that the aim of *Leviathan* is "to describe the nature of this artificial man."

and, subsequently, in the English Revolution of the seventeenth century. It is perhaps not surprising, therefore, to find that both the ideology of state power and the new terminology employed to express it provoked a series of doubts and criticisms that have never been altogether stilled.

Some of the initial hostility derived from conservative theorists anxious to uphold the old ideal of *un roi, une foi, une loi*. They wished to repudiate any suggestion that the aims of public authority should be purely civil or political in character, and thereby to reinstate a closer relationship between allegiance in church and state. But much of the hostility stemmed from those who wished to uphold a more radical ideal of popular sovereignty in place of the sovereignty of the state. Contractarian writers sought in consequence to keep alive a preference for speaking about the government of civil or political society,[103] while the so-called commonwealthmen maintained their loyalty to the classical ideal of the self-governing republic throughout much of the eighteenth century.[104]

It is true that, at the end of the century, a renewed counter-revolutionary effort was made to neutralize these various populist doubts. Hegel and his followers in particular argued that the English contractarian theory of popular sovereignty merely reflected a failure to distinguish the powers of civil society from those of the state, and a consequent failure to recognize that the independent authority of the state is indispensable if the purposes of civil society are to be fulfilled. But this hardly proved an adequate reassurance. On the one hand, the anxiety of liberal theorists about the relationship between the powers of states and the sovereignty of their citizens generated confusions which have yet to be resolved. And on the other hand, a deeper criticism developed out of these Hegelian roots, insisting that the state's vaunted independence from its own agents as well as from the members of civil society amounts to nothing more than a fraud. As a result, sceptics in the tradition of Michels and Pareto, no less than socialists in the tradition of Marx, have never ceased to insist that modern states are in truth nothing more than the executive arms of their own ruling class.

Given the importance of these rival ideologies and their distinctive vocabularies, it is all the more remarkable to observe how quickly

[103] Benjamin Hoadly, for example, continues to speak about "the civil power," "civil government" and "the power of the civil magistrate" rather than about the state. See "The Original and Institution of Civil Government, Discussed" in Hoadly (1773, vol. II: 189, 191, 201, 203 *et passim*).

[104] See the usages in Robbins (1959: 125, 283) and cf. Kramnick (1968, esp. pp. 236–60) and Pocock (1975, esp. pp. 423–505).

the term "state" and its equivalents nevertheless became established at the heart of political discourse throughout western Europe. By the middle of the eighteenth century the new terminology had become virtually inescapable for all schools of thought. Even so nostalgic an exponent of classical republicanism as Bolingbroke found himself constrained in his pamphleteering of the 1720s to talk about the authority of the state, and about the need for the state to be supported, protected, and above all reformed (1967a: 19, 43, 93, 131). By the time we come to Hume's essays of the 1750s,[105] or Rousseau's *Contrat social* of a decade later,[106] we find the concept of the state and the terms *état* and *state* being put to work in a consistent and completely familiar way.

The immediate outcome of this conceptual revolution was to set up a series of reverberations in the wider political vocabularies of the western European states. Once "state" came to be accepted as the master noun of political argument, a number of other concepts and assumptions bearing on the analysis of sovereignty had to be reorganized or in some cases given up. To complete this survey, we need finally to examine the process of displacement and redefinition that accompanied the entrenchment of the modern idea of the state.

One concept that underwent a process of redefinition was that of political allegiance. A subject or *subditus* had traditionally sworn allegiance to his sovereign as liege lord. But with the acceptance of the idea that sovereignty is lodged not with rulers but with the state, this was replaced by the familiar view that citizens owe their basic loyalty to the state itself.

This is not to say that those who originally advanced this argument had any desire to give up speaking of citizens as *subditi* or subjects. On the contrary, the earliest theorists of the state retained a strong preference for this traditional terminology, using it as a means of countering both the contractarian inclination to speak instead about the sovereignty of the *populus* or people, and the classical republican contention that we ought to speak only of *civitates* and *cives*, of cities and their citizens. Hobbes, for example, with his usual cunning, maintains in the first published version of his political theory that he is writing specifically "about the citizen" – *de cive*. Yet he makes it one of his most important polemical claims that "each

[105] Hume's main discussions of state power occur in his essays "Of Commerce" and "That Politics may be Reduced to a Science." See Hume (1875, vol. I: 100, 105 and 289, 294–5).

[106] See Rousseau (1966, "De l'état civil", pp. 55–6). On "état" in the political vocabulary of Rousseau and his contemporaries see Derathé (1950: 380–2) and Keohane (1980, esp. pp. 442–9).

citizen, as also every subordinate civil person" ought properly to regard himself as "the subject of him who hath the chief command" (Hobbes 1983: 90).

Hobbes is in complete agreement with his radical opponents, however, when he goes on to argue that citizens ("that is to say, subjects") ought not to pay allegiance to those who exercise these rights of sovereignty, but rather to the sovereignty inherent in the state or commonwealth itself (Hobbes 1983: 151). Hotman and later "monarchomach" theorists had already insisted that even holders of offices under a monarchy must be viewed as councillors of the kingdom, not of the king, and as servants of the crown, not of the person wearing it.[107] Hobbes simply reiterates the same argument when he declares with so much emphasis in *De cive* that the "absolute and universal obedience" owed by each and every subject is due not to the person of their ruler, but rather "to the city, that is to say, to the sovereign power" (Hobbes 1983: 186).

A further and closely connected concept that was comparably transformed was that of treason. As long as the concept of allegiance was connected with that of doing homage, the crime of treason remained that of behaving treacherously towards a sovereign lord. By the end of the sixteenth century, however, this came to seem less and less satisfactory. Even in the case of England, still bound by the Statute of 1350 which defined treason as compassing or imagining the king's death, the judges began to place increasingly wide constructions upon the meaning of the original Act. The aim in almost every case was to establish a view of treason essentially as an offence against the king in virtue of his office as head of state.[108] Meanwhile the political writers of the same period, untrammeled by the need to wrestle with precedents, had already arrived by a more direct route at the familiar view of treason as a crime not against the king but against the state. As always, Hobbes states the new understanding of the concept most unequivocally. As he declares at the end of his analysis of dominion in *De cive*, those who are guilty of treason are those who refuse to perform the duties "without which the State cannot stand"; the crime of treason is the crime of those who act "as enemies to the Government" (Hobbes 1983: 181).

Finally, the acceptance of the state as both a supreme and an impersonal form of authority brought with it a displacement of the more charismatic elements of political leadership which, as I indicated at the outset, had earlier been of central importance to the

[107] See Hotman (1972, e.g. pp. 254, 298, 402).
[108] On this process see Holdsworth (1925: 307–33).

theory and practice of government throughout western Europe.

Among the assumptions that suffered displacement, the most important was the claim I began by stressing: that sovereignty is conceptually connected with display, that majesty serves in itself as an ordering force. Machiavelli, for example, still assumes that a ruler can expect to derive protection from *la maestá dello stato*, from a connection between his own high state of stateliness and his capacity to maintain his state.[109] It proved impossible, however, for such beliefs about the charisma attaching to public authority to survive the transfer of that authority to the purely impersonal agency – the "purely moral person," in Rousseau's phrase[110] – of the modern state. By the start of the eighteenth century, we already find conservative writers lamenting that, as Bolingbroke (1967b: 333) puts it, "the state is become, under ancient and known forms, an undefinable monster," with the result that a monarchy like England finds itself left with "a king without monarchical splendour" as head of state.

It was of course possible to transfer these attributes of majesty to the state's agents, permitting them to conduct state openings of parliament, to be granted state funerals, to lie in state, and so forth. Once it became accepted, however, that even heads of state are simply holders of offices, the attribution of so much pomp and circumstance to mere functionaries came to be seen not merely as inappropriate but even absurd, a case not of genuine pomp but of sheer pomposity. This insight was first elaborated by the defenders of "free commonwealths" in their anxiety to insist that, in Milton's phrase, rulers should never be "elevated above their brethren" but should "walk the streets as other men" (1980: 425). More's *Utopia*, for example, contains an early and devastating portrayal of public magnificence as nothing more than a form of childish vanity (1965: 152–6). Ponet's *Politic Power* includes a more minatory reminder of the punishments God visited upon the Israelites for demanding "a gallant and pompous king" (1942: 87). And Milton in *The Ready and Easy Way* condemns with deep disdain those rulers who aspire "to set a pompous face upon the superficial actings of state" (1980: 426).

One outcome of distinguishing the authority of the state from that of its agents was thus to sever a time-honoured connection

[109] Machiavelli (1960: 74, and cf. also pp. 76, 93). The same applies even more strongly to Machiavelli's contemporaries among "mirror-for-princes" writers. See for example Pontano (1952: 1054–6), Sacchi (1608: 68).

[110] Rousseau (1966: 54) on "la personne morale qui constitue l'Etat."

between the presence of majesty and the exercise of majestic powers. Displays of stateliness eventually came to be seen as mere "shows" or "trappings" of power, not as features intrinsic to the workings of power itself.[111] When Contarini concedes, for example, that the Doge of Venice is permitted to uphold the dignity of his office with a certain magnificence, he emphasizes that this is just a matter of appearances, and uses a phrase that Lewkenor translates by saying that the Doge is allowed a "royal appearing show."[112] Speaking with much greater hostility, Milton (1980: 426, 429) agrees that a monarch "sits only like a great cypher," with all his "vanity and ostentation" being completely inessential to the ordering force of public authority.

Finally, for the most self-conscious rejection of the older images of power, as well as the most unambiguous view of the state as a purely impersonal authority, we need to turn once more to Hobbes. Discussing these concepts in chapter 10 of *Leviathan*, Hobbes deploys the idea of an effective power to command in such a way as to absorb every other element traditionally associated with the notions of public honour and dignity. To hold dignities, he declares, is simply to hold "offices of command"; to be held honourable is nothing more than "an argument and sign of power" (Hobbes 1968: 152, 155). Here, as throughout, it is Hobbes who first speaks, systematically and unapologetically, in the abstract and unmodulated tones of the modern theorist of the state.

[111] On the distinctiveness of this conception of public power see Geertz (1980: 121–3).

[112] See Lewkenor (1969: 42), translating "specie regia" from Contarini (1626: 56).

For invaluable help with earlier drafts I am greatly indebted to John Dunn and Susan James.

REFERENCES

Aquinas, St. Thomas. 1963. *Summa theologiae*, 3 vols., edited by P. Caramello. Turin: Marietti.

1966. *In octo libros politicorum Aristotelis expositio*, edited by R. Spiazzi. Turin: Marietti.

Bacon, F. 1972. *Essays*, edited by M. Hawkins. London: Dent.

Baron, H. 1966. *The Crisis of the Early Italian Renaissance*, 2nd edn. Princeton, NJ: Princeton University Press.

Bartolus of Sassoferrato. 1562. *Digestum novum commentaria.* Basel.

Beroaldo, F. 1508. "Libellus de optimo statu." In *Opuscula*. Venice, fos. x–xxxiiii.

Bodin, J. 1576. *Les Six Livres de la république*. Paris.

1586. *De republica libri sex*. Paris.
1962. *The Six Books of a Commonweale*, translated by R. Knolles and edited by K. McRae. Cambridge, MA: Harvard University Press.
Bolingbroke, Lord. 1967a. "A Dissertation upon Parties." In *The Works*, 4 vols., vol II. London: F. Cass, pp. 5–172.
1967b. "Letters on the Study and Use of History." In *The Works*, 4 vols., vol. II. London. F. Cass, pp. 173–334.
Bossuet, J.-B. 1967. *Politique tirée des propres paroles de l'Ecriture Sainte*, edited by J. Le Brun. Geneva: Droz.
Budé, G. 1966. *De l'institution du prince*. Farnborough: Gregg.
Burke, E. 1910. *Reflections on the Revolution in France*, Everyman edn. London: Dent.
Calasso, F. 1957. *I Glossatori e la teoria della sovranitá*. Milan: Giuffrè.
Campano, G. 1502. "De regendo magistratu." In *Opera omnia.* Venice, fos. xxxxiii–xxxxviii.
Cassirer, E. 1946. *The Myth of the State*. New Haven, CT: Yale University Press.
Castiglione, B. 1960. *Il libro del cortegiano*. In *Opere*, edited by C. Cordié. Milan: R. Ricciardi, pp. 5–361.
Chabod, F. 1962. *L'idea di nazione*, 2nd edn. Bari: G. Laterza.
Chiappelli, F. 1952. *Studi sul linguaggio del Machiavelli*. Florence: F. Le Monnier.
Church, W. 1972. *Richelieu and Reason of State*. Princeton, NJ: Princeton University Press.
Cicero. 1913. *De officiis*, translated by W. Miller. London: Heinemann.
1914. *De Finibus*, translated by H. Rackham. London: Heinemann.
1927. *Tusculanae Disputationes*, translated by J. King. London: Heinemann.
Condren, C. 1985. *The Status and Appraisal of Classical Texts*. Princeton, NJ: Princeton University Press.
Contarini, G. 1626. *De republica Venetorum*. Lyons.
Cosenza, M. 1962. *Biographical and Bibliographical Dictionary of the Italian Humanists*, vol. V: *Synopsis and Bibliography*. Boston, MA: G.K. Hall.
Cranz, F. 1978. "The Publishing History of the Aristotle Commentaries of Thomas Aquinas." *Traditio* 34: 157–92.
Dante Alighieri. 1966. *Inferno*, edited by G. Petrocchi. Milan: A. Mondadori.
Delaruelle, L. 1907. *Guillaume Budé*. Paris: H. Champion.
D'Entrèves, A. 1967. *The Notion of the State*. Oxford: Oxford University Press.
Derathé, R. 1950. *Jean-Jacques Rousseau et la science politique de son temps*. Paris: Presses Universitaires de France.
Dowdall, H. 1923. "The Word 'State.'" *The Law Quarterly Review* 39: 98–125.
Dunn, J. 1969. *The Political Thought of John Locke*. Cambridge: Cambridge University Press.
Elliott, J. 1984. *Richelieu and Olivares*. Cambridge: Cambridge University Press.
Erasmus, D. 1974. *Institutio christiani principis*, edited by O. Herding. In *Opera*

omnia, part IV, vol. I. Amsterdam: North-Holland, pp. 95–219.
Ercole, F. 1926. *La politica di Machiavelli*. Rome: Anonima Romana Editoriale.
Fell, A. 1983. *Origins of Legislative Sovereignty and the Legislative State*, vol. I. Cambridge, MA: Atheneum.
Fernandez-Santamaria, J.A. 1977. *The State, War and Peace*. Cambridge: Cambridge University Press.
Fink, Z. 1962. *The Classical Republicans*, 2nd edn. Evanston, IL: Northwestern University Press.
Franceschi, E. 1966. "Oculus pastoralis." *Memorie dell' accademia delle scienze di Torino* 11: 19–70.
Franklin, J. 1973. *Jean Bodin and the Rise of Absolutist Theory*. Cambridge: Cambridge University Press.
Froissart, J. 1824–6. *Chroniques*, 14 vols., edited by J. Buchon. Paris: Vordière, J. Carez.
1972. *Chroniques: début du premier libre*, edited by G. Diller. Geneva: Droz.
Geertz, C. 1980. *Negara*. Princeton, NJ: Princeton University Press.
Giannardi, G. 1942. "Le 'Dicerie' di Filippo Ceffi." *Studi di filologia italiana* 6: 27–63.
Gilbert, F. 1965. *Machiavelli and Guicciardini*. Princeton, NJ: Princeton University Press.
Giovanni da Vignano. 1974. *Flore de parlare*. In Matteo dei Libri, *Arringhe*, edited by E. Vincenti. Milan: R. Ricciardi, pp. 229–325.
Giovanni da Viterbo. 1901. *Liber de regimine civitatum*, edited by C. Salvemini. In *Bibliotheca iuridica medii aevi*, 3 vols., edited by A. Gaudenzi, vol. III. Bologna: Società Azzoguidiana, pp. 215–80.
Grotius, H. 1625. *De iure belli ac pacis*. Paris.
Guicciardini, F. 1932. *Dialogo e discorsi del reggimento di Firenze*, edited by R. Palmarocchi. Bari: G. Laterza.
1933. *Scritti politici e ricordi*, edited by R. Palmarocchi. Bari: G. Laterza.
Haitsma Mulier, E. 1980. *The Myth of Venice and Dutch Republican Thought in the Seventeenth Century*, translated by G. T. Moran. Assen: Van Gorcum.
Hamilton, B. 1963. *Political Thought in Sixteenth-century Spain*. Oxford: Clarendon.
Harrington, J. 1977. *The Political Works of James Harrington*, edited by J. Pocock. Cambridge: Cambridge University Press.
Hertter, F. 1910. *Die Podestalitteratur Italiens im 12. und 13. Jahrhundert*. Leipzig. B.G. Teubner.
Hexter, J. 1973. *The Vision of Politics on the Eve of the Reformation*. New York: Allen Lane.
Hoadly, B. 1772. *The Works*, 3 vols. London: W. Bowyer and J. Nichols.
Hobbes, T. 1968. *Leviathan*, edited by C. Macpherson. Harmondsworth: Penguin.
1983. *De cive: The English Version*, edited by H. Warrender. Oxford: Clarendon.
Holdsworth, W. 1925. *A History of English Law*, vol. VIII. London: Methuen.

Hotman, F. 1972. *Francogallia*, edited by R. Giesey and J. Salmon. Cambridge: Cambridge University Press.

Hume, D. 1875. *Essays*, 2 vols., edited by T. Green and T. Grose. London: Longmans Green.

Humphrey, L. 1973. *The Nobles, or Of Nobility*. In *The English Experience*, no. 534. New York: Da Capo Press.

Kantorowicz, E. 1957. *The King's Two Bodies*. Princeton, NJ: Princeton University Press.

Keohane, N. 1980. *Philosophy and the State in France*. Princeton, NJ: Princeton Unversity Press.

Kramnick, I. 1968. *Bolingbroke and his Circle*. Cambridge, MA: Harvard University Press.

Laslett, P. 1967. "Introduction." In Locke 1967: 1–120.

Latini, B. 1948. *Li Livres dou trésor*, edited by F. Carmody. Berkeley, CA: University of California Press.

Lewkenor, L. 1969. *The Commonwealth and Government of Venice*. In *The English Experience*, vol. 101. New York: Da Capo Press.

Livy. 1962. *Ab urbe condita*, vol. VIII, translated by F. Moore. London: Heinemann.

1966. *Ab urbe condita*, vol. VI, translated by F. Moore, London: Heinemann.

Lloyd, H. 1981. "The Political Thought of Charles Loyseau (1564–1610)." *European Studies Review* 11: 53–82.

1983. *The State, France and the Sixteenth Centiry*. London: George Allen and Unwin.

Locke, J. 1967. *Two Treatises of Government*, edited by P. Laslett, 2nd edn. Cambridge: Cambridge University Press.

Machiavelli, N. 1960. *Il principe e discorsi*, edited by S. Bertelli. Milan: Feltrinelli.

Maffei, R. de. 1964. "Il problema della 'Ragion di Stato' nei suoi primi affioramenti." *Rivista internazionale di filosofia del diritto* 41: 712–32.

Mansfield, H. 1983. "On the Impersonality of the Modern State: A Comment on Machiavelli's Use of *Stato*." *The American Political Science Review* 77: 849–57.

Maravall, J. 1961. "The Origins of the Modern State." *Journal of World History* 6: 789–808.

Marsilius of Padua. 1956. *The Defender of Peace*, translated by A. Gewirth. New York: Columbia University Press.

Matteo dei Libri. 1974. *Arringhe*, edited by E. Vincenti. Milan: R. Ricciardi.

Mayer, T. 1985. "Faction and Ideology: Thomas Starkey's *Dialogue*." *Historical Journal* 28: 1–25.

Meinecke, F. 1957. *Machiavellism*, translated by D. Scott. London: Routledge and Kegan Paul.

Milton, J. 1962. *The Tenure of Kings and Magistrates*. In *Complete Prose Works*, vol. III, edited by M. Hughes. New Haven, CT: Yale University Press, pp. 190–258.

1971. *History of Britain*. In *Complete Prose Works*, vol. V, edited by F. Fogle. New Haven, CT: Yale University Press.

1980. *The Ready and Easy Way to Establish a Free Commonwealth*. In *Complete Prose Works*, vol. VII, edited by R. Ayers, revised edn. New Haven, CT:Yale University Press, pp. 407–63.

Mochi Onory, S. 1951. *Fonti canonistiche dell' idea moderna dello stato*. Milan: Società Editrice 'Vita e pensiero.'

Mommsen, T. (ed.). 1970. *Digesta*, 21st edn. Zurich: Weidmannes.

More, St. Thomas. 1965. *Utopia*. In *The Complete Works of St. Thomas More*, vol. IV, edited by E. Surtz and J. Hexter. New Haven, CT: Yale University Press.

Muratori, L. (ed.). 1741. "Gratulatio." In *Antiquitates Italicae*, vol. IV. Milan: Arretti, pp. 131–2.

Patrizi, F. 1594a. *De institutione reipublicae*. Strassburg.

1594b. *De regno et regis institutione*. Strassburg.

Petrarch, F. 1554. *Opera quae extant omnia*. Basel.

Pocock, J. 1975. *The Machiavellian Moment*. Princeton, NJ: Princeton University Press.

Ponet, J. 1942. *A Short Treatise of Politic Power*. Reprinted in W. Hudson, *John Ponet*. Chicago, IL: University of Chicago Press, pp. 131–62.

Pontano, G. 1952. "De principe." In *Prosatori latini del quattrocento*, edited by E. Garin. Milan: R. Ricciardi, pp. 1023–63.

Post, G. 1964. *Studies in Medieval Legal Thought*. Princeton, NJ: Princeton University Press.

Raab, F. 1964. *The English Face of Machiavelli*. London: Routledge and Kegan Paul.

Raleigh, W. 1661. "Maxims of State." In *Remains of Sir Walter Raleigh*. London: W. Sheares, pp. 1–65.

Rinuccini, A. 1957. *Dialogus de libertate*, edited by F. Adorno. In *Atti e memorie dell' accademia toscana di scienze e lettere La Colombaria* 22: 265–303.

Robbins, C. 1959. *The Eighteenth-century Commonwealthman*. Cambridge, MA: Harvard University Press.

Rousseau, J.-J. 1966. *Du contrat social*, edited by P. Burgelin. Paris: Garnier-Flammarion.

Rowen, H. 1961. ' "L'état, c'est à moi.' Louis XIV and the State." *French Historical Studies* 2: 83–98.

Rowley, G. 1958. *Ambrogio Lorenzetti*, 2 vols. Princeton, NJ: Princeton University Press.

Rubinstein, N. 1952. "Florence and the Despots. Some Aspects of Florentine Diplomacy in the Fourteenth Century." *Transactions of the Royal Historical Society*, 2: 21–45.

1971. "Notes on the word *stato* in Florence before Machiavelli." In *Florilegium historiale*, edited by J. Rowe and W. Stockdale. Toronto: University of Toronto Press, pp. 313–26.

Sacchi, B. 1608. *De principe viro*. Frankfurt.

Sallust. 1921. *Bellum Catilinae* translated by J. Rolfe. London: Macmillan.

Salmon, J. 1973. "Bodin and the Monarchomachs." In H. Denzer (ed.), *Bodin*. Munich: Beck, pp. 359–78.

Sardo, R. 1845. *Cronaca Pisana*. In *Archivio storico italiano* 6, part II: 73–244.

Scala, B. 1940. *De legibus et iudiciis dialogus*, edited by L. Borghi. In *La Bibliofilia* 42: 256–82.
Seneca. 1964. *De beneficiis*, translated by J. Basore. London: Heinemann.
Shadwell, L. (ed.). 1912. *Enactments in Parliament Specially Concerning the Universities of Oxford and Cambridge*, 4 vols. London: Clarendon.
Shennan, J. 1974. *The Origins of the Modern European State, 1450–1725*. London: Hutchinson.
Skinner, Q. 1978. *The Foundations of Modern Political Thought*, 2 vols. Cambridge: Cambridge University Press.
Sommerville, J. 1982. "From Suarez to Filmer: A Reappraisal." *The Historical Journal* 25: 525–40.
1986. *Politics and Ideology in England, 1603–1640*. London: Longman.
Sorbelli, A. 1944. "I teorici del reggimento comunale." *Bullettino dell' istituto storico italiano per il medio evo* 59: 31–136.
Starkey, T. 1948. *A Dialogue between Reginald Pole and Thomas Lupset*, edited by K. Burton. London: Chatto and Windus.
Strayer, J. 1970. *On the Medieval Origins of the Modern State*. Princeton, NJ: Princeton University Press.
Suarez, F. 1612. *Tractatus de legibus, ac Deo legislatore*. Coimbra.
Tanner, J. 1930. *Constitutional Documents of the Reign of James I*. Cambridge: Cambridge University Press.
Tierney, B. 1982. *Religion, Law and the Growth of Constitutional Thought, 1150–1650*. Cambridge: Cambridge University Press.
Topham, J. *et al.* (eds.). 1783. *Rotuli Parliamentorum*, vol. III. London.
Tuck, R. 1985. "Warrender's *De cive*." *Political Studies* 33: 308–15.
Tully, J. 1980. *A Discourse on Property*. Cambridge: Cambridge University Press.
Ullmann, W. 1968–9. "Juristic Obstacles to the Emergence of the Concept of the State in the Middle Ages." *Annali di storia del diritto* 12–13: 43–64.
Vespasiano da Bisticci. 1970–6. *Le vite*, 2 vols., edited by A. Greco. Florence: Nella sede dell' istituto nazionale di studi sul rinascimento.
Vettori, F. 1842. *Parero* [On the Government of Florence, 1531–2]. In *Archivio storico italiano* 1: 433–6.
Villani, G. 1802–3. *Istorie fiorentine*, 8 vols. Milan: Società tipografica dei classici italiani.
Wahl, J. 1977. "Baldus de Ubaldis and the Foundations of the Nation-State." *Manuscripta* 21: 80–96.
Waley, D. 1978. *The Italian City-republics*, 2nd edn. London: Longmans.
Warrender, H. 1983. "Editor's Introduction." In Hobbes 1983.

6

Representation

HANNA FENICHEL PITKIN

Words and the world vary together, but not in any simple one-to-one correlation. When we imagine the introduction of a new word, we tend to think of examples like the explorer naming a newly discovered land or the chemist making a newly discovered or created substance. But such examples are profoundly misleading, for most words are not names, and human beings can as easily discuss what does not exist as what does. In the realm of social, cultural, and political phenomena, the relationship between words and the world is even more complex, for these phenomena are constituted by human conduct, which is profoundly shaped by what people think and say – by words. In order to understand how words and the world vary together, then, one must – to borrow a famous Wittgensteinian phrase – *look and see* in particular cases (Wittgenstein 1968, § 66).

The concept of representation is an instructive case because its meaning is highly complex and, from very early in the history of this family of words, has been highly abstract. It is thus a useful corrective to our fantasies about explorers and chemists. Representation is very much a cultural and political, a human phenomenon. Accordingly the "semantic map" of the English words in the "represent-" family does not correspond well to those of cognate terms in even closely related other languages. For example, German has three words – *vertreten*, *darstellen*, and *repräsentieren* – all of which are usually translated by the English "represent."[1] *Darstellen* means to depict or stand for; *vertreten* means to act for as an agent. *Repräsentieren* is close to the latter, but more formal and elevated in its connotations. (German political theorists sometimes argue that

[1] This example is taken from my *Wittgenstein and Justice* (Pitkin 1972). Much of the rest of this essay is reprinted, with minor revisions, from my *The Concept of Representation* (Pitkin 1967).

mere selfish private interests can be *vertreten*, but the common good or the good of the state must be *repräsentiert*.) *Repräsentieren*, however, is not at all close in meaning to *darstellen*. So, for an English speaker, the way a painting or a painter or a stage actor represents is obviously part of the same concept as the way an agent or an elected legislator represents; for a German speaker it is not. The history of legal, artistic, political, and other representation among German-speaking peoples of course also differs from the corresponding history among English-speaking peoples, but not in a way that correlates simply or neatly with such semantic differences.

Telling the full story of the concept of representation, then, would really require detailed parallel accounts of verbal and social, political, and cultural history, a task far beyond the scope of this essay. Its focus is limited primarily to etymological history, with only occasional forays into the sociopolitical; and its primary interest is in political representation, though that focus is treated in relation to the many other realms of meaning of this family of words.

Although the ancient Greeks had a number of institutions and practices to which we would apply the word "representation," they had no corresponding word or concept. The term is of Latin origin, although in Latin, too, its original meaning had nothing to do with agency or government or any of the institutions of Roman life which we might consider instances of representation. The Latin *repraesentare* means "to make present or manifest or to present again," and in classical Latin its use is confined almost entirely to inanimate objects (Lagarde 1937; Hauck 1907: 479). It can mean to make them literally present, bring them into someone's presence; accordingly it also comes to mean appearing in court in answer to a summons, literally making oneself present. It can also mean the making present of an abstraction through or in an object, as when a virtue seems embodied in the image of a certain face. And it can mean the substitution of one object for another, instead of the other, or the hastening of an event, bringing it into the present. Thus it can mean "to perform immediately" and even "to pay in cash." It has nothing to do with people representing other people or the Roman state.

In the Middle Ages the word is extended in the literature of Christianity to a kind of mystical embodiment, "applied to the Christian community in its most incorporeal aspects."[2] But its real expansion begins in the thirteenth and early fourteenth centuries, when the Pope and the cardinals are often said to represent the

[2] Lagarde (1937: 429n.), my translation. See also Tierney (1955: 4, 34–6, 45).

persons of Christ and the Apostles.[3] The connotation is still neither of delegation nor of agency; the church leaders are seen as the embodiment and image of Christ and the Apostles, and occupy their place *per successionem*. At the same time, medieval jurists begin to use the term for the personification of collective life. A community, although not a human being, is to be regarded as a person (*persona repraesentata*, *repraesenta unam personam*, *unium personae repraesentat vicem*). The stress is on the fictive nature of the connection: not a real person but a person by representation only (*persona non vera sed repraesentate*).

Meanwhile there is current among glossators the notion, derived from Roman law, that the prince or the emperor acts for the Roman people, stands in their place, looks after their welfare. In the thirteenth century the canonists begin to adopt this idea, to sharpen and develop it and apply it to religious communal life. Neither the glossators nor the canonists yet use the word "representation" in developing these Roman law ideas; but the parallel with allegorical church thought is close enough so that, by the middle of the thirteenth century, a writer familiar with both disciplines can argue that the magistrate represents the image of the whole state.[4] Here representation of an allegorical or imagic kind is applied to a secular magistrate.[5]

A similar development seems to have taken place in French. According to the *Littré*, at least, *représenter* was used for images and inanimate objects embodying abstractions long before it came to

[3] My information in this and the following paragraph comes from Lagarde (1937).

[4] Roffredus, *Quaestiones Sabbathinae*, cited by Lagarde (1937: 429n.). Georges de Lagarde has discovered a very interesting passage in the writings of a late-thirteenth-century jurist, in which the sense of imagic representation of a community meets, as it were, head on with a notion of legal agency. The jurist Albert de Gaudino inquires whether a community can plead through an attorney (*par procureur*) in a criminal case. In a sense, he says, one is tempted to answer no, since every private person must appear in person, and a collectivity (*universitas*) is to be regarded as a person. But, in another sense, the attorney represents just the fictive person of the community. Therefore, if he appears, it is as though the community appeared in person. Here we have not only the collectivity that is taken to be one person by a fiction (*unius personae repraesentat vicem*) but also the attorney who appears in the place of this person (*qui repraesentat vicem universitatis*). The ordinary activities of an attorney in court are not yet called "representing" at this time; Gaudino uses *intervenire* for the way in which a magistrate or attorney stands and acts for the community.

[5] Lagarde (1937: 433 and n.). Tierney (1955: 126) suggests that the concept of a proctor may figure significantly in the transition from image or embodiment to authoritative action.

mean anything like one person acting for others.[6] But by the thirteenth century a bailiff can be spoken of representing the person of his lord.

The same sequence of development reoccurs in English, after the word "represent" appears, probably late in the fourteenth century.[7] At that point, according to the *Oxford English Dictionary*, it is used to mean "to bring oneself or another into the presence of someone," "to symbolize or embody concretely," "to bring before the mind." The adjective "representative" means "serving to represent, figure, portray or symbolize." During the fifteenth century, the verb "represent" expands to mean also " to portray, depict, or delineate." It comes to be applied to inanimate objects which "stand in the place of or correspond to" something or someone. And it means "to produce a play," apparently a sort of depicting on the stage. At the same time, the noun "representation" appears, meaning "image, likeness, or picture." Now human beings are not entirely absent from these early uses; they appear in two ways. Firstly, representation can be an inanimate object or image standing for a human being. Secondly, representing is a human activity, but not an acting for others; it is the activity of presenting, of depicting, of painting a picture or staging a play. Not until the sixteenth century does one find an example of "represent" meaning "to take or fill the place of another (person), substitute for"; and not until 1595 is there an example of representing as "acting for someone as his authorized agent or deputy."[8]

Did the development in the meaning of "represent" that took place in Latin in the thirteenth and early fourteenth century, and that was at least under way in French in the thirteenth century, really

[6] Littré (1875). The Latin development probably had a greater influence on French than it did on English. C.H. MacIlwain (1932: 689) cites an early-fourteenth-century summons from the French king to the clergy of Tours, ordering them to come in person or send "exvobis unum nobis ad premissa mittatis, qui vicem omnium representet et omnium habeat plenariam potestatem." Corresponding documents in England do not seem to use *repraesentare*.

[7] "Probably," because it is never safe to assume that a word or a usage suddenly appears at the time of its first exemplification in the *Oxford English Dictionary*. Often there will be earlier instances that did not come to the attention of Gilbert Murray and his dictionary-making crew. Nevertheless, for convenience, I continue to write in the rest of this essay as if new usages appear at the time of their first dictionary exemplification.

[8] When a word of Latin origin was introduced into English fairly late by way of Old French, it was often used particularly in formal contexts, especially if the new word paralleled an older Anglo-Saxon word already in use, with nearly the same meaning. Thus "liberty" and "freedom", "justice" and "fairness," "commence" and "begin," "initiate" and "start." See Ziff (1960: 190).

not take place in English until the sixteenth century? Or does the *Oxford English Dictionary* simply lack earlier examples though the change came earlier? It is possible that legal, juristic, and political works, in which representing in the sense of "acting for" would be most likely to occur, were not written in English until this later time, even in England. Such writings may rather have been formulated in Latin or French. Despite a statute of 1362 that English was to be used in the law courts, records of court decisions from as late as 1500 are still in French.[9] And the statutes were written in Latin throughout the fifteenth century.[10] The earliest known petition in English dates from 1414 (Chrimes 1936: 132).

To understand how the concept of representation moved into the realms of agency and political activity, one must keep in mind the historical development of institutions, the corresponding development in interpretive thought about those institutions, and the etymological development of this family of words. It is now generally accepted that the summoning of knights and burgesses to meet with the king and lords in parliament began as a matter of administrative and political convenience to the king.[11] The knights and burgesses came to assent to taxes, give information, "bring up the record" from the local court in disputed cases, and carry information back to their communities (Cam 1944, chap. 15; MacIlwain 1932: 669; Chrimes 1936: 142–5). At first the crucial thing was that they came with authority to bind their communities to the taxes to be imposed. Somewhat later they began to be used by the communities as a way of presenting grievances to the king, and there were attempts to insist on redress of grievances before consenting to taxes. With this development began a gradual recognition that the member could further the interest of his community, in addition to committing it to taxation (Cam 1944: chap. 15; Pollard 1926: 158–9). Knights and burgesses who went to parliament began to be thought of as servants or agents of their communities. They were paid by the communities and, when they returned, might be required to give an account of what they had done in parliament (Cam 1944, chaps. 15 and 16, esp. pp. 230–2; McKisack 1932: 82–99; Brown 1939: 23–4; and Emden 1956: 12).

[9] The statute is in Lodge and Thornton (1935: 268). Stanley Bertram Chrimes (1936) presents excerpts from Year Book Cases through the fifteenth century, all still in French.

[10] For example, those cited in Lodge and Thornton (1935).

[11] For a clear discussion of the rival theories, see MacIlwain (1932) and Cam (1944, chap. 15). The fact is substantiated by the reluctance of early knights and burgesses to serve in parliament: Pollard (1926: 109, 158–9); Beard and Lewis (1932: 230–3); Ford (1924: 101n.); Hogan (1945: 142–3).

They came to parliament with authority to commit their communities, but often there were specific limits on this authority, or instructions that came with it. And some members had to consult with their communities before consenting to an unusual tax (McKisack 1932: 130).

From the fourteenth to the seventeenth century there was a gradual development of unified action by the knights and burgesses in parliament.[12] They found that they had common grievances, and began to present common petitions instead of only separate ones. They came to be called "members" of parliament. This joint action went hand in hand with an increasing awareness of themselves as a single body. Parliaments lasted longer, and members were re-elected, and so came to know each other and work together. Their joint action was often in opposition to the king, and they found strength to oppose him by acting as a corporate group. This development culminated in the period of the Civil War and the Protectorate and Commonwealth, when there was no king to oppose or consent to. Suddenly there was only parliament to govern the nation and even to pass judgment on the ruler in the name of the nation.

The development of political theory, of interpretations of what parliament was doing, paralleled these developments in fact. In the early period the knights and burgesses were regarded as the servants or attorneys or procurators of their communities (Cam 1944: chaps. 15 and 16; Chrimes 1936: 131–3; Luce 1930: 434). They were not called representatives because the word did not yet have that meaning; legal attorneys in court were not said to represent either. By the fifteenth century, as the Commons came to act as a unified body, the members were occasionally spoken of as being, jointly, "procurators and attorneys of all the counties . . . and of all the people of the realm" (Chrimes 1936: 131; the citation dates from 1407). They began to think of themselves, and be thought of, as those who "were commen for the Communalte of the Londe" (Chrimes 1936: 132; from about 1470). This idea is still compatible with the view that each member speaks for his particular district; the group thus adds up to the equivalent of the whole nation. Still later came the further elaboration that each member acts for the entire nation. This principle was recognized by the early seventeenth century, when Coke wrote in the *Institutes*: "it is to be observed though one be chosen for one particular county, or borough, yet

[12] On this development see MacIlwain (1932: 671–3); Brown (1939: 25, 32, 36); De Grazia (1951: 14–18); Chrimes (1936: 131); Bailey (1835: 3); Leibholz (1929: 54–5); Pease (1916: 25–6); Hatschek (1905: 241).

when he is returned, and sits in parlament, he serveth for the whole realm, for the end of his coming thither as in the writ of his election appeareth, is generall."[13]

These changing views of the function of parliamentary members became linked with two other traditions of thought: the idea that all men are present in parliament, and the idea that the ruler symbolizes or embodies the whole realm. The former is essentially a legal fiction, probably originating in the medieval *quod omnes tangit* doctrine from Roman law, that parties who have legal rights at stake in a judicial action are entitled to be present or at least consulted in its decision (Pitkin 1967, chap. 4, esp. n. 89). Thus the presumption was that parliament, being considered a court rather than a legislative agency, had the consent and participation of all taxpayers. By the fourteenth century a judge could argue that ignorance of the law is no excuse, since everyone is taken to be present when parliament acts (ibid.). This is not, of course, a democratic doctrine at the time.

The other idea that comes to enrich the tradition of thought about parliament is that the whole nation is somehow embodied in its ruler, as the church is in Christ or in the Pope after Him. It is a medieval and mystical conception: the king is not merely the head of the national body, not merely the owner of the entire realm, but he *is* the crown, the realm, the nation.[14] The idea goes beyond either representation or symbolization as we now conceive them, and involves a mystic unity which "theoretical analysis can scarcely divide."[15] The Latin word *repraesentare* comes gradually to be used in connection with this cluster of ideas. Then, as the authority of parliament grows, and its role in pronouncing the law is more widely

[13] Sir Edward Coke (1809, chap. 1: 14). There is (understandably) much disagreement about just when this doctrine originated. Hatschek (1905: 238) produces a passage of parliamentary history from 1415 that seems to articulate it. Hallam (1871: 265) dates it from a parliamentary debate of 1571. Writers who do not cite a single specific instance nevertheless vary considerably as to the period in which members of parliament first thought of themselves as each acting for the whole nation. Chrimes (1936: 131) suggests the fifteenth century; Brown (1939: 24–5) the seventeenth; Emden (1956: 5) the eighteenth. The idea must have emerged gradually, and we might expect to find instances of it when it was by no means the main constitutional doctrine. Hatschek's and Hallam's early instances seem limited because each occurs in a rather specialized context. Coke's is the first I have found in which the doctrine is clearly and broadly articulated as constitutional principle.

[14] Gierke (1913, pt.2, chap. 4); also, more generally, his (1881); Kern (1939, pt. 1); Hauck (1907); Hintze (1929–30: 230); Lagarde (1937); Lewis (1954, vol. I: 195, 242, 263–4; vol. II: 415); Kantorowicz (1957).

[15] Kern (1939: 141). Cf. Clarke (1936: 290), who says the idea "resists analysis"; and Wolff (1934: 13–16).

recognized, this symbolic position is ascribed to the king-in-parliament jointly, as a single body or corporation (Wilkinson 1949: 502–9; Brown 1939: 29; Hatschek 1905: 239). Thus the king-in-parliament that governs the realm is also seen as its mystic equivalent or embodiment.

These various ideas and doctrines converge quite naturally. The king-in-parliament is the mystic equivalent or embodiment of the whole realm, and everyone in the realm is to be considered present in it. The Lords and bishops and the king himself are present in person; the Commons as a whole (as an estate, for a time) are present through their procurators as a group (Chrimes 1936: 81–126). Finally, each knight or burgess is thought of as acting for all the common people, and for the entire realm.

A neat summary of the state to which these ideas had developed by 1583 can be found in Sir Thomas Smith's *De republica Anglorum*, of that year.[16] Smith's work is also one of the earliest known applications of the English word "represent" to parliament. Smith uses the word only once, but in a crucial position, writing of "the Parliament of Englande, which representeth and hath the power of the whole realme, both the head and the bodie. For everie Englishman is entended to be there present, either in person or by procuration and attornies . . . And the consent of the Parliament is taken to be everie man's consent" (Smith 1906: 49). Smith says that parliament represents the whole realm (or is it that it represents the power of the whole realm?), but he does not apply the word to the members of parliament or to those particular members who are there as procurators and attorneys for the Commons. This seems to be the pattern in all the early applications of the word to parliamentary institutions in England; it is the parliament as a whole (often including the king) that represents the whole realm.

Almost half a century passes after Smith's work before parliament is again said to "represent," but in the intervening time there begins a remarkable flowering of meanings and forms in this family of terms. In particular, in the second quarter of the seventeenth century, no doubt spurred by the pamphleteering and political debate that preceded, accompanied, and followed the Civil War, the "represent-" family become political terms. But the flowering is by no means confined to politics. In the period from Smith's work to the Glorious Revolution, English is enriched by "representator" (1607), "representant" (1622), "representee" (1624), "representance" (1633), "representatory" (1674), "representativer" (1676), "repre-

[16] The work was actually completed in 1565.

sentamen" (1677), plus many new meanings for pre-existing words in this family. Obviously, many of these innovations did not make it into modern English; some of them did not last beyond the seventeenth century. Nevertheless, the politicization of the idea of representation seems to have occurred against the background of a general expansion and fluidity in this conceptual region.

The etymological evidence is not entirely clear, but it suggests that the whole family of terms seems first to be applied to parliament as a whole, or to the Commons as a group.[17] And the meanings are obviously in transition from the earlier standing for others by way of substitution, to something like acting for others. The terms seem first to be used as an expression of, and as a claim to, authority, power, prestige. Let the Lords take heed: the Commons represent the whole kingdom. Let the king take heed: the parliament represents the realm. At no time during this period are these words used to express the relation of an individual member of the Commons to his particular constituency, his duty to obey the wishes of those he represents, his power to commit them, or anything of the sort. The idea that members of parliament are attorneys or agents of their communities exists, or course, but it is not expressed by the term "representation."

The earliest application I have come across of the noun "representative" to a *member* of parliament occurs in 1651, when Isaac Pennington, the younger, writes: "The fundamental right, safety and liberty of the People; which is radically in themselves, derivately in *the* Parliament, their substitutes or representat*ives*" (cited in Chisholm 1910–11: 109; emphasis mine). It is applied in this way with increasing frequency in the Protectorate parliaments, until eventually this becomes the noun's major meaning, and various rival terms become obsolete.[18]

But 1651 is also the year in which Hobbes published the *Leviathan*, the first examination of the idea of representation in political theory. Twice before, in 1640 and 1642, Hobbes had completed arguments similar to that of *Leviathan*, deriving sovereignty and

[16] The work was actually completed in 1565.

[17] Chisholm (1910–11: 109); Hintze (1929–30: 235). Some writers, however, argue that the term "representation" was applied first to the activities of attorneys and agents, and hence to individual members of parliament insofar as they were thought of as agents, and only derivatively to parliament as a whole. See esp. Hermens (1941: 5); Lewis (1877: 97–8). Perhaps these views rest on some confusion between the use of the Latin and the English word in this period.

[18] According to the *Oxford English Dictionary*, none survives the seventeenth century, though of course the lack of later dictionary examples is not proof. For examples of the new usage in the Protectorate parliaments and after, see Brown (1939); Emden (1956: 15).

political obligation from a social contract made in a prior state of nature.[19] Somehow, in the intervening decade and in the midst of the semantic turmoil in the "represent-" family, Hobbes saw a brilliant way to apply representation to his argument.

In *Leviathan*, he defines representation in terms of the formal aspects of legal agency, specifically in terms of authorization: a representative is someone given authority to act by someone else, who is then bound by the representative's action as if it had been his own. Representation may be "limited," with only certain specific actions under specific constraints being authorized, or it may be "unlimited." The latter kind gives rise to sovereignty:

> A commonwealth is said to be instituted, when a multitude of men do agree, and covenant, every one with every one, that to whatsoever man, or assembly of men, shall be given by the major part, the right to present the person of them all, that is to say, to be their representative; every one . . . shall authorize all the actions and judgments, of that man, or assembly of men, in the same manner, as if they were his own.
>
> Hobbes 1839–45, vol. III: 159–60.

This action welds the multitude of individuals into a single, lasting whole, "the person of them all." The sovereign represents that single, public person; indeed, it is because he represents it that it can be considered a unit.

By Hobbes's formalistic definition, a representative as such acquires only new rights or powers in being authorized; the represented acquires only new obligations. But insofar as the term applied to individual agency in ordinary usage by this time at all, it surely already included implications of some obligations or standards constraining what a representative as such is supposed to do, how the activity of representing is conducted. Indeed, despite his formalistic definition, Hobbes himself on occasion uses the word in this ordinary way. And, whether or not he consciously intended the effect, his political argument about sovereignty trades on the discrepancy between his formal definition and ordinary usage. By calling the sovereign a representative, Hobbes constantly implies that the sovereign will do what representatives are expected to do, not just whatever he pleases. Yet the formal definition assures that this expectation can never be invoked to criticize or resist the sovereign for not representing his subjects as he should. Indeed,

[19] *The Elements of Law*, completed in 1640, was not published until 1650. *De cive*, completed in 1642, was first published in Latin and did not appear in English until 1651, the year of publication of *Leviathan*.

within the explicit definition there is no such thing as (not) representing *as one should*.

Although the etymological development of the modern concept of representation, at least in its politically significant aspects, was essentially completed before the end of the seventeenth century, its development in political theory had barely begun. There, its elaboration continued against the background, firstly, of the great democratic revolutions of the late eighteenth century, and then of the protracted nineteenth-century political and institutional struggles: over suffrage and districting and apportionment, over political parties and interests and policies, over the relationship between legislative and executive functions, legislative and executive institutions. These political struggles precipitated a sizeable body of literature, from time to time systematized, enriched, and redirected by political theory. From that welter of material, only two interrelated conceptual issues can be discussed here: the "mandate–independence controversy" and the relationship of representation to democracy.

The "mandate–independence controversy" is one of those interminable theoretical debates that never seem to get resolved, no matter how many thinkers take positions on the one side or the other. It may be summarized in the dichotomous choice: is a representative to do what his constituents want, or what he thinks best? The dispute grows out of the paradox inherent in the very meaning of representation: making present in *some* sense what is nevertheless *not* literally present. But in political theory the paradox is overlaid by a number of substantive concerns: the relationship among representatives in a legislature, the role of political parties, how local and partial concerns fit into the national good, how deliberation relates to voting and both to governing, and so on.

Without a doubt, the most famous theoretical spokesman for the "independence" side of the controversy was Edmund Burke, whose complex and sometimes inconsistent views are epitomized in his speech to the electors of Bristol, his own constituents, whom he told:

> Parliament is not a congress of ambassadors from different and hostile interests, which interests each must maintain, as an agent and advocate, against other agents and advocates; but Parliament is a deliberative assembly of one nation, with one interest, that of the whole – where not local prejudices ought to guide, but the general good, resulting from the general reason of the whole. You choose a member, indeed; but when you have chosen him he is not a member of Bristol, but he is a member of Parliament. Burke 1949c [1774]: 116

Since the relationship of each member is to the nation as a whole, he stands in no special relation to his constituency; he represents the nation, not those who elected him.

This view fits with Burke's more general understanding of government as a trusteeship:

> The king is the representative of the people; so are the lords; so are the judges. They are all trustees for the people, as well as the commons; because no power is given for the sole sake of the holder.
>
> Burke 1949b [1770]: 27–8

The single most important consideration is that rulers should be virtuous and wise, however they are chosen. But the only reliable way of producing such leadership, Burke thinks, is the complex, traditional system of upbringing, education, and character development he associates with a "natural aristocracy."[20] In this vision of governance, more ordinary understandings of representation – election, the very existence of a House of Commons – seem to have no part.

But this is by no means the whole of Burke's theory of representation. He does after all assign the House of Commons a special role, favor elected members of parliament, favor (some) parliamentary reform and extension of suffrage, and support the American colonies' complaint they are oppressed because excluded from representation. "The virtue, spirit, and essence of a House of Commons," Burke says, "consists in its being the express image of the feelings of the nation." Its task is not so much to govern as to control the government on behalf of the people. "It was not instituted to be a control *upon* the people . . . [but] as a control *for* the people." And it cannot fulfill that controlling function unless its members "are controlled themselves by their constituents" (Burke 1949b [1770]: 28).

Burke distinguishes between what he calles "virtual" and "actual" representation. The latter means actually having a voice in the choice of representative; the former means:

> a communion of interests and a sympathy of feelings and desires between those who act in the name of any description of people and the people in whose name they act, though the trustees are not actually chosen by them.
>
> Burke 1949f [1792]: 495

While the doctrine of virtual representation can be used to oppose electoral reform or extensions of the suffrage, Burke himself used it in the opposite way: to support extension of the suffrage to Irish

[20] Pitkin (1967: 169 and nn.).

Catholics who, he maintained, were represented neither virtually nor actually, since those purporting to represent them shared neither their interest nor their feelings and desires. Where he saw actual, practical grievances unattended, Burke supported electoral reform, but he opposed extensions of the suffrage based on nothing more than abstract principle or "natural right."

Burke does not think of "interests" as shifting and personal, a mater of individual choice. He conceives of relatively few, broad, fixed, and objective interests that together make up the welfare of the whole. These interests are largely economic, and are associated with particular localities whose livelihood they characterize. He speaks of a mercantile interest, an agricultural interest, a professional interest (but recognizes also a distinct interest of Irish Catholics as a group). A locality "partakes of" or "participates in" such an interest; neither a locality nor an individual "has" an interest.

The representative is, indeed, a spokesman for the interest of his district – for instance, for the mercantile interest if he represents Bristol. But this implies neither that he must consult the people of Bristol nor that his votes must favor Bristol over Britain. Consultation is not necessary because interests are objective and utterly different from opinions. The representative owes his constituents "a devotion to their interests *rather than* to their opinion."[21] By and large, people know when something is wrong in their lives, so information about their complaints and needs must be transmitted by a sympathetic representative; but about causes and solutions people are hopelessly ignorant.

> The most poor, illiterate, and uninformed creatures upon earth are the judges of a *practical* oppression. It is a matter of feeling; and as such persons generally have felt most of it, and are not of an over-lively sensibility, they are the best judges of it. But for *the real cause*, or *the appropriate remedy*, they ought never to be called into council.[22]

Nor is the representative an agent of the particular interest in which his district participates, for the real task of the legislature is deliberation rather than voting. The true, great interests of the nation in principle fit together; it is the task of wise and virtuous statesmen to reason out how they fit, how existing troubles may best be remedied. When they have finished deliberating, the result should scarcely require a vote. Government is a matter of reason, not of will, of duties and not of arithmetic.

[21] Canavan (1960: 155). See also Parkin (1956: 43); and Burke's "Speech at the Conclusion of the Poll," cited in Hogan (1945: 189).

[22] Burke (1949f: 492–3). See also Burke (1949b: 8; 1949g: 119; 1949e: 393). Also Burke (1963 [1765]: 213); Gibbons (1914: 36); Parkin (1956: 39).

Burke does also acknowledge the existence of an altogether different understanding of representation, which he calls "personal representation," the representing of each individual person through universal suffrage in electoral districts based on population (Burke 1949d [1782]: 229). This view Burke rejects unequivocally, as a creature of abstract philosophical speculation based on the idea of natural rights.

But the idea of personal representation was to triumph over Burke's representation of fixed interests; even in his time the theorists of liberalism on both sides of the Atlantic were articulating a theory of the representing of persons who have interests. In America, representation was clearly to be of persons, and interests became an inevitable evil, to be tamed by a well-constructed government. In England, Utilitarianism not only favored the representation of persons, but made interest an increasingly personal concept.

Alexander Hamilton, John Jay, and James Madison in the *Federalist Papers* introduce representative government as a device adopted instead of direct democracy, because it is impossible to assemble large numbers of people in a single place; representation is "a substitute for the meeting of the citizens in person."[23] But they do not regard it as a second-best substitute; indeed, it promises unprecedented possibilities for the government of America.

For the authors of the *Federalist*, the concept of interest is much more pluralistic and unstable than it was for Burke, and essentially pejorative. Interests are identified with "faction," and are evil. While Madison still recognizes a "landed interest" and a "manufacturing interest," these may be subdivided almost indefinitely, and the resulting economic groupings are cross-cut by others "founded on accidental differences in political, religious, or other opinion, or an attachment to the persons of leading individuals" (Madison 1953 [1787]: 17, 42). Interests are something people "feel," and they are as various and shifting as feeling, fundamentally subjective (Hamilton, Madison, and Jay 1948, no. 10: 45).

Nevertheless the *Federalist* does also assume the existence of something larger and more objective, "the public good" (Hamilton, Madison, and Jay 1948, no. 10: 45; see also no. 63: 324). Representation is superior to direct democracy precisely because it can secure the public good without distraction from the various conflicting particular interests, or "factions." A faction is

[23] Hamilton, Madison, and Jay (1948, no. 52: 270). The original papers appeared in 1787 and 1788.

> a number of citizens, whether amounting to a majority or a minority of the whole, who are united and actuated by some common impulse of passion, or of interest, adverse to the rights of other citizens, or to the permanent and aggregate interest of the community.
>
> Hamilton, Madison, and Jay 1948, no. 10: 42

A republic or government based on representation "promises the cure" for the evils of faction.

> First, representation itself acts as a kind of filter to refine and enlarge the public views, by passing them through the medium of a chosen body of citizens, whose wisdom may best discern the true interests of their country, and whose patriotism and love of justice, will be least likely to sacrifice it to temporary or partial considerations.
>
> Hamilton, Madison, and Jay 1948, no. 10: 45

This sounds almost Burkean, but Madison does not really have much faith in this mechanism. "Enlightened statesmen will not always be at the helm" (Hamilton, Madison, and Jay 1948, no. 10: 44). Far more promising is the fact that representation makes possible a *large* republic and, in a large republic, interests will be multiple and diverse, and therefore less likely to combine for effective factious action.

> Extend the sphere, and you take in a greater variety of parties and interests; you make it less probable that a majority of the whole will have a common motive to invade the rights of other citizens; or if such a common motive exists, it will be more difficult for all who feel it to discover their own strength and to act in unison.[24]

As Madison sees it, the danger is in political action, the safeguard in stalemate. Factions' interests are to be "broken," "controlled," and "balanced" against each other to produce "stability" (Beer 1957: 629; Padover 1953: 17; De Grazia 1951: 96, 99–100). On those rare occasions when public action is required, Madison assumes, there will be no difficulty in securing a substantial majority to support it. Representation not only makes possible a large republic, but it is a way of bringing dangerous social conflict into a single central forum where it can be controlled and rendered harmless by balancing. Only if each representative in fact pursues the interests of his constituents will the requisite balancing take place.

The Utilitarians' concept of interest is even more subjective, and ultimately personal to each individual. They argue variously that all

[24] Hamilton, Madison, and Jay (1948, no. 10: 47). The same point is made in nos. 51, 60, and 63, pp. 267, 307, 323; in a speech by Madison on June 6, 1787, cited in Padover (1953: 18); and in Farrand (1927: 136, 431). Cf. Padover's (1953: 17) interpretation; and Riemer (1954: 37).

people are always or most people are usually motivated by their own interests, and that, as Bentham puts it, "There is no one who knows what is for your interest, so well as yourself."[25] It follows that each individual is the only reliable guardian of his own interest, whether because others are too selfish to guard it, or because they cannot know it.

This might seem to make representation impossible, but that is not in fact the conclusion reached by the Utilitarians. All of them recognize the existence of a "common," "universal," or "general" interest, the good of the whole society.[26] Sometimes Bentham says it is simply the "aggregate" or "sum of the interests of the various members who compose" the society but, in the context of legislation, Bentham acknowledges that each person has both a public and a private interest, both a social and a self-regarding interest.[27] The public or social interests of each add up to the "universal interest"; the private or self-regarding interests do not. Unfortunately most people mostly prefer these. The exceptions are so rare, Bentham says in a revealing comparison, that they "cannot reasonably be regarded as being so frequently exemplified as insanity."[28]

But here the legislator intervenes. His job is to attach rewards to socially desirable but individually unattractive actions, and punishments to socially undesirable but individually attractive ones, so that self-interest will become aligned with the public good. What motivates the legislator to do this? In his early writings, Bentham seems mostly to imagine a hypothetical, single, master-legislator (perhaps himself), who would be one of those rare individuals genuinely motivated by altruism. But for the later Bentham, and certainly for James and John Stuart Mill, the legislator is replaced by an elected legislature, and altruism must be replaced by institutional mechanisms, particularly representation.

Since "the community cannot have any interest opposed to its interests," James Mill argues, all that is required is for "the interests of the representatives to be identified with those of their com-

[25] Bentham (1843g: 33; 1954: 438). Compare James Mill (1955: 69); John Stuart Mill (1947, chap. 3: 208; 1947: 133); Bailey (1835: 68); Adam Smith (1937: 497); Halévy (1955: 491); Stoke (1937: 80).

[26] Bentham (1843c: 2; 1843d: 269; 1843b: 446, 450–2); James Mill, cited in Ford (1924: 145); J.S. Mill (1947, chap. 6: 248, 255); Bailey (1835: 69, 71, 137); Halévy (1955: 15–17, 118–19, 405, 489–90). Cf. Ayer (1954: 255).

[27] Bentham (1843b: 453–5; 1843f: 6, 53, 60–2, 67; 1843e: 475; 1954: 428–33). Cf. J.S. Mill (1947, chap. 6: 248–55); Bailey (1835: 137).

[28] Bentham (1843f: 61). See also Bentham (1954: 432).

munity."[29] Mill thinks this can be achieved if there is frequent rotation in office, so that legislators know they will have to live under the laws they enact. Bentham adds the "principle of dislocability," the familiar notion that, because legislators want to be re-elected, they will do what the voters want (Bentham 1843f: 63, 103, 118, 155). And in his context Bentham claims that what the voters want is the public interest. Bentham was impressed with the example of America, and took it to prove by experience that

> on the part of the electors – at any rate, on the part of the majority of them – there *does* exist the disposition to contribute towards the advancement of the universal interest, whatsoever can be contributed by their votes.[30]

But this is the same Bentham who thought insanity more frequent than the willingness to sacrifice selfish for public interest!

John Stuart Mill wrestles with much the same dilemma. He, too, thinks it a "universally observable fact" that an individual will prefer his "selfish interests to those which he shares with other people, and his immediate and direct interests to those which are indirect and remote" (J.S. Mill 1947, chap. 6: 252). Indeed, for this very reason, Mill advocated representative government, universal suffrage, and proportional representation:

> It is important that everyone of the governed have a voice in the government, because it can hardly be expected that those who have no voice will not be unjustly postponed to those who have.
>
> J.S. Mill 1874: 21

At the same time Mill recognizes that a representative government will fail under conditions where

> nobody, or only some small fraction, feels the degree of interest in the general affairs of the State necessary to the formation of a public opinion, [where] the electors will seldom make any use of the right of suffrage but to serve their private interest, or the interest of their locality.[31]

Sometimes John Stuart Mill thinks even a minority of public-spirited citizens would suffice, if the representative system is so organized that selfish interests are balanced evenly against each other, cancelling each other like Madisonian factions. Mill defines "class" almost exactly as Madison does faction:

[29] Cited in Ford (1924: 146); James Mill (1955: 69).

[30] Bentham (1843b: 455); on the U.S., Bentham (1843b: 437, 445, 447) and Halévy (1955: 412).

[31] J.S. Mill (1947, chap. 4: 219). Again, in contrast to Burke, the Utilitarian takes interest to be something people "feel."

> If we consider as a class, politically speaking, any number of persons who have the same sinister interest – that is, whose direct and apparent interest points towards the same description of bad measures; the desirable object would be that no class, and no combination of classes likely to combine, should be able to exercise a preponderant influence on the government.[32]

Then there can emerge a minority in each class in whom class interest "would be subordinate to reason, justice, and the good of the whole," and these minorities together might prevail over the stalemated class interests (J.S. Mill 1947, chap. 6: 255).

Thus for all forms of liberalism there is, after all, such a thing as the objective public interest, which must somehow include and encompass the true, long-range best interest of each. Accordingly, despite Utilitarian claims to the contrary, each individual is not the best judge of his own interest. Indeed, if the judgment of interest were truly subjective and personal to each individual, meaningful representation would seem impossible.

This is the position adopted by Jean-Jacques Rousseau. Rousseau argues in terms not of interest but of will, and will is truly personal. One person can will instead of others, but there is no guarantee of the will of the one coinciding with the will of those others. Accordingly, people are free only when self-governing; they are legitimately bound only by laws which they have "ratified in their own person," enacted by their own will expressed in direct participation (Rousseau 1974: 260).

Of course, the public has to have various officials who "represent" it by carrying out administrative, judicial, and executive tasks, but "the People, in its legislative function, cannot be represented" (Rousseau 1974: 261). As soon as a people introduces legislative representation, it ceases to be free. Thus,

> The English people think that they are free, but in this belief they are profoundly wrong. They are free only when they are electing members of Parliament. Once the election has been completed, they revert to a condition of slavery: they are nothing. Making such use of it in these short moments of their freedom, they deserve to lose it.
>
> Rousseau 1974: 260

For the most part, later thinkers ignored Rousseau's view as bizarre and idiosyncratic. Almost no one who favored democracy doubted that representation was its modern form, its indirect equivalent. If representative government had faults, those faults were attributed

[32] J.S. Mill (1947, chap. 6: 254–5). Cf. Bentham's "sinister interests" (1843b: 446, 450–1).

to the particular electoral system, or party system, or the exclusion of some group from suffrage. Even most socialist critics of liberal democracy questioned not representation as such but its genuineness under capitalism.

Only in recent decades have a number of thinkers again begun to question these assumptions, to resurrect those few, faint voices – some socialist, some anarchist, all more or less bizarre and deviant – which continued to challenge the idea of representation itself, to challenge not just its superiority to, but even its substitutability for the older ideal of direct, participatory democracy. These thinkers have suggested that participation in public power and responsibility may be intrinsically and not just instrumentally valuable, necessary to the good of life and to the full development of human beings. They have suggested that only a politically involved and active people is free, and that representative institutions, initially designed to open the public realm to the previously excluded common people, have in fact served to discourage active citizenship.

As long as politics is equated with government, and government regarded as a means for achieving private purposes and reconciling conflicting private claims in a generally acceptable manner, rightly designed representative institutions may serve its purposes very well. But if its real function is to direct our shared, public life, and its real value lies in the opportunity to share in power over and responsibility for what we jointly, as a society, are doing, then no one else can do my politics "for" me, and representation can mean only the exclusion of most people from its benefits most of the time.

Thus, as Hannah Arendt (1965: 239) has argued, the

> question of representation, one of the crucial and most troublesome issues of modern politics ever since the [eighteenth-century] revolutions, actually implies no less than a decision on the very dignity of the political realm itself.

Only direct democratic participation provides a real alternative to the horns of the mandate–independence dilemma, in which a representative is either a mere agent of private concerns or else a periodically elected usurper of popular freedom. In the former case, no one at all has access to a public life, for there is none. In the latter case,

> the age-old distinction between ruler and ruled . . . has asserted itself again; once more, the people are not admitted to the public realm, once more the business of government has become the privilege of the few . . . The result is that the people must either sink into "lethargy, the

forerunner of death to the public liberty," or "preserve the spirit of resistance" to whatever government they have elected, since the only power they retain is "the reserve power of revolution."

Arendt 1965: 240

REFERENCES

Arendt, Hannah. 1965. *On Revolution*. New York: Viking.

Ayer, A.J. 1954. *Philosophical Essays*. London: Macmillan.

Bailey, Samuel. 1835. *The Rationale of Political Representation*. London: R. Hunter.

Barker, Sir Ernest (ed.). 1951. *Essays on Government*. Oxford: Clarendon.

Beard, Charles A. and John D. Lewis. 1932. "Representative Government in Evolution." *American Political Science Review* 26 (April): 223–40.

Beer, Samuel H. 1957. "The Representation of Interests." *American Political Science Review* 51 (September): 613–50.

Bentham, Jeremy. 1843a. *Works*, edited by John Bowring. Edinburgh: William Tait.

1843b [1809]. "A Plan of Parliamentary Reform." In Bentham 1843a, vol. III: 433–557.

1843c [1789]. "An Introduction to the Principles of Morals and Legislation." In Bentham 1843a, vol. I: 1–154.

1843d [1830]. "Leading Principles of a Constitutional Code." In Bentham 1843a, vol. II: 267–74.

1843e [1824]. "Book of Fallacies." In Bentham 1843a, vol. II: 375–488.

1843f [1830–2]. "Constitutional Code." In Bentham 1843a, vol. IX.

1843g [1825]. "Manual of Political Economy." In Bentham 1843a, vol. III: 33–84.

1954 [1817]. "The Psychology of Economic Man." In W. Stark (ed.), *Bentham's Economic Writings*, vol. III. London: George Allen and Unwin, pp. 419–50.

Brown, Louise Fargo. 1939. "Ideas of Representation." *Journal of Modern History* 11 (March): 23–40.

Burke, Edmund. 1949a. *Burke's Politics*, edited by Ross J.S. Hoffman and Paul Levack. New York: Alfred A. Knopf.

1949b [1770]. "Thoughts on the Cause of the Present Discontents." In Burke 1949a: 5–45.

1949c [1774]. "Speech to the Electors." In Burke 1949a: 113–17.

1949d [1782]. "Speech on the State of the Representation." In Burke 1949a: 224–32.

1949e [1791]. "Appeal from the New to the Old Whigs." In Burke 1949a: 391–400.

1949f [1792]. "Letter to Langriche." In Burke 1949a: 477–511.

1949g [1777]. "Letter to a Member of the Bell Club." In Burke 1949a: 117–20.

1963 [1765]. "Fragments of a Tract Relative to the Laws against Popery in Ireland." In *Selected Writings and Speeches*, edited by Peter J. Stanlis. Garden City, NY: Doubleday, pp. 210–227.

Cam, Helen M. 1944. *Liberties and Communities*. Cambridge: Cambridge University Press.

Canavan, Francis P. 1960. *The Political Reason of Edmund Burke*. Durham, NC: Duke University Press.

Chisholm, Hugh. 1910–11. "Representation." *Encyclopaedia Britannica*, 11th edn. vol. XXIII: 108–16.

Chrimes, Stanley Bertram. 1936. *English Constitutional Ideas*. Cambridge: Cambridge University Press.

Clarke, Maude V. 1936. *Medieval Representation and Consent*. London: Longmans, Green and Co.

Coke, Sir Edward. 1809 [1644]. *The Fourth Part of the Institutes of the Laws of England*. London: W. Clarke and Sons.

De Grazia, Alfred. 1951. *Public and Republic*. New York: Alfred A. Knopf.

Emden, Cecil S. 1956. *The People and the Constitution*, 2nd edn. Oxford: Clarendon.

Farrand, Max (ed.). 1927. *The Records of the Federal Convention of 1787*, vol. I. New Haven, CT: Yale University Press.

Ford, Henry J. 1924. *Representative Government*. New York: Henry Holt and Co.

Gibbons, Philip Arnold. 1914. *Ideas of Political Representation in Parliament 1651–1832*. Oxford: Blackwell.

Gierke, Otto von. 1881. *Das deutsche Genossenschaftsrecht*, vol. III. Berlin: Weidmann.

1913. *Johannes Althusius*. Breslau: M. und H. Marcus.

Halévy, Elie. 1955. *The Growth of Philosophical Radicalism*. Boston, MA: Beacon.

Hallam, Henry. 1871. *Constitutional History of England*, vol. I. New York: Widdleton.

Hamilton, Alexander, James Madison and John Jay. 1948 [1787–8]. *The Federalist*, edited by Max Beloff. Oxford: Blackwell.

Hatschek. Julius. 1905. *Englisches Staatsrecht*, vol. I. Tübingen: J.C.B. Mohr.

Hauck, Albert. 1907. "Die Rezeption und Umbildung der allgemeinen Synode im Mittelalter." *Historische Vierteljahrschrift* 10: 465–82.

Hermens, F.A. 1941. *Democracy or Anarchy?* South Bend, IN: University of Notre Dame Press.

Hintze, Otto. 1929–30. "Typologie der ständischen Verfassungen." *Historische Zeitschrift* 141: 229–48.

Hobbes, Thomas. 1839–45. *English Works*, edited by Sir William Molesworth. London: Longmans, Brown, Green and Longmans.

Hogan, James. 1945. *Election and Representation*. Cork: Cork University Press.

Kantorowicz, Ernst. 1957. *The King's Two Bodies*. Princeton, NJ: Princeton University Press.

Kern, Fritz. 1939. *Kingship and Law in the Middle Ages*, translated by S.B. Chrimes. Oxford: Blackwell.

Lagarde, Georges de. 1937. "L'Idée de représentation." *International Committee of the Historical Sciences Bulletin* 9 (December): 425–51.

Leibholz, Gerhard. 1929. *Das Wesen der Repräsentation*. Berlin: Walter de Gruyter.

Lewis, Ewart. 1954. *Medieval Political Ideas*. New York: Alfred A. Knopf.

Lewis, George Cornwall. 1877. *Remarks on the Use and Abuse of Some Political Terms*. Oxford: James Thornton.

Littré, M.P.E. 1875. *Dictionnaire de la langue française*. Paris: Hachette.

Lodge, Eleanor C. and Gladys A. Thornton (eds.). 1935. *English Constitutional Documents 1307–1485*. Cambridge: Cambridge University Press.

Luce, Robert. 1930. *Legislative Principles*. Boston, MA: Houghton Mifflin.

MacIlwain, C.H. 1932. "Medieval Estates." In *Cambridge Medieval History*, vol. VII: *The Decline of Empire and Papacy*. Cambridge: Cambridge University Press, pp. 665–715.

McKisack, May. 1932. *Representation of the English Boroughs during the Middle Ages*. London: Oxford University Press.

Madison, James. 1953 [1787]. Speech on June 6, 1787; Letter to Thomas Jefferson of October 24, 1787. In Padover 1953: 17–18; 42.

Mill, James. 1955 [1823; 1824–5]. *An Essay on Government*. New York: Library of Liberal Arts.

Mill, John Stuart. 1874. "Thoughts on Parliamentary Reform." In *Dissertations and Discussions*, vol. IV. New York: Henry Holt, pp. 1–46.

1947. "On Liberty" [1859] and "Consideration on Representative Government" [1861]. In *Utilitarianism, Liberty and Representative Government*. London: J.M. Dent, pp. 65–170; 175–393.

Padover, Saul K. 1953. *The Complete Madison*. New York: Harper.

Parkin, Charles. 1956. *The Moral Basis of Burke's Political Thought*. Cambridge: Cambridge University Press.

Pease, T.C. 1916. *The Leveller Movement*. Washington, DC: American Historical Association.

Pitkin, Hanna Fenichel. 1967. *The Concept of Representation*. Berkeley, CA, Los Angeles, CA and London: University of California Press.

1972. *Wittgenstein and Justice*. Berkeley, CA, Los Angeles, CA and London: University of California Press.

Pollard, A.F. 1926. *The Evolution of Parliament*. London: Longmans, Green.

Riemer, Neal. 1954. "James Madison's Theory of the Self-destructive Features of Republican Government." *Ethics* 65 (October): 34–43.

Rousseau, Jean-Jacques. 1974 [1762]. "The Social Contract," translated by Gerard Hopkins. In *The Social Contract*, edited by Sir Ernest Barker. London: Oxford University Press, pp. 167–307.

Smith, Adam. 1937 [1776]. *An Inquiry into the Nature and Causes of the Wealth of Nations*, vol. IV. New York: Modern Library.

Smith, Sir Thomas. 1906 [1583]. *De republica Anglorum*. Cambridge: Cambridge University Press.

Stoke, Harold W. 1937. "The Paradox of Representative Government." In

John M. Mathews (ed.), *Essays in Political Science in Honor of W. W. Willoughby*. Baltimore, MD: Johns Hopkins University Press, pp. 77–99.

Tierney, Brian. 1955. *Foundations of the Conciliar Theory*. Cambridge: Cambridge University Press.

Wilkinson, B. 1949. "The Political Revolution of the Thirteenth and Fourteenth Centuries in England." *Speculum* 24 (October): 502–9.

Wittgenstein, Ludwig. 1968. *Philosophical Investigations*, translated by G.E.M. Anscombe, 3rd edn. New York: Macmillan.

Wolff, Hans J. 1934. *Organschaft und juristische Person*, vol. II. Berlin: Carl Heymanns.

Ziff, Paul. 1960. *Semantic Analysis*. Ithaca, NY: Cornell University Press.

7

Party

TERENCE BALL

Party – the word and the concept – is a relatively recent addition to the vocabulary of politics. Perhaps because it is widely believed to be an institution instead of an idea, "party" has been largely ignored by historians of ideas. As J.A.W. Gunn observes, "Liberty, justice and equality – not to mention representation, the majority, and the separation of powers – all have their intellectual histories; but party seems to be an institution singularly bereft of intellectual parentage" (1972a: 1). To trace its paternity would be to tell an important and heretofore largely missing part of the story of political theory and practice in the West.[1] A comprehensive history of "party" being well beyond the bounds of the present essay, I shall merely sketch some of the more noteworthy contours of the concept's pre-history, focusing in particular upon the changing imagery and distinctions that preceded its emergence in anglophone political theory and practice in the late seventeenth and early eighteenth centuries. My conceptual pre-history therefore ends just where a proper conceptual history would begin, with the recognizably modern conception of party as a principled and loyal opposition.

My archaeological excavation of a series of long-abandoned political sites proceeds in the following way. After briefly outlining the approach against which I shall be arguing, I go on to show that the modern idea of party emerged haltingly and haphazardly from a long pre-history in which an older political vocabulary was gradually transformed. This transformation in its turn permitted a series of

For criticizing an earlier version of this essay, I am grateful to J.A.W. Gunn, James Farr, and Russell Hanson.

[1] Two indispensable collections of original sources are Beattie (1970) and Gunn (1972a); both contain valuable introductions. Useful surveys are also to be found in Robbins (1958), Hofstadter (1970), Sartori (1976), and Von Beyme (1978).

shifts in political perceptions. These stemmed not only from arguments about what is legitimate and permissible but from a changing stock of political metaphors, among which the shift from organic or bodily imagery to contractual notions proved to be particularly important.

I

One way of writing the history of "party" is to take the ahistorical tack of suggesting that parties have always existed even though they were until quite recently regarded as an illegitimate species of political organization. The history of "party" then becomes not the story of conceptual-cum-political change and innovation, but an account of changing attitudes toward something that has always existed. This is the view advanced, for example, by Harvey Mansfield, Jr., who holds that "Parties are universal, but party government is the result of the recent discovery that parties can be respectable. Because the reason for partisanship is so simple and compelling, the respectability, not the existence, of party is the distinguishing mark of party government" (Mansfield 1965: 2). Two things are presupposed in such an account. The first is the nominalist view that political concepts – in this case "party" – function merely as names or labels attached by convention to independently existing phenomena. The second supposition is that an emotivist theory of meaning offers an adequate account of the way in which moral and political terms actually function in discourse. According to the emotivist view, what matters for purposes of political analysis and historical understanding is not names but the changing feelings or attitudes of political agents toward the thing named. Thus the difference denoted by calling some grouping a "party," instead of, say, a "sect" or a "faction," is a psychological difference of feeling or attitude. Simply stated, a party is a faction of which one approves, and a faction a party of which one disapproves. The history of party is therefore a nominalist story about changing labels and a psychological story about changing attitudes toward the phenomenon to which these labels have been attached.

In the case of "party," however, the foregoing account gets matters exactly backward. Far from functioning as labels attached to independently existing phenomena, as suggested by a nominalist account of language, political concepts are themselves partially *constitutive* of those phenomena. And, contrary to the emotivist theory, feelings and attitudes are more the products than the sources of our conceptually constituted world. Thus, for example, we don't call an action "unjust" because we disapprove of it; rather, we disapprove of it because we have reason for believing it to be unjust. And we do not designate an organization as a political party because we approve of it (or, conversely, as a faction because we disapprove of it); rather, we mean to mark an actually existing, politically pertinent – and distinctly nonpsychological – difference between parties and factions.

To see how this process works in the case of "party" let us imagine an eminently rational political agent who is eager to exhibit his behavior as legitimate.[2] Let us further imagine that he wishes to act in some new or otherwise untoward way. If he is to satisfy both *desiderata* he must be able to describe the latter in terms recognizable within the limits set (however loosely) by the former. It then follows that linguistic form constrains political content; linguistic limitations limit political possibilities. As a speaker or writer who wishes to communicate with others our ideally rational agent cannot, like Humpty Dumpty, make words mean whatever he wants them to mean. And this, for a *political* agent, is a consideration of surpassing importance. For, *qua* political agent, he necessarily wishes not only to communicate but if possible to persuade others to follow his new route. Hence he needs to be able to call upon an already existing stock of concepts, if his appeal is to be at all intelligible, much less persuasive. By argument, analogy, metaphor, and other means he might, with sufficient skill, be able to alter or extend the range of reference of some of the concepts constitutive of the political discourse of his day. But however skilful he is, he will not be able to create concepts *ex nihilo* but must instead work within an already established universe of discourse. Hence, as Skinner notes, "the problem facing an agent who wishes to legitimate what he is doing at the same time as gaining what he wants cannot simply be the instrumental problem of tailoring his normative language in order to fit his projects. It must in part be the problem of tailoring his projects in order to fit the available normative language" (1978, vol. I: xii–xiii). Although the "ordinary language" that a theorist inherits is rarely his last word, it must of necessity be his first word, lest he be unintelligible to himself and to others.

Even so, conceptual change is not reducible to or identical with linguistic change – that is, the making of new distinctions, the

[2] The following account is adapted from Skinner (1974; 1978, vol. I: xii–xiii).

coining of new terms or extending or altering the criteria used in applying older terms. Conceptual change and political innovation are as much a matter of nondiscursive myths, metaphors, symbols, images, and overarching world pictures as of linguistic extension. As Isaiah Berlin reminds us:

> Men's beliefs in the sphere of conduct are part of their conception of themselves and others as human beings; and this conception in its turn, whether conscious or not, is intrinsic to their picture of the world. This picture may be complete and coherent, or shadowy or confused, but almost always . . . it can be shown to be dominated by one or more models or paradigms: mechanistic, organic, aesthetic, logical, mystical, shaped by the strongest influence of the day – religious, scientific, metaphysical or artistic. This model or paradigm determines the content as well as the form of beliefs and behaviour.
>
> Berlin 1979: 154

Indeed, as George Armstrong Kelly notes, "One may observe throughout the long history of political science that it periodically, perhaps even paradigmatically, attaches itself to root metaphors from other surrounding bodies of knowledge and achieves its discourse in them" (1968: 9). Political innovation and conceptual change are therefore linked, inevitably and inextricably, to large-scale, and often gradual and unconscious, shifts in the models and metaphors that dominate our lives and our thought (see Lakoff and Johnson 1980).

Until the late seventeenth century there was neither the vocabulary nor the necessary stock of images in which anything like the recognizably modern notion of party could be conceived, much less publicly articulated and discussed. The appropriate imagery, along with an allied vocabulary – including the ideas of an irreducible plurality of political interests, a legitimate and loyal standing opposition, and the like – was a long time in the making.

II

The ancients had no concept corresponding to our "party." Even though democratic Athens in the fifth century BC was well acquainted with factions of various stripes, it knew nothing of parties as we understand them. "There were [in Athens] no parties in anything like the modern sense, " writes A.H.M. Jones, "either among the politicians or among the general public." Although "there were groups or cliques among the politicians," these "were probably based on personalities rather than principles, and seem to have been temporary."[3] And while there were also the more persistent factions formed along class lines, as described by Aristotle in *The Politics*, these were by no means parties. The polis is a compounded whole that is greater than the sum of its several "parts" (*meros* or *morion*), including individuals, families, and other partial associations whose interest coincides with that of the whole. A "faction" (*stasis*), by contrast, aims at its own good rather than the community's and acts to the detriment of the whole. Thus faction or *stasis* represents an unnatural reversal of the proper ordering of the whole and its several parts.

Later writers were long content to follow Aristotle's lead on this matter. Even among Roman writers like Cicero we find no significant departure from this feature of Aristotelian doctrine. The *res publica* was said to embody the shared or public interest of the whole, not the partial interest of any individual "part" or "party." Significantly, the terms "party" and "faction" have entirely different origins. "Faction" derives from *factio*, making, which is connected to the verb *facere*, to do or act. Thus a faction was any group bent on taking matters into their own hands and making them conform to their own designs. By contrast, "party," which comes from *partire*, was simply a "part" of some larger association composed of several parts or parties. Although there were in the Roman republic factions and intrigues aplenty, these were not political parties, properly speaking. *Optimates* and *Populares* did not correspond to oligarchs and democrats or to conservatives and progressives but referred instead to groups consisting of "leading political figures and their followers." Such unprincipled personal entourages and familial factions scarcely deserve to be termed parties (Adcock 1959: 60–2).

Later Christian writers (Augustine to the contrary notwithstanding) were not inclined to doubt the wisdom of Aristotle's analysis of faction and tyranny. So far as faction is concerned, they were in the main content to repeat the teachings of "the philosopher," or, as Dante called him, "the master of them that know." The end of wisdom, says St. Thomas, is the bringing of order into human affairs. This order may be of two types. The first consists of arranging separate parts into a coherent and useful whole; this is the sort of order that the builder brings in constructing a dwelling. The second and altogether "different sort of order exists between things which are united by some common end." Such is the order of the

[3] Jones (1957: 130–1). Perhaps the closest modern counterpart to such political groupings would be the "parties" formed by and around charismatic leaders like the late Juan Perón and Charles de Gaulle.

commonwealth. And since the whole is prior to the parts (*partis*), the latter cannot properly be said to exist except insofar as they serve and help to constitute the whole. Thus "there is no action of the parts which is not also action of the whole," and vice versa (Aquinas 1965: 189–93). Should any individual "part" seek its own advantage instead of the good of the whole it ceases to be a part, properly speaking, and becomes instead a faction intent upon tyranny.

Even as late as the fourteenth century, in the writings of Remigio de'Girolami, Bartolus of Sassoferrato, and Marsiglio of Padua, Aristotle's account of faction remains essentially unchanged. All are agreed that internal divisiveness or "faction" poses the single greatest threat to the liberty and security of city-repubics, and all see the prevention or elimination of faction as the surest means of muting civil strife and promoting the public good (see Skinner 1978, vol. I: 53–65). Moreover, they took very seriously – and sometimes quite literally – the classical imagery of a unified political body. The body politic could be healthy only as long as its "members" or "parts" cooperated and fulfilled their respective functions. No body, corporeal or political, could long survive if its members constantly worked at cross-purposes.

The point is perhaps made most vividly in Marsiglio's *Defensor pacis*. Invoking the authority of Aristotle's *De motu animalium* Marsiglio writes that "the well-ordered animal" cannot move in response to conflicting commands. "For if there were many of these principles and they gave contrary or different commands at the same time, the animal would either have to be borne in contrary directions or remain completely at rest." In either case "it would . . . lack those things, necessary and beneficial to it, which are obtained through motion." And, as with animal bodies, so with political ones: "The case is similar in the state properly ordered, which [is] analogous to the animal well formed according to nature. Hence, just as in the animal a plurality of such principles would be useless and indeed harmful, we must firmly hold that it is the same in the state." The moral that Marsiglio draws is that factions or partial associations, each attempting to impart motion and direction to the political body, can bring only chaos and disorder. A well-ordered body politic must therefore have a single unified government. Justice is the harmonious ordering of the several parts or members for the good of the whole (Marsiglio 1967: 83–4).

Renaissance writers continued to maintain that the presence of factions, sects, and cabals tended to undermine the unity and security of the state. Guicciardini, for one, reiterated the traditional view that factions are disruptive of civic stability and a prime source of political corruption (Pocock 1975: 261–3). In his *Ricordi* he hails the "praiseworthy and useful citizen" who "renders good service to his country" by eschewing "faction or usurpation (*sette e usurpazione*)" (Guicciardini 1949: 2–3). Machiavelli's account is rather more complex. Some "divisions" (*divisioni*), he maintained, are injuirious and others not. The former include all factions or sects formed for private purposes; the latter include any portion, part, or partisans (*partigiani*) of the society "which maintains itself without cabals or factions (*sette*)" (Machiavelli 1843b: 149). And while Machiavelli traced the creation and maintenance of Roman republican liberty to the conflict between the nobles and the plebeians, these contending *divisioni* or "parts" were by no means parties in any of our several modern senses. Nor were they factions or sects in the sense familiar to Machiavelli and his contemporaries. Nobles and plebeians were not small, short-lived sectarian factions but were, rather, larger, longer-lived natural divisions within Roman society, each exemplifying different "tempers" within the body politic. Out of the clash of these "two different tempers (*umori diversi*)" came the compromises and "the laws favorable to liberty" (1843a: 261).

The venerable imagery of a civic body made medical analogies featuring physicians and remedies almost as commonplace among Renaissance writers as they were among classical authors. Guicciardini in his *Dialogo* complains of the difficulty of finding the *medicina appropriata* for curing the ailments afflicting different parts of the political body (Pocock 1975: 252, n. 71). Machiavelli develops his medical metaphors in even more lurid detail. Just as leeches may be required to relieve the human body of its blood-borne ill-humors, he says, so may the ills of the body politic require equally drastic remedies. Factions are most likely to be formed when this natural outlet is blocked; "and when these ferments cannot in some way exhaust themselves, their promotors are apt to resort to some extraordinary means, that may lead to the ruin of the republic." By contrast, "nothing renders a republic more firm and stable, than to organize it in such a way that the excitement of the ill-humors that agitate a state may have a way prescribed by law for venting itself." One of the sources of faction being the absence of legal remedies for "enabling the people to exhaust the malign humors that spring up among men," the wise republic will provide legal home remedies to prevent any disgruntled sectarians from calling upon the even more malign ministrations of foreign physicians (Machiavelli 1843a: 265–6). Like Guicciardini, Machiavelli warned that "there is no surer way of corrupting the citizens, and to divide the city against itself, than to foment the spirit of faction that may prevail there." If it is to be long-lived a republic must be "united and without antagonistic parts (*unite e senza parti*)" (1843a: 394). Even as he reiterates the traditional warnings about the evils of faction Machiavelli avers that controlled conflict among the "parts" can have beneficial consequences, including the prevention of political corruption and the promotion of liberty.[4]

Despite his fulminations against Aristotle and his repeated railings against "the darknesse of School distinctions," Thomas Hobbes did not doubt that factions or formed oppositions of any kind are among "those things that weaken, or tend to the dissolution of a commonwealth." It is ironic that Hobbes, who derided any thinker who relied upon metaphors and other "abuses of speech," should himself have had recourse to that hoariest of metaphors, the body politic, and its accompanying medical imagery, in a way that exceeds even Machiavelli. The "infirmities of the commonwealth," Hobbes insisted, "resemble the diseases of a naturall body." Such "internall diseases" and "intestine disorder" weaken, and eventually kill, the political body. Political convulsions

> not unfitly may be compared to the Epilepsie, or Falling-sickness . . . For as in this disease there is an unnaturall spirit, or wind in the head that obstructeth the roots of the nerves, and moving them violently, taketh away the motion which naturally they should have from the power of the soule in the brain, and thereby causeth violent, and irregular motions, which men call convulsions, in the parts . . . so also in the Body Politique

which internal convulsions must "either overwhelm . . . with oppression, or cast . . . into the fire of a Civil Warre." From this it follows that "mixed government" is a contradiction in terms; for "such government, is not government, but division of the commonwealth into . . . independent factions." This results in a monstrously misproportioned body.

> To what disease in the naturall body of man, I may exactly compare this irregularity of a Common-wealth, I know not. But I have seen a man, that had another man growing out of his side, with an head, armes, breast, and stomach, of his own: If he had had another man growing out of his other side, the comparison [with mixed government] might then have been exact.

[4] An altogether different account of Machiavelli's views on party and sect is supplied by Mansfield (1972) and criticized tellingly by Phillips (1972) and Gunn (1972b). See, further, Gilbert (1949), who casts his net more widely still.

Any association whose presence is perceived to pose a threat to sovereign authority "are as it were many lesser Common-wealths in the bowels of a greater, like wormes in the entrayles of a naturall man." These "little wormes, which physicians call *ascarides*," must be expelled lest the political body perish (1968, chap. 29).

Anyone who expects unity to emerge from faction, Hobbes says in *De cive*, is as deluded as the daughters of Pelias:

> They going to restore the decrepit old man to his youth again, by the counsel of Medea they cut him into pieces, and set him in the fire to boil; in vain expecting when he would live again. So the common people, through their folly, like the daughters of Pelias, desiring to renew the ancient government, being drawn away by the *eloquence* of ambitious men, as it were by the witchcraft of Medea; divided into *faction* they consume it rather by those flames, than they reform it.
>
> 1972: 255

Here Hobbes is of course speaking of "faction," not "party." But even when he does use the word "party" – as in "the king's party" – he refers merely to those who took the king's part, or side, in the English Civil War (1839: 316). That even an apparently radical innovator like Hobbes did not envision anything like "party" in our sense is scarcely surprising. For he – no less than the dreaded Schoolmen, much less Marsiglio, Machiavelli, and Guicciardini – remained wedded, with subtle reservations, to the traditional idiom and imagery of the body politic, with its attendant aversion to anything that threatens its health and organic integrity. Just how subtle, and how momentous, these reservations were, we shall see shortly.

More surprising, perhaps, is that Hobbes's *bêtes noires* – Levellers like Lilburne and Overton, Diggers like Winstanley, and other radical sectarians – neither favored faction nor formulated any notion of a legitimate opposition party. To peruse Puritan tracts in search of some recognizable precursor of the political party is to look in vain. The body politic and its allied imagery remained pretty firmly intact in Puritan political discourse. Even the most utopian tracts – Winstanley's *The Law of Freedom* foremost among them – envisioned a good society in which no provision was made for parties or organized opposition. Hence it is anachronistic to suggest that Winstanley wrote "the first socialist utopia formed in the hopes of becoming a party program" (Sabine 1941: 5). And although the Levellers were without doubt a democratically organized political movement it is surely stretching credulity to claim that theirs "was the first political party . . . to organise itself on a pattern of democratic self-government" (Brailsford 1961: 317). An opposition movement it surely was, and some of the organizational features of the modern party it surely had; but there is little evidence to suggest that the Levellers operated with anything like our modern understanding of a legitimate opposition party.

What is true of radical English puritans was by and large true of their more moderate American brethren. Describing "a due forme of Government both civill and ecclesiasticall," John Winthrop repeats the old maxim that "the care of the publique must oversway all private respects . . . for it is a true rule that perticuler estates cannott subsist in the ruine of the republique" (Morgan 1965: 90). Winthrop went so far as to sanctify the body politic, comparing the Christian commonwealth to the body of Christ:

> There is noe body but consistes of partes and that which knitts these partes together gives the body its perfeccion, because it makes eache parte soe contiguous to other as thereby they doe mutually participate with eache other, both in strengthe and infirmity in pleasure and paine, to instance the most perfect of all bodies, Christ and his church make one body: the several partes of this body considered aparte before they were united were as disproportionate and as much disordering as soe many contrary quallities or elements but when Christ comes and by his spirit and love knitts all these partes to himself and each to other, it is become the most perfect and best proportioned body in the world.
>
> Morgan 1965: 84

It is precisely because individual Christians and their communities are or aspire to be "partes" of one perfect body – the body of Christ – that there is no place or function for disputatious parties, sects, or factions. Nor, despite the deep internal schisms occasioned by the Antinomian controversy, were sectaries like Roger Williams wont to question this piece of conventional wisdom. Far from repudiating the older organic imagery, orthodox Puritans and Antinomians alike accepted and even embellished it.

III

Given the widespread agreement about the evils of faction, one might well wonder how the modern political party ever appeared at all. At least part of the answer is to be found in the various ways in which the older organic imagery began to give way to newer pictures of political association. To put it crudely, the idea of the body politic as a natural body began to give way to the notion that it was an artificial body created by contract and agreement. The beginnings of this shift can be seen already in the Puritans, with their resurrection of the old Hebrew idea of a community created by covenant. But the shift is perhaps more readily discernible in their arch-foe Hobbes, whose account of the commonwealth combines elements of the older and newer pictures.

Hobbes's subtle shift in perspectives begins with the assertion that the ills of the body politic resemble those of the natural body. This amounts to saying that the body politic is – *pace* Aristotle – not a natural body at all, but a "body" of an altogether different sort. While the body politic may resemble a natural body in some respects – having, for example, "members," a "head," and "arms," and liable to "intestine disorders" – it is in fact an artificial body. Men are not only "members" but the "makers and orderers" of the commonwealth. And they create this artificial body by entering into a covenant. By human art and artifice is created the great Leviathan. The irony is that this "mortall god" is itself the creation of its own devotees and worshippers. Little wonder, then, that Hobbes the absolutist should have been suspected by many monarchists of being a seditious wolf attired in royal purple. For he made the bond between sovereign and subjects conditional, resting upon an agreement among his subjects that they would obey him as long as, and no longer than, he should protect them.

It is scarcely an exaggeration to suggest that the emergence of this picture – of a political society created consciously and by contract – marks a momentous shift in political self-understanding in the West.[5] Instead of depicting a society founded by the solitary lawgivers and heroic founders of antiquity, Hobbes paints a picture of many individuals joining together for the purpose of self-preservation. Far from merging their individual identities into some greater organic whole, each member remains readily identifiable. This is perhaps most vividly portrayed in the original frontispiece to the 1651 edition of *Leviathan*, in which the body of the sovereign is shown to consist of the clearly discernible bodies of the individual

[5] The "contractual" picture of the origins of the state is, of course, very old. A rudimentary version of social contract theory was advanced by Sophists like Lycophon and was put into the mouth of Glaucon in Plato's *Republic* (358 e–362; cf. *Laws* 683 c–694). This contractual view is introduced, however, only in order to be refuted. Likewise Aristotle denies that the polis is an artificial or temporary alliance (*koinonia symmachia*) resting upon the prior agreement of the contracting parties and dissolvable at will (*Politics*, 1280b 10; 1962: 119). Cicero makes much the same point in his *De re publica* (1929, bk. I, chap. 25; bk. III, chap. 13). That this anti-contractarian orthodoxy met with no successful challenge until the seventeenth century might be explained less in terms of the perceived inadequacy of Aristotelian arguments than in the breakdown of bodily or organic imagery that underlay and served to sustain those arguments.

members. His body exists by virtue of their agreeing to create it by making a covenant among themselves.

But what, exactly, does all this have to do with the conceptual history of "party"? Just this: one of the crucial characteristics of a covenant, or contract, is that there must be "parties" to it, i.e. people who take part or participate in making and keeping it. This is the sense in which the term is used, even today, in ostensibly nonpolitical activities. Thus lawyers, for example, draw up contracts referring to the signers or participants as "parties" (as in "the party of the first part agrees to convey to the party of the second part . . ."). And when one reserves a table in a restaurant one will quite likely be asked how many people are in one's party. The question is not, of course, a political one.[6]

In fact, "party" was not much used in political contexts until the seventeenth century. I want to suggest that one – though by no means the only – reason why "party" came to be conceived as a political concept was that politics came in some quarters to be pictured in England after 1660 increasingly in contractual terms. Whereas bodies – including bodies politic – have parts, contracts have "parties." Although contractual relations are relations among parties, these are not yet parties in our modern sense(s) of the term. The contracting parties are, rather, still understood as "parts" of the larger society which, despite their disagreements, agree to live according to some rule of common equity. If these are not yet "parties" in our sense, neither are they properly describable as factions or sects. The danger, however, is that one of the parties will break faith with the others and attempt to dominate them for its own private purposes. Such a party would then have ceased to be a party or "part," becoming instead a faction in the older sense.

This distinction became increasingly clear in the course of the Exclusion Crisis of 1679–80, during which the names of Tory and Whig were heard for the first time (Beattie 1970: 5). Most Tories took the older Cavalier view that the king, ruling as he does by divine right, was not party to any contract and could not be bound by its terms. The Whigs – the name comes from the Whiggamores, radical Scots covenanters of the 1640s – argued that by allowing the accession of his Catholic brother James II to the throne, Charles II had violated the terms of the Restoration Settlement of 1660. Charles's several attempts at compromise having failed, he dissolved

[6] Although it could be mistaken for one, with predictably amusing results. The following story is told about a Soviet diplomat newly arrived in Washington, DC. Making reservations at a fashionable Washington restaurant, he was asked how many people were in his party, whereupon the surprised diplomat replied, "Seventeen million."

parliament in 1681, ruling until his death in 1685 without one. When James succeeded his brother he in effect attempted to repeal not only the specific terms of the Settlement but the very idea that the relations between crown and country could be pictured in contractual terms. The Glorious Revolution of 1688 amounted to a militant reaffirmation of the Whiggish or contractarian view that monarchs too are "parts" who are as it were parties to an agreement by which they are constitutionally bound. It was this principle, more than any other, that gave rise to and served to sustain the distinction between Whigs and Tories, the first divisions even remotely resembling modern political parties.

Perhaps the most subtle, abstractly theoretical, and radical defence of the Whig picture is to be found in Locke's *Second Treatise*. "Tis not a change from the present state," says Locke, "which perhaps Corruption, or decay has introduced, that makes an Inroad upon the Government, but the tendency of it to injure or oppress the People, and to set up one part, or Party, with a distinction from, and an unequal subjection of the rest" (1963, § 158). Any "part, or Party" attempting such a move ceases to be a proper party to the contract and becomes a "rebel." The rebel, in effect, makes his part or party into a faction inimical in its operation to a previously agreed upon conception of the common good. This, says Locke in a faint but audible allusion to the older organic imagery of the body politic, is the justification for "cutting off those Parts, and those only, which are so corrupt, that they threaten the sound and healthy" (1963, § 171). That Locke, himself a doctor, should have relied so infrequently upon medical analogies surely says a good deal about the demise of the older organic imagery and its replacement by newer notions of contract, consent, and agreement amongst distinct "parties" or "parts."

IV

The somewhat less theoretical tracts of the late seventeenth and early eighteenth century also suggest that, so far as party and partisanship were concerned, a subtle shift in political self-understanding was beginning to take place. To be sure, there was as yet no defense of party *per se*, nor was there any well-articulated idea of a loyal opposition. "Party" is sometimes taken to be virtually synonymous with faction, whose mischiefs are frequently decried, and political opposition is often equated with treason. This mainstream view is found, for example, in "The Trimmer" Halifax's *Political Thoughts and Reflections* (*c.* 1690). "The best Party," wrote

Halifax, "is but a kind of a Conspiracy against the rest of the Nation" (Gunn 1972a: 44).

This and other oft-repeated warnings were turned by "Real Whig" polemicists in a different direction. Invoking the names of Machiavelli, Harrington, and Locke, among others, the Real Whigs or Commonwealthmen sought to consolidate and extend an emerging English republican tradition (Robbins 1968). John Toland's *The Art of Governing by Partys* (1701) begins conventionally enough by resurrecting the imagery of the political body wracked by the disease of partisanship: "of all the Plagues which have infested this nation . . . none has spread the contagion wider, or brought us nearer to utter ruin, than the implacable animosity of contending Partys . . . it is the most wicked masterpiece of tyranny purposely to divide the sentiments, affections, and interests of a people" (Beattie 1970: 19–20). But Toland then goes on to argue that partisan divisions, though often evil, need not always be so. It is not parties *per se* but their "implacable animosity" that poses the greatest political threat to the nation. What may therefore be needed is not the abolition of parties but their being put to some better public purpose. Factiousness and freedom go hand in hand; the point is to keep both from getting out of hand. This view Toland developed in his *Memorial of the State of England* (1705) and at greater length in *The State Anatomy of Great Britain* (1716). "Every division," he wrote in *The State Anatomy*, "is not simply pernicious: Since Parties in the State, are just of the like nature with Heresies in the Church: sometimes they make it better, and sometimes they make it worse; but held within due Bounds, they always keep it from stagnation" (Gunn 1972a: 54).

In warning of the dangers of stagnation Toland echoed the Machiavellian (and Harringtonian) view that divisions or "parts" are not inherently evil but can, under the appropriate circumstances, be beneficial in allowing the political body to vent its ill humors. This, minus the medical imagery, had also been the central theme of Robert Molesworth's *Account of Denmark* (1694). Molesworth had seen in the factionless state of Denmark the peace of the grave. "Where there are no Factions, nor Disputes about Religion which usually have a great influence on any Government," he wrote, the possibilities for political reform and renewal were stifled. Though this uniformity of opinion be a "vast convenience to any Prince," it precludes popular reform and leads inevitably to political stagnation (Molesworth 1694: 25–51). In a similar spirit Walter Moyle asked, "who is there that would not prefer a factious liberty before a settled Tyranny?" (1726: 112–14).

Although such unorthodox views met with widespread opposition we see in this period the first glimmerings of the idea that at least some political divisions are based upon principles of some sort, however odious or mistaken or disingenuously proclaimed, and that such divisions, however dangerous, may even be unavoidable in a free state. More significant still, some writers were going so far as to suggest that honest and honorable men might disagree about what the common interest was and how it might best be served. Thus while warning of the evils of faction the anonymous author of *The State of the Parties* (1692) averred that the differences between Whigs and Tories stemmed not from one's serving the common interest and the other's not, but from their having different conceptions of the common interest of the nation to which both were loyal after their fashion. Such partisan contentiousness came to be taken by some as an identifying feature of the English national character. The unnamed author of *The Political Sow-Gelder* (1715) averred that Englishmen were and would remain as varied in their politics as England was in her climate. And the author of *The Freeholder's Alarm to his Brethren* (1734), usually attributed to Henry Fielding, remarks that parties and partisans were inevitable in a political climate in which freedom and liberty prevailed (1734: 8).

Among political philosophers like Hobbes and Locke one expects a certain degree of self-consciousness about linguistic or conceptual change. Perhaps surprisingly, however, one finds among political pamphleteers of the period a remarkably similar sensibility. John Toland, for example, notes that "Patriots and loyalists, court and country-parties, tho in themselves words significant enough, yet they are become very equivocal, as men are apt to apply them: whereas Whig and Tory cannot be mistaken; for men may change, and words may change, but principles never" (Toland 1716: 18). Along with the emerging idea that parties, properly understood, stand for principles of some sort came an appreciation of the mutability of our moral and political concepts and an awareness that meanings, like minds, can be changed through political argument.

The arguments in favor of party were neither legal nor logical but political and rhetorical ones in which actions were redescribed, new distinctions made, and old ones recast or abandoned. Chief among these was, of course, the distinction between faction and party. To defend faction and factiousness, as Molesworth and Moyle had done, doubtless had a certain shock value; but such a defense could scarcely be sustained, given the prevailing views about the evils of faction. Hence the importance of drawing the distinction in ways that might prove politically acceptable. The distinction was drawn in different ways, some writers preferring to focus upon their respective members' motives, others upon organizational features or political functions, and still others upon some combination of these. In *An Enquiry into the State of the Union of Great Britain* (1717), for example, William Paterson reports on the (perhaps imaginary) meeting of "the Wednesday's Club in Friday-street," as follows:

> You say you are for Parties; Are you for Factions too?
> By no means (reply'd Mr. Grant) these are wicked things.
> A very nice Distinction (reply'd Mr. Ford) pray wherein do your parties and factions differ? Since I confess my self so wise as not to know.
> The difference is manifest several ways (said Mr. Grant) particularly your natural Parties are things consisting only of Members without Heads, but your Factions, or in other Words provoked unnatural Parties, have Heads.
> By what other Properties can we distinguish them? (said Mr. Ford).
> Your natural Parties are pretty tame, . . . (reply'd Mr. Grant) but the others are always wild and voracious; the first is capable of Good, as well as Hurt, of Love as well as Hatred, and frequently produce Emulation, a very good thing. But instead thereof, your unnatural Parties [or factions] hate, but love not, are hurtful in the Nature, and chiefly produce Enmity, a dangerous Quality in Men.
>
> Gunn 1972a: 82–3

Although other defenders of party drew the distinction in other ways, the central point, politically speaking, was that distinctions were being drawn and that party was accordingly coming to be viewed by some as a novel, acceptable, and even a valuable English political institution.

Opponents of party, by contrast, were intent upon reinstating and defending older distinctions or at any rate disputing new ones. This strategy consisted, in the main, of attempting to show that parties were nothing new under the sun, but an old phenomenon parading under a new name. Numerous anti-party pamphleteers purported to show that parties were really factions after all, or, failing that, that parties tended to degenerate into factions. But it remained for Bolingbroke, "the classic anti-party writer" and "fountainhead of anti-party thought" (Hofstadter 1970: 18), to construct a last-ditch defense against the encroachment of party.

Bolingbroke ingeniously deployed an array of "Old Whig" arguments to criticize parties and partisanship. The crown having been captured by the corrupt ministry of Walpole and the "New Whigs," Bolingbroke appealed to earlier Whig defenses of the Glorious Revolution, in hopes of creating a "Patriot King" freed from the snares of party politics and partisan narrowness. Such a king could "defeat the designs, and break the spirit of faction, instead of partaking in one and assuming the other" (1749: 62). And while he might temporarily favor one party over another, he would remain aloof from both. The irony in this defense of royal prerogative is that the conditions that make it possible must be brought about by a new kind of party – a "country party" – devoted not to narrow partisan interests but to "principles of common interest." Cutting across the distinction between Whig and Tory, Bolingbroke's country party would include men of good will from both parties and therefore would not be a party, strictly speaking. "A party thus constituted," he maintained in "A Dissertation upon Parties" (1735), "is improperly called party. It is the nation speaking and acting in the discourse and conduct of particular men" (1841: 48).

Bolingbroke's idea of a nonpartisan party was advanced as a temporary expedient and a necessary evil, not an inevitable feature of constitutional government. But in advancing and defending the idea of a party to end all parties Bolingbroke conceded the necessity, the importance – and the justifiability – of such an institution. And in so doing he had to acknowledge that there could, in principle, be "parties" of different kinds and that party was not necessarily synonymous with faction. Indeed by asserting that "parties" inevitably "degenerate into absolute factions" (1749: 47) he further reinforces the latter point – since, strictly speaking, something (an acorn, a party) can hardly be said to be identical with the thing that it eventually becomes (an oak, a faction). Too ingenious by half, Bolingbroke's argument against parties proved in the end to be singularly self-subverting.

In "Of Parties in General" and "The Parties of Great Britain" (1742) David Hume brought together a number of earlier arguments in a novel synthesis. Hume's argumentative and rhetorical strategy was to concede that "parties" are "factions" but that factions come in several different varieties, not all of which are equally noxious. He begins by reaffirming the traditional view that factions are evil "weeds." But like Molesworth and the Real Whigs, Hume held that factions are "plants which grow most plentifully in the richest soil," i.e. "they rise more easily, and propagate themselves faster in free governments." Different forms of free government give rise to factions of quite different kinds. "Personal factions," for example, "arise most easily in small republics. Every domestic quarrel, there, becomes an affair of state" (1985: 56). Such personal or familial factions as those of republican Rome and Florence are however, he concedes, increasingly rare in the modern state. More common nowadays are "parties" or "real factions" which "may be divided into those from *interest*, from *principle*, and from *affection*." The first, says Hume, "is the most reasonable, and the most excusable" (1985: 59). The third – "parties from affection" – "are founded on the different attachments of men towards particular families and persons, whom they desire to rule over them" even though "they are in no wise acquainted . . . and from whom they never received, nor can ever hope for any favour" (1985: 63). But it is the second sort of party which is truly novel. "Parties from *principle*, especially abstract speculative principle, are known only to modern times, and are, perhaps, the most extraordinary and unaccountable *phaenomenon*, that has yet appeared in human affairs" (1985: 60). Parties professing to stand for some set of political or philosophical principles represented an entirely new wrinkle. Hume was among the first to note that this development was rapidly becoming commonplace. Indeed, as he remarks in "of the Original Contract," "no party, in the present age, can well support itself, without a philosophical or speculative system of principles, annexed to its political or practical one" (1985: 465). Hume ably described, if he did not altogether approve of, this development.[7] Such parties being unavoidable in a free state, the cure would then be worse than the disease. Like it or not, parties from principle were becoming a familiar feature of the political landscape.

By the time Samuel Johnson published his *Dictionary of the English Language* in 1755, his definition of party was already out of date. Swimming against an ever stronger current of conceptual change Johnson defined "party" as "a number of persons confederated by similarity of designs in opposition to others, a faction; . . . side, persons engaged against each other, as, of your *party*; cause, side." Then as now, dictionaries follow fashion; they do not dictate it. Johnson, however, followed political and philosophical fashion at a considerable distance.

The phenomenon that Hume found extraordinary and unaccountable and Johnson ordinary and unacceptable was soon to be justified by means of an argument at once principled and pragmatic. In *Thoughts on the Cause of the Present Discontents* (1770) Edmund Burke defended the practice of partisan "connection" against the anti-party fulminations of the Earl of Chatham (William Pitt).[8] As prime

[7] On this much, at least, Hume and Bolingbroke were agreed, even if the distance between them was in other respects profound (Jäger 1971).

[8] For insightful inquiries into the rhetorical structure of Burke's argument, see Boulton (1963, chap. 5) and Reid (1985).

minister, Chatham claimed to be interested in "measures, not men," and had had some success in luring partisans away from their parties, including the Rockingham Whigs with whom Burke was affiliated. Once separated from their party, they could then be more readily manipulated by the Chatham ministry. Seeing through this strategy of divide and conquer Burke proceeded to denounce nonpartisanship and to defend the idea of principled opposition.[9] This was now practicable in part, Burke argued, because the older and politically disastrous division between monarchists and parliamentarians no longer existed. But although "the great parties which formerly divided and agitated the kingdom are known to be in a manner entirely dissolved," there remains a politically ambitious and corrupt "court faction" or "cabal" which while hiding behind a façade of nonpartisanship seeks to advance its own interests at the country's expense (1826: 220). "This cabal has, with great success, propagated a doctrine which serves for a colour to those acts of treachery." That "doctrine," says Burke, is "that all political connexions are in their nature factions, and as such ought to be dissipated and destroyed; and that the rule for forming administrations is mere personal ability, rated by the judgment of this cabal upon it." The wilful failure to distinguish between faction and party "connection" is politically pernicious:

> That connexion and faction are equivalent terms, is an opinion which has been carefully inculcated at all times by unconstitutional statesmen. The reason is evident. Whilst men are linked together, they easily and speedily communicate the alarm of any evil design. They are enabled to fathom it with common counsel, and to oppose it with united strength. Whereas, when they lie dispersed, without concert, order, or discipline, communication is uncertain, counsel difficult, and resistance impracticable. Where men are not acquainted with each other's principles nor experienced in each other's talents, . . . no personal confidence, no friendship, no common interest, subsisting among them; it is evidently impossible that they can act a publick part with uniformity, perseverance, or efficacy.

Part and party are intertwined, in that one cannot reasonably hope to "act a publick part" outside of one's party:

> In a connexion, the most inconsiderable man, by adding to the weight of the whole, has his value, and his use; out of it, the greatest talents are wholly unserviceable to the publick. No man . . . can flatter himself

[9] Burke's master, the Marquis of Rockingham, articulated very succinctly the then-new connection between the older concept of "part" and the modern "party" dedicated to particular political principles and committed to playing the part of a loyal opposition. "We and *only we* of all the parts now in Opposition," he said in 1769, "are so on principle" (quoted in Foord 1964: 315).

> that his single, unsupported, desultory, unsystematick endeavours are of power to defeat the subtle designs and united cabals of ambitious citizens. When bad men combine, the good must associate; else they will fall, one by one, an unpitied sacrifice in a contemptible struggle.
>
> Burke 1826: 329–30

The "parties from principle" which Hume found so unaccountable are for Burke paradigmatic of party *per se*. "Party," as Burke defines it, "is a body of men united, for promoting by their joint endeavours the national interest, upon some particular principle in which they are all agreed" (1826: 335). With this the pre-history of party ends and we enter a world recognizably modern and akin to our own.

Where pre-history ends history begins. Much more could of course be said about party and opposition in the eighteenth century, particularly in the England of George III (Brewer 1976), about the development of a party system in the United States (Hofstadter 1970; Ladd and Hadley 1978), about the (almost Bolingbrokean?) Leninist vision of a vanguard party to end all parties (Meyer 1962) and the emergence of single-party states in the twentieth century in Africa and elsewhere (Zolberg 1966), and about the allegedly declining importance of political parties in the Western democracies (Broder 1972). It must suffice to say that the present essay is not intended to be a comprehensive history of party but a small and selective contribution to a story which is still unfolding and a history which remains to be written.

REFERENCES

Adcock, F.E. 1959. *Roman Political Ideas and Practice*. Ann Arbor, MI: University of Michigan Press.

Anon. 1692. *The State of the Parties*. London.

Anon. 1715. *The Political Sow-Gelder*. London.

Aquinas, St. Thomas. 1965. *Selected Political Writings*, edited by A.P. D'Entreves. Oxford: Blackwell.

Aristotle. 1962. *The Politics*, edited and translated by Ernest Barker. New York: Oxford University Press.

Beattie, Alan (ed.). 1970. *English Party Politics*, 2 vols., vol. I: *1600–1906*. London: Weidenfeld and Nicolson.

Berlin, Isaiah. 1979. *Concepts and Categories*. New York: Viking.

Bolingbroke, Henry St. John, 1st Viscount. 1749. *The Idea of a Patriot King*. London: (Reproduction. Menston: Scolar Press, 1971.)

1841 [1735]. *A Dissertation upon Parties*. In *Works*, vol. II. Philadelphia, PA: Carey and Hant, pp. 5–172.

Boulton, James T. 1963. *The Language of Politics in the Age of Wilkes and Burke*. London: Routledge and Kegan Paul.

Brailsford, Henry Noel. 1961. *The Levellers and the English Revolution*, edited by Christopher Hill. Stanford, CA: Stanford University Press.
Brewer, John. 1976. *Party Ideology and Popular Politics at the Accession of George III*. Cambridge: Cambridge University Press.
Broder, David. 1972. *The Party's Over*. New York: Harper and Row.
Burke, Edmund. 1826 [1770]. *Thoughts on the Cause of the Present Discontents*. In *Works*, vol. II. London: C. and J. Rivington, pp. 215–344.
Cicero, Marcus Tullius. 1929. *On the commonwealth*, translated by G.H. Sabine and S.B. Smith. Indianapolis, IN: Bobbs-Merrill.
Fielding, Henry. 1734. *The Freeholder's Alarm to His Brethren*. London.
Fleisher, Martin (ed.). 1972. *Machiavelli and the Nature of Political Thought*. New York: Atheneum.
Foord, Archibald. 1964. *His Majesty's Opposition, 1714–1830*. Oxford: Clarendon.
Gilbert, Felix. 1949. "Bernardo Rucellai and the Orti Oricellari, a Study of the Origin of Modern Political Thought." *Journal of the Warburg and Courtauld Institutes* 12: 101–31.
Guicciardini, Francesco. 1949. *Ricordi*. New York: S.F. Vanni.
Gunn, J.A.W. (ed.). 1972a. *Factions No More: Attitudes to Party in Government and Opposition in Eighteenth Century England*. London: Frank Cass.
1972b. "Commentary [on Mansfield 1972]." In Fleisher 1972: 275–81.
Hobbes, Thomas. 1839. *Behemoth*. In *English Works*, edited by William Molesworth, vol. VI. London: John Bohn, pp. 165–418.
1968. *Leviathan*, edited by C.B. Macpherson. Harmondsworth: Penguin.
1972. *De cive*. In *Man and Citizen*, edited by Bernard Gert. Garden City, NY: Anchor Books, pp. 87–386.
Hofstadter, Richard. 1970. *The Idea of a Party System*. Berkeley, CA; and Los Angeles, CA: University of California Press.
Hume, David. 1985. *Essays Moral, Political, and Literary*, edited by Eugene Miller. Indianapolis, IN: Liberty Press.
Jäger, Wolfgang. 1971. *Politische Partei und Parlementarische Opposition: eine Studie Zum Politischenen Denken von Lord Bolingbroke und David Hume*. Berlin: Duncker und Humboldt.
Johnson, Samuel. 1755. *Dictionary of the English Language*. London: John Williamson and Co.
Jones, A.H.M. 1957. *Athenian Democracy*. Oxford: Blackwell.
Kelly, George Armstrong. 1986. "Mortal Man, Immortal Society? Political Metaphors in Eighteenth-Century France." *Political Theory* 14 (February): 5–29.
Ladd, Everett Carll, Jr., and Charles D. Hadley. 1978. *Transformations of the American Party System*, 2nd edn. New York: Norton.
Lakoff, George, and Mark Johnson. 1980. *Metaphors We Live By*. Chicago, IL: University of Chicago Press.
Locke, John. 1963. *Two Treatises of Government*, edited by Peter Laslett. Cambridge: Cambridge University Press.
Machiavelli, Niccolò. 1843a. *Discorsi*. In *Opere Complete*. Florence: Alcide Parenti, pp. 255–411.

1843b. *Istorie Fiorentine*. In *Opere Complete*. Florence: Alcide Parenti, pp. 9–195.
Mansfield, Harvey, C., Jr. 1965. *Statesmanship and Party Government: A Study of Burke and Bolingbroke*. Chicago, IL: University of Chicago Press.
1972. "Party and Sect in Machiavelli's Florentine Histories." In Fleisher 1972: 209–66.
Marsiglio of Padua. 1967. *The Defender of the Peace*, translated by Alan Gewirth. New York: Harper Torchbooks.
Meyer, Alfred G. 1962. *Leninism*. New York: Praeger.
Molesworth, Robert. 1694. *Account of Denmark*. London: T. Goodwin.
Morgan, Edmund S. (ed.). 1965. *Puritan Political Ideas, 1558–1794*. Indianapolis, IN: Bobbs-Merrill.
Moyle, Walter. 1726. "An Essay on the Roman Government." In *Works*, vol. I. London: Printed for J. Darby, A. Betterworth, F. Fayram, J. Osborn, and T. Longman, pp. 1–148. (Repr. in Robbins 1969: 201–59.)
Phillips, Mark. 1972. "Comment [on Mansfield 1972]." In Fleisher 1972: 267–75.
Pocock, J.G.A. 1975. *The Machiavellian Moment*. Princeton, NJ: Princeton University Press.
Reid, Christopher. 1985. *Edmund Burke and the Practice of Political Writing*. Dublin: Gill and Macmillan.
Robbins, Caroline. 1958. " 'Discordant Parties': A Study of the Acceptance of Party by Englishmen." *Political Science Quarterly* 73 (December): 505–29.
1968. *The Eighteenth Century Commonwealthman*. New York: Atheneum.
(ed.). 1969. *Two English Republican Tracts*. Cambridge: Cambridge University Press.
Sabine, George H. (ed.). 1941. *Works of Gerrard Winstanley*. Ithaca, NY: Cornell University Press.
Sartori, Giovanni. 1976. *Parties and Party Systems*, 2 vols. Cambridge: Cambridge University Press.
Skinner, Quentin. 1974. "Some Problems in the Analysis of Political Thought and Action." *Political Theory* 2: 277–303.
1978. *The Foundations of Modern Political Thought*, 2 vols. Cambridge: Cambridge University Press.
Toland, John. 1701. *The Art of Governing by Partys*. London: B. Lintott.
1705. *Memorial of the State of England*. London: The Booksellers of Westminster.
1716. *The State Anatomy of Great Britain*. London: John Philips.
Von Beyme, Klaus. 1978. "Partei, Faktion." In *Geschichtliche Grundbegriffe: Historisches Lexikon juristisch-sozialen Sprache in Deutschland*, edited by Otto Brunner, Werner Conze, and Reinhart Koselleck, vol. IV. Stuttgart: Klett-Cotta, pp. 677–733.
Winthrop, John. 1630. "A Model of Christian Charity." In Morgan 1965: 75–93.
Zolberg, Aristide R. 1966. *The Party-states of West Africa*. Chicago, IL: Rand McNally.

8

Patriotism

MARY G. DIETZ

I

Contemplating his retirement from political life in 1796, yet wishing to leave the American people with some sentiments vital to their identity, George Washington wrote: "Citizens by birth or choice, of a common country, that country has a right to concentrate your affections. The name of American, which belongs to you, in your national capacity, must always exalt the just pride of Patriotism" (Washington 1948: 631). Though the exact words of Washington's Farewell Address may be forgotten, the idea he exalted is not. So commonplace are appeals to patriotism – not only in the United States but in most nations – that the concept seems, everywhere, to be a timeless artifact, a spirit that transcends historical moment and is impervious to political change. In reality, however, patriotism is not an evanescent entity but a relatively new word of eighteenth-century origin whose linguistic life, brief though it is, involves dramatic change over time. When Washington appealed to "patriotism" in 1796, for example, he invoked a highly specific political virtue and a set of particular political practices barely remembered in the rush of subsequent American history. In telling the story of "patriotism," then, I wish not only to narrate changes of language, politics, and principle, but also to reveal that the "just pride" Washington urged Americans to exalt is almost extinct in these "nationalistic" times, and with it a conception of civic virtue is nearly lost as well.

II

"Patriotism" is a relatively new word, but its cognate "patriot" is older and their etymological root, *patria*, is more ancient still. In Greek and Roman antiquity *patria* referred chiefly to the city. But for the Greeks, who thought of themselves as *politai* or citizens, and conceived of political membership in terms of participation in the life of the polis, *patriotai* were barbarians – foreigners named after their country, not citizens of distinctive city-states. Without question, the Greeks had deep emotional attachments to and pride in their native cities (one need only recall Homer's epics, Pericles' Funeral Oration, or Socrates' tribute to Athens in the *Crito*) but they did not primarily associate politics with the preservation of a "fatherland" or a moment of founding. Aristotle's remark that "the identity of a *polis* is not constituted by its walls" is at least partly indicative of the extent to which territory alone was not the focal point of Greek political identity or loyalty (Aristotle 1958: 98).

As Hannah Arendt (1958: 120–4) has observed, it was in Rome that the full meaning of the word *patria* and its emotional resonance came into being; the *patria*, Rome itself, was the site and symbol of all values – moral, religious, political, and ethical – for which a soldier or citizen might care to live and die. The powerful symbolism of heroic self-sacrifice for the glorious fatherland, so much a part of modern patriotism, had its roots in Roman history. Cicero asked, "What good citizen would hesitate to welcome death if it were profitable for the *patria*?" (Kantorowicz 1957: 242). He also declared *Patria mihi vita mea carior est*, "Fatherland is dearer to me than my life" (Kantorowicz 1957: 244). The most Roman of all conventions, the law, abounded with ethics concerning the *patria*. The Digest distinguished between two *patriae*, the individual city (*patria sua*) and the city of Rome (*communis patria*). In the empire, all subjects, regardless of their membership in a *patria sua*, recognized Rome as their common fatherland (Kantorowicz 1957: 246–7). As the empire expanded, allegiance to *patria* became an increasingly abstract matter. Love of fatherland was tied less to the specific locale of the city and more to an idea (e.g., the imperial *pater patriae*) which the empire represented and numerous political symbols and religious doctrine reinforced (Finley 1984: 50–70, 122–41).

Nothing, however, more systematically undermined the sense of *patria* as a specific locale and a political entity than Roman thought, particularly Stoicism, where the concept assumed a thoroughly philosophical and religious meaning. Epictetus's declaration, "You are a citizen of the universe," captured the Stoic understanding of *patria* as cosmos, the universal society to which all humans belonged (Wolin 1960: 77–82). Although the concept *patria* was still a part of the political language of citizenship, loyalty, and community, that political language was strained to its breaking point; for some time two conceptions of *patria* competed in Rome: the secular–political one of the Roman empire as fatherland, and the philosophical–religious one of the universe as the locus of human membership. In the end, material and intellectual events conspired to render the political meaning of *patria* virtually valueless by the time of the late empire. The growth of the large-scale, impersonal cosmopolis of Rome weakened all meaningful sense of "ties" to the fatherland; then Christianity demolished that understanding completely; for worldly territory had minimal relevance for the Christians' understanding of themselves as members of a shared community. The earthly city could not wrest from them the emotional commitment that characterized Cato's *pugna pro patria* or Cicero's devotion to Rome. Following the teachings of the Fathers, the Christians had become citizens of another world. The writer of the *Letter to Diognet* observed, "Every place abroad is their fatherland, and in their fatherland they are aliens," which is simply to say that, for the Christian, *patria* had lost all political significance (Kantorowicz 1951: 475).[1] They would "render unto Caesar" but they would not worship him or glorify the land of their birth. The transvaluation of *patria* from a secular to a spiritual entity was a part of the political task of early Christianity, one Hannah Arendt has characterized as the attempt "to find a bond between people strong enough to replace the world" (Arendt 1958: 53). And no one took up that task with more vigor and altered the concept of *patria* more decisively than St. Augustine. In his monumental effort to articulate the religious identity of Christianity, Augustine vividly transformed the conception of heroic self-sacrifice and with it the conception of the object of such sacrifice. More than any other work of late antiquity, *The City of God* loosened the concept of *patria* from its political moorings and rendered it spiritual, the object of devotion for the new models of self-sacrifice – the saints, the martyrs, and the holy virgins (Kantorowicz 1951: 474–5). No longer were those who pledged devotion and died for Rome the paragons of heroic glory, for in Augustine's theory of *ordo* Rome was but a minor part of a vast and hierarchically ordered cosmic whole. Those who looked to

[1] The Christian's minimal attachment to an earthly home is perhaps no more vividly evident than in Augustine's account of his mother's death. In response to Augustine's brother's lament that she die not in a foreign land but in her own country, Monica says, "Put this body away anywhere . . . I ask only this of you, that you remember me at the altar of the Lord, wherever you may be" (Augustine 1960: 223).

Rome as the fatherland, as the source of their identity and their life, were destined to remain helplessly trapped in the *civitas terrena*.[2] Hence, the political community diminished in importance; the celestial city and the soul of the communicant took on a grandeur unprecedented in the history of political thought, not to mention the life of the citizen.

If in the late empire the emergence of *patria* as a primarily spiritual entity was the result of the increasing influence of *ecclesia* and the depreciation of the political order, then the low Middle Ages and the rise of feudalism did nothing to reverse that trend; indeed, the centuries of Western feudalism exacerbated it. What we find following the collapse of the Roman empire is a shift in the nature and meaning of territorial identification. As civilized urban centers receded and medieval baronies and feudal estates developed, people no longer thought of themselves as members of anything larger than a town or village, and one's loyalty as knight, warrior, or vassal was offered up to the lord and master rather than in the name of a territory, an empire, or a "state" (Kantorowicz 1951: 476–7). Though the concept of *patria* itself still existed, it was almost always used in secular practice with reference to one's immediate locality. In the intellectual and theological life centered in the monasteries, *patria* retained its exalted Augustinian meaning.

As is so often the case in the history of conceptual change, the usage of the word is in part conditioned by the material conditions of the times. *Patria* had lost the emotional content and the rhetorical power it had in antiquity, much as the ancient city itself had ceased to exist. In its place stood the church, the only great source of institutional coherency throughout the low Middle Ages. The classical emotional values of *patria* were recovered, however, in the twelfth and thirteenth centuries, as new political territories developed. And the church itself, or at least church doctrine, played an important role in the recovery.

The story of how *patria* once again became identified with political–territorial loyalty – only now directed toward a national kingdom rather than an ancient city and legitimized by Christian doctrine – is a long and complicated one (Post 1953). The briefest of

[2] Augustine does grant that Rome is or was a commonwealth. But he is also unambiguous about the "common interest" that binds the people of a political commonwealth – it is decidedly inferior to the love (*caritas*) which binds the Christian community to God, just as the political *patria* is but a shadow of the *patria aeterna* (1960: 478).

sketches will have to suffice. Two phenomena are of importance in understanding the revitalization of *patria*: the rise of national territories or "kingdoms" from about the ninth century onward, and the institution of the tax *ad defensionem natalis patriae*, "for the defense of the native fatherland" (or *pro defensione regni*, "for the defense of the king") (Kantorowicz 1951: 479).[3] By the early twelfth century, the concept *patria* was mobilized (most effectively in 1124 by Louis VI of France) for both religious and political purposes: to solicit the funds necessary for the waging of the Holy War and to recruit the services of potential defenders of the realm. The kings began to demand taxes and services in the name of the fatherland (*communis patriae*) and, by the late thirteenth century, *patria* acquired a recognizably modern sense, evocative not only of national territory but also of an emotional commitment to "fatherland" which itself was perceived of as sacred (*corpus mysticum*) and, most importantly, was associated with the person of the king.[4]

In short, the late twelfth and thirteenth centuries were decisive turning points in the Western world for the early beginnings of national consciousness and the reclamation of *patria* as an entity worthy of self-sacrifice. A theological standard of *amor patriae* was allied with the conception of an organic body politic; Cato's declaration was revived and reiterated time and again. Death *pro patria* was no longer considered a pagan act but rather a glorious sacrifice animated by Christian virtues.[5] Although it took some time before the claims of the jurists and the arguments of the scholastics found their equivalent in popular expression, the groundwork was now laid for a conception of *patria* that would flourish in the Renaissance, namely, the idea that the homeland (whether monarchic territory, princedom, or city-state) deserved a love and loyalty that

[3] So, for example, in 1302 after the French defeat at Courtrai, Philip IV asked for aid from the clergy: "ad defensionem natalis patrie proqua reverenda patrum antiquitas pugnare precepit, eius curam liberorum preferens caritati" ("For the defense of the native fatherland which the venerable antiquity of our ancestors ordered to fight for, because they preferred the care for the fatherland even to the love for their descendants") (Kantorowicz 1951: 479).

[4] The influence of popular songs, poetry, and prose cannot be underestimated – in the case of France, the *Chansons de geste* and, in England, Geoffrey of Monmouth's *History of the Kings of England* served as nationalistic literature and historiography, respectively, in the Middle Ages. We also find a related development, the differentiation of one's own land from others' and scorn for the latter, what Koht somewhat anachronistically calls the beginnings of "nationalism" during this era (1946–7: 276).

[5] Tolomeo of Lucca even placed *amor patriae* in a rank of honor "above all other things," and St. Thomas asserted that *pietas* was the power animating devotion to both parents and *patria* (Kantorowicz 1951: 489; 1957: 243).

took precedence over the family, the individual, and even the transcendent spirit of the Christian believer.[6] The expression, "I love my native city more than my own soul," common among the Renaissance humanists although brought most vividly to life in the political writings of Machiavelli, indicated the emergence of a new normative vocabulary. As human beings increasingly turned their attention toward the concrete political, social, and ideological manifestations of their allegiance to *patria*, they began to deliberate upon the nature of their obligation to act as "patriots." To no small extent these deliberations revolved around the coherence between court and country which the medieval world had certified in the form of the king (*pater patriae*). Early modern patriotism is primarily a story of emotional and political revaluation of this coherence – of the idea of the king as *pater patriae* and, correspondingly, of the conception of *patria* as the king.

III

"Patriot" came into early modern English around the sixteenth century, a verbal borrowing from the French *patriote*.[7] Originally, it referred simply to a fellow-countryman (in 1596 Lombarde wrote of "our honest patriote Richard Harrys") though it retained the appraisive character of its root in both popular literature and poetry. Thus in *Volpone* (1605) Ben Jonson observed, "such as were known patriots, sound lovers of their country" (*Oxford English Dictionary*). Until near the end of the seventeenth century, however, "patriot" lay relatively idle in English political discourse, including that of the Civil War. The Stuart kings staked no claim upon it, nor do we find the word appropriated by any of the opponents of the crown. Neither the regicides nor any of the host of lesser but no less voluble defenders of the law of freedom and the common weal declare themselves "patriots." There was, however, one exception, found in the popular press of the day. In 1643, following his death in battle

[6] Expressions regarding the timelessness of national territory (e.g., *la France éternelle*) belong to the period of the late fourteenth and early fifteenth centuries. Expressions concerning the primacy of "the fatherland" emerge as well. Consider the humanist Coluccio Salutate's declaration: "if such would be expedient for the fatherland's protection or enlargement, it would seem neither burdensome and difficult nor a crime to thrust the axe into one's father's head, to crush one's brothers, to deliver from the womb of one's wife the premature child with the sword" (Kantorowicz 1957: 245).

[7] The German *Patriotismus* and *Patrio* also come from the French *patriote*, at about the same time. From this point on, I will deal primarily with the development of patriotism in its Anglo-American context.

against the king's Cavaliers, the parliamentarian John Hampden was memorialized in the *Weekly Account* as "that noble patriot of his country, whose losse is infinitely lamented in all places" (Karsten 1978: 23–4).[8] This seemingly minor moment of eulogistic history had immense significance for the role that "patriot" came to play in the political rhetoric of late-seventeenth and eighteenth-century England. Beginning with the commendation of Hampden, the word was increasingly appropriated for various political purposes (i.e. not simply in reference to those who share a homeland and a romantic love of it) and so began a career of ambiguous and, at times, equivocal meaning.[9]

The site for the emergence of "patriot" as a fully-fledged part of English political discourse was the radical Whig rhetoric of the late 1680s and 1690s, during and following the Glorious Revolution of 1688. Two events of rhetorical significance occurred. First, "patriot" was tied to a particular set of political principles: the defense of liberty and the rights of Englishmen against tyranny, the laws and constitution of England against the king and court, and "revolutionist" or Whig (as understood in 1688) as opposed to conservative or Tory sensibilities. Secondly, the word was linked in Whig rhetoric to political martyrdom, only now the defender of *patria* or "patriot" was he who opposed the tyranny and excesses of the king. Thus the link between king and *patria* was rhetorically severed, and the "patriot," at least in English political discourse, took his stand with country (or, more exactly, with the constitution) and against absolutist kings.

As examples of "patriot" self-sacrifice, the Whigs chose John Hampden and the republican Algernon Sidney, beheaded for treason under Charles II in 1683. Both were enshrined in poem, pamphlet, and private gatherings as martyrs to the cause of liberty in England.[10] Thus, beginning in 1693 yearly celebrations were held at the Calves Head Club to roast (the Stuart) calf and toast Hampden, Sidney, and other "patriots who killed the tyrant" (Karsten 1978: 21–4). In his tract *Sydney Redivivus* (1689) Humphrey Smith noted

[8] Cromwell also called Hampden (his cousin) "the Patriot," although Cromwell himself did not fare so well as a model for patriots; in both England and the colonies he was too closely linked with the danger of a standing army (Karsten 1978).

[9] Consider Maxwell's derisive observation in 1644, concerning "the specious and spurious pretences of our glorious Reformers and zealous patriots"and, in 1677, Hicks' claim that patriots will be the ruin of the church (*Oxford English Dictionary*).

[10] There is at this time a resurgence of interest in Cato, whose proclamation *pugna pro patria* is taken up by the Whigs. Trenchard and Gordon defended the cause in the *London Journal* under the by-line "Cato" (Karsten 1978: 21–4).

"the Blood of patriots is the seed of Asserters of the People's Liberty." Some years later the poet James Thomson extolled in a tribute to Sidney "the Patriot's noble Rage / Dashing corruption down through every worthless age" (Karsten 1978: 184, 40, 33).

The symbolic use of the "Twin Patriots" that extended into the eighteenth century in both England and America is truly remarkable, but the "patriotic" import of this exercise in hagiography should not be overlooked.[11] Though associated with certain founding principles – liberty, constitutional rights, and property – "patriot" became an ideological tool of legitimation forged in the fires of Whig and Tory animosity. During this episode, at least, the story of the concept turns less on radical shifts in its meaning than on what Quentin Skinner (1980: 566) calls its "specific moral light," or what we might term the specific *political* lights and allegiances the concept was enlisted to defend. In the turbulent politics of early modern Britain, "patriot" assumed an appraisive and an "existentially contested" character. It was appropriated as a political attribute by Whig and Tory alike but, more importantly, the conception was a part of two larger, competing perspectives on political reality. At stake, then, in the Whig and Tory debates, was not only the "right" to the title "patriot" but the legitimacy of one political vision, governmental program, and party over another. This contest for legitimacy was played out in the language of patriotism.

Thus in 1681, the poet John Dryden, an arch-Tory, discredited the parliamentarians' use of the term and seemed to reject it (at least in its new guise) altogether: "Gull'd with a Patriot's name, whose Modern sense / Is one that wou'd by Law supplant his Prince." But in 1699 he sought to reclaim it: "A patriot both the King and Country serves / Prerogative and privilege preserves" (*Oxford English Dictionary*). Dryden's poetic attempt at conceptual recovery was followed by Alexander Pope's in 1716: "An honest Courtier yet a Patriot too / Just to his Prince and his Country true"; although his comment "A patriot is a fool in ev'ry age" is perhaps better known (*Oxford English Dictionary*).

The poets and essayists were not the sole reliquaries of Tory patriotism, however. Perhaps the most determined theoretical effort to wrest the word from Whig control was Bolingbroke's pamphlet of 1738, *The Idea of a Patriot King* (1917b). Bolingbroke imagined a monarch who would "respect great principles," "lift no

[11] For a helpful though apolitical treatment of the deluge of patriotic poetry in early-eighteenth-century England, see Bonamy Dobrée (1978). For the poets, patriotism had to do with love of the country as a natural environment.

party" nor "list himself in any." The patriot king would avoid factions and rest his authority on "the spirit and the strength of the nation" (1917b: 53, 51). Like the Whigs, Bolingbroke fixed the "spirit of the nation" in the English constitution, and *The Idea of a Patriot King* had its impact.[12] In the middle of the eighteenth century at least, "patriot" was an appraisive term in both the Tory and Whig lexicon. Bolingbroke used it with great skill against Walpole, and the Tory Samuel Johnson defined it in the 1755 edition of his *Dictionary* as "one who maintains and defends his country's freedom and rights," while at the same time noting its use "ironically for a factious disturber of the government."[13] At least until the latter half of the nineteenth century, then, the term "patriot" retained a clear meaning and a favorable evaluation. Whigs and Tories might have disagreed as to whether one or the other truly *was* a patriot or not, but the association of the concept with the past, the defense of constitutional liberties, and the fight against corruption was not in dispute.

Not surprisingly, much the same set of usages attended the word "patriotism," an extension of "patriot" that came on the scene of English politics along with a host of other "-isms" in the eighteenth century. Although he did not coin the term, Bolingbroke wrote a series of letters in 1736–8 "on the spirit of patriotism" in which he invoked Cato and "the true principles of liberty" (Bolingbroke 1917a).[14] Shortly thereafter, in 1750, Bishop Berkeley published his "Maxims Concerning Patriotism," intended to disassociate the "fop," the "epicure," and the "factious man" from the "patriot" (1953). Yet the Tories' attempt to legitimize their position and

[12] The specifics of Bolingbroke's program (never accomplished) included: independent parliaments, frequent elections, no placemen, non-party government, and a militia instead of a standing army. As Betty Kemp (1966: 40) notes: "under the patriot program 'the modern party system' could not have developed, in so far as its pre-requisites were placemen and patronage." The Whigs, for all their patriot rhetoric, had no theorist comparable or superior to Bolingbroke writing on the meaning of "patriot." Their pre-eminent theoretical voice, Locke, made no reference to patriots or patriotism in the *Second Treatise*, an especially surprising omission, since Locke was a compatriot of Algernon Sidney and sympathetic to the cause for which Sidney was martyred and enshrined as a "patriot hero."

[13] There is a substantial literature on Bolingbroke's opposition to Walpole's administration, and much of it concerns the ideological implications of his professions of patriotism. The debates (at least implicitly) raise a conceptual issue concerning the status of "patriotism" (was it a commonplace slogan, or did it represent a specific set of political ideas and principles? or was it both?) that has relevance for any historical interpretation of Bolingbroke's opposition to Walpole. See, especially, Quentin Skinner (1974).

[14] The *Oxford English Dictionary* cites the first usage of "patriotism" as Bailey's definition (1726): "the acting like a Father to his country."

secure their political goals by appealing to "patriotism" seems to have diminished in the last quarter of the century. It was almost as if they conceded the Whigs' hegemony of "patriot" rhetoric and then sought to turn a hitherto commendatory term into a condemnatory one. Contrary to the maxims of the good Bishop, patriotism became the stock-in-trade of factious men. The reasons for this shift in rhetoric are not entirely clear (nor is the rhetoric itself entirely consistent), but perhaps the Tories' turn can be better assessed if we shift our historical gaze from British party politics toward America. For across the Atlantic, "'patriot" and "patriotism" were taking on more radical connotations and acquiring more revolutionary force than anything in the standard fare of Whig and Tory discourse in England.

IV

Although the English colonists called themselves "Americans," referred to their country as "America," and exhibited, in prose and verse, a genuine love of the land long before the War of Independence, the concepts of "patriot" and "patriotism" did not come alive until the "Great Awakening" of the 1760s and 1770s. Only with the stirring of the movement for independence did the language of "patriotism" emerge in American life: the reality of a new land, the development of a distinct collective identity, and, most decisively, a growing perception of a "conspiracy against liberty," fuelled by the revolutionary literature of the period, set the stage for the radicalization of "patriotism." At first the term was associated with the defense of liberty and property against tyrant kings and corrupt ministers, a legacy the colonists drew from the Whig symbolism of Hampden and Sidney. Hence, in 1770 John Adams declared: "If oppression is warranted by law, the Patriot is much more likely to fall victim than the pimp or the pander. Hampdens will stain the scaffold with blood" (Karsten 1978: 48). In the same year, Benjamin Franklin and James Burgh compared the resistance of the colonist to taxation without representation to "the conduct of the brave Hampden" (ibid.). American essayists and pamphleteers who increasingly opposed the crown venerated Sidney as "our patriot" and hailed him as a "martyr to liberty" (Karsten 1978: 42–6). But the appeal to "patriotism" did not end with references to the memory of the British "twins" and their fight against corrupt kings. Soon "patriotism" stood for opposition to any sort of king, especially an English one. By 1775, "patriot" rhetoric was enlisted in defiance of

British authority in its entirety – king, parliament, England itself were declared corrupt, fallen from liberty, and no longer deserving of allegiance. Essays, pamphlets, newspapers, broadsides, songs, and poems took up the cause of revolution against the crown, and their authors either appropriated the name "patriot" for themselves or became known as supporters of the "patriot cause." So Sam Adams wrote of those who would fight for independence: "All are not dead, and where there is a spark of patriotik fire, *we* will enkindle it" (Davidson 1941:5). No wonder that, back in Britain, Samuel Johnson declared patriotism "the last refuge of a scoundrel."

The term "patriot" and "patriotism" did not simply reflect a set of emerging political developments. The concepts themselves enkindled the political movement and fired the imaginations of the participants. The language of patriotism served at least two political purposes in America: first, it established the boundaries of revolutionary political practice in a far more decisive manner than in eighteenth-century England. None of the ambiguity that enveloped the use of the word in Whig and Tory discourse arose in the colonies. By 1776, the American revolutionary alone was a "patriot"; all others were "loyalists," defenders of the mother-country and the English constitution.[15] Secondly, the concepts of "patriot" and "patriotism" were clearly affixed to a particular set of ideological, constitutional, and political principles: a free republic, love of liberty, sanctity of property, limited government, and the foundation of a new body politic, and to a distinctively *political*, public spirit that evolved from the experience of a shared struggle and self-sacrifice for a common cause. It was precisely this political spirit, and not simply a romantic attachment to country, that Washington alluded to in his Farewell Address, which was, in essence, a meditation on patriotism. In short, if in eighteenth-century England the language of patriotism had become the hard currency of party rhetoric, then in America (for a time, at least) "patriotism" was the vital consciousness of a revolutionary movement, the generative force of a new people and, as Tocqueville later wrote, a "reflective" spirit of self-government.

V

As we turn to the nineteenth century, we find that from 1790 until 1850 the language of patriotism in England was primarily appropriated

[15] The "loyalists" themselves called the American revolutionaries "rebels," but with rare exceptions, like Chalmers's response to Paine, *Plain Truth*, they laid no claim to the title "patriot."

not by Tories or Whigs but by Chartists, Dissenters, trade-unionists, and Anti-Corn Law Leaguers who defended "the rights of Englishmen" against a new set of social and economic conditions. They condemned the slavery of factory labor, pressed the rights of workers, the poor, and the unemployed, and warned against the encroachments of state power. More importantly, they viewed themselves, initially at least, not as Chartists or Dissenters, socialists or trade-unionists, but as "patriots" defending a familiar set of patriot concerns – liberty, property, and constitutional rights – only in an environment exceedingly different from that of their seventeenth-century counterparts and even of their American compatriots, from whom they drew inspiration. The "patriot cause" now involved opposition to the increasingly centralized state and the growing capitalist economic order. The patriots' call was for reform.[16]

Thus at the turn of the century, patriotic clubs were formed, *Patriot* newspapers appeared, and songs proclaimed the patriotism of the radical reformers. In 1843, the Chartist Henry Vincent lectured at Leeds and called for the awakening of "the patriotic feelings of every English heart" (Karsten 1978: 127). In 1853, the funeral of Ben Rushton was a major public event. The Chartist was eulogized as a "noble patriot" whose life had been spent in opposition to the power of the English church and state. All of this led the Tory Richard Oastler to coin a new definition: "He will be the greatest patriot who can produce the greatest dissatisfaction" (Cunningham 1982).

Of course it would be mistaken to assume that during this brief period of English radicalism and opposition to government the claim to "patriotism" was not heard in any other quarter. Radical patriotism was neither unopposed nor completely dominant during these years, but it did mark a moment, soon to be lost, when "patriotism" was firmly anti-statist, *internationalist* in its leanings, and on the side of one of the largest social movements in modern history. The "patriot" stood for political equality and social justice in national life. What Karl Polanyi says of England after the decline of Chartism – that "[it] had become poorer by that substance out of which the Ango-Saxon ideal of a free society could have been built

[16] Prominent in the early Chartist movement was an identification with historical "patriots" elsewhere – including the American revolutionaries and the French *patriote* party of 1789. Many of those who called themselves patriots and argued that England had forfeited political liberty cited *La Patriote Françoise* as their model, following the French revolutionaries' own use of the term.

up for centuries to come" – could equally be said of the concept of patriotism (Polanyi 1944: 167).[17]

By the late nineteenth century, a transformation of political and economic forces and the related rise of more potent "statist" symbols significantly diminished the meaning of patriotism in the special sense of constitutional reform and (in its Chartist manifestation) economic egalitarianism. As patriot rhetoric became increasingly assimilated into the emerging vocabulary of "state" and "nation," and its central idea underwent a transference to the national, party, and racial doctrines of the modern age, it lost its earlier, critical sting. Indeed, it seems that at a certain moment in history, patriotism ceased to be the springboard for opposition to a government's program or policies in the name of constitutional principles, and became instead the basis for uncritical support of the "my country right or wrong" variety.[18] At the root of this decisive shift in the meaning of patriotism is a phenomenon John Dunn (1979: 55) has called "the starkest political shame of the twentieth century," and John Schaar, "patriotism's bloody brother" (1981: 285). The phenomenon is "nationalism" and though its own distinctive history cannot be fully traced here, we must say something about it, for nationalism weighs heavily upon the meaning of patriotism in our age.

Nationalism did not become a part of our political discourse until the middle of the nineteenth century. As Ernest Gellner notes, "nationalism owes its plausibility and compelling nature only to a very special set of circumstances, which do indeed obtain now, but which were alien to most of humanity and history" (1983: 125). The material pre-conditions Gellner has in mind – the rise of the state, the growing power of national institutions, a developing world-market and centralized economies, imperialist expansionism, and new forms of social organization based on deeply internalized, education-dependent, high culture – all served to foster what might be loosely called "secular religions" of national identity. A collective spirit rooted in a sense of national supremacy and "ersatz greatness" (as Simone Weil once put it) reinforced the idea of the nation as the

[17] Karsten (1978: 133) also notes that with the passing of Chartism "neither Hampden nor Sidney served again as champions of the people."

[18] The *Oxford English Dictionary* cites *Fraser's Magazine* (1844) with the earliest usage (a condemnatory one): "nationalism is another word for egotism." (The full reference to the quotation is: "Our country! In her intercourse with foreign nations may she always be right, but our country right or wrong," by Stephen Decatur in 1816.)

ultimate object of political loyalty, and of the state as the embodiment of the nation. This nationally predicated political sentiment was invigorated by mass education, in which the mystification of the nation's past played a significant role. Doctrines of particular political parties served to reinforce national loyalty as well, and to associate it with certain ideological (but rarely constitutional) principles. And, most ominously, warfare, "the great motor of nationalist expansion," used nationalist fervor as its generating force.[19]

The pervasiveness of these social and political conditions, which in fact prevail in the modern world and nowhere else, have had profound implications for our current understanding of patriotism. The transference of nationalistic sentiments into the language of patriotism is readily apparent in the contemporary discourse of politicians, presidents, and public relations experts, not to mention the ordinary language of the citizen.[20] Quite clearly, the older idea of the patriot as one who defends constitutional rights, reveres liberty, agitates for an end to corruption, and struggles against the outrages of centralized power, has been thoroughly eroded. What Tocqueville called "reflective patriotism" and characterized as self-government and the exercise of political rights seems no longer to be remembered as a virtue – if it is remembered at all. Likewise, the republican values that fired the insurgent imaginations of such diverse patriots as Algernon Sidney, Sam Adams, Tom Paine, or Ben Rushton have been largely drowned out in the shrill rhetoric of modern "patriotism." Indeed, patriotism itself has become more of an expression than a practice, but if at all a practice, surely not one informed by a reverence for public liberty or a skepticism toward the state, much less a proclivity for Adams's "enkindling" of revolutionary sentiments.

[19] The phrase is John Dunn's (1979: 67). Equally cogent comments on the relationship between the state, the nation, war, and nationalist consciousness in the twentieth century can be found in Randolph Bourne (1977).

[20] It seems, however, that the word has been officially obliterated from the vocabulary of social science. *The Encyclopedia of Social Sciences* makes no mention of it. Nor does Raymond Williams include it in *Keywords* (1983), though "nationalism" merits an entry. Even when "patriotism" is not obliterated, however, as in *The Blackwell Encyclopaedia of Political Thought* (Miller 1987), its political meaning is forgotten. The entry notes that patriotism "has often been confused with nationalism but it is a far older idea, and carries with it less theoretical baggage," and (even more dubiously), "Patriotism is really a sentiment rather than a political idea, but one that can be pressed into service by needs of many different sorts, most notably in times of war" (p. 369). Contrary to this view, I have argued that patriotism has long been a political idea, and that its "service" as a concept to various creeds is not an accidental, but an integral part of its public, political meaning. It is instructive – albeit disturbing – that even political theorists overlook this conceptual point.

The moral light of patriotism, along with its meaning, has been cast in drastically different hues: in terms of a sense of duty and service to the state, the uncritical support of government programs and policies, and the veneration of the nation as an absolute value. Without question, "patriotism" and "patriot" are still compelling parts of political rhetoric, but one need only consider their current usage and range of reference to understand how the "rhetoric of state" has absorbed them, and how far removed they are from their eighteenth-century roots in the radical defense of liberty, constitutional rights, reform, and revolution.

Ernest Gellner would assess this condition by having us think of nationalism as "a very distinctive species of patriotism" (1983: 138). But I believe this suggestion stands in danger of collapsing two historically rooted forms of political practice whose differences we ignore at our own peril. The blurring of patriotism into nationalism, or even the acknowledgement of nationalism as a "species" of patriotism, reveals that we have literally lost touch with history, with a very real past in which real patriots held to a particular set of political principles and their associated practices – to a conception of citizenship that bears scant resemblance to modern nationalism.

To put this another way, patriotism as a particular "way-of-being" in the world – as an active, and often radically participatory form of citizenship rooted in a concern for the good of one's own country – is nearly lost to us, and the damages that result from this failure of memory are not negligible. In this respect, maintaining a distinction between patriotism and nationalism is more than just an exercise in semantics or arid conceptual analysis. For the more patriotism's past recedes from our collective political imaginations the less are we able to "think what we are doing" – to evaluate the sort of citizens and "patriots" we are in the present and to assess the examples we set for the future. In fact, without some awareness of the attitudes and practices that constituted patriotism before the rise of the centralized nation-state, we are unlikely to appreciate the extent to which our contemporary patriotic discourse and practices are historically contingent (and in many ways demoralized) phenomena, not inherent attributes of humanity or universal necessities beyond reproach. Our failure to appreciate such things and thereby engage in the critical reappraisal of our own patriotic presuppositions and nationalist presumptions is nothing short of a failure of citizenship. That is why remembering patriotism's past can itself be understood as a patriotic act – as an attempt to revivify and perhaps restore a more virtuous understanding of the relation between self and country than our current conception allows and our current practices reflect.

Exactly how the practice of patriotism might be reconceptualized or reconstructed is a subject fit for the future labors of political theorists who are concerned with questions of civic virtue, loyalty, dissent, citizenship, obedience, liberty, and the manifold complexities associated with "love of country."[21] And while this brief conceptual history provides no final answers, it does serve to remind us that, at its root, the "problem of patriotism" is not simply a rhetorical or an analytical matter, but a historical reality, in need of our remembrance.

[21] Some political theorists (although not many) have taken up this issue with varying verdicts on whether or not "patriotism" can be revitalized. For a rare and particularly intriguing treatment of patriotism and the case of France in the 1940s, see Simone Weil (1952). Also see Schaar (1981), MacIntyre (1981), Janowitz (1983), and Anderson (1983).

REFERENCES

Anderson, Benedict. 1983. *Imagined Communities*. Thetford: Thetford Press.

Arendt, Hannah. 1958. *The Human Condition*. Chicago: University of Chicago Press.

Aristotle. 1958. *Politics*, edited by Ernest Barker. Oxford: Oxford University Press.

Augustine of Hippo, St. 1960. *Confessions*, edited by J. Ryan. New York: Doubleday.

Berkeley, Bishop George. 1953 [1750]. "Maxims Concerning Patriotism." In A.A. Luce and J.E. Jessop (eds.), *The Works of George Berkeley*, vol. VI. London: T. Nelson and Sons, pp. 251–5.

Bolingbroke, Viscount Henry St. John. 1917a [1736]. *Letters on the Spirit of Patriotism*, Oxford: Clarendon.

1917b [1738]. *The Idea of a Patriot King*, edited by S. Jackman. Indianapolis and New York: Bobbs-Merrill.

Bourne, Randolph. 1977. *The Radical Will: Selected Writings 1911–1918*, edited by O. Hansen. New York: Urizen Books.

Cunningham, Hugh. 1982. "Will the Real John Bull Stand up, Please?" *Times Literary Supplement* 19 (February 19).

Davidson, Philip. 1941. *Propaganda and the American Revolution 1763–1783*. Chapel Hill, NC: University of North Carolina Press.

Dobrée, Bonamy. 1978. "The Theme of Patriotism in the Poetry of the Early Eighteenth Century." *Proceedings of the British Academy* 25: 49–65.

Dunn, John. 1979. *Western Political Theory in the Face of the Future*. Cambridge: Cambridge University Press.

Finley, M.I. 1984. *Politics in the Ancient World*. Cambridge: Cambridge University Press.

Gellner, Ernest. 1983. *Nations and Nationalism*. Ithaca, NY: Cornell University Press.

Janowitz, Morris. 1983. *The Reconstruction of Patriotism*. Chicago: University of Chicago Press.

Kantorowicz, Ernest. 1951. "*Pro Patria Mori* in Medieval Political Thought." *American Historical Review* 56: 472–92.

1957. *The King's Two Bodies: A Study in Medieval Political Theory*. Princeton, NJ: Princeton University Press.

Karsten, Peter. 1978. *Patriot–Heroes in England and America*. Madison, WI: University of Wisconsin Press.

Kemp, Betty. 1966. "Patriotism, Pledges, and the People." In M. Gilbert (ed.), *A Century of Conflict*. London: Hamish Hamilton, pp. 37–46.

Koht, Thomas. 1946–7. "The Dawn of Nationalism in Europe." *American Historical Review* 52: 265–80.

MacIntyre, Alasdair. 1981. *After Virtue*. Notre Dame, IN: University of Notre Dame Press.

Miller, David (ed.). 1987. *The Blackwell Encyclopaedia of Political Thought*. Oxford: Blackwell.

Polanyi, Karl. 1944. *The Great Transformation*. Boston, MA: Beacon Press.

Post, G. 1953. "Two Notes on Nationalism in the Middle Ages." *Traditio* 9: 281–320.

Schaar, John. 1981. *Legitimacy in the Modern State*. Brunswick, NJ: Transaction Press.

Skinner, Quentin. 1974. "The Principles and Practice of Opposition: the Case of Bolingbroke versus Walpole." In Neil McKendrick (ed.), *Historical Perspectives: Studies in English Thought and Society in Honour of J.H. Plumb*. London: Europa Publications, pp. 93–128.

1980. "Language and Social Change." In L. Michaels and C. Ricks (eds.), *The State of the Language*. Berkeley, CA: University of California Press, pp. 562–78.

Washington, George. 1948 [1796]. "Farewell Address," In S. Commins (ed.), *Basic Writings of George Washington*. New York: Random House, pp. 627–43.

Weil, Simone. 1952. *The Need for Roots*. Boston, MA: Beacon Press.

Williams, Raymond. 1983. *Keywords: A Vocabulary of Culture and Society*, revised and expanded edition. London: Fontana.

Wolin, Sheldon. 1960. *Politics and Vision*. Boston, MA: Little, Brown.

9

Public interest

J. A. W. GUNN

The concept of the "public interest" first gained sustained academic attention in the late 1950s. At that time it was commonly singled out as one of those political expressions whose demise would unclutter the mass of unresolved meanings that bedevil our language. We have now, no doubt, passed through the worst of the obsession with scouring political words in order to render them operational and so the danger of discarding "public interest" because people used it in different senses is more likely now to seem quaint rather than threatening. Philosophy and intellectual history have both, in their different ways, contributed to an appreciation that one of the uses of the language of politics is to bring different concerns and emphases together in a single "contested" concept. Or, to do justice to the work of intellectual historians, we now have reason to expect that even concepts that appear to have existed time out of mind will partake of the various specific circumstances in which they have been used and will thus be more complex entities than a specious continuity of usage would suggest.

But whatever lessons have been learned at a general level still need detailed application to the individual concepts that constitute political discourse. For though we may now be better informed about possible unsubtleties in treating political terms, we still know too little about what people were saying when they wrote of the "public interest." By neglecting the concept's history, modern enquiry has made the task of understanding more difficult. For the notion of public interest is burdened with certain connotations and turns of phrase the meaning of which has been established by past usage. Since traditional formulae for discussing the relation of partial interests to those of the community still set the terms of modern debate, we would do well to consult that history.

Recent as is its prominence in academic circles, the notion of "public interest" and its equivalents were known to the world from a very early time. Not surprisingly, the law of ancient Rome possessed a vocabulary for referring to matters of concern to the whole community as opposed to those that affected particular persons only, though surviving formulations suggest, with varying emphasis, some connection between the two conditions (Steinwenter 1939; Gaudemet 1951). Medieval political language maintained and elaborated such distinctions. What serves to distinguish the early-modern period from earlier ones is that it was only with the rise of individualism that the full resources of the concept came to be explored through the process of political controversy. English law thus knew of a relevant formulation in the dictum that some matters – especially those involving the government's power of eminent domain – were "affected with a public interest." In such cases, private property rights were deemed to give way before the claims of the community. The same consideration figured in treatises on law and morals without seeming to occasion much comment. But not until events led controversialists to draw upon such understandings did the concept of the public interest become a contested one and so a significant weapon in political argument.

First in Britain and then later in France a perspective on the public interest that came from below challenged the pretensions of autocratic government. It was thus the middle-class revolutions of the seventeenth and eighteenth centuries that served as the heroic age of public interest and these centuries provide the setting for much of the present account. It is not that the public interest then fell into disuse, for modern governments still expropriate and still use the old rationale. Nor are we unaware of that hardy resort of the hard-pressed politician, that certain disclosures would not be in the public interest. But this is not the stuff of significant history. Public interest reached the forefront of political debate only in the era where the relation of the community to the concerns of individuals and groups was undergoing those changes that we now associate with the onset of political liberalism and economic individualism. The process continued, of course, through the nineteenth century but the issue of public interest played only a modest part in that age's great systems of social theory. Finally, abstracted from the circumstances that had given it life, the concept came to inform the discourse of twentieth-century political science.

In the world of affairs, talk of "public interest" still figures, for instance, in public policy regulating telephone rates or restrictive trade practices; it has, however, receded from its earlier prominence in the language of controversy. Our ongoing revision of (or autopsy on) liberalism has given rise to thoughts on the nature and benefits of community (see Unger 1975; Taylor 1985) that may yet return debate about public interest to its erstwhile centrality. For the present, though, the early-modern period, chiefly in Britain and France, must supply the bulk of evidence about the use of the concept.

Any such double-barreled political concept offers, in its conjunction of adjective and noun, twin challenges to analysis. The first is the uncertainty that has resided in "interest" at least since the introduction of this French word into English political vocabulary around 1640. To have an interest – be it of an individual person, a class or group or state – may either suggest that its possessor subjectively feels a concern, and may thus actively promote it, or it may convey the claim of some observer that the welfare of the party addressed is objectively affected by certain factors whether or not the situation has prompted any felt need. Applied to individuals, the notion of "interest" invites the philosopher's question as to whether we should comply with the request of our suddenly mad friend to return his chain saw. Class interest, even more complex than that of individuals – if only from the difficulty of first identifying the unit that allegedly bears the interest – has led us to the knotty problems of true and false consciousness.

But, originally at least, the interest of the community entailed no such pitfalls. The interest of states was the business of statesmen and French treatises on statecraft made clear that only they were politically competent. To be enjoyable, perhaps, by all, the public interest implied no mental state on the part of the bulk of an early-modern populace. It belonged to the province of reason, specifically the reason of state, a form of wisdom embodied in maxims and founded upon restricted information, that would at least preserve the community against major disasters. Even outside the realm of high politics it held sway, as evidenced by those documents from the reign of Charles I that condemned enclosures in the name of national welfare, despite the telling admission that such enclosures would, in fact, satisfy all of those who were in a position to articulate views (Gunn 1969: 217). In that judgment we find compressed the essence of traditional paternalism – its good as well as its bad side. Public interest was a claim that belonged largely to non-participant, if not absolute, governments and its objective dimension was emphasized.

The time of the Puritan Revolution, more than any other, brought to the fore the radical potential of the political word "interest." Initially men challenged a serenely absolutist view of policy-making with the mild assertion that, even though the bulk of the people might be undiscerning about national priorities, they could still feel the weight of their burdens. Common folk could not see, but they could feel, as a dictum of the 1640s had it. Soon, however, this concession to the *arcana imperii* was withdrawn and one finds the republican, James Harrington, specifically appealing to that suffrage view of truth that is sometimes credited to Locke. The people could indeed "see" and whether one wished to identify physical objects of sensation or elements of national policy, the majority's vision was the surest guide. One passage from his pamphlet *Politicaster* would be echoed, albeit unconsciously, for centuries:

> if a man know not what is his own interest, who should know it? And that which is the interest of the most particular men, the same being summed up in the common vote, is the public interest.

Whatever his faults, one cannot complain that Harrington failed to provide an operational definition of the public interest. As Algernon Sidney said late in the seventeenth century, men could be enjoined to care for the public only by having a part in it.

Republican formulations of public interest embodied a number of discrete claims, all of which sometimes appeared in less revolutionary guise. Most importantly, the case for rooting national objectives in the concerns of the people struck a blow at ancient doctrines on the nature of social duty. The superiority of the common good over private advantage had long been a favorite theme throughout Christendom for homilies on the need for virtue and self-abnegation. A corrective to such austerity was to question the truth of that psychological premise that assumed the possibility of taking no thought of one's self. The sophisticated defense of self-regard found an ample foundation in Hobbes's materialism and flourished through the efforts of a host of literary figures towards the close of the *grand siècle*. So there were philosophical grounds for arguing that man might be so constituted that he could not know any other concern with that certainty and intensity with which he experienced the demands of his own nature. Confined by his sense organs, man might then necessarily respond to his own pleasures and pains, for perhaps he could do no other. But however powerful the arguments of the philosophical high road to self-interest, they were not needed by the rank and file of seventeenth-century pamphleteers who contented themselves often with the simple observation that it was simply reasonable that private persons should be able to seek their own benefit. Indeed, the Hobbesian doctrine of an ineradicable self-interest was apt to prove awkward for purposes of public discourse, for it sloughed over the appealing distinction between ordinary selfishness and a legitimate quest for defensible goals, often perceived not just as interests but also as "rights." Hobbes's focus on the sovereign and his interest also had more in common with French thought of the time than English. The Hobbesian argument did not, of course, disappear and came to serve the cause of emerging social science in the form of the maxim that "interest will not lie" (Gunn 1968a). It was even more conspicuous, but less useful, in the brittle philosophy – ably criticized by Bishop Butler in his sermons preached in the Rolls Chapel (*c.* 1720) – that falsely equated "interest" with all human intentions.

The task of sustaining a new vision of public affairs needed less offensive materials and these were readily discovered in the adjective "public." Central to the new individualism was thus the notion that in reality a community was but an aggregate of particular persons. This inspiration owed something to medieval nominalism, but it had been suggested as well by certain renderings of the Roman *utilitas publica*. Francisco Suarez had preserved a stronger medieval version of the claim when he wrote of two forms of public good – that which addressed the general welfare of the state and that which took the form of "bonum commune mediante privato," or a common good founded upon the welfare of individuals. The distinction, appearing in Suarez's *De legibus* (1613), was an innocent explanation of a received distinction about two different sorts of laws and was not, it seems, associated with Jesuitical schemes of popular sovereignty. Nevertheless, the idea contained the means of reversing the traditional way of perceiving social wholes. If it were true that the community were reducible to its constituent parts, then the priority of the common good ceased to pose a barrier to at least some private ambitions.

The poet, George Wither, made the point effectively and without theoretical flourish when he observed that a commonwealth could not prosper when the members were, one by one, destroyed (Gunn 1975: 111). No plea for a clever libertinism, this was but a sober requirement that complaint should yield reform. Such pleas were in no way dependent upon emphasizing either man's anti-social propensities or the falsity of claims for the pre-eminence of a common good. Writers of Hobbesian inspiration thought, at times, of an atomized community, as might advocates of an extreme economic individualism. By contrast, the advocates of a popularly-based public interest were quite content to rely upon the light of nature, and the rights of self-preservation. When Wither identified the common good as a "compound being" or Marchamont Needham wrote of "that apprehension which every particular man hath of his own immediate share in the public interest," they were presenting their cause as a righteous one quite consistent with the requirements of community. The traditional realm, a thing of organic structure, with a real presence and a will that was independent of its subjects, was turning into the "public" – a collection of imminent wills and consciences. The change was a subtle one, however, and seventeenth-century individualism remained grounded in familiar beliefs.

In order to appreciate the point of individualism in the revolutionary period, one must examine the substance of complaints and thereby create a better understanding of the limits of the case being made. A continuing source of ambiguity is that it is one thing to argue that the public interest was reducible to the interests of individuals and quite another to say that therefore any particular interest was necessarily compatible with that of the community. Fortunately, we possess a mass of evidence demonstrating that no such extreme conclusion was usually inferred. The merest glance at seventeenth-century popular sentiments will make clear that political argument was directed at the promotion – and often merely the preservation – of recognized rights. Chief among these was the right to property in the ample seventeenth-century sense. In keeping with the general parliamentary case, private citizens were encouraged to argue that it was government that tended to usurp prerogatives and that their demands for consideration were but applications of well-known principles.

The ancient appeal to *salus populi* thus played a major role in fitting out a popular program, especially early in the 1640s; later one more often heard the frank avowal that to unsettle private men's estates and expectations or to render the populace poor could not be an intelligible rendering of public good. Nothing in this case challenged the primacy of the community. Instead, proponents of private concerns aligned themselves with the supposed interests of the great mass of the people. Far from discarding the familiar injunctions to prefer the common good, they tried to bring themselves within its terms. This was the more readily done by the explicit recognition that the crucial factor in rendering rights secure was that the security be made universal. In an era of negative rights, it made sense to perceive private claims as non-competitive and thus each person might be seen as enjoying protection against official tyranny by virtue of his neighbor's similar immunity.

Naturally, it helped if one could supply examples of a view of public interest that fitted less well with community needs. The desideratum was present in the Continental notion of "reason of state" – a fairly recent import, since the very word "state" seems to have found its way into English political language only in the sixteeenth century. Bacon, with his notion of judicial "lions under the throne," the earl of Strafford, and Archbishop Laud were associated with that view of policy, but it found few articulate friends in English public life after 1641 and was to suffer further discredit with the Glorious Revolution (Moore 1906, chap. 1). Harrington did try to adapt reason of state to republican government, but most writers chose rather to abandon such courtly words in favor of the domestic concerns of private citizens. Military power, dynastic ambition, and the more mercantilistic understandings of the purposes of national wealth were the casualties in this process. By emphasizing the few beneficiaries of such criteria, proponents of the more popular view might better accentuate the measure in which their cause was genuinely social, and not dismissable as special pleading for selfish interests. With the Restoration, certain traditional arguments were revived, but talk of reason of state remained rare.

Though the fashionable word "interest" encouraged all sorts of anti-social possibilities, most debate in the seventeenth century was focused upon defining an interest more genuinely "public" than that which had obtained hitherto. Exceptions occasionally appeared in economic argument where enthusiastic advocates of free trade sometimes alleged that if a particular merchant profited, the commonwealth of which he was a part necessarily gained. But in political argument this was rare and the efforts to found public interest upon the concerns of the populace was more firmly based in logic. So appealing did it become, in fact, that a sermon of January 30, 1716, interpreted the martyrdom of Charles I as private rights overridden by unsound appeals to public good. This took argument from rights absurdly far, but the principle was familiar:

> it being something hard to conceive, how the Public can be happy . . . when the particular Members whereof it consists, are not secure in their Rights and Properties. "R.S." 1716: 9

While the British tradition had been adjusting its vocabulary in the direction of liberalism, French practice had been to refine that court idiom so decisively rejected in England. It would seem, moreover, that the era of Richelieu saw a conscious redirection of categories, away from the threadbare moralizing – and recognized hypocrisy – involved in asserting the superiority of a common good. Though the pious language of preferring the common good certainly did not disappear, it was supplanted in political writings by the interest of the prince and of the state (Keohane 1980: 154–5, 182). The new technical vocabulary – consciously distanced from the language of social duty – may have allowed for a greater frankness in political discussion, but it cannot have assisted in the major task of reconciling subjects to sovereigns. In fact, the lack of humanitarian impulse in the tradition of "reason of state" would appear to account for the major thrust in French thought about the public interest prior to the Revolution. Early in the eighteenth century the busy earnestness of the Abbé de Saint-Pierre had seen the need of making private men content with their private concerns and so the more available to unite in a public one. Whether or not this fusing of interests was possible became a topic of debate between the *philosophes* and their opponents.

The school of the Physiocrats took up the banner of a national good conceived in terms hostile to traditional reason of state. Theirs was a curious case, if only because they lacked any hostility to the royal court and wished only to teach the king – and then all others – the truth that the public interest did not lie in martial exploits, glory or even in commerce, but in their economic program. This teaching was tendentious, no doubt, but in the physiocratic insistence that the right of property served to connect the interests of all persons and in the allied assumption that, in other respects, the different interests of individuals would check each other, they had a formula comparable to that developed in England in the previous century. Turgot wrote, in 1753, of a public interest that was "la somme des intérêts particuliers" (Turgot 1966, vol. II: 680) – and Mercier de la Rivière echoed the theme. So the language of a sum of interests gained new life in public debate.[1]

French argument was not limited to rehearsing the substance of English ideas of the previous century, for the physiocratic position was an odd blend of economic individualism and political authori-

[1] The aggregative formula appeared in certain French works as early as the 1740s.

tarianism. Nor was hostility to its rather tendentious form of individualism confined to spokesmen for the status quo. One critic was Rousseau, who denied that public good or ill was but a sum of particular portions as in a "simple aggregation" (Rousseau 1964, vol. III: 284). A riposte to Rousseau's position had already come from a churchman, not noted for his radicalism, who regretted that modern republicans were excessively committed to an ideal of Spartan virtue that left too small a place for healthy self-regard (Bonnaire 1758, vol. III: 547–51). It is also true that claims for social discipline and submission to royal authority retained a remarkably forbidding form, so much so that even neutral and seemingly innocuous use of the expression "bien public" suggested to some a dangerous challenging of the king's exclusive authority (Griffet 1778, vol. II: 101).

The persistence of absolutist doctrine in a very stern version encouraged, in addition, degrees of dissent. Thus the Marquis de Chastellux took a utilitarian view of public good in combatting the traditional emphasis upon national power, still found in the works of Muratori and the Abbé Gros de Besplas (Muratori 1772: 260–1; Gros de Besplas 1768: xii, 8). For Chastellux the problem lay in an excessive attention to the growth and duration of empire, with administrators forgetting that the happiness of individual people and the prospering of government were not synonymous (Chastellux 1774, vol. II: 124). However, the republican zealot, Brissot de Warville, in turn chided Chastellux for still having too traditional an understanding of public good (Brissot de Warville 1786: 69). The claim that the general interest was, in effect, a sum of particular (and uniform) interests continued to be affirmed during the Revolution. We know, of course, that Benjamin Constant's liberalism consisted, in part, in a profound distrust of calls for sacrifice to the public good; he had seen too much of Robespierre's vision of unity. But it was the authoritarian position on the matter that became unfashionable, while Constant's views did not lack for company until the intellectual climate of the new century deprived old disputes of their meaning.

French political economy of the latter half of the eighteenth century was much more politicized than was the case in Britain, for in the *ancien régime* questions such as the grain trade provided opportunities, not otherwise available, to take stock of the society as a whole. The nature of a public interest was thus more prominent in such debates than in the well-known British equivalents. Adam Smith did indeed say, in the same passage as that in which he wrote of an invisible hand, that he had never known much good to be done by merchants who affected to trade for the public good. But this was not intended as the preliminary to a general statement of the priorities of British society. More technical than the French equivalent, British economic literature had not the same commitment to political comment. The point is of some importance in tracing usage, since it has often been assumed that any document recording *laissez-faire* proposals might serve equally to illustrate an individualistic rendering of the public good.

This is by no means true, as is attested by long-standing confusion about Bernard Mandeville's thoughts about the public and its welfare. Because the famous *Fable* presented the paradox that private self-indulgence was the foundation of public benefit, it has been too readily assumed that Mandeville identified the personal interests of individuals with that of the state. All that he said, however, was that some forms of so-called vice were productive of national greatness. His emphasis was on the causal connection between private activity and public welfare and not upon any individualistic criterion of that public welfare (Gunn 1975: 114). Indeed, Mandeville associated public good with the strength of national institutions, the flourishing of national honor and the aggrandizement of nations in terms measured by military strength and an already old-fashioned bullionism. At the same time he wrote, not of the prosperity or happiness of private citizens, but of the consequences of their carrying out their designs. Here public prosperity was often based on private ruin. British economic liberalism did not have to assail a court-centered conception of the public interest, for even as the basic writings of physiocracy were coming from the press, the case of *Entick* v. *Carrington* (1766) struck down the plea of state necessity in English law.

One factor encouraging misconceptions about views of the public interest was Elie Halévy's emphasis on a natural harmony of interests in economic life (Halévy 1955: 89). But this should not foster the belief that there was necessarily any important understanding of public interest in economic argument. If anything, the promptings of economic individualism discouraged talk about the public interest for, as Smith pointed out, merchants were not prone to think about it and did none the worse for that. The same sentiments exactly informed the writings of Smith's fellow economist, Sir James Steuart, when he said in 1767

> I expect . . . that every man is to act for his own interest in what regards the public; and, politically speaking, every one ought to do so. It is the

> combination of every private interest which forms the public good, and of this the public, that is, the statesman, only can judge.
>
> Steuart 1767, vol. I: 164

Steuart readily accepted, with Smith, the need for laws to command obedience on some matters and neither really subscribed to Halévy's natural harmony of interests. Both assumed some situations where serving the public good allowed private concerns to flourish and allowed that there would always be some private concerns incompatible with public good.

The categories of individualism remained prominent in nineteenth-century discourse, but some of the factors that had once served to render intelligible talk of a sum of interests were no longer available. Natural rights played no great role in British political vocabulary and the holism that characterized much of European thought afforded less friendly soil than had the setting of the eighteenth century. Nor was the language of class conducive to visualizing the convergence of individual ambitions on a single range of conditions, such as those perceived as securing private rights. True as well that the presence of legislatures, popularly elected, banished in large measure those images of arbitrary power that had made so attractive a public good rooted in the interests of ordinary people. Tensions between the parts and the social whole were expressed still, but with public debate increasingly a matter of challenging those very rights of property that had been the palladium of the original individualism, neither of the main traditions for discussing the public interest was readily available. There remained a place for "public interest" in the *laissez-faire* economics of J.R. McCulloch but he relied neither upon traditional elevation of a national interest hostile to particular interests nor upon a reduction of public good to an aggregate of lesser ones. Rather the economist cheerfully allowed that there was a place for government intervention in the name of public interests and also some potential that policies might "sacrifice the interests of community to those of a favoured few" (McCulloch 1849: 50). Herbert Spencer echoed pre-industrial struggles in writing of "the man versus the state" but the energy seems to have deserted the concept of public interest as the bearer of his brand of individualism. It is perhaps significant that the facile eighteenth-century position that reduced public interest to individual interests was well preserved in the arguments of Simon Gray, an English Physiocrat, loyal to the formula of the French school. Few other Englishmen can be found arguing the sanctity of private interests and the remoteness of official ones with that fervor typical of earlier times.

Even on the Continent, enthusiasm for redefining the public interest is most easily discovered early in the nineteenth century, as in the writings of Gaspar de Jovellanos (Jovellanos 1806; Polt 1971: 101–2). Liberal revulsion towards state necessity understandably arrived late in Spain. Bastiat, the fervent advocate of *laissez-faire*, did not, of course, publish his major work until 1850. However, his bland formula – to the effect that the good of each was favorable to the good of all and the good of all was equally favorable to that of each – avoided the difficult issues (Bastiat 1964: 84). It lacked only the twentieth-century reference to General Motors that graced an equivalent statement of the 1960s.

One strain that linked the centuries was utilitarianism and the thought of Jeremy Bentham provided the crucial documents. Bentham has always earned low marks for social insight by virtue of his notorious claim that the interest of the community was somehow an aggregate of the interests of its members. Placing Bentham in the history of thought about the public interest now allows us to view him, not as the advocate of an anti-social hedonism, but rather as a late representative of the cause of reducing national goals to fit the concerns of private citizens. In common with so many before him, Bentham relied heavily upon a supposed universal interest in the security of person and property as the means of knitting private and public good together. Like others, he condemned the courtier's conception of national advantage for its haughty irrelevance to the lives of ordinary folk. At the same time, Bentham was a systematic thinker who could not afford to misrepresent the nature of government and society in order to sustain a slogan. Thus his works attest to the fact that communities did indeed possess some interests irreducible to the concerns peculiar to identifiable persons. Bentham realized both that government had to address such matters and that the political process could, at best, improve the articulation of diverse concerns – of individuals and of organized groups. It could not smooth out all clashes of interest (see Gunn 1968b). For too many commentators, Bentham appears to stand as the isolated ideologue of an extreme social atomism. Only when firmly located in a tradition of political argument does his case regain that life and meaning that it had for others. Perhaps one would have managed better to get the hang of Bentham on the public interest were it not for the fact that the great assault on the bastions of the aristocratic state was indeed in its late stages when he wrote. Complementing this interpretation of Bentham's thought, but emphasizing a different issue, was James Mill's claim that people had both private, selfish interests and a "community interest."[2] Whatever confusion this consideration introduces into utilitarian psychology, it certainly speaks against the assumption that the school was incapable of making sense of the good of the community.

The other great landmark of nineteenth-century Anglo-Saxon liberalism is provided by the thought of John Stuart Mill and specifically a passage in his *Utilitarianism*. Here the old problem of the aggregative nature of the public good is framed by a signal instance of what seems to be the fallacy of composition. For Mill chose to discuss the principle of utility in terms of moving from a general desire for one's own happiness to an apparent desire for the general happiness. Modern commentators are now sometimes inclined to be indulgent about Mill's alleged howler, citing the probability that his version of the general happiness was weaker than one might suppose and so it might be viewed as no more than a simple aggregate of satisfactions (West 1982). This late exoneration indicates with what difficulty the individualism of which Mill was the heir has been understood, especially when the point was made, as by Mill, in a form that was independent of specific controversies. But examples of this mode of reasoning are legion in the record of political and economic thought. Nor did most contributors exercise the same care as Mill in setting out their philosophical assumptions.

Consider the following statement in 1786 by Matthew Robinson, later to become 2nd Baron Rokeby:

> Every individual desires necessarily his own welfare: The collective body of the people therefore seek of course the general good.
>
> Robinson 1786: 137

In the absence of a careful analysis of that general good itself, Rokeby's claim looks fallacious. His intent here was to provide cautious support for the responsibility of the *vox populi*. Had it been to defend a rendering of the public good, arguments were available to make the transition from a rational self-interest to that public good. Nor, if challenged, would Rokeby probably have disputed that there were dimensions of the public good that were but remotely related to individual interests or wholly incompatible with at least some of them.

The late nineteenth century saw a further development in the idea of public interest and one of the few that did not relate directly to the relation of individual interests to public good. European social

[2] This theme figures in Mill's common-place books, now being prepared for publication by Professor R.A. Fenn. I have employed Fenn's transcription.

theorists contemplated societies deeply divided by classes, beset by competing ideologies, and manipulated by elites, and proclaimed the falsity of the public interest. Though the claim was not new, it had usually surfaced as the skeptical evaluation of certain interests masquerading as the interest of the community. A German pamphlet of 1647 had made the point (cited in Kraus 1959: 237), as would Marx in *The German Ideology*. Neither source explicitly said, however, that "public interest" was always used in efforts to deceive. But in Mosca's "political formula" and in Pareto's "derivations," the public interest was no more than a fiction. This too was the message of Ludwig Gumplowicz as he surveyed European conflict, and his conclusion appears to have influenced A.F. Bentley's relegation of the concept to the realm of spooks. It was Bentley's position that eventually had such influence on political science with its pronounced disrespect for talk about the public interest. Gumplowicz's views about conflict are not very similar in tone to behavioral social science, but those two strains of thought were united at least in a tough-minded condemnation of political idealism. Neither position, it should be noted, was forced, by a profound awareness of the strength of particular interests, to reject the public interest as a concept. Bentley's contemporary, Albion Small, preceded him in writing of interests in the American political process, and yet retained the normative concept of a common interest by which the lesser ones were measured.

We turn now to our own times. Amidst behavioral demands that the language of public interest be jettisoned, there have been suggestions that the process whereby "spurious" versions of the public interest compete for favor is indeed a valuable one. This had led to the notion that though it may rarely be an appropriate mode of speech for social scientists to identify specific policies as being in the public interest, one might so identify a process of making decisions. (See Smith 1960: 159; Lane 1964: 192.) Public interest as procedure is a point of view characteristic of modern academic analysis and has few antecedents in traditional polemics. Undoubtedly this offers more than the simple demand to make the concept operational or scrap it; still it suffers from a worrisome disjunction between the perspectives of citizen and scientist.

When French writers of the seventeenth century attempted to create a technical political vocabulary they de-emphasized the normative language in which the good of the community had usually been treated. Because that normative language expressed something more than the convenience of writers about politics, it could not be suppressed and eventually it was the reason of state that passed from the ranks of acceptable concepts. The twentieth-century animus against the public interest was to a much greater extent inspired by the needs of science. Sustained by no absolute governments, the animus has now, it seems, receded. But if hostility to the concept has declined, reasons for perplexity flourish still. (See Gerber 1982; Ward 1983.)[3] Chief among sources of concern has been the difficulty of making sense of inherited traditions about the relation of the public interest to particular ones. For the ancient formula that announced the superiority of the public interest seemed difficult to contemplate in liberal–democratic systems, while the liberal alternative, as associated for instance with Bentham, has seemed unintelligible. A second concern has underlined the protean vocabulary that leaves scope, for instance, for noting how "common good" bears connotations different from those of "public interest." A further source of obscurity has resisted an apparent fusion of descriptive and normative elements in claims for public interest. Philosophical correctives to a naive positivism assist in resolving some difficulties. However, if the position taken here has any merit, more attention must be paid to the actual place of this concept in the history of argument. When professors come actually to direct questionnaires to each other to elicit views on the subject (see Leys 1962: 237–8), simultaneously making do with the thinnest sort of historical awareness, some effort at redressing the balance is overdue.

The concept of a "public interest" is, in its normal use, a normative expression (Meyer 1975: 3–15) and one likely to be employed rather differently depending upon circumstances. That is what makes it so difficult to specify a given thinker's position on the public interest. Any thinker with ample occasion to use the concept will, like Suarez, or Harrington, or English jurists arguing in the 1680s about the dispensing power (Gunn 1969: 295–6), vary the emphasis. Perhaps it is its very complexity that accounts for the curious fact that the place of the concept in intellectual history has been widely misunderstood, while, at the same time, the philosophical record has been muddied by expectations that a crucial term for political discourse be neutral and descriptive. Even ordinary strategies for getting one's own way seem to be blunted in the presence of the public interest. Of what other political concept has such a mountain of commentary been written, much of it for the ostensible purpose of discountenancing its use?

[3] These theses contain recent surveys of the literature.

REFERENCES

Bastiat, Frédéric. 1964 [1850]. *Economic Harmonies*, edited by G.B. de Huszar. Princeton, NJ: Van Nostrand.

Bonnaire, Louis de. 1758. *La Règle des devoirs que la nature inspire à tous les hommes*, 4 vols. Paris: Briasson.

Brissot de Warville, J.P. 1786. *Examen critique des voyages dans l'Amérique septentrionale de M. le Marquis de Chastellux*. London.

Chastellux, F.J. de. 1774 [1772]. *An Essay on the Public Happiness*. London: T. Cadell.

Gaudemet, J. 1951. "Utilitas publica." *Revue historique de droit français et étranger* 4th series: 465–99.

Gerber, Mitchell. 1982. "The Utility of the Concept of Public Interest in Liberal Political Theory." Unpublished Ph.D. Dissertation, New York University.

Griffet, Henri de. 1778. *Mémoires pour servir à l'histoire de Louis, dauphin de France . . .avec un traité de la connoissance des hommes fait . . .en 1758*. Paris: P.G. Simon.

Gros de Besplas, Joseph. 1768. *Des causes du bonheur public*. Paris: S. Jorry.

Gunn, J.A.W. 1968a. "Interest Will Not Lie: A Seventeenth-Century Political Maxim." *Journal of the History of Ideas* 29: 551–64.

1968b. "Jeremy Bentham and the Public Interest." *Canadian Journal of Political Science* 1: 394–413.

1969. *Politics and the Public Interest in the Seventeenth Century*. London: Routledge and Kegan Paul.

1975. "Mandeville and Wither: Individualism and the Workings of Providence." In Irwin Primer (ed.), *Mandeville Studies*. The Hague: M. Nijhoff, pp. 98–118.

Halévy, Elie. 1955 [1901–4]. *The Growth of Philosophic Radicalism*. Boston, MA: Beacon.

Jovellanos, G.M. 1806. *L'identité de l'intérêt général avec l'intérêt individuel*. St. Petersburg: F. Drechsler.

Keohane, Nannerl O. 1980. *Philosophy and the State in France*. Princeton, NJ: Princeton University Press.

Kraus, Wolfgang H. 1959. "The Democratic Community and the Problem of Publicity." In C.J. Friedrich (ed.), *Community*. New York: Liberal Arts Press, pp. 225–55.

Lane, Edgar. 1964. *Lobbying and the Law*. Berkeley, CA and Los Angeles, CA: University of California Press.

Leys, Wayne A.R. 1962. "The Relevance and Generality of the Public Interest." In C.J. Friedrich (ed.), *The Public Interest*. New York: Atherton Press, pp. 237–56.

McCulloch, J.R. 1849. *Principles of Political Economy*, 4th edn. London: Longman.

Meyer, William J. 1975. *Public Good and Political Authority: a Pragmatic Proposal*. Port Washington, NY: Kennikat Press.

Moore, W.H. 1906. *Act of State in English Law*. London: J. Murray.

Muratori, Lodovico. 1772 [1749]. *Traité du bonheur public*. Lyons: Reguilliat.

Polt, John H.R. 1971. *Gaspar Melchor de Jovellanos*. New York: Twayne.

Robinson, Matthew. 1786. *The Dangerous Situation of England, or an Address to our Landed, Trading and Funded Interests on the Present State of Public Affairs*, 2nd edn. London: Stockdale.

Rousseau, J.-J. 1964 [*c.* 1760]. "Contrat Social" [Geneva Manuscript]. In *Oeuvres complètes*, 4 vols., vol. III, edited by B. Gagnebin and M. Raymond. Paris: Gallimard, pp. 279–346.

"R. S.," Revd. Dr. 1716. *Particular Men not to be Injur'd for the Publick Good*. London: J. Morphew.

Smith, Howard R. 1960. *Democracy and the Public Interest*. Athens, GA: University of Georgia Press.

Steinwenter, Artur. 1939. "Utilitas publica – utilitas singulorum." In *Festschrift Paul Koschaker*, 3 vols., vol. I. Weimar: H. Böhlaus, pp. 84–102.

Steuart, Sir James. 1767. *An Inquiry into the Principles of Political Economy*, 2 vols. London: Miller and Cadell.

Taylor, Charles. 1985. "Atomism." In *Philosophical Papers, I: Philosophy and the Human Sciences*. Cambridge: Cambridge University Press, pp. 187–210.

Turgot, A.-R.-J. 1966 [1753]. "Lettres sur la tolérance." In vol. II, *Oeuvres*, 2 vols., edited by E. Daire. Osnabrück: Zeller, pp. 675–87.

Unger, Roberto M. 1975. *Knowledge and Politics*. New York: Free Press.

Ward, Edward John. 1983. "An Exploration of the Public Interest Concept." Unpublished Ph.D. Dissertation, Claremont Graduate School.

West, Henry. 1982. "J. Mill's Proof of the Principle of Utlity." In H.B. Miller and W.H. Williams (eds.), *The Limits of Utilitarianism*. Minneapolis, MN: University of Minnesota Press, pp. 23–34.

10

Citizenship

MICHAEL WALZER

A citizen is, most simply, a member of a political community, entitled to whatever prerogatives and encumbered with whatever responsibilities are attached to membership. The word comes to us from the Latin *civis*; the Greek equivalent is *polites*, member of the polis, from which comes our "political." But we have taken more from Greek and Latin than a vocabulary. What may be called the ideology of citizenship is essentially an early-modern (neoclassical) interpretation of Greek and Roman republicanism, and the current legal understanding of the concept has its sources in the later Rome of the empire and in early-modern reflections on Roman law.

We can best engage the ideology *in medias res*, not, for the moment, in its origins or early intellectual history, and not in its later decline and intermittent revivals, but at the height of its vigor, during the French Revolution. In its Jacobin phase, the revolution is best understood as an effort to establish citizenship as the dominant identity of every Frenchman – against the alternative identities of religion, estate, family, and region. The replacement of the still honorific title *Monsieur* with the fully universal *citoyen* (and also, though less significantly, *citoyenne*) symbolizes that effort. Citizenship was to replace religious faith and familial loyalty as the central motive of virtuous conduct. Indeed, citizenship, virtue, and public spirit were closely connected ideas, suggesting a rigorous commitment to political (and military) activity on behalf of the community – *patria*, not yet *nation*. Activity (meetings, speeches, public service) was crucial; this was an emphatically positive conception of the citizen's role. A distinction between active and inactive citizens, drawn on economic rather than political lines, was introduced in the constitution of 1791 but suppressed a year later (Brinton 1934: 42–3). In Jacobin ideology, citizenship was a universal office; everyone was to serve the community. Thus the *levée en masse* (1793), which goes well beyond all subsequent conscription laws; it literally conscripts everybody, setting tasks for men and women of all ages. "Young men will go to the front; married men will forge arms and transport foodstuffs; women will make tents, clothes, will serve in the hospitals; children will tear rags into lint; old men will get themselves carried to public places, there to stir up the courage of the warriors, hatred of kings, and unity in the republic" (Brinton 1934: 128). The mood is best captured by the *Marseillaise*, "Aux armes, citoyens!"

The inspiration for all this was classical, that is, it derived from the reading of Aristotle, Plutarch, Tacitus, and so on. But the ideology is clearly a neoclassical, early-modern production. Machiavelli, Harrington, Montesquieu, and Mably are key theorists, but it is Rousseau (and, a little later, Kant) who gives citizenship its modern philosophical grounding, connecting it to the theory of consent. The citizen, in *The Social Contract*, is the free and autonomous individual, who makes, or shares in the making of, the laws he obeys: "obedience to a law which we prescribe to ourselves is liberty" (*Social Contract*, bk.I, chap.8; 1950). Only the political community provides a suitable arena for this ethical self-creation. Only the activist citizen, who "flies to the public assemblies," can be both free and moral (righteous, upright, or just, rather than naturally good).

For Rousseau, the republic would be successful only if each citizen found the greater proportion of his happiness in public rather than in private activity (*Social Contract*, bk.III, chap.15). For then the pursuit of happiness would strengthen the structures of virtue. In the expanding bourgeois world of the eighteenth century, however, private activity – especially in the market and the family – was a more likely source of happiness. Wealth and affection, rather than power and glory, seemed to most men and women the more realistic, perhaps also the more desirable, goals. And some of them, at least, could actually accumulate wealth and win affection – not, however, as citizens in Rousseau's sense but as entrepreneurs, lovers, and parents, *monsieurs* rather than *citoyens*, members of civil society rather than of the political community. But then civil society was a threat to the republic, for it drew its members away from politics; now they flew homewards rather than to the assemblies. It followed that citizenship and virtue required either the repression of civil society or the reduction of its scope and appeal. This project is already implicit in Rousseau's theory; Jacobin politics makes it explicit.

"Revolutionaries must be Romans," declared the Jacobin tribune Saint-Just (1957: 197). They must be citizens in the style of the classical republics. But this would require what Marx, writing about the Jacobin Terror of 1793, called the "sacrifice" of bourgeois values – industry, competition, private interest, and self-enjoyment. Indeed, the revolutionary state can impose the sacrifice; it can "abolish" the exuberance and corruption of civil society, but "only in the way it abolishes private property by . . . confiscation . . . or only in the way it abolishes life by the guillotine" (Marx 1963: 16). There is no road that leads back to Greek or Roman citizenship except the road of coercion and terror, because modern civil society does not breed citizens but rather, in Marx's philosophical jargon, "self-alienated natural and spiritual individuality" (Marx and Engels 1956: 164) – men and women who need occasionally to imagine themselves as citizens but whose everyday actions are governed by the imperatives of the market. Jacobinism enacts an inauthentic autonomy, and fails because it cannot sustain the enactment without continuous violence.

This failure to establish political life as the "real life" of ordinary men and women comes early in modern history, and it is not necessarily definitive. But it does invite us to look back, to look behind neoclassical republicanism, as it were, and to study its ancient and more authentic models. *What was citizenship?* The answer to this question is much disputed among contemporary scholars of Greece and Rome, though it is increasingly clear that we need to be skeptical of idealized accounts of public spiritedness and political participation in the ancient republics. There too citizenship stood in some tension with family, religion, and private economic interest. There too citizens were often self-absorbed and apathetic. But the city-state was a far less complex and differentiated society than our own. And for many of its male citizens, the city itself, the political community, was indeed the focal point of everyday life. In its public squares, its courts and assemblies, they might well find the greater part of their happiness.

The minimal range of social differentiation is crucial here. Citizenship in Periclean Athens, for example, was doubly endogamous, and so the body of citizens was something like an extended family, an urban tribe. Socrates could plausibly describe the city and its laws as the parents of the citizens. "We have brought you into the world," he has the Laws say, "and reared you and educated you, and given you and all your fellow-citizens a share in all the good things at our disposal" (*Crito*, 51c; 1954). The standard religion was a civil religion (as Rousseau understood), providing local gods and a myth of origins. The privacy of faith was unknown; religious rituals were performed by public priests in public temples. Though Athens was an imperial center and possessed a significant population of resident aliens and foreign slaves, the sense of place and the attachment to homeland were strong among its citizens. Precisely because of the presence of aliens and slaves, class divisions among the free and native-born, though visible enough, were never overriding and took no legal form; in the assembly every citizen was the equal of every other. All this made for the moral unity of the city and lifted citizenship to what was probably primacy among self-conceptions.

Ancient citizenship was the experience of this primacy, not occasionally but every day, in political discussion, participation in the juries and councils, universal military service, and common worship. Perhaps most important of all was the rotation of citizens through the chief magistracies. Aristotle understood citizenship in terms of eligibility for office (much as we might understand it in terms of the vote): "The citizen in the strict sense is best defined . . . [as] a man who shares in the administration of justice and in the holding of office" (*Politics*, 1275a; 1948). When he went on to describe democratic citizens as men who rule and are ruled in turn, he was referring not to the legislative function, making laws and then obeying them, but rather to the executive function, holding office and then submitting to other office-holders. Once again, the character and scale of the community were crucial. In the city-state, citizens were likely to know (or at least know of) one another, and so they were ready to trust one another in office, even allowing particular choices to be made by lottery (in Athens only generals and public physicians were elected) – a strong expression indeed of moral unity.

When the scale of political organization changes, unity and trust collapse and a different understanding of citizenship is required. The requirement is most visible, perhaps, in modern bourgeois society, but it is apparent already in the Roman empire; it is in the first instance the product of imperial inclusiveness. Rome expanded by granting citizenship to the peoples it conquered – at first only to some and by degrees; in 212, by an edict of Caracalla, to all subjects of the empire except the very lowest (chiefly rural) classes. This extension did not alter the formal definition of citizenship, still expressed in terms of office-holding, but it did alter the political and legal realities. When St. Paul claimed to be a Roman citizen, he was imagining himself not as an active and involved member of the political community, certainly not as a potential magistrate, but rather as the passive recipient of specific rights and entitlements (Acts 23: 27). A citizen was more significantly someone protected by the law than someone who made and executed the law. On this understanding, citizenship was relatively easy to extend to a large and heterogeneous population whose members had no knowledge of one another and shared neither history nor culture. Henceforth the body of Roman citizens included people ethnically different from the original Romans, with different religions, different conceptions of political life, who lived elsewhere, and so on. Citizenship for such people was an important but occasional identity, a legal status rather than a fact of everyday life.

So it remained throughout the feudal period, when even the legal status had only a bookish existence, replaced in actual social relationships by such private-law identities as serf, villein, vassal, lord, and so on. But the absolutist states of the late medieval and early-modern period, seeking to impose their authority on heterogeneous populations, returned to the (imperial) Roman experience. Jean Bodin, the sixteenth-century jurist, an early theorist of sovereign power, was reflecting on this experience when he defined the citizen as "one who enjoys the common liberty and protection of authority" (Bodin 1945: 158). "Enjoy" might mean "rejoices in," but I suspect that it is an entirely passive relationship that Bodin intended to describe. In his view, the citizen is not himself an authority; rather he is someone to whose protection the authorities are committed. Their commitment, insofar as it is serious, rules out the arbitrary use of political power; hence it makes for the kind of liberty sometimes called "negative" – the liberty of private life and individual choice.

Early-modern liberalism is an effort to explore and expand the Bodinian commitment. "Political liberty," wrote Montesquieu, "consists in security or . . . in the opinion that we enjoy security" (*Spirit of the Laws*, bk.XII, chap.2; 1949). To share in the "common liberty" is to be protected against various sorts of danger – posed sometimes by other people, sometimes by the authorities themselves. It is to be made secure in one's physical life (Hobbes) or in family and home (Bodin and Montesquieu) or in conscience and property (Locke). But this search for protection assumes the primacy of what is protected, namely, the private or familial world. It is there that men and women find the greater part of their happiness; they "enjoy" protection but rejoice in something else. They are not political people; they have other interests, in salvation or business or love or art and literature. For them, the political community is only a necessary framework, a set of external arrangements, not a common life.

Citizenship as enjoyment still dominates contemporary law. Citizens are distinguished from aliens by the added protection to which they are entitled (sometimes also by the added obligation of military service), not by their right to hold office. In democratic states, of course, the vote is part of the citizen's title, but politics has largely dropped out of the general understanding. Thus *Webster's International Dictionary*: "A citizen as such is entitled to the protection of life, liberty, and property at home and abroad, but is not necessarily vested with the suffrage or other political rights."

Jacobin radicalism represented a full-scale revolt against the early-modern version of this passive citizenship – a reassertion of republican values against the claims of empire and the monarchic or liberal state. But this is an ideological reassertion and a failed revolt because the Jacobin intellectuals never took the measure of their own society. France was no city-state. Vast in scale (by ancient standards), heterogeneous and divided, the country did not provide an appropriate social base for an activist citizenship. And yet, republican politics survived the Jacobin experiment as it survived the fall of the ancient cities; it has had a long after-life, and even today it suggests an alternative, whether practical or utopian, to the largely apolitical existence of modern citizens.

Dualistic constructions are never adequate to the realities of social life. It will be useful, nonetheless, to summarize this particular dualism of republican and imperial or liberal citizenship before trying to see what lies beyond it. We have, then, two different understandings of what it means to be a citizen. The first describes citizenship as an office, a responsibility, a burden proudly assumed; the second describes citizenship as a status, an entitlement, a right or set of rights passively enjoyed. The first makes citizenship the core of our life, the second makes it its outer frame. The first assumes a closely knit body of citizens, its members committed to one another; the second assumes a diverse and loosely connected body, its members (mostly) committed elsewhere. According to the first, the citizen is the primary political actor, law-making and administration his everyday business. According to the second, law-making and administration are someone else's business; the citizen's business is private.

The first understanding of citizenship, Marx argued, is appropriate to "the ancient, realistic, and democratic republic based on real slavery" while the second is appropriate to "the modern spiritualist . . . representative state which is based on emancipated slavery, on bourgeois society" (Marx and Engels 1956: 164). But that distinction, like the fundamental dualism itself, is too rigid. By "realistic," Marx means that citizenship among the ancients was a concrete and actual experience; by "spiritualist," he means that citizenship under modern conditions is an ideology and an illusion. In fact, however, ancient realism was at least partly ideological, for there were many citizens who were inactive or ineffective in action (and many more non-citizens upon whom political silence was imposed). And modern spiritualism is at least partly real, for ordinary citizens are sometimes mobilized in parties and movements that change the shape of the larger society.

To understand citizenship in the United States today, and in Western democracies more generally, we must focus on this partial reality. It has its origin in two simple facts of political life: firstly, the security provided by the authorities cannot just be enjoyed; it must itself be secured, and sometimes against the authorities themselves. The passive enjoyment of citizenship requires, at least intermittently, the activist politics of citizens. And, secondly, whenever an activist politics is possible, the definition of "common liberty" is certain to be contested. Democratic politics since the French Revolution is essentially this contest, sometimes fought to a settlement, but always renewed. The contestants are not Jacobin (or Greek or Roman) citizens, but they are also not the mere recipients or consumers of political protection – if they were that they would get much less protection than they do.

"Common liberty" is an idea subject to expansion. The expansion is of two sorts. The number and range of people in the "commonality" grows by invasion and incorporation. Slaves, workers, new immigrants, Jews, Blacks, women – all of them move into the circle of the protected, even if the protection they actually get is still unequal or inadequate. And, at the same time, the number and range of "liberties" or entitlements also grows, and citizenship comes gradually to entail not only the protection of life and family but also the provision, in one or another degree, of education, health care, old age pensions, and so on. Both these expansions are contested; both involve organization and struggle, and so citizenship as political participation or "ruling" and citizenship as the receipt of benefits go hand in hand. At least, they go hand in hand until a full range of benefits is finally provided for a full range of citizens. Then there may be nothing left to organize and struggle for, no contest worth contesting. But that time seems a long way off. Meanwhile citizenship is simultaneously active and passive, requiring the exercise of ancient virtues if only for the enjoyment of modern rights.

But the number of citizens actually involved in political organizations, actually holding political office, is fairly small, and the willingness of ordinary men and women to devote time and energy to politics is fairly minimal. Democratic citizenship in its contemporary form does not seem to encourage high levels of involvement or devotion. Hence the periodic reappearance of ancient citizenship in ideological dress, the expression of a hand-wringing sense that something vital has been lost. Indeed, the primacy of politics has been lost and with it the exhilarating sense of civic or urban camaraderie bred in the Greek and Roman cities (never really shared by their rural members). But "lost" is a strange verb here, for this sort of thing has never been "found" in a fully modern setting – except perhaps in those parties and movements that championed the expansion of democratic citizenship. The labor movement, the civil rights movement, the feminist movement, have all generated in their time a sense of solidarity and an everyday militancy among large numbers of men and women. But these are not, probably cannot be, stable achievements; they don't outlast the movement's success, even its partial success. Citizenship is unlikely to be the primary identity or the consuming passion of men and women living in complex and highly differentiated societies, where politics competes for time and attention with class, ethnicity, religion, and family, and where these latter four do not draw people together but rather separate and divide them. Separation and division make for the primacy of the private realm.

REFERENCES

Aristotle. 1948. *The Politics*, translated by Ernest Barker. Oxford: Oxford University Press.

Bodin, Jean. 1945 [1566]. *Method for the Easy Comprehension of History*, translated by Beatrice Reynolds. New York: Columbia University Press.

Brinton, Crane. 1934. *A Decade of Revolution 1789-1799*. New York: Harper and Brothers.

Marx, Karl. 1963. *Early Writings*, translated by T. B. Bottomore. London: C. A. Watts.

Marx, Karl and Friedrich Engels. 1956 [1844]. *The Holy Family*, translated by R. Dixon. Moscow: Foreign Languages Publishing House.

Montesquieu. 1949 [1748]. *The Spirit of the Laws*, translated by Thomas Nugent. New York: Hafner.

Plato. 1954. *Crito*, translated by Hugh Tredennick. In *The Last Days of Socrates*. Harmondsworth: Penguin, pp. 53-70.

Rousseau, Jean-Jacques. 1950 [1762]. *The Social Contract and Discourses*, translated by G. D. H. Cole. New York: E. P. Dutton.

Saint-Just, Louis Antoine Léon de. 1957. *Discours et rapports*, edited by Albert Soboul. Paris: Editions Sociales.

11

Corruption

J. PETER EUBEN

> Men passed their lives in governing themselves. Democracy could not last except through the incessant labor of all citizens. Let their zeal diminish ever so little, and it perished or became corrupt.
>
> Coulanges 1957: 336

> The variety of definitions employed by contemporary social scientists interested in corruption fortunately does not cover as wide a span as those given in the *OED*.
>
> Heidenheimer 1970: 4

> Corruption is but one problem our society faces, and it is far from the most serious one.
>
> Johnston 1981: 183

I

The conceptual history of "corruption" is uncertain. While the word clearly derives from the Latin *corrumpere* and its cognates, the meaning of the term as found in the republican tradition and the *Oxford English Dictionary* is wider than anything found in the Roman authors of antiquity. Almost always the latter use corruption either in reference to a specific human activity (bribery) or in the more general sense of destroy, lay waste, adulterate or spoil in reference to organic matter such as food. In those few instances where the general meaning was extended to human beings in ways that could mean systemic moral decline, the usage was metaphoric and referred to groups with less than full citizen status, such as women and children. For example, when Livy talks about the corruption of Rome, he uses a set of specific moral and political terms which later, but not with him, jointly constitute structural corruption. There are a few instances[1] where corruption has this extended meaning of political decline and it may be that later writers seized on these instances to elaborate the metaphorical meaning in ways that made it possible for corruption to become the crucial term it did for the English republicans and American revolutionaries.

If we are to recover the origins of the republican understanding of corruption, we might be better off beginning (as the republicans themselves sometimes did) with Greek authors, which is what I propose to do. After a brief elaboration of the etymology of corruption as it appears in the *Oxford English Dictionary*, I will turn to Thucydides' portrait of *stasis* at Corcyra and Aristotle's views on citizenship and politics. Having sketched this republican understanding of political corruption, I offer a contrasting sketch of a "liberal" understanding as that derives from (or can be reconstructed in terms of) Hobbes and Madison. In the final section I look at the meaning and status of corruption in contemporary social science.

The point of my contrast is not to extol "the" ancients at the expense of "the" moderns; still less to excoriate liberalism one more time. There is more to say in criticism of "the" ancients and of republicanism than I will say, more to say for Hobbes and Madison than I shall say, and far more to liberalism than Hobbes and Madison. My object in being so schematic is to make the disinherited in our history co-founders of our polity and full participants in the contemporary debate over the meaning of political corruption. This suggests that what follows is more a "thin conceptual genealogy" than a "thick conceptual history." It is genealogical insofar as it loosens the hold of the social scientific present over the historical past; disturbs the "metahistorical deployment of idea signification and indefinite teleologies" (Foucault 1977: 140); and helps establish the claims to attention of local, disenfranchised, disqualified knowledges "against the claims of a unitary body of theory which would filter, hierarchise and order them in the name of some true knowledge and some arbitrary idea of what constitutes a science and its objects" (Foucault 1980: 83). It is a "thin" genealogy because though offering no global theory, it does imply norms (and so normalization) and is insufficiently attentive to historical detail and discontinuities.

[1] Quo perniciosius de re publica merentur vitiosi principes, quod non solum vitia concipiunt ipsi, sed ea infudunt in civitatem, neque solum obsunt, quod ipsi corrumpuntur, sed etiam quod corrumpunt, plusque exemplo quam peccato nocent. atque haec lex dilatata in ordinem cunctum coangustari etiam potest; pauci enim atque admodum pauci honore et gloria amplificati vel corrumpere mores civitatis vel corrigere possunt. Cicero, *Laws* III. 14. 32

II

In the *Oxford English Dictionary* corruption has several related meanings having to do with decay, degeneration, disintegration, and debasement.[2] Corruption implies decay, where the original or natural condition of something becomes infected. If the infection goes far enough, the infected body begins to decompose until unrecognizable. In this sense corruption entails a loss of identity and definition. A people who lose what is distinctive to and about them become amorphous, then anonymous, and historical victims rather than actors. A person who loses his composure loses his capacity to act and speak.

Decay also implies a wasting away or wearing down. In this respect corruption involves enervation, a loss of health and power. Such loss leads to decadence or even death. Decadence implies self-indulgence, luxury and excess, where men and women lack concern for or commitment to each other and collective ideals. Decadence points to a violation of time, as if some natural rhythm of life is displaced by an artificial speeding up or a slowing down of life or culture. Decadence is like entropy: it involves homogenization and loss of energy (as in thermodynamics) and fragmentation and loss of energy (as in communications theory).

Corruption also implies degeneration and disintegration. A people degenerates when it sinks to a lower standard of behavior than the generations which preceded it. This decline signals an enfeeblement of the culture's animating principles and a departure from the highest ideals of its collective life. A culture disintegrates when it breaks apart into factions and incoherence. A person or a people without integrity is bereft of focus, or of organizing aim. More specifically, someone without integrity is dishonest. Lacking an element of sound character he or she becomes easily seduced from fidelity to the discharge of a public duty.

Corruption is not only the absence of an element or principle; it may involve the presence of some foreign element that debases or undermines the whole. The base or basis of something is its foundation, or fundamental and constituting principles, the starting point from which action and analysis proceed. In these terms political corruption involves the altering of the foundations or constitution of something (or someone) in a manner which lowers it (or them) in dignity, quality, character or value.

In sum, political corruption is a disease of the body politic. It has

[2] The next few paragraphs are drawn from my essay (Euben 1978).

less to do with individual malfeasance than with systematic and systemic degeneration of those practices and commitments that provide the terms of collective self-understanding and shared purpose. In a corrupt society each part pretends to be the whole; each interest to be the common one; each faction to make its view and voice exclusive. Under such circumstances the common good is seen (and so comes to be) a ruse for fools and dreamers while the political arena is a place where factions, like gladiators, fight to the death.

In the republican tradition factions are the death of politics and the surest sign of corruption. Their presence always signifies a polity divided against itself, one that can no longer be recognized or act as a single body. Unless someone of extraordinary *virtù*(e) can heal the fissure by recalling the city to its founding principles and so renew its dedication to a common life, everything is lost. No narrative makes this point better than Thucydides' description of the *stasis* at Corcyra.

III

The root sense of *stasis* is placing, setting, position, standing, and station. Its range of meanings includes party, party formed for seditious purposes, faction, discord, and civil war or revolution. In this sense *stasis* is political corruption in its "purest" sense. M.I. Finley calls *stasis* "one of the most remarkable words to be found in any language." That is because though its root sense does not imply negative connotations, its use in a political context is always pejorative. The "inescapable implication" is that a partisan position "is a bad thing, leading to sedition, civil war and the disruption of the social fabric."[3]

The word is remarkable for another reason Finley does not explore, but his discussion suggests. *Stasis* is the opposite of moderation, in the sense of balance, deliberateness and limit. Thus Thucydides' Athenians are immoderate in their intellectual boldness, political daring, and ceaseless movement. But there is a different, somewhat paradoxical kind of immoderation present in Spartan culture. Traditionalism, parochialism, and religiosity can become a kind of lethargy which, if unchecked, infects the body politic as fatally as excessive restlessness. As Aristotle's criticism of Plato and Machiavelli's praise of Rome suggest, *stasis* and political corruption can be a matter of too much stability as well as too little,

[3] My discussion of *stasis* is taken from Finley (1962).

of staying too much in one place as well as never being in the same place.

This ambiguity is brought out nicely by the English words Finley chooses to define *stasis*. I take "standing" as an example, though "position," "setting," "placing," and "station" would do as well. "Standing" can refer to social standing, having appropriate credentials (which gives one standing), making a stand (as in warfare), taking a stand (in argument), standing for something, standing still (as opposed to movement), or standing upright as opposed to sitting down or collapsing. We stand by, with, down, and aside; have standoffs and stand-outs; stand up to, and stand for something or even someone. We can, of course, be too rigid about the stand we take, or lack the courage of our convictions and take no stand at all. Societies can have rigid social hierarchies or treat all as individuals independent of any "socially prescribed" characteristics. The point is not merely that meaning is use, but that the political meaning of *stasis* in Thucydides has a double critical thrust which is echoed in the republican understanding of corruption.

Thucydides is concerned mainly with *stasis* or political corruption in Athens. That is because he regards the growth of Athenian power as the true cause of the war and the factionalism at Athens as the true cause of its ending and Athenian defeat. Since Athens is the most important city in the *History*, the whole *History* is about political corruption and *stasis*. But there is one particular incident that captures that whole with claustrophobic intensity: the civil war at Corcyra. The moral bankruptcy, annihilating passions, limitless carnage, and conceptual chaos which surface there with singular ferocity disclose a world corrupt at its very core. All that my etymology suggests and *stasis* can mean Thucydides evokes. And it is an evocation that foreshadows the collapse of all Hellas. For Corcyra is not only a turning point in the war and the *History*; it is a preview of the brutal excess which later revolutions refined with perverse ingenuity. And to the degree that Hobbes's state of war is a contemporary extrapolation of this version of *stasis* from which he draws anti-republican conclusions, my emphasis on Corcyra provides a preface to my contrast between the republican and liberal conceptions of corruption.

Stasis releases ambition, envy, greed, and the lust for power driving men to pitiless extremes until they become oblivious to the importunements of justice, honor, mercy, and those "common laws (koinous . . . nomous) to which all alike can appeal for salvation should they be overtaken by adversity" (*History*, 3.84). Everything is inverted and so perverted. Reason and courage are reduced to animal cunning; established institutions become instruments for the pursuit of private ends. Everything is a weapon, everyone an instrument, every act other than it seems. Nothing is stable or certain; all is of, by, and for the moment.

Under such conditions religion, law, family, and morality become instruments in their own destruction. Oaths are temporary strategies adopted only when one is outmaneuvered or outmanned by an opponent. Since blood is weaker than party, partisan slogans excuse patricide. Morality and justice are rhetorical diversions which disguise secret hatreds and excuse private revenge. Since any offense, however trivial, ancient or imagined, becomes a motive for vengeance, no one can trust even their closest friends. Since everyone is a potential enemy, isolation is the only guarantee against surprise attack. In the beginning of civil war, men killed their enemies with the assistance of their party. But as the *stasis* intensified the number of potential enemies increased and the number of possible friends decreased until the only trustworthy friend was oneself and the only safe party was a party of one.

Language too becomes an instrument in its own destruction. During civil war "Words were forced to change their ordinary meaning and to assume a significance that distorted the extraordinary deeds now undertaken" (*History*, 3.82). This is not only a matter of saying one thing and doing or meaning another: it is also seeing how language itself is part of the social fabric unraveling before us and that the social fabric is unraveling because the preconditions for discourse are being killed as surely as the men and women of Corcyra. Not only at Corcyra but at Athens; not only among the actors in the *History* but the Athenian historian. The conceptual and political corruption at Athens is suggested by the narrative structure of book VIII.

That book reveals an Athens torn by faction, physically divided between military forces on Samos declaring themselves to be the true city and oligarchs in the city itself. The ruling oligarchy itself is split between the more extreme and moderate factions and rent by individual rivalry. We can no longer consider the Athenians as a unit or the city's political life as a series of choices among policies or leaders. This absence is reflected in the narrative of the book. There is no brilliant character or pairing which might give the book a center around which events could be given form. Civic disintegration and moral atomism brought about by *stasis* and corruption have their literary analogue in the disintegration of the units of and techniques upon which much of the earlier portions of the *History* have been built (Connor 1984: 214-17). The impotence of Athenian political and military leaders is reflected in Thucydides' shift from offering confident assessments of motives and strategies to what W. Robert Connor (1984) calls a "meditative approach." He is no longer the omniscient narrator and so we are no longer omniscient readers but are inquirers, as modest in what we can say here as Thucydides was about what could be known about the causes of the plague.

It is by now a cliché, at least among critics of positivistic social science, that language helps constitute the world. Thucydides does not say that, but he certainly shows us what it means to say it, and how the collapse of language is the collapse of the world. We can see in and through his *History* how we are defined by our concepts even as we define them, whether the "we" are actors in the public arena or theorists writing about them. As lenses through which we see and structure the world, language is the bond and bounds that make us whole. We can be communicants and friends rather than excommunicants and enemies only when the community of speech and the speech of a community remain generally intact. This does not preclude vagueness or opacity. Indeed without them speech would lack purpose. Nor does it preclude the possibility that some speech, such as Thucydides' own, is partly outside the conceptual disintegration it depicts and evokes. But it does presume that statements about conceptual incoherence must themselves be coherent; that claims about incompatible modes of discourse must themselves refer to a discourse in which such incompatibilities can be described.

Political theorists have often made such claims for their own statements. Certainly Plato did. And it is Plato who completes Thucydides' analysis of *stasis*. Where the *History* shows how the admittedly imperfect unity of Hellenic states against Persia collapsed first into a war between Greek cities, then a war within cities, and finally a war of all against all, Plato shows how an individual can be at war with himself or herself. It is no accident that warlike Polemarchus, whose idea of justice is helping friends and harming enemies, is made to see that we are often our own worst enemies, and never more so than when seeking domination over others. With Plato the failure of Hellenic unity is visited in every Hellene. The civil war that destroyed the capacity of the polis to act collectively destroys the individual soul's capacity for coherent action. In the end political corruption entails psychic corruption.

For all the differences between Thucydides and Aristotle it is possible to read the latter's *Politics* as an elaboration of the republican understanding of political corruption implicit in the *History*. But there is a tension in Aristotle's conception of political corruption; a tension that ultimately derives from the ambiguous connections between philosophy and politics, *sophia* and *phronesis*, which mark his thought as a whole. In book I of the *Politics*, Aristotle sets out the *telos* of a political association. In this "ideal" picture of the polis, corruption is a constitution's falling short of the final end implicit in its being. But since most (perhaps all) regimes confront practical impediments to this "natural" growth, Aristotle adopts a less stringent, but still moral, definition of corruption. In this second, more historical and pragmatic understanding, political corruption is defined in terms of the ideals of a specific regime. When a constitution systematically falls short of the paradigms of action, character, and justice which give it unity and definition, it is corrupt.

Despite (or because of) this tension, the sense of political health and decay emanating from the *Politics* has helped define the republican tradition and, depending on one's interpretation of Marx, Habermas, Gadamer, and MacIntyre, contemporary discussions of political economy, social theory, and moral philosophy as well.

For Aristotle a healthy polity is, first of all, a city in which citizens share in the administration of justice, though who is and who is not a citizen, the degree of sharing, and what justice is, depend on historical and geographic circumstances. What is independent of circumstances is the fact that politics is a moral activity in which men realize what is distinctively human about them and to them. Because the polis is the highest, most comprehensive and self-sufficient association, political activity is intrinsically, rather than instrumentally, valuable. Since men become politically educated and morally complete only by living a public life, representation makes no sense. If politics is a partnership in virtue, how could I designate someone to be virtuous for me? No one can act for me or in my name, not because he or she will misrepresent my interests, but because such designation is a resignation of my humanity. A polis which is less than a partnership in virtue, which fails to regard public life as a moral activity, degenerates into a mere alliance, aggregation, commercial collaboration or a contractual agreement guaranteeing rights or stipulating principles of mutual forbearance. Unlike these relationships which leave men morally unchanged and politically disconnected beyond temporary bonds based on instrumental purposes, political activity changes the character of the men engaged in it. However they come to political participation, they leave different beings. "If," Aristotle writes, "the spirit of their participation and the nature of their interaction is the same after they have come together as it was before they left their separate spheres, their community would not be a polis" (*Politics*, 1280b).

Secondly, a healthy polity requires that all commercial transactions be rigorously subject to the moral purposes of household management which are themselves subject to the more comprehensive moral ends of the polis. Economic transactions in which the aim is profit rather than the replenishment of needs undermine friendship and so communal life. Conversely, when men are no longer friends and their economic exchange is disembedded from face-to-face relations, they treat each other as instrumentalities. In these terms a corrupt city is one where gain is valued over friendship, private interest is valued over the common good, and materialist ideologies and motives are the animating forces of individual and collective life.[4]

Thirdly, a healthy polity depends on a plurality of contributions and points of view. Though each citizen must alike be committed to the common good, the need for and possibility of politics exists only when individuals see that good through different eyes. In fact it is this shared vision of a common good which allows mere difference to become recognized diversity, including diversity about what is or should be the common good. Thus a healthy city is obliged to promote unity and diversity, while a corrupt one fosters either community without politics or a "politics" without community. With his overemphasis on unity and stability, Plato makes the first error; with their insistence on unfettered economic activity, advocates of the free market make the second one.

As this implies, a healthy polity is, fourthly, one based on equality, though once more, who is and who is not equal and the respect in which they are depends on the particular characteristics of a regime: whether, for instance, it is oligarchic or democratic. What matters is that equals be treated equally and unequals be treated unequally, *and* that this equality be determined by contributions to the common good in particular (as defined by a constitution) and in general (as defined by the idea of a polis).[5] Those who contribute most to the

[4] Aristotle did not oppose private property; he did oppose the exclusively private use of private property.

[5] The tension between these two definitions leads to several difficulties: what to do with the good man in a less than good city; how to treat the supremely virtuous man justly without turning the city into a family; how much to strengthen a corrupt regime; the status of Aristotle's ideal state, etc.

common good, who most fully exemplify and elaborate the collectively defined ends of the community, deserve the highest praise and greatest rewards the community can offer. In these terms a corrupt society is one which regards all actions and ideals of character as equal, or discriminates against those whose contributions to the common good warrants greater consideration.

A fifth criterion of political health derives from Aristotle's view that lesser, more partial, and private interests or associations must be subordinate to higher, more inclusive public interests and associations. A society is corrupt whenever a part determines or rules the whole, or a lower principle rules a higher one, or a man of inferior character rules a man of superior character. It is this principle of inclusion that gives the polity its superiority over the two corrupt regimes which compose it. While democracy values numbers and free birth and oligarchy values wealth, a polity recognizes both contributions. By doing so it creates a whole more virtuous than that represented by either part. The more principles, contributions, and points of view a polis includes without losing its coherence or vitiating its moral end, the more it becomes a whole, in the same way that the more experience and previous thought a theory takes into account the more impartial it becomes.[6] A mixed constitution, like a mixed theory, is superior to a constitution based on one principle.

Finally, a healthy polity is one in which citizens are soldiers and soldiers are citizens. This is less a love of war and combat – Aristotle is highly critical of both Spartan militarism and imperialist ventures which distract from improving the moral quality of public life – than a statement about political responsibility. A soldier must think of himself as a citizen first and soldier second for the same reasons that a barterer must be guided by criteria of friendship rather than profit. In the same way that men who seek gain are unfit citizens, a soldier who seeks his own individual renown is an unfit comrade-in-arms. A free people fight for their freedom in the double sense of standing together against a common external enemy and seconding each other's moral strength against the temptations of private interest, and economic dependency. And only a free people willingly fight for their common inheritance. Unlike professional soldiers who are subject to an authority which they do not help constitute, or those who value political participation for extrinsic ends, free men die for their country not because it protects their private lives but because it is their life. When Machiavelli said he loved his country more than

6 Impartial but not objective, since it is never the case that a political theory can be as comprehensive as a science.

his soul, he implied, among other things, that his country was his soul. In this he was giving voice to a very old idea, though one which, in the altered context of a putative Christian Italy, was seen as revolutionary if not blasphemous.

IV

Except for some laudatory remarks about the *Rhetoric*, Thomas Hobbes has almost nothing good to say about Aristotle. He rejected Aristotle's metaphysics, politics, and idea of morality, regarding him as one of (if not *the*) culprits whose teachings were responsible for the English Civil War. Central to Hobbes's rejection was a repudiation of the Aristotelian – republican understanding of political corruption as I have summarized it in the previous section. In this respect Hobbes was a pivotal figure in the liberal transvaluation of corruption, despite his admiration for Thucydides and his illiberal defense of sovereign power.

Hobbes's strategy is twofold: he undercuts the metaphysical, epistemological and moral foundations of the republican idea of corruption making it appear as simultaneously superfluous, dangerous, and unintelligible to the modern sensibility he is helping and hoping to define; and he offers an alternative scientific paradigm where the remnants of the republican idea are inserted into a new conceptual cluster and projected practices which divest that idea of its critical legacy. The first tactic deconstructs republican politics and political theory; the second helps construct what became the liberal idea of politics and political theory.

In chapter 19 of *Leviathan* Hobbes offers a traditional delineation of three forms of government: monarchy, aristocracy, and democracy. But when it comes to taking the next traditional step of distinguishing legitimate from illegitimate versions of these forms as had Aristotle (as well as Cicero and Machiavelli), he not only demurs but launches an attack on the very idea of legitimacy. What had been regarded as perversions – tyranny, oligarchy, and anarchy – are "not the names of other forms of government, but the same form misliked." To call a regime corrupt is to say something about the speaker's preferences, not about the regime itself.[7] Moral judgments

[7] In chapter 6 of *Leviathan* Hobbes writes: "But whatsoever is the object of any man's Appetite or Desire; that is it, which he for his part calleth Good . . . For these words of Good, Evill, and Contemptible, are ever used with relation to the person that useth them: There being nothing simply and absolutely so."

are projections of interests and a stratagem for achieving power just as they were at Corcyra.

Notice how this dissolves the rhetorical force of calling a government or citizen corrupt. Corruption cannot be the triumph of private interest over the public good since attributing corruption to a regime is already a private interest and the public good is simply the private good of the one man who retains his natural liberty when the rest of us renounce ours. It may be that he will treat us well. If he does that is not because we are his judges or have power over him, or because he is a man of character or reason, but out of a fear of violent death. We are his private property and the source of his power in his continued war with other sovereigns, and so it is in his private interest to restrain himself from those capricious acts which reduce the commonwealth's power and increase his vulnerability. In these terms, the moralists who follow Aristotle (or Cicero or Machiavelli) and insist on the critical content of "corruption" are themselves immoral. They ignore how their name-calling exacerbates the political violence and linguistic chaos of civil war. Their error is not merely a matter of propounding an unreasonably high standard of public conduct, though it is true that Hobbes's sovereign is absolutely unexceptional and that he thought Plato too demanding. It is rather that there is no standard of public conduct except how the sovereign does in fact conduct himself.[8] Or to put it more generally, the sovereign defines a morality which is moral because it is sovereign rather than the other way around.

The sovereign is chosen not for his *virtù* or virtue, not because of his intellectual gifts, qualities of character, expert knowledge or generosity of spirit, but essentially by lot. His authority derives from the nature of his empowerment, not from anything in or about himself or his acts. His legitimacy rests on the consent of contracting individuals who are his complete equals at the moment of contract and his complete unequals afterwards. Thus he represents us in the double sense of re-presenting, that is mirroring us, and in the sense of being authorized by us to act in our name.

Hobbes's view of representation, like his views of citizenship, liberty, political education, equality, and diversity, is less a direct

[8] The situation is necessarily more complicated. Because we join the commonwealth to save our lives, the contract is one-sided in theory only. We cannot help but judge the sovereign's success in maintaining the conditions of peace and commodious living. To provide reasons for doing something, as Hobbes does for contracting, necessarily provides criteria for judging the adequacy of what is done in the name of those reasons. The dilemma is sharpened in times of war when the outcome of a crucial battle is in the balance.

refutation of Aristotle than part of a theory in which Aristotle's categories and arguments make no sense. Once men are seen as irremediably egoistic subjects rather than potentially activist citizens, as sharing a nature which fragments them rather than a history which unites them, as requiring an absolutely sovereign ruler rather than a sharing of power, we confront a political and conceptual universe in which republican political theory is irrelevant.

Given Hobbes's egoism (together with his physicalism and nominalism) men remain self-enclosed and undisclosed. Like billiard balls in constant motion, they collide with each other, push each other around and aside, but lack any internal connections. What we can infer by hypothetical reasoning, realize from introspection, confront in our dreams, and know from the way we actually live (armed, suspicious, fearful, hostile, and aggressive) is that we are all alike. We share a nature, not a history, replicate rather than modify each other in the course of collective action and deliberation. Men cannot and should not seek to alter who they are through and in public life. Such political education intensifies those destructive passions which make collective life fragile if not impossible. We remain strangers rather than friends or comrades, united by temporary alliances and permanent contracts, egoists and sons of egoists. If we have little peace with ourselves, we have a kind of peace with each other.

It barely needs saying that in Hobbes's system the Aristotelian definition of a citizen as ruling and being ruled in turn, or participating in the administration of justice, loses its point and meaning. Insofar as men become moral by authorizing the actions of another rather than acting themselves; to the degree that the public interest is simply the private interest of the sovereign; if men are irremediably egoistic in speech and deed; then political participation is unnecessary if not destructive.

For Aristotle political participation was the way in which diversity and unity were recognized, sustained, and reconciled. As each citizen brought a contrasting point of view to the common deliberation, he came to appreciate how diversity presupposed unity and unity preserved diversity. But if all men are egoistic and all points of view are equally the expressions of private interests, then the rationale for Aristotelian diversity and unity disappears. And if, furthermore, all regimes aim at physical survival and stability above all else, then Aristotle's principle of distributive justice becomes an argument for obedience. Those who contribute most to the ends of a

Hobbesian state are those who care least about honor, politics and political education.

Hobbes's disagreement with and dismissal of Aristotle's views on unity and diversity finds further expression in his rejection of a mixed constitution and his idea of theory. For Aristotle the superiority of the polity lies in its mixture of political principles, classes, and forms of power. Within limits, the more inclusive a community's deliberation, the more it becomes the whole. But for Hobbes a mixed constitution divides sovereignty, increases instability, and leads to civil war. His "mixture" of egoistic individuals, each of whom embodies the same political principles and idea of power, means that deliberation must be the clash of interests.

The principle of inclusion extends to Aristotle's understanding of political theorizing. His attention to what has been said and done before attests to his belief that a theorist needs to consider the accumulated wisdom of statesmen and thinkers. For him, as for Machiavelli, political theory is a mixture, which is to say that both commend republican theorizing as well as republican politics.

In the "Introduction" to book I of the *Discorsi* Machiavelli declares his intention to "open a new route." It is a route he hopes others will follow, for the task before him and them, the revival of republican politics and republican political theory, is difficult and necessarily collaborative. As this implies, Machiavelli understood theorizing as analogous to political founding and the power of theory as analogous to republican political authority. In both cases the aim is the further politicizing of the people as opposed to rendering them quiescent or permitting their ambitions to disintegrate into a riot of private demands. Leader, founder, and theorist initiate actions which others must complete or, in the case of the leader and theorist in a republic, they help complete and sustain actions already initiated. While the common people understand what they can feel and the features of their immediate landscape, they are less adept and more easily deceived about more remote and distant matters.[9]

One thing Machiavelli learned about political theory as an activity from the great founders he admires (or around whom he constructs a mythology for the Prince to admire) is that political and theoretical power requires a sharing of responsibility. Rome's greatness came

[9] "The function of republican leadership [and I would add of republican political theory and founding] is to reconnect the abstract generality of policy options and political principles with the lived experience and practical skill of the led" (Pitkin 1984: 88).

from the sharing of authority among Romulus, Numa, the Senate and, later, the people. That sharing is institutionalized in Rome's mixed constitution in which each class embodies a social principle and political commitment (to unity, inherited wealth or popular liberty) and view of the common good as part of a collaborative but also confrontational politics.

Because the mixed constitution provided Rome with multiple perspectives, she had a unique ability to adapt to the times. It is precisely this capacity that Machiavelli claims for himself in the *Prince*, where he likens himself to a landscape painter who is able, as the Prince and people separately are not, to see each from the other's point of view. This implies that a healthy republic with a mixed constitution makes theory superfluous, and that conversely political theory is needed only in times of corruption.

Hobbes has a very different understanding of theory, though that theory, like Machiavelli's, is analogous to a (very different) understanding of politics. Hobbes does not want or expect others to complete his task (except in the sense of implementing it) any more than he expects the sovereign to be divided. If preachers and teachers would make it the new Bible and *Republic*, there would be an end to pernicious doctrines and *stasis*.

Part of Hobbes's originality and power rests on his arguments for and appeal to method and science (by which he meant the geometrical science of the Paduan school). The scientific method was a model not so much for the study of politics as for the remaking of it. Hobbes understood what later American social scientists practiced: that one could better contain popular activism and radical theory if the methods of study helped constitute and conform to the methods of doing politics. Method also permitted Hobbes to exempt himself from the charge of self-interest which his own argument claimed to be behind any theory or theology. He, unlike others, was disinterested, because he, unlike them, simply followed scientific rules by which politics could be deduced from psychological egoism, itself derived from principles of physics.

The problem with method is that it may not impress those who do not understand its nature. Since this includes a majority, most men would be unconvinced by the reasoning Hobbes uses in book I of *Leviathan*. But this is not a serious obstacle, since all they need do is to look into themselves and remember their dreams. For such men it is not the precision of science that will move them but an evocative prose which makes the nightmares of their waking lives as vivid as their dreams. Better yet, the power of language can energize human passions such that men relive civil war in their imaginations so they remain committed to its prevention in reality. In an effort to achieve all this, Hobbes's masterpiece incorporates into a single edifice the poetry and parables of a Christian people living with a classical legacy in an emerging commercial society.

The *Leviathan* uses the full resources of language (including those it condemns) to appeal to all political factions and the full range of human passions. At a minimum it hopes to convince everyone on every ground that it offers a language in which each can talk to the other without fear of disadvantage. More substantially it speaks to each faction in its own "dialect," whether that be scientific or commercial, royalist or revolutionary, Catholic or Puritan, classical or modern – within a single work which would be a vehicle for linguistic and so national reconciliation. Yet *Leviathan* uses diverse rhetorical strategies and multiple discourses to argue for and to create a single politically antiseptic language. Only with the success of such a project could cacophony be transformed into conversation.[10] So whatever its own language, the language *Leviathan* commends is geometrical, precise, and quantitative. However intense and evocative its prose, it seeks to defuse the intensity of speech in order to flatten public speech and prevent civil war. Ideally such a language would help make political controversies as peripheral as mathematical ones,[11] and leave us if not with community then with *détente*.

All this suggests once more how far Hobbes's understanding of political corruption is from the etymology of corruption, from Aristotle, and from the republican tradition. In that tradition corruption and virtue had been the controlling terms of public discourse. But Hobbes regards this as moralism. For him moral judgments are manifestations of interests narrowly conceived, morality is what the sovereign says it is, virtue is correct reasoning which leads sane men to prefer obedience to dissent and passivity to activity, and corruption is transformed from a standard of judgment to a standard judged in terms of its contribution to stability, peace, and commodious living.

Of course republican theorists cared about stability, unity, and order too. Machiavelli's praise of the confrontational politics that

[10] In these respects the *Leviathan* seeks to be like the sovereign: it would like to represent us and be authorized to speak for us through a contract in which we assent to its propositions as we did to those of the sovereign. If Machiavelli saw political theory as analogous to political action, Hobbes sees politics as an extension of his conception of theory.

[11] This is the argument of a man who thought of mathematical disputes in terms of warfare.

energized Rome (but decimated Florence) presupposed a strong civic religion to provide object and limit for such confrontations. As Aristotle's critique of Plato indicates, what matters is that the order be a *political* order. An order built on hierarchy and dependency, privatism and passivity, the absence of public liberty and ambition, the domination of a single person or class, and a preoccupation with material rewards rather than a common good, is corrupt no matter how orderly it may be. A *political* order requires the sharing of power, which is why Aristotle understands his definition of citizenship to fit a democracy best.[12]

V

For purposes of this essay the *Federalist Papers* can be read as developing and refining Hobbes's critique of the Aristotelian–republican understanding of political corruption, despite Hobbes's mercantilist tendencies and royalist sympathies and Publius's insistence that by adapting republicanism to the exigencies of the moment and the imperatives of the age, the republicans were saving republicanism rather than rejecting it. Though I think the republicans' repudiation of civic humanism more complete for being less obvious and explicit, I would not wholly deny J.G.A. Pocock's (1975: 526–7) claim that the republican idea of corruption "persisted in American thought, not merely as a survival slowly dying after its tap-root was cut, but with a reality and relevance to elements in American experience that kept it alive and in tension with consequences from its partial abandonment." If, as he insists, "America was born in a dread of modernity itself, of which the threat to virtue by corruption was the contemporary ideological expression," then even this partial abandonment was reluctant.[13]

The argument that the republican understanding of corruption remained alive after the liberal triumph and in tension with it helps explain how our rhetorical tradition has sustained both a dominant discourse, which regards corruption narrowly as individual malfeasance or not at all, and a subjugated discourse, in which corruption is an important political term and understood in systemic moral terms. In times of disarray, the latter emerges as a contestant for

[12] Aristotle's preferences for democracy are matters more of practical experience than of principle. For instance, one advantage of democracy over oligarchy is that the poor who care for wealth have greater possibilities for civic education than do the wealthy who love honor.

[13] Pocock (1975: 509). If true, then the modernization literature takes on a wholly new dimension.

redescribing the dominant interpretation of corruption. This dialectic helps explain why social scientists even now find it necessary to criticize Aristotle's "moralistic" definition of corruption and how, more parochially, they can write about corruption as they do and I can criticize them as I shall do.

Despite the legitimacy of Pocock's warning, it still seems to me that Madison gutted so much of the infrastructure of republican theory and politics that "partial abandonment" becomes a pun. Moreover, it is perfectly possible, as the case of Locke illustrates, to fear modernity, yet insist that its realities (and promise) be courageously faced and accepted. Finally, I think Pocock underestimates the degree to which the middle-class radicals in the last decades of the eighteenth century based their arguments on natural rights, were preoccupied with modern socio-economic grievances, and defined virtue and corruption in terms of productivity, specialization, industriousness, professionalism – anything that distinguished them from the corruption of the idle nobility and the wretched poor – rather than in terms of citizenship and the public quest for a common good. "Self-centered economic productivity," Isaac Kramnick (1982: 662) writes, "not public citizenship, became the badge of the virtuous man."

To claim, as I do here, that the *Federalist Papers* are built on Hobbesian political metaphysics[14] seems inconsistent with the obvious fact that Hobbes insists that only an absolute sovereign could maintain peace and economic well-being. Clearly such a sovereign would be as odious to liberty as to anarchy. The separation of powers, checks and balances, social fragmentation, and federalism as a whole, are all designed to divide sovereignty while maintaining a strong state.[15] And while it is true that "the people" are sovereign, this is not one people but many. They are divided against each other and themselves so as better to guard against a permanent majority faction.

Yet the authors of the *Federalist Papers*, especially Hamilton, are, like Hobbes, anxious to enhance the powers of a centralized state at the expense of local attachments to place, persons, and tradition. Both, moreover, regard the principal tasks of that state as military security and economic prosperity. "The chief ends of government" are insuring American independence of foreign domination, regu-

[14] I say "Hobbesian," not "Hobbes's," because I am less interested in historical influence than I am in analogies and parallels.

[15] A strong state does not preclude individual rights, as long as those rights are maintained by the state itself and derive from no independent moral source that would justify revolution.

lating interstate commerce, supervising taxation, and maintaining a militia to prevent domestic convulsions brought on by economic disputes. Government has no substantive good of its own. It exists to provide men with the opportunity to choose their own private goods.

The Federalists are what Hobbes wished to be: founders of a new nation. For this reason (and others) they have little interest in elaborate scientific scaffolding, methodological exegesis, theological disputations or hypothetical states of nature. Nevertheless, they do emphasize the scientific foundations of their republican revisionism and understand, as Hobbes did, that this new science is possible only when men are seen to have a common nature rather than a shared history. History is of little use except to provide object lessons and so there is little need to pay attention to recent political experiments or ancient practices and thinkers. Finally, the Federalists speak of the revolutionary remnants around them in language reminiscent of Hobbes's state of nature. The revolution has reconfirmed their view that men are generally ambitious, vindictive and rapacious, usually governed by momentary passions and immediate interests and often driven to politics by depravities endemic to their condition.[16]

The way to contain human nature is through a well-designed system which defuses passion and diffuses interests. Like Hobbes's sovereign, the citizen in that system would not even aspire to self-governance. Since egoism cannot be changed by policy or political education, the only hope for a stable society is to use egoism against itself. If men cannot be persuaded to curb their egoism in the interest of balancing liberty and authority, they can nevertheless attain the balance despite their intentions. The originality of the proposal is its claim to contain corruption (in the sense of disintegration and decay) without having to stimulate *virtù*(e). This severing of virtue and corruption amounts to a repudiation of the conceptual constellation that had defined republicanism.

But this is not wholly true or quite fair. The authors of the *Federalist Papers* did not regard themselves as discarding republican principles but as uncovering a "powerful means" by "which the excellences of republican government may be retained and its imperfections lessened or avoided."[17] Given the "horror and disgust" which the constant agitations between tyranny and anarchy of ancient Italy and Greece engender, it is necessary to save republican principles from the charge that "all free government [is] inconsistent with the order of society." The task then is to save

[16] See *Federalist*, no. 6, 15, 28, 37. [17] Hamilton in *Federalist*, no. 9.

republicanism from itself and from its critics; from its history and its theorists; from its tendency to degenerate into anarchy and corruption. The history of mankind reveals that it is republicanism that is most prone to corruption. Hobbes is right.

One way republicanism could be saved from its excesses, its enemies, and its history, was rhetorical: assign the pejorative connotations of republicanism to popular regimes while assigning its positive connotations to the new representative system.[18] Such a rhetorical division made the democratic component of the mixed constitution (collective wisdom and commitment to public liberty) part of corruption rather than part of a solution to it. This helps account for the fact that in less than a generation democratic Athens and republican Rome went from being exemplars to object lessons.

A second way in which republicanism could be saved was by relying on the traditional virtue of the founders. The Federalists regarded themselves as a group of men who, by character, learning, circumstance, and opportunity were exempt from the corruption of their contemporaries and progeny. Given their power and virtue, they could seize the moment to instantiate that virtue in a regime that would live after among people incapable of emulating their character or achievement. This problem of sustaining the virtue of founders is a familiar one in republican political theory. Machiavelli, for instance, thought that the founders could become civic only through the establishment of a civic religion which both stimulated heroic deeds analogous to the founding act and assured that the referent of such deeds was the public good. Political (and theoretical) foundings required continual renewal and rededication by acts which imitated the founding act itself.

The Federalists' solution (though not necessarily their intent) is surprisingly similar and radically different: similar because it relied on the perpetuation of founding *virtù*(e) in a civic religion which celebrated the virtue of the founders and the system they consecrated; different because this civic religion of system was meant not to inspire future deeds of similar character but to make them unnecessary. While the founders' virtue was manifest in their lawgiving, collective wisdom, and dedication to public good and public liberty, subsequent generations would need "virtues" of a very different sort: law-abidingness, private liberty, self-interest.

A third way of saving republicanism was to institute the political reforms discovered by the improved science of politics. Foremost

[18] This is Richard Krouse's (1983) argument.

among these was a theory of representation and fragmentation which would make it possible for a republic to exist over great spaces and a long period of time, in contrast to the republics of antiquity.

Prior to the *Federalist Papers* common wisdom dictated that a "large republic" was a contradiction in terms and in form. Any large centralized regime inevitably fostered privatism and apathy, preoccupation with status and wealth, and a citizenry who thought of themselves as benefit-receiving subjects rather than participants defining benefits in and for the public. Madison turned this whole argument upside down. A large republic was not a contradiction in terms; it was the only way republicanism could be made viable. Only a centralized state in which the government controlled the governed and itself[19] could save society from the tyranny of faction, by which Madison meant a minority or majority of citizens united by some "common impulse of passion, or of interest, adverse to the rights of citizens, or to the permanent and aggregate interests of the community."[20]

It was precisely the merit of Madison's representative version of republicanism that it solved the problem of faction. The only way of removing the cause of faction is to destroy liberty (a cure worse than the disease); or "to give every citizen the same opinion, the same passions and the same interests." This is impossible as long as men have unequal "faculties of acquiring property," and are ruled by partiality and passion rather than disinterested reason. Since they always are, the causes of faction are sown in the nature of men. Thus the only realistic possibility is to control the effects of faction, either by preventing the same passion or interest from uniting a majority, or by rendering such a majority incapable of concerted action. But if "the impulse and the opportunity be suffered to coincide, we well know that neither moral nor religious motives can be relied on as an adequate control."

A large republic can control the effects of faction in both these ways. The larger the number of people choosing a representative, the more interests he has to represent. The more interests he has to represent, the less likely he is to represent a single interest or unite a

[19] See *Federalist*, no. 51.

[20] From *Federalist* no. 10, as is the exposition which follows. In contrast to Madison's argument on faction, republicans insisted that the commonwealth "must stand outside class or other factional interests" because its aim was moral and achievable only by political education, morally exemplary conduct, disinterested legislation, and mature judgment in the choice of leaders. See Finley (1962: 6).

single faction. A similar principle of division pervades the life of individual citizens. As Madison puts it in *Federalist*, no.51: "This policy of supplying, by opposite and rival interests, the defect of better motives, might be traced through the whole system of human affairs, private as well as public." The more diverse and diffuse the interests, the more tenuous and tentative become allegiances to or dependencies on particular groups, institutions, persons, traditions or locales. The more people are free of such particular attachments, the more they accommodate to each other in shifting national coalitions, for plural if not incompatible ends. If, by some fluke, a majority faction does form, there are institutional arrangements designed to check, balance, and dissipate their power.

Notice how this argument legitimates faction as the mode in which a decreasingly virtuous people perceives and pursues its interests in public, whether the people are conceived of as individuals seeking a private good or as groups seeking a more inclusive but still particular good. This admittedly reluctant legitimation contrasts sharply with the republican belief that factionalism was the death of politics, because a faction, unlike a particular viewpoint on or contribution to a whole, was a part and partial view imposing itself on a whole.

Notice too how Madison revolutionizes the republican views on unity and diversity in two ways: through revising the idea of a mixed constitution and through a form of anti-political education. For Machiavelli the one, the few, and the many embodied distinctive rights, privileges, and principles of government. But where there was no monarch, no inherited or (more disappointingly) natural aristocracy, and where the people seemed intent on trampling down the liberty of others, one needed to balance not principles or social classes but interests and the institutional forms through which the people chose to be represented.[21] While this recasting of a mixed constitution might not create substantive relations of virtue, it did have two important benefits: it would prevent the acquisition of so much power by some that others would become dependent; and it allowed for an infinitely expanding republic, since the number of interests the system could absorb was, in principle, unlimited.

A second way in which Madison recasts the relationship between diversity and unity leads back to the issue of political education. In Aristotelian terms Madison can be accused of fostering too much unity wrongly conceived, and too much diversity wrongly conceived. For Madison was implicitly proposing what he explicitly

[21] See the discussion of this point in Pocock (1975: 517ff.).

denied was possible: giving the people the same interest and opinion.

That interest was an interest in interest, an opinion that men are by nature self-interested animals incapable of civic virtue and that any realistic politics must respect that nature without imposing any substantive good, except perhaps the good that there is no substantive good. But of course such a shared interest and good, while it may treat (or even make) us alike, dissociates rather than unifies. It fosters a homogenizing ideology of interest which fragments us much as Madison hoped to accomplish by controlling the results of faction. In these terms the critique of small republics, as presupposing cultural consensus and social homogeneity, and the praise of large states, as pluralistic, may have things backwards.

By helping shape similar opinions about the nature of politics and the proper way to study it, *Federalist Papers* have provided an oblique political education much as republican theorists sought to do directly.

Of course this is an exaggeration. Not all people regard politics and its study in Madisonian terms. But one place where they do is in the contemporary scholarship on political corruption.

VI

Most contemporary social scientists regard political corruption as a matter of particular officials violating their public trust by placing private gain above public duty, rather than as a general loss of civic virtue. If corruption is merely the failure of a few miscreants to adhere to bureaucratic rectitude, then the problem is easily solved by removing them from positions of authority.

It may be that the general repudiation of the republican understanding of structural corruption this signifies is due to our having solved the problem as republican authors understood it. Or, it may be that we have difficulty understanding it in their terms; that we have "solved" the problem by narrowing corruption's range of reference and association in ways that blunt its critical edge, curing the disease by making it difficult to diagnose.[22] At the very least the overall (but not total) deflation of "corruption" disconnects us from

[22] Livy (1.1) laments that his contemporaries live in a darkness where "we can neither endure our vices nor face the remedies needed to cure them"; where "wealth has made us greedy, and self-indulgence has brought us, through every form of sensual excess to be . . . in love with death both individual and collective." Machiavelli too thought that one sign of corruption was an inability to recognize its presence.

the beginnings of political science and the origins of our polity.

A good argument can be made that political science and theory were "invented" as a response to, a way of making sense of, and in hopes of ameliorating the political corruption that plagued classical Athens. Thucydides' *History* focuses on it, Socrates was tried for it, the *Republic* is about it, and Aristotle's understanding of it shaped a tradition that provided the primary terms of American political self-understanding until at least the last decades of the eighteenth century. It is clear that the debate then over what America was and ought to be took place in the language of corruption and virtue. In these terms present scholarly attitudes cut us off from resources of understanding contained in our conceptual and political origins.

Of course if one believes in methodological and political modernization as progress, then those "resources" are obstacles to understanding and policy. Some such belief underlies the present effort by political scientists to develop a politically neutral, methodologically respectable, operationally viable definition of corruption.[23] That effort is built on the rejection of the republican understanding of corruption as moralistic and subjective. There is no point in dealing with the "moral aspects of corrupt behavior" when an "empirical examination of consequences is certain to contribute more to an understanding of political corruption than the roundest condemnation."[24] To see corruption as a "disease" infecting the body politic ignores the fact that it can be functional in its facilitating of entrepreneurship, stability, modernization, and integration of new elites.[25]

This view rests on an implicit standard of systemic corruption and health even as it explicitly rejects such a standard. A good society is a modernizing one; a corrupt society is one that inhibits "develop-

[23] See for instance Leys (1965); Nye (1967); and van Klaveren (1970).

[24] That is the claim of LeVine (1975: xii-xiii). J.S. Nye (1967: 567) opposes moral judgment and political analysis, and Johnston (1981: 173) rejects the idea of systemic corruption. Cf. Samuel Huntington (1968), who is critical of identifying modernization with political development.

[25] More specifically, corruption can be functional when it helps a political system adapt to innovation, increases economic efficiency, prolongs a society's existence even when "formally inadequate," produces "favourable decisions," provides entrance for disenfranchised groups and accommodates rising classes, and enlists the support of leaders who would otherwise remain outside the regime. A frequently cited instance of corruption helping a political system to function more smoothly is the urban machines in America, which purportedly delivered both material and symbolic benefits to the urban poor, thus easing the trauma of urbanization and industrialization. Even if the benefits were not as extensive as claimed and did not flow to all the poor on the basis of need, "there were benefits, widely distributed": Johnston (1981: 5, 174); Friedrich (1972: 139); and Wilson (1966).

ment." But because the ends of modernity are regarded as inevitable, impersonal, and/or rational, they cannot themselves be the subject of rational dispute or "subjective" prescriptions. In the end republican moralists are simply on the wrong side of history, which is itself a process whereby struggle, contradiction and dissonance are transformed into hidden harmonies brought about by providential design, secular progress, and science.

In these terms a corrupt society is one which inhibits intellectual progress (i.e., the growth of science and social science), discourages social differentiation and the division of labor, stifles individual initiative, lacks stable mechanisms to insure system maintenance, and has a fragmented authority structure. In sum, a corrupt society imposes political restraints on economic development and traditional restraints on political development. Conversely, a noncorrupt society is one that maintains political order as a precondition for economic disorder understood as "development."

There is much that can be said in criticism of the substance and grounding of this standard of corruption, but I should like to make just two comments. The first is to note what may seem obvious: that while advanced industrial societies (notably the United States) remain the *telos* toward which developing countries (do and should) aim, aspire or tend, the "findings" about corruption in those nations serve to redefine that *telos* in ways that further marginalize the republican understanding of systemic corruption. Or to put it in more fashionable terms, the construction of the other is also a reconstruction of the self. Secondly, the still largely uncritical celebration of modernization upon which that marginalization rests has come under incisive criticism by "post-modernist" writers such as Michel Foucault.

Foucault argues that modern disciplinary society is no less a system of subjugation and subjection than the regime it replaced.[26] Because this society incorporates the rhetoric of liberation, self-realization, demystification, and rights into its disciplinary strategies, its form of domination may be a particularly insidious one. Certainly its reliance on a unified subject as the bearer of rights and rational interests against the encroachment of others and a potentially repressive government ignores the process by which such an epistemologically and morally privileged subject is constituted by disciplinary strategies and normalizing tactics. Fearing the paternalism of kings and the abuse of absolute sovereigns, modern liberal

[26] See especially Foucault's *Discipline and Punish* (1979) part III, chapter 3, and part IV, chapter 3, as well as his "Afterword" (1982).

society has fostered a micro-domination of everyday life which confounds its fondest hopes and largest claims.

I am not arguing that Foucault is right in insisting that Bentham's Panopticon is the appropriate metaphor for contemporary society. Still less am I claiming him as an ally in my invocation of republicanism since that too is for him a normalizing discourse. But insofar as Foucault dramatizes the ways in which the modern liberal state is unable to provide significant political content to its own values of consent, individuality, freedom, and rights; to the extent that he correctly claims that we are as "unfree" as the older communities liberalism sought to and thought it had overcome: to that extent there may be good reason to look at aspects of those older communities and traditions as ways of sustaining even liberal values. More particularly, it may be that only a strong republican understanding of systemic corruption can sustain either the liberalism of Hobbes and Bentham or that of J.S. Mill (whose *On Representative Government* comes close to acknowledging this point). The irony of republican communities as the focus for sustaining liberal values is that it turns on its head Madison's argument that only a large centralized state could salvage republicanism.

REFERENCES

Connor, W. Robert. 1984. *Thucydides*. Princeton, NJ: Princeton University Press.

Coulanges, Fustel de. 1957. *The Ancient City*. Garden City, NY: Doubleday.

Euben, Peter. 1978. "On Corruption." *The Antioch Review* 36 (1): 103–18.

Finley, Moses. 1962. "The Athenian Demagogues." *Past and Present* 21: 3–24.

Foucault, Michel. 1977. "Nietzsche, Genealogy, History." In Donald F. Bouchard (ed.), *Language, Counter-memory, Practice: Selected Essays and Interviews*. Ithaca, NY: Cornell University Press, pp. 139–64.

1979. *Discipline and Punish: The Birth of the Prison*. New York: Random House.

1980. "Two Lectures." In Colin Gordon (ed.), *Power/Knowledge*. New York: Pantheon Books, pp. 78–108

1982. "Afterword." In Hubert L. Dreyfus and Paul Rabinow, *Michel Foucault: Beyond Structuralism and Hermeneutics*. Chicago: University of Chicago Press, pp. 208–26.

Friedrich, C.J. 1972. *The Pathology of Politics: Violence, Betrayal, Corruption, Secrecy and Propaganda*. New York: Harper and Row.

Heidenheimer, Arnold J. (ed.) 1970. *Political Corruption: Readings in Comparative Analysis*. New York: Holt, Rinehart, and Winston.

Huntington, Samuel. 1968. *Political Order in Changing Societies*. New Haven, CT, and London: Yale University Press.

Johnston, Michael. 1981. *Political Corruption and Public Policy in America*. Monterey, CA: Brooks/Cole.

van Klaveren, Jacob. 1970. "Corruption: The Special Case of the United States." In Heidenheimer 1970: 269–75.

Kramnick, Isaac. 1968. *Bolingbroke and his Circle: The Politics of Nostalgia in the Age of Walpole*. Cambridge, MA: Harvard University Press.

1982. "Republican Revisionism Revisited." *The American Historical Review* 87 (3) (June): 629–64.

Krouse, Richard. 1983. "'Classical' Images of Democracy in America: Madison and Tocqueville." In Graeme Duncan (ed.), *Democratic Theory and Practice*. Cambridge: Cambridge University Press, pp. 58–78.

LeVine, Victor T. 1975. *Political Corruption: The Ghana Case*. Stanford, CA: The Hoover Institution Press.

Leys, Colin. 1965. "What Is the Problem about Corruption?" *Journal of Modern African Studies* 3: 215–24.

Nye, J.S. 1967. "Corruption and Political Development: A Cost–Benefit Analysis." *American Political Science Review* 61 (2) (June): 417–27.

Pitkin, Hanna Fenichel. 1984. *Fortune is a Woman*. Berkeley, CA, and Los Angeles, CA: University of California Press.

Pocock, J.G.A. 1975. *The Machiavellian Moment: Florentine Political Thought and the Atlantic Republican Tradition*. Princeton, NJ: Princeton University Press.

Wilson, James Q. 1966. "Corruption: The Shame of the States." *The Public Interest* 66 (2) (Winter): 28–38.

12

Public opinion

J. A. W. GUNN

To have opinions is a universal trait of humanity and to contemplate the opinions of that body sometimes called the "public" is scarcely less commonplace. In order to isolate a political idea of which a history may be written, retreat from such universality is essential. Not that one may readily identify a form of political discourse about opinion that owes nothing to more general themes; rather one must try to decide at what points awareness of the sentiments of others matured into a formula similar to our modern notion. By this test, Alcuin's maxim, "Vox populi, vox dei," does not mark a significant development in political expectations. Often employed as a sentimental invocation of the virtues of ordinary people, the divine connection conferred none of the powers that it had bestowed on kings. Applied to politics, *vox populi* might serve merely to remind rulers that subjects' complaints warranted attention. Rarely were the identity of the people or the mode of its being heard specified. Surviving documents usually condemn the *vox populi*; Pope, for an educated man, was being moderate when he remarked on the oddity that this voice both was and was not divine. Comments, more positive and more political, surface in the literature of the English Civil War of the 1640s or of the Fronde in France. In 1709–11 *vox populi* figures prominently in the vocabulary of British political argument arising in the debate over party addresses (Gunn 1983: 76–7). But other forms of expression provided the continuing language of discussion.

For there has been an awkwardly large number of ways of alluding to matters of common report – the early *sensus communis*, Machiavelli's *publica voce* and the French *opinion commune*. The last carries the strongest credentials as direct ancestor of modern expression and meaning, but there are formidable difficulties in rendering Renaissance "opinion" as public opinion. For the *opinio* of the Latin humanists was a philosophical term to describe a product of the imagination to be contrasted with the more reliable judgments derived from reason. What survived this epoch was the maxim that opinion was "queen of the world." The thought may have been that of Jerome Cardan, polymath and skeptic; the editor of Cardan's autobiography, Gabriel Naudé, popularized it in a political context. Further spread abroad from its use by Pascal, it consequently gained two centuries more of life, for Pascal's text was cited in the major French dictionaries of the early eighteenth century. Few were the French writers who thereafter could mention the subject without invoking its regal status, though often this cliché was a barrier to useful confrontation with the phenomenon.

The most familiar scholarly judgment about the early history of the concept must be qualified. Sir William Temple, we often hear, said something significant when he noted that all governments rested on opinion. Now, by virtue of its dominance over all things, opinion no doubt prevailed too in government; "mundus regitur opinionibus" was another current saw. So Temple's insight may not be remarkable. More specifically, however, the thought was already familiar in the works of writers who had explored the various provinces of that worldly empire commanded by opinion. One of these was Barnaby Rich, writing in the reign of James I, who said that it was "Opinion that placeth Men in Office and Authoritie" (Rich 1613: 1416). Sir Walter Raleigh's *Cabinet Council* made the same point by stressing that the physical weakness of a single man dictated a basis other than force for government. Hobbes agreed and referred specifically to "opinion," while Temple's contemporary, Lord Delamere, related authority to the "good opinion" that subjects entertained of rulers (Warrington 1694: 44–7). Temple's insight was thus shared by much of his century. Nor did the observation distinguish between governments that might defer to public sentiment and those that did not. As a pamphleteer of 1780 would write, even the ruler of the Ottoman empire might occasionally sacrifice a grand vizier to the mob's fury.

But this is not what we mean by government resting upon public opinion, and Pascal's contrast between force and the gentle rule of opinion may have a stronger parental title. Still, it was Temple's dictum that was carried into the next age when Charles Davenant, Bishop Berkeley, and David Hume all used it. Hume's thoughts on the subject subsequently influenced James Madison. But the well-traveled dictum arrived largely empty, almost as devoid of sound content as Cardan's maxim. Evidence for the ambiguity of both of these thoughts may be culled from a book of 1631 by François Cauvigny which paid its respects to the queen, opinion, and then proceeded to show how the French king employed that engine to overawe his adversaries (Colomby 1631: iii–iv). Far from being a shield protecting subjects, opinion was a sword to be wielded in the name of royal power and did not entail limited government. Indeed, in light of the contempt with which learned men of the time treated the opinions of the masses, there was an unresolved tension in the appeal to their opinion as the support of power. Only in the eighteenth century would schemes for enlightening the public mind serve to reduce the anomaly.

Where then are the roots of our concept? In the satirical literature on manners largely inspired by La Bruyère and in British polemics of the 1730s. In France, we find what appear to be the earliest literal references to *l'opinion publique* as early as Montaigne's *Essais* of the 1580s. But the expression became in any way commonplace only in essays of Theophrastan characters, dating from the early years of the eighteenth century. These tended to display the state of society and to protest against the tyranny exercised by modes and opinions. This theme occasioned the thought of Morvan de Bellegarde (in 1702) that "l'opinion publique" was not a guarantor of real merit, or the argument in an anonymous work that man responded not to independent taste, but only to "l'opinion publique" (Bellegarde 1702: 181; Anon. 1700: 133, 218).[1] To make sense of these comments, one must appreciate that there existed in Britain and especially in France a recognized public. Chiefly an audience for writers and dramatists, its exact contours and the justness of its mind were much disputed. The power of this "tribunal" was exercised over individual reputations, influencing the individual both as artist and as moral being. Literary men at once courted the public and condemned the inauthentic conduct induced by attention to its caprice. Because of the intellectual's affected disdain for popular opinion, a positive connotation for *l'opinion publique* was associated with views more stable and responsible than the latest enthusiasm of the town. In 1715 Louis de Sacy limited the name to the unanimous voice of all men – something close to a moral consensus (Sacy 1716: 56–62, 150). Only in this durable form could it be said that God explained himself through the voice of the people.

Sacy's insistence on lasting unanimity as the basis of a useful

[1] Both P.-J. Brillon and an *avocat* known only as Alleaume have been credited with writing this.

public sentiment would continue to haunt French understanding. This literature's focus on personal reputation was also politically relevant. For in an age without organs for collecting opinion, the reputation of rulers afforded the point of entry into politics. Sometimes writers suggested that rulers were manipulative in striving to regulate opinion; others stressed how the sanction of opinion might rule the destinies of ministers. In the largest sense, the literature of characters dealt with "moeurs," a category embracing both private ethics and social mores. As the century progressed the social, even political, nature of *moeurs* was underlined, but in the reign of Louis XIV the main avenue of social commentary had created an expression – "l'opinion publique" – and had, if only obliquely, contemplated its political relevance.

In Britain, meanwhile, private foibles were less savored and public issues more fully aired. The French vogue for treating "opinion" as an abstract and impersonal force was not as evident, though several essayists – among them John Selden, Henry Peacham, Owen Felltham, and Matthew Prior (Selden 1927; Peacham 1962; Felltham 1661; Prior 1970) – followed Rich in this vein. What the English produced in abundance were weekly political essays in which party champions contested the issues of the day. In the 1730s the words and the meaning of our expression "public opinion" both appeared. Understandably, major treatments of the substance of public opinion fail to call it that and some examples of use deal with nonpolitical sentiment. *The Weekly Register*, a paper supporting Walpole from the fringes of partisan controversy, seems to have been one of the first to use the term regularly. A comment of 1731 on Bolingbroke's political reputation said, for instance, "After all, the publick Opinion must be determin'd by the Publick itself" (*Weekly Register* 69, August 7, 1731).[2] Chiefly it was the government press that led in examining the nature, scope, and legitimacy of public opinion. Temple's too-famous thought that all government rested on opinion was qualified by spelling out the receptivity of British institutions to popular influences.

James Pitt, who writing as "Francis Osborne" was the most inspired of the journalists, portrayed George II as governing but by "the Management of other People's Opinions, Prejudices, Passions and different Views in Life." It was good, said Osborne, that the king was in touch with the opinions of an electorate of some 600,000 (Pitt's estimate). The task of a minister, if unpopular, was to

[2] See too *Weekly Register* 65 (July 10, 1731); 104 (April 8, 1732); and 202 (January 19, 1734).

"struggle with popular Opinion till he have satisfied the Publick" (*Daily Gazetteer* 216, March 6, 1736; *London Journal* 1759, January 12, 1733–34). The "Sense of the People" was not the voice of disaffection and was to be taken from the votes in parliament. Tests based on opinion without doors came at elections and by noting the state of public credit. The right of petitioning gained ample acknowledgment but insolent commands of the populace were out of order. Nor were members of parliament delegates. The mere fact of Opposition rhetoric or of ferment continued to win dispraise from Walpole's writers. Appeal to the public in defense of the government's case was but "a fair and rational Design in a Free Country; where as all Publick Measures are submitted to the Opinion of all, they may consequently be liable to the Misapprehension of Many." Or again, with a more traditional notion of the legitimate scope of opinion,

> It is excusable for Private Men to be carried away by the torrent of Publick Opinion, but hopeless is the Nation which hath in view anything below National Concerns.
>
> 1739–40; *Daily Gazetteer* 1439, January 30; 1495, April 4, 1740

Bolingbroke too led the Opposition into a new vocabulary, writing that his political views would "stand, or fall in the publick Opinion, according to their merit" (*Craftsman* 13: 327).

Undoubtedly, Britain was then the home of public opinion, though of a small public, and the phenomenon had been labeled in terms already modern. What stood in the way of embracing it without reserve was the place of parliament; the nation that enjoyed representative institutions could afford to ignore unofficial pretenders to the people's voice. There is also that curious pattern whereby court journalists were most likely to remark upon the novel features of politics. The name and nature of public opinion thus gained recognition largely through the efforts of those who defended party, influence, and a ministerial press as necessary means of ensuring that a volatile people did not overwhelm its government. The expression "public opinion" would never thereafter quit English usage, but the concept lacked scrutiny for another half century.

In France, by contrast, one detects more concern about the status of public opinion, perhaps for the very reason that there was no electorate to consult, no legislature to express indignation at irresponsible grumblings, no free comment in the press and, in sum, little that Britons would see as a political process. Thus arises a curious situation and room for misunderstanding. Literary evidence of interest in the phenomenon would grow in France, contrasting with a very matter-of-fact British acceptance of the presence of an articulate public. The salience of a political concept may turn not on the presence of the condition of which it speaks, but on its absence, a fact not always noted by those who exaggerate Gallic contributions to understanding public opinion. Nor is an element of wish-fulfillment an ideal basis for such understanding. British documents suggest that much may be taken for granted and that a process and vocabulary for understanding it need not accompany each other, though that nation did in fact develop, haltingly, categories meaningful for its situation.

In the France of Louis XV efforts to relate "opinion" to domestic politics came from the Abbé de Saint-Pierre, his friend d'Argenson, one-time minister of foreign affairs, and from Antoine Pecquet, the chief clerk in that ministry. But Rousseau, who is sometimes credited, quite wrongly, with introducing the term "public opinion" into English, is the major figure (see Ganochaud 1980). In fact, the English knew of public opinion without Rousseau's help. Rousseau's credentials as innovator are strongest in contemplating a legislator who managed public opinion and directed it to the great end of reforming *moeurs*. The affirmation in the *Contrat social* that modern governments ignored public opinion as an agent of reformation was too bold. Rousseau's identifying the managing of public opinion as a lost art may have helped, however, to advance the concept from one for incidental mention to an object of contemplation in its own right. Ambitions to reform *moeurs* were not new, but study of the relation between laws and manners had gained vitality with Montesquieu's *Esprit des lois* and there had followed that wave of social self-examination in which works by Charles Pinot Duclos and Toussaint were but the most prominent. The folkways of interest were directly relevant to the quality of public life and the notion of *moeurs publiques* grew fashionable. The same thought led Duclos to write, in 1751, that *moeurs* in Paris correspond to what was called the spirit of government in London.

Like Duclos, Rousseau saw opinions as forming the content of *moeurs*, but his marked disdain for existing attitudes muted his respect for influences upon government; rather, the public appears less as an actor than as the object on which the judicious ruler was to act. So despite recognition that the people should have a censorial power – a function serving to distinguish public opinion from the legislative role of the general will – Rousseau's conception of public opinion was dominated by the need to provide citizens with the right opinions. Until the public voice spoke true, Rousseau worried lest an ignorant consensus confine superior persons. The specific issues that had invited thoughts on public opinion were the ordinary ones of the day – the scandal of the aristocratic code of honor, for instance. This had served as the focus for reflection on the public mind before Rousseau broached it in his *Lettre à d'Alembert* (1758). Duclos's dictum of 1747 that it was the clash (*choc*) of opinions that lit the light of truth (Duclos 1968: cxxviii–ix) immediately entered the language, but Rousseau was too ambivalent towards the subject to coin a comparable phrase. Nor would a simple clash of freely expressed opinions have left him content.

A pattern was emerging in the 1760s and two schools of thought offered programs that were at once more concrete and, in the short run, more influential than were Rousseau's musings. First came the Physiocrats with a clear doctrine of *l'opinion publique* and the need to channel it toward their measures. In writings of Le Trosne and of Le Mercier de la Rivière one finds the queen of the world reduced to the status of a tame courtier in the retinue of an enlightened despot. In this cause, public opinion was to be the object of a series of transitive verbs – to fix, to enlighten, to direct. This partook of Rousseau's vision of legislators who reshaped their peoples. Even Turgot, whose career shows a willingness to consult popular prejudices, feared the people. A letter of 1778 called popular tyranny the worst of all because other forms could be checked either by remorse or by public opinion. A multitude, however, did not know remorse and was equally beyond the check of opinion (Turgot 1966: 806).

Less equivocal in its message was the voice of militant anticlericalism as expressed by Baron d'Holbach and his coterie. Here, the queen of the world was a blind queen, the guise in which popular ignorance presented itself. As d'Holbach slyly put it, the people's voice was said to be God's, only because God could not fail to endorse opinions dictated by the priesthood. Critical of the despot who placed himself above opinion, d'Holbach wished rulers to consider the public mind only as a preliminary to changing it. Opinion was due to be displaced as ruler of all things; significantly, d'Holbach sometimes referred to the new sovereign power as *la raison publique*. When Voltaire or d'Alembert lauded the man of letters for supplying the public with opinions, they were but asserting another means of effecting control over the minds of the masses. In either version, contempt for untutored opinion led to viewing the public as pliant material for the legislator's will. More sympathy for spontaneous opinions is found in the clerical party. Pascal, with his studied awareness of the limits of reason, had been rather friendly to opinion, as were the views of those eighteenth-century churchmen who resisted the prejudice that the public needed philosophical instruction in order to lose its prejudices.

Long before the *prérévolution*, the aim of mastering opinion had made its way from the council chamber to become the common design of all parties. It found clear statements in the works of Jacob-Nicolas Moreau, later an historiographer-royal of France, and the age's most erudite defender of absolutism. Before Rousseau regretted the failure to shape opinion, Moreau's *Moniteur françois* (1760) had said the same. Why, he asked, did one hesitate to lead a people such as the French, so amenable to fashion and opinion? Light and vivacious, French attitudes might be more readily conducted into patriotic channels than those of the sombre, stiff-necked English. The French were easily governed, but failed to generate the partisans of public betterment who abounded across the Channel. So the very silence of the French people suggested to Moreau a certain *incivisme* (Moreau 1760, vol. I: 16–17, 27–34). Without neglecting the importance of having the people's voice reach the sovereign, Moreau gave priority to social animation conducted by that very sovereign. In 1789, Moreau adhered still to his original prescription and denied that current discussions could yield a model for national regeneration. In his equation of public opinion with the "universal wish of the nation" (Moreau 1789, vol. I: 17; vol. II: 200), Moreau reflected an expectation that dominated the immediate future.

To Jacques Necker history has assigned a major part in familiarizing Europe with the centrality of public opinion, and indeed the Swiss-born minister of finance, as much from his genius for self-promotion as from the content of his ideas, did manage to excite interest in the forbidding world of public finance. Necker's interest in public opinion arose naturally from its relevance to economic markets, but his was more than a concern with the *ditti di borsi*, for he insisted that rulers had to consult opinion. Unlike many contemporaries, Necker had no plan to improve the public mind. Rather, he reflected that the dismayingly childlike character of public judgment was but the price of essential inequalities. Still, this left him unhappy with French opinion, regretting the absence of sophistication of Britain where "le Peuple est moins Peuple." Most curious was the theme that public opinion was more powerful in monarchies than in republics. This entailed the assumption that subjects, excluded from making laws, somehow managed to recoup, gaining all their influence through the tribunal of opinion. Citizens of republics were apparently denied such an influence by virtue of their identification with government. The argument was not without a defensive air as when Necker's *De l'administration des finances* (1784) suggested that foreigners tended to underestimate the potency in France of the invisible power (Necker 1775, vol. I: 223; 1784, vol. I: lxi). Here Necker was typical of people who so argued, for the claim was based on assumptions both about the institutional superiority of monarchy and the nature of the French character. Fluctuations of opinion, however manifested, were indeed monitored and one only need recall that eloquent testimony to the decline of royal popularity as recorded by a diarist: when Louis XV was ill in 1744, six thousand masses were paid for at Notre Dame, but when he was on his deathbed there were but three (Véri 1933, vol. I: 471n.)![3] Nevertheless, Necker's suggestion that a people without formal means of expressing its views had a powerful weapon in public opinion seems to place undue faith in the murmurs of crowds or the witticisms of the drawing-room.

Necker's work of 1784 probably did most to popularize the notion of public opinion but his book of 1775 on the grain trade had also treated the subject. The claim that monarchy was peculiarly friendly to public opinion was also argued by others, especially in the 1780s (see Gunn 1985). Nor did the argument go unchallenged, as by the young Brissot de Warville – probable author of the jibe that property was theft. A Montesquieu-like comparison between monarchies and republics asserts that they differed greatly in the publicity afforded to acts of state and that, whereas citizens' opinions were precious in a republic, public opinion in a monarchy was confined to matters irrelevant to government or threatening to its purposes. The future Girondin had already gone well beyond the cautious truisms that occupied other writers. Brissot acknowledged the influence both of Jeremy Bentham and of David Williams and probably British experience colored his understanding here (Brissot de Warville 1782–5, vol. IV: 87n.; vol. X: 348).

The French Revolution is often portrayed as marking the birth of public opinion. This can hardly be true, though the events reflect an unprecedented eruption of public sentiment. By November 1788, the historian J.P. Papon saw a revival of "public opinion," long suppressed in France. What was so called might either be the traditional censor of individual morals or it might be a sentiment fixed upon *la chose publique*; it was the latter that interested Papon, and he must surely

[3] From an unpublished portion of the diary of Siméon-Prosper Hardy, cited in this edition of another diary of the period.

be one of the first clearly to distinguish between the two. He defined public opinion, in the relevant meaning, as the prevailing idea about the governors and the state of the nation. The impression had to be general; in fact, by emphasizing its irresistibility, Papon suggested something close to unanimity (Papon 1789: 4).[4] It is the last observation that dominates the period.

Admittedly, the extremists in the clubs had no monopoly on talk about public opinion and in the early period of the constituent assembly it was language probably most often in the mouths of anglophile royalists such as Jean-Joseph Mounier. But a century of characterizing opinion as an irresistible torrent and decades of calls to reform manners now took effect. Opinion came to be widely perceived as a condition that should affect everyone in the same way. No doubt this assumption owed much to the initial impression created before the emergence of factions within the Revolution. Thus one finds Thomas Jefferson reporting, in a letter of March 1789, on the near unanimity of the French public mind. As divisions increased, the ideal of a single and united opinion became more precious. At the end of the century, Christoph Wieland, one of the writers who did much to acquaint Germans with *öffentliche Meinung*, still wrote of public opinion as though nations had but one mind and but one voice.

The revolutionary search for an enlightened public had many facets. There was Saint-Just's effort to compress the opinion of any nation into a single objective – conquest at Rome or indolence in India (Saint-Just 1908: 276, 279–80)! Robespierre serves as the usual measure of Jacobin thought and he succumbed to the mirage of a unanimous public (Cobban 1968: 172–87).[5] By 1792 he sought guidance for opinion, while still remaining unhappy about Roland's alleged interference with it, through the ministry of the interior. The difficulty of Robespierre's situation is illustrated by noting that modern critics cite the program of patriotic festivals as tyrannical imposition on opinion, whereas a populist such as Babeuf condemned him as an enemy of free opinion because he abolished some such observances. One of the best statements in favor of opinion, freely formed, came in an article (probably by J.B. Salaville) in the *Annales patriotiques*. The writer attacked Robespierre and insisted that freedom of opinion demands diversity and opposition, for opinion

[4] A fuller version of the argument appeared when the pamphlet was reprinted in Rulhière 1819 (vol. II: 203–74).

[5] Cobban's interpretation is noteworthy for the sympathy shown to Robespierre's position.

at once free and unanimous was a contradiction. Still the critic could not resist asking for some *opinion commune* (Delacroix [1794]: 394–8). This had been Robespierre's object, but he had been unwilling to await the results of slow processes.

Part of the revolutionary effort to make sense of public opinion entailed consideration of the companion notion of public spirit. Familiar in English by the late seventeenth century, the concept brought visions of patriotic, disinterested freeholders. In 1786, Sébastien Mercier noted its naturalization, by which time it had long been current in France. In the writings by the future Count Roederer, the Abbé du Chatellier, Dieudonné Thiebault of the Berlin Academy and many others, one finds a ballet of abstract nouns – *esprit national*, *esprit public*, *volonté générale*, *sentiment public*, *caractère national* – all somehow related to public opinion. Rich in concepts, thin in institutional specifics, this literature sought, in vain, to define a national rallying-point. Roederer's *Journal de Paris* and his *Journal d'économie publique* even carried a feature on *l'esprit public*, in the manner of weather reports. This left public opinion in the days of the Directory as the locus of a disappointed hope, the exact nature of which had never been agreed upon. Jean-François Sobry, who had striven to understand public opinion under the old *régime*, averred that it had been Necker, with his self-interested manipulation of opinion, who had first wrested the scepter of opinion from the people. The past had seen earned reputations, formed by a genuine public mind, but efforts to force public acclaim had wrecked the social order (Sobry 1799/1800: 42–5). The Abbé Morellet, a champion of a free press from as early as the 1760s, offered an analysis of that French expectation that there would be a clear public voice. In France one said "on dit" meaning not, as in England, that someone said, but rather that many are saying or "everyone is saying" (Morellet 1818). Morellet was an unregenerate admirer of the role of opinion in Britain.

In Britain, meanwhile, institutions flourished and concepts rested. Not even extra-parliamentary activity could prompt the British to revamp political vocabulary. From the Middlesex election in 1769 to the emergence of the country associations at the end of 1779, discussion centered upon what constituted the "sense" of the people and whether it could be collected other than in parliament. This expression carried the right suggestions of a rough, not a mechanical or exact, summation of views. Neither unanimity nor absolute truth was implied and it avoided the speculative air that surrounded the word "opinion." In 1780 Charles James Fox reneged on his earlier view that the people's sense was to be found only in the Commons and called upon parliament to hearken to "public opinion" in the country. That same year saw the passage of Dunning's motion seeking a diminution of the influence of the crown, thus suggesting to some that the popular voice was already stronger than the palace. Two major factors affected British understanding of public opinion in the 1780s (see Gunn 1974). These were, firstly, the revival in more sophisticated form of defenses of royal influence in the Commons and unreformed representation and, secondly, the constitutional lessons that accompanied the fall of the North–Fox coalition. The former emerged in 1780 and lasted until 1832. Its message was little different from that of writers in the 1730s: influences of all sorts now met in the Commons and, as a sort of trade-off, one was invited to accept the legitimacy of public opinion and Opposition parties to counter-balance royal and aristocratic influences. The best examples of the genre for purposes of giving due weight to public opinion came quite late – not before the 1790s. Still normally to be discovered in parliament, now, however, opinion without doors was assumed to be a matter of which all actors were aware. Yet another change was entailed by the breaking of the septennial convention governing the life of parliament – first in 1780 and then again in 1784. The defeat of Fox's India Bill and the ensuing election of 1784 had been precipitated by the king's not being content with the ministers thrust on him by the Commons. It was thus claimed that the electorate had now assumed guardianship of the constitution. This, at least, was the message spelled out by the *English Review*, the source of the best political commentary in the 1780s. Not only did the *Review* grant public opinion a high place in the political order, it also drew upon the philosophical history of the previous decades to link the popular voice to improvements in transport, communication and literacy, and the rise of associations. The accidents of the decade thus assumed a new dignity and became the march of civilization. The *Edinburgh Review* of the nineteenth century still expressed itself in these terms.

If none of this attention ranks much above daily journalism, one may note that from 1771 the Revd. David Williams had been interested in the phenomenon and, spurred by new forms of organization and new levels of disorder, had pondered how sentiment might organize and express itself. Bentham too was aware of the place of public opinion as early as 1780, though his greatest contributions to the subject date much later and have been rather overpraised by admirers. Both men were doubtless influenced by French thought and influenced it in turn. There is no better way of accounting for the absence of sustained attention to public opinion than by citing John Stuart Mill's reply, of May 1835, to a question from Tocqueville about British views of administration. The English, Mill said, were resistant to general ideas and so had not grouped administrative tasks together, apparently from a failure to perceive that they belonged to the same species. This had arisen "from our sheer inability to comprehend general ideas on the subject of government or anything else" (Schleifer 1980: 158). Similarly, it may be suggested, the British elite argued about petitions, addresses, freedom of the press, and the rights of the electorate, but rarely subsumed these causes under a rubric of "public opinion."

In France the coming of the Charter brought recognition of public opinion in a form appropriate to parliamentary government. Finally opinion could be related to a set of institutions, and it was, by Necker's daughter, Mme. de Staël, and by Benjamin Constant among others. Gone for the time being were efforts to identify irrefutable signs of public opinion; rather people stressed the institutions that were its prerequisites and in this the literature is almost British in its empiricism. Public opinion had become, in the words of the ultra-royalist Baron de Vitrolles, the essence of representative govern ment (Vitrolles 1815: 4; Oechslin 1960: 107–11). But what, apart from a parliament, did government by opinion require? Largely, one learned, a public spirit on the part of the people, a possession long perceived as distinctively British. A flood of essays explored the notion of *l'esprit public* and the ways of British public life. One of the best of these was by an anonymous *ancien consul* who recommended to his countrymen that *capacité politique* displayed by the British and spelled out its details in a form very similar to modern notions about social pluralism and its political contribution (L*** 1815: 14–19). Acclaim was not, to be sure, unanimous and Joseph Fiévée, a Bonapartist, devoted several treatises to the argument that public opinion in the modern sense had shattered the traditional rule of opinion as mediated by men of letters. A liberal reviewer was respectful, but found the argument incomprehensible (Fiévée 1809; 1816; *Journal des débats* September 4, 12, 20, 1815).

Nor did old habits die easily. Tocqueville's concerns about public opinion as instrument of the tyranny of the majority – a notion reflected in Mill's essay "Civilisation" (1836) and James Fenimore Cooper's *The American Democrat* (1838) – turned on the French propensity to reify the public as though it were an indissoluble unit. Americans of the 1840s, wishing to banish this bogey, reached for

James Madison's brilliant vision of multiple and shifting majorities. A more bizarre proof that the eighteenth-century attitudes were still abroad was Comte's quaint preference for public opinion that would flourish, not in newspapers or journals, but in the fashionable salon. Despite such survivals the France of Charles X saw an understanding of public opinion that proceeded along much the same lines as in Britain. Opinion remained an addle-pated queen prone to alienating admirers and so the concept still had a thin time of it amongst the makers of political dictionaries.

In Britain there was no watershed comparable to the Bourbon Restoration, for the great Reform Bill was more the product of opinion than its cause. Peel's famous description of public opinion as "folly, weakness, prejudice, wrong feeling, right feeling, obstinacy, and newspaper paragraphs" had been written in 1820. Subsequent comment tended especially to focus upon the press as the organ of public opinion. British observers of opinion were largely hostile, as a selection of views from the 1850s demonstrates. David Urquhart, traveler and specialist on foreign policy, vacillated between saying that public opinion was ineffectual because indefinite in content and that it was malign. He emphasized the dearth of analyses of the concept and attributed it to opinion's being subject either to uncritical admiration or to loathing. Joseph Moseley, who devoted three chapters of a book on politics to the topic, observed that all parties both loved and hated public opinion, for eventually it deserted them all. For R.W. Barnes, an Exeter clergyman, the complaint was that public opinion was not each person's private opinion collected, but rather an imposition by the press, especially *The Times*. Perhaps its least hostile analyst of the decade was Homersham Cox whose treatise on British government allowed that public opinion might work well were it not hindered by political parties (Urquhart 1855: 14–20; Moseley 1852: 220–1; Barnes 1855: 12–20, 58–64, 238; Cox 1854: 220–31). Caught between charges that, on the one hand, it was the magnified voice of faction and, on the other, that it would overwhelm the cultivated minority, public opinion could please only rarely.

Twentieth-century students of public opinion have been most interested in gaining precision on the state of the public mind, and their judgments on the phenomenon have moderated both the hopes and the fears of earlier times. One of the first to attempt a scientific study was Gabriel Tarde, whose work brought a new coherence to a long-standing French concern for social imitation and its significance. In the eighteenth-century writers on "la mode" and its tyranny one finds the antecedents of Tarde's laws of imitation. Other commentators, such as Graham Wallas and Walter Lippmann, emphasized, in particular, the imperfections of a public that was confined in its information and subject to irrational behavior. Fear of public opinion in its guise of a tyranny of the majority was another prominent theme of the early theorists of the modern era and it is amply reflected in James Bryce's *American Commonwealth* (1888).

On some of these alleged problems a measure of conceptual clarification has emerged from more recent studies. Thus John Dewey, in *The Public and its Problems* (1927), improved upon Madison's insights to emphasize that in complex societies there are really many publics, not a single, menacing hydra-headed beast. A related refinement in understanding has been to insist that the opinion of interest is that of all holding views and is not to be associated with unanimity or even a majority view (Hennessy 1965, chap. 5; Childs 1965: 15–19). Had traditional rhetoric honored this consideration, the history of the concept would have been very different. One may also observe that modern research has done little to alter inherited notions about the identity of the politically relevant public, for rarely had the concept been confined to the electorate or *pays légal*. This is because British and French usage had already assumed – sometimes to a degree bordering on paradox – that public opinion was the opinion of very ordinary people and not just that of an informed elite. Had this not been so, there would have been little point in proposing to form and educate opinion, as in France, or to ignore it in favour of parliament's decisions, as in all but the final decades of eighteenth-century Britain.

Social scientists have undoubtedly experienced frustration at the variety of definitions of public opinion and this has been accompanied by a desire to "operationalize" the concept. But there has never, it seems, been the widespread insistence – so apparent in relation to the concept of "public interest" – that one should discard a term that is too burdened with unclear meanings. Indeed, research on public opinion has sometimes been perceived as the antidote to idle talk about the public interest (Leiserson 1968: 201–2).

Perhaps the most challenging recent interpretation relevant to conceptual change has come from Elisabeth Noelle-Neumann, the senior figure in survey research in the German Federal Republic. Using her concept of the "spiral of silence" – the social–psychological process whereby people with opinions that diverge from apparent majority positions tend not to proclaim their views – she has reconstructed the history of public opinion. Central to her argument is that what is called "public opinion" refers, in a primary sense, to that sentiment which, using the pervasive fear of social isolation, induces conformity. Sometimes this interpretation suggests that our twentieth-century understanding of public opinion as a tribunal that controls government is simply a misconception without historical antecedents. More defensibly, it suggests that modern students of the subject have explored only that dimension of the phenomenon, whereas the public's power over the individual was better understood in the past (Noelle-Neumann 1984: 94–6). Certainly, one cannot readily accept that expectations about the public's influence on government is a new one. Papon, in 1789, left no doubt, for instance, that the important and interesting aspects of opinion took the form of judgments about government and a host of other documents, from as early as the seventeenth century, confirm the political relevance of opinion. But the historical record also reveals, even in the political wranglings of Britain in 1730s, an awareness that opinion had a much wider province than the relations between the people and its government. If Papon announced the centrality of political opinion, his contemporaries, Sobry and Fiévée, can be seen as lamenting the passing of older connotations of the expression. The new analysis thus usefully underlines how opinions entertained about national issues are themselves molded by the moral censorship exercised by the public. From such a perspective, fears about the tyranny of the majority gain life anew. Similarly, the emphasis – especially in French thought – about the desired unanimity of public opinion takes on added meaning. So too does the element of official manipulation of sentiment, both factors pointing to that moral censorship recognized as commanding all individuals, long before it was supposed that the community might regularly and systematically instruct its governors.

This is no antiquarian quibble that suggests how lore from the past may affect our understanding of the origins of public opinion. Rather, it calls attention to universal processes of social control that still act, but whose empire has escaped due recognition by investigators who fail to ground the narrowly political relation of citizen and government in more general social processes. Sometimes Noelle-Neumann seems too dismissive of the modern presumption to hold governors on the leash of opinion and too insensitive to the history of this ambition over at least two centuries. But, in her insistence that pressure to conform to the social consensus is the dominant fact in explaining the dynamics of public opinion, she effects a happy partnership of social science and intellectual history, gratifying to the intellectual historian because it demonstrates how understanding the history of concepts may inform our current use of them.

Earlier scholarship on the historical place of public opinion has also been dominated by Germans – Ferdinand Toennies and Wilhelm Bauer. Their selection of the canon exaggerates the French contribution, without sufficiently recognizing that it differed significantly from the Anglo-Saxon tradition that has triumphed, at least for the time being, in our modern understanding of public opinion.

REFERENCES

Anon. 1700. *Suite des caractères de Théophraste et des moeurs de se siècle*. Paris: Michallet.

Barnes, R. W. 1855. *Public Opinion, Considered in Letters* . . . Truro and London: Netherton, Mozley.

Bellegarde, J. B. Morvan de. 1702. *Lettres curieuses de littérature et de morale*. Paris: Guignard.

[Brissot de Warville, J. P.] 1782–5. *Bibliothèque philosophique du législateur*, 10 vols. Berlin and Paris: Desauges.

Childs, Harwood L. 1965. *Public Opinion: Nature, Formation and Role*. Princeton, NJ: Princeton University Press.

Cobban, Alfred. 1968. "The Political Ideas of Robespierre, 1792–5." In *Aspects of the French Revolution*. New York: Braziller, pp. 158–91.

Colomby, François Cauvigny, Sieur de. 1631. *De l'authorité des roys*. Paris: Du Bray.

Cox, Homersham. 1854. *The British Commonwealth: or a Commentary on the Institutions and Principles of British Government*. London: Longman.

The Craftsman. 1737. 14 volumes. London,

Daily Gazetteer. 1736–40. London.

Delacroix, J. V. [1794]. *Le Spectateur françois pendant le gouvernement révolutionnaire*. Paris: Buisson, l'an III.

Duclos, Charles Pinot. 1968 [1747]. "Discours prononcé à l'académie française . . ." In *Oeuvres*, 9 vols., edited by M. Auger, vol. I. Geneva: Slatkine, pp. cxxiii–cxxxviii.

Felltham, Owen. 1661 [1623]. "Of Opinion." In *Resolves: Divine, Moral, Political.* London: P. Dring, pp. 103–5.

Fiévée, Joseph. 1809. *Des opinions et des intérêts pendant la révolution*. Paris: Normant.

1816. "Des doctrines et des opinions." In *Correspondance politique et administrative*, pt. IV. Paris: Normant, letter 9.

Ganochaud, Collette. 1980. *L'opinion publique chez Jean-Jacques Rousseau*. Lille and Paris: Champion.

Gunn, J. A. W. 1974. "Influence, Parties and the Constitution: Changing Attitudes, 1783–1832." *The Historical Journal* 17: 301–28.

1983. *Beyond Liberty and Property: The Process of Self-recognition in Eighteenth-century Political Thought*. Kingston and Montreal: McGill-Queen's University Press.

1985. "Public Opinion: A Study in Conceptual Change." Unpublished paper presented at the meeting of the American Political Science Association, New Orleans, LA.

Hennessy, Bernard C. 1965. *Public Opinion*. Belmont, CA: Wadsworth.

Journal des débats. 1815. Paris.

L***. 1815. *Essai sur l'esprit public*. Paris: Delaunay.

Leiserson, Avery. 1968. "II: Public Opinion." In *Encyclopedia of the Social Sciences*, vol. XIII. Cromwell, Collier and Macmillan, pp. 197–203.

London Journal. 1733–4. London.

Moreau, J. -N. 1760. *Le Moniteur françois*. Avignon.

1789. *Exposition et défence de notre constitution monarchique françoise*. Paris: Moutard.

Morellet, André. 1818. "Remarques philosophiques grammatico-morales sur la particule 'ON' [*c*. 1786]." In *Mélanges de littérature et de philosophie du 18e siècle*, 4 vols., vol. IV. Paris: Lepetit, pp. 219–30

Moseley, Joseph. 1852. *Political Elements, or the Progress of Modern Legislation*. London: Parker and Son.

Necker, Jacques. 1775. *Sur la législation et le commerce des grains*, 2 vols. Paris: Pissot.

1784. *De l'administration des finances de la France*, 3 vols. [Paris].

Noelle-Neumann, Elisabeth. 1984. *The Spiral of Silence: Public Opinion – Our Social Skin*. Chicago, IL, and London: University of Chicago Press.

Oechslin, J. -J. 1960. *Le Mouvement ultra-royaliste sous la restauration*. Paris: Librairie générale de droit et de jurisprudence.

Papon, Jean-Pierre. 1789. *De l'action de l'opinion sur les gouvernmens*. [Paris?].

Peacham, Henry. 1962 [1638]. "Of Opinion." In *The Complete Gentleman, The Truth of Our Times*, edited by V. B. Veltzel. Ithaca, NY: Cornell University Press, pp. 196–8.

Prior, Matthew. 1970. [1721]. "Opinion." In *The Literary Works*, 2 vols., edited by H.B. Wright and M.K. Spears, vol. I. Oxford: Oxford University Press, pp. 586–99.

[Rich, Barnaby]. 1613. *Opinion Deified, Discovering the Ingins, Traps and Traynes, that are set in this Age, whereby to Catch Opinion*. London: Adams.

Rulhière, Claude de. 1819. *Oeuvres*, 2 vols. Paris: Menard et Desenne.

Sacy, Louis de. 1716 [1715]. *Traité de la gloire*. Paris: Huet.

Saint-Just, Louis Antoine de. 1908. "Esprit de la révolution et de la constitution de France." In *Oeuvres complètes*, 2 vols., edited by C. Vellay, vol. I. Paris: Charpentier et Fasquelle, pp. 250–345.

Schleifer, James T. 1980. *The Making of Tocqueville's Democracy in America*. Chapel Hill, NC: University of North Carolina Press.

Selden, John. 1927 [1689]. "Opinion." In *Table Talk*, edited by Sir Frederick Pollack. London: Quaritch, pp. 87–8.

Sobry, J. -F. 1799–1800. *Discours sur les réputations*. Paris, l'an VIII.
Turgot, A. -R. -J. 1966 [1778]. "Lettre au docteur Price." In *Oeuvres*, 2 vols., edited by E. Daire, vol. II. Osnabrück: Zeller, pp. 805–11.
Urquhart, David. 1855. *Public Opinion and its Organs*. London: Trübner.
Véri, Joseph A., Abbé de. 1933–4. *Journal*, 2 vols., edited by Baron Jehan de Witte. Paris: Tallandier.
[Vitrolles, Eugène, Baron de]. 1815. *Du ministre dans le gouvernment représentatif*. Paris: Dentu.
Warrington, Henry Delamere, Earl of. 1694. *Works*. London: Lawrence and Dunton.
Weekly Register. 1731–4. London.

13

Ideology

MARK GOLDIE

I

The word "popery" was coined in English in the 1520s. It became a pervasive term in the language of the Protestant Reformation and remained so until the nineteenth century. The word "priestcraft" was first used in the 1650s and became commonplace in the 1690s. It was a characteristic term in the language of the Enlightenment. The word "ideology" appeared in the 1790s, becoming familiar with Marx's usage of it in the 1840s. It is a characteristic concept in modern social and political theory. Each of these three terms offered a powerful conceptual tool in the political vocabulary of its era. Arguably each evinces a recognizably similar conceptual apparatus. We shall see that historically the latter two terms are heirs to the first. If this is so, then the conceptual history of "ideology" turns out to offer more than an etymological excursion to the 1790s, and more than a record of momentary proleptical intimations, in Francis Bacon or the *philosophes* or whomever, of a notion which has been so much vaunted as a peculiar cognitive achievement of modern political science. More particularly, the Enlightenment critiques of priestcraft, often referred to in sketches of the background to Marx's notion of ideology, will no longer seem quaint and narrowly circumscribed premonitions of a modern doctrine. On the contrary, the criticism of religion, as Marx himself insisted, was the premise of the criticism of all ideology. If the concept of ideology ultimately became secularized, it did so within the unfolding of Christian reformism. It is an outgrowth of the Reformation in its epistemically skeptical mood, in its explorations of the sociology of religious error. We must first sketch the classical theory of ideology, and then turn to explore the historical connection between the philosophical critique of knowledge and the evangelical critique of popery.

II

The beliefs people hold may be considered in two ways. We may, with the philosopher, ask whether those beliefs are true or false. Or we may examine them from the standpoint of the practical needs of those who hold them. To do the latter is to engage in a familiar practice of the social sciences; it is to have a theory of ideology. Those needs have been variously identified as economic, social, political, and psychological. Beliefs have been said to serve the interests of class, party, or tribe, or to sustain people in their hopes and console them in their anxieties. Theorists of ideology have offered many candidates for the crown of pre-eminent human need, but all have asserted that, under the pressure of needs, beliefs become other than simply propositional. They become instruments or therapies in the practices of life. Accordingly, the classical theory of ideology offers an understanding of our values grounded in knowledge of the natural facts about our needy selves.

Formally, at least, the social theorist takes no stand on questions of philosophical truth. The political scientist, the anthropologist, the historian, all customarily declare that their disclosure of the motivational and functional setting of systems of belief implies no judgment upon their veracity. Yet this suspension of judgment about the truth of propositions has not historically been well sustained. For most of its career the concept of ideology has been deployed pejoratively. It has been a theory about cognitive contamination, an insistence that once we grasp the compelling nature of needs and circumstances, we shall see that our judgments are badly distorted by our prejudices, that our moralities are parochial when they pretend to be universal, that our values are rooted in the physical when they purport to be metaphysical. To expose a belief as ideological has generally been part of a strategy of exposing such belief as false. Such falsehoods may be thought, at worst, to be implausible figleaves covering undesirable motives, or, at best, necessary myths which cement the social fabric.

At its most acidic, therefore, the theory of ideology corrodes philosophy, because the simple pursuit of the truth comes to seem naive in the face of the pervasive evidence for the circumstantial conditioning of thinking. The theorists of ideology are apt to claim that adequate philosophy cannot be done until the obstacles in its way are properly understood. It is not, they say, that the task of philosophy, properly understood, is inappropriate, but that philosophy as hitherto practiced has been premature and misconceived. The path to adequate philosophy has yet to be cleared of ideological distortion. Only with the end of ideology will there be a trustworthy philosophy. The theorist of ideology accordingly claims to be a clearer of the ground. But this propaedeutic task has too easily become the chief preoccupation. In laying out the preconditions for adequate human knowledge, it comes to dwell on the causes of our present ignorance: it hence offers a sociology of human error, and a conjectural history of the cognitive career of the species. Social theory has therefore traveled not in parallel with but in different tracks from philosophy; it is a child of philosophy which turned against its parent. The theory of ideology is philosophy become curious about the history and sociology of error.

The classical theory of ideology is coterminous with the heroic age of sociology, which in turn was grounded in the epistemic endeavors of the seventeenth century. It offered the world the prospect of freedom from ideology, for it offered a "science" of society, in place of superstition and intellectual flummery. It urged "experimental," "empirical," or "positive" knowledge, and it took itself to be deposing "metaphysics," which it derided for failing to be grounded in natural knowledge. It held out the hope of transparent self-understanding, and it has persistently done so by elaborating the conditions of our present ignorance, our intellectual servitude to the toils of ideology. In its heroic phase – and examples can be found from the time of Bacon early in the seventeenth century to the heyday of American Parsonian sociology in the 1930s to 1950s – it offers a vision of New Epistemic Man, standing bravely, face set firmly towards the future, intellectually fearless in his newly disenchanted world, able to construct his life without illusion. Its putative cognitive history of the species reduces to a simple two-stage story, a celebration of epistemic parturition, of a revolutionary enlightenment which overthrows an intellectual *ancien régime*, and brings humanity out of its pre-history of darkness.[1] The classical theory of ideology has a mood of knowingness, of epistemic masterfulness. It debunks. Its language has been one of disclosure, demystification, disillusionment, unmasking, disenchantment. The

[1] For a minor, but remarkably late and striking example of the genre, see Lane (1966).

theorist of ideology guards the citadel of knowledge against the agents of darkness, the usurpers of reason for, when reason is usurped, we live in a world of illusion.

III

It is the project of the Enlightenment. And a straightforward reason for adducing an Enlightenment paternity is the fact that the word "ideology" was devised by a group of intellectuals in Revolutionary France, who owed their outlook and ambitions to the *philosophes* of the preceding generation. In 1796 Destutt de Tracy proposed a new science, to be called *idéologie*, which would investigate the natural origins of our ideas. He did not use the word pejoratively: "ideology" was for him the science which would expose illusionary thought. For Marx and later writers "ideology" was the name for such illusions themselves. The terminology has migrated, but the idea has remained substantially the same.

The furniture of the human mind, de Tracy contended, is shaped by sensory experience. Our values are generated through assessments of the satisfactions and pains experienced by the organic self, and they are sustained by the machinery of social approval and disapproval of actions according as they succor the social organism. The names "good" and "evil" are conventional appellatives for the things which conduce to sensory satisfactions and pains. They are not transcendental absolutes. Systems of morals and ideas are accordingly reducible to psychological phenomena, and proper understanding of these facts was the key to social and material progress. The ideologists' faith in the possibilities of progress in knowledge and in the plasticity of human nature yielded a sanguine prospect for the perfectibility of humankind. Theirs was a positivist conception of human science, for, like so many in the Enlightenment, they aspired to be Newtons of the moral world. They aspired to a unified science, presuming that knowledge of the human world was of the same mode as knowledge of the physical. The science of ideology was rooted in Lockean empiricism. For something to be true it had to be verifiable in sense experience. Knowledge is "read off" from the facts of the world. Truth is manifest to the clear-sighted, and when people perceive things properly they will produce agreed knowledge. To the honest and effortful, social knowledge will become pellucid and uncontroversial. It will not be compromised or bounded by a "point of view," for it would be an accurate representation of how things are. And anything which cannot be "read off" from our perceptions does not have the status of knowledge. True philosophy offered a mirror to nature.

The ideologists offered not only a science of human knowledge, but a diagnosis of human ignorance. For if truth is univocal natural knowledge, then the fact of ignorance and disagreement becomes especially puzzling. The enthusiasts for a positivist political science have often been more conspicuous in their contributions to the sociology of ignorance than in their contributions to the achievement of substantive new social knowledge. This is the outcome of their own conception of the task of philosophy. For they followed Locke in being, in his phrase, "underlabourers," ground clearers. They attacked traditional philosophy for weaving fabrics or propositions about matters where no certain knowledge can be had, and where only dogma and prejudice can subsist. Philosophy cannot go beyond knowledge of the physical; hence there should be no metaphysics. The true philosopher dissolves metaphysics on behalf of science. But the obstacles to science by no means lay merely in lack of intellectual application. Ignorance was more systematic than that: it had its origins in the prejudice and self-interest of those in power who had an advantage in the ignorance and blindness of others. Metaphysics is a miasma invented to gull the credulous and to impose chains of darkness: it is delusion pretending to be philosophy. The new natural knowledge will put power and self-determination into people's hands; self-understanding offered self-mastery. Knowledge was hence the enemy of the old entrenched power, of systems of domination. Ignorance and falsehood are the instruments of men of power; they rule by fabricating illusions; they clothe naked power with their icons and idols. The intellectual task of unmasking is therefore the ally of political liberation. De Tracy and his colleagues were the philosophical servants of the French Revolution: they unmasked the ideational instruments of *ancien régime* power.[2]

IV

That mental laziness, stupidity, concupiscence, habit, intellectual fashion, and deference to authority often lead people to hold wrongheaded beliefs is not an insight which could escape any generation, and so not one which could be said to have a history. Why, then, do we flatter the Enlightenment's self-regard by

[2] For comments, of different kinds, upon the Enlightenment project see: Popper (1966); Rorty (1980); Shklar (1957). On de Tracy's school see: Acton (1966); Lichtheim (1965).

implying that it has a special place in the history of human self-understanding?

Nobody doubts that an adequate grasp of what we ought to believe is difficult. At issue is whether that difficulty is just intrinsic to our limited capacities for adequate reasoning, or whether it has contingent social causes. To hold the latter view is to have a theory of ideology. Our ignorance and illusions are said to be the product of human agency, conscious or unconscious. By implication, the barriers to knowledge are removable. Error stems from inadequate circumstances or from the misuse of power, and the critique of error is therefore intimately connected with a critique of power. Hence there is a politics, a sociology, and a history of knowledge.

To hold the former view, on the other hand, and to deny that there is a politics of knowledge, is to take what might be called the Augustinian view. For St. Augustine human reason is limited, and thinking is muddled groping after insight. Ignorance and disagreement are an unavoidable part of the human predicament; we cannot avoid unlikemindedness, and this fact perpetually estranges us from each other. On this account, the theorist of ideology is accused of holding things to be temporary and oppressive, which ought rather to be said to belong to the human condition. The doctrine of ideology attributes to social conditions that which is properly owed to epistemic sin. It lacks intellectual humility, it fails to recognize that just as the poor are always with us, so too is intellectual poverty. The existence of error is therefore perennial, not historical. Yet in the Enlightenment, intellectuals began to argue that it was indeed historical, and that there could be a political program for its removal. The ideologist, according to this view, falsely offers a secular eschatology, for he promises an epistemic epiphany on this earth, a coming of translucency, a liberation from darkness into light. A theory of ideology is thus "any doctrine which presents the hidden and saving truth about the evils of the world in the form of social analysis" (Minogue 1985: 2). For the Augustinian, this activist eschatology is a dangerous falsehood, for the claim to have found the means to the fruit of the Tree of Knowledge is a usurpation of God. It is Promethean. The catastrophe of modern political theory is said to lie in this hubristic aspiration for complete knowledge, an abandonment of a sense of the intellectual Fall. For the Augustinian there is a terrible danger in the doctrine that ignorance and delusion are contingent and historical facts. It leads to political messianism, to faith that political action can end such imperfection, to faith in a secular state that will at last allow people to improve themselves with cognitive clarity. It constructs a civil religion. To have a *theory of* ideology therefore is, paradoxically, a slippery slope to having "an ideology," in its more general and most pejorative sense. Thus, in particular, Marx is held both to have launched the modern concept of ideology, in *The German Ideology* of 1846, and to have unleashed "an ideology," a catastrophic secular messianism.[3]

The conservative critique of the theory of ideology has generally been expressed in Augustinian terms, whether literally or metaphorically intended. To cast the matter in theological terms is appropriate. It calls our attention to religion. There can be little doubt that the concept of ideology in its modern form had its main provocation in the confrontation between a skeptical, secular consciousness and the manifest fact that most people at most times have been religious. It is hard to be curious about the social or psychological origins of religious beliefs if such beliefs are taken for granted as certain knowledge. When philosophical doubt arises it provokes sociological curiosity. The suspicion that the most precious of people's convictions are incapable of being shown to be demonstrably true generates an acute sense of the yawning gap between the pressure of human cognitive needs and the human incapacity for certitude. When intense belief is found radically wanting by the canons of natural knowledge, then its presence must be accounted for existentially, economically, or politically: as consoling the fearful, galvanizing the oppressed, or justifying the successful. Religious belief comes to be identified not as propositions about God but as fundamentally about something else, about humanity and society. The Sacred Propaganda comes to be seen as just that.

The Enlightenment *philosophes* were especially concerned to dethrone religious speculation and to show that orthodox religion was merely ideology, mythologies devised to cheat the credulous for the sustaining of the social order. They deposed gods and priests. They denounced "priestcraft" as the paradigm of what we would now call ideology. But the mood of critique need not be that of a militant atheist demythologizer. It may be just that mood of knowingness, of having grasped what religion is *really* about, so

[3] Instances, albeit diverse ones, of what I here call the Augustinian view are: Acton (1955); Aron (1957); Benda (1969); Minogue (1985); Shklar (1957); and Tucker (1961). Benda remarked: "The modern clerks have preached to men the religion of the practical by means of their theology, through the image of God they have set before them"; they have made God a "physical and not a metaphysical existence"; they have forgotten how to say "My kingdom is not of this world" (Benda 1969: 155, 43).

pervasive in modern historical or sociological discourse when it addresses itself to evidence of religious conviction. Puritanism, it is for instance said, purports to be a view about eternity, but is "really" the sustained ideology of capitalism; or Methodism is "really" the sigh of the proto-industrial oppressed.

The reduction of religion to its social and psychological substratum is the archetype of the intellectual labors of the theorist of ideology. Confronted by the efforts of theology to discern transcendental truths, the theorist of ideology will find a scrambled code, an inverted panorama, which, once decoded, displays not God but human power, aspiration, and frustration. If the theorist of ideology is to offer an end of cognitive self-estrangement, an end of ideology, then he must above all propose an end to theology. Religious belief is the miasma which social theory will dispose of, a "snakeskin cast off by history."[4] To have faith, so it seems, is to repudiate the ideological insight, and much of the self-esteem of the sociological tradition has rested upon its dethronement of theology, a relentless anxiety to dissociate science from religion, to attest the untainted credentials of an illusion-free episteme. Its instinctive weapon is the accusation that any system of ideas which cannot be grounded in natural knowledge is "theological," "metaphysical," and hence illusory, a mystification. "The Natural History of Religion" is the name of a book by a late-seventeenth-century deist: it might also be a generic name for a host of scholarly enterprises since. When it writes its own history, the secular intellect fondly dwells upon the heroic thought-acts of a Bacon, a Hobbes, a Hume, in slaying the dragon of theology, so that humankind can get on with the proper intellectual tasks of its maturity. It is the view of Condorcet, de Tracy's colleague in the 1790s (Condorcet 1955). It is the view in countless nineteenth-century schemas of the intellectual phylogeny of humankind. And it is a view still repeatedly purveyed. The concept of ideology is grounded in the intellectual supersession of theology, in the conviction that the best life consists in humanity kicking away its cognitive crutches and standing on its own epistemic feet.

But if it is correct to see the theory of ideology as fundamentally a kind of anti-clericalism, as a distinctive part of the intellectual culture of secularist social theory, it is not correct to see it wholly in contradistinction to traditions within Christianity. The "Augustinian" criticism of theories of ideology abets this presumed contradistinction:

[4] Marx, *On the Jewish Question*: quoted by Minogue (1985: 161).

the theory of ideology is said to stand in opposition to the deepest of Christian insights; that our capacity for adequate knowledge is flawed by our Fallen nature, and not merely by social contingencies. But we shall see that, on the contrary, the theory of ideology is as much the outgrowth of, as a rebellion against, Christian theology.

V

The Christian religion has been unusual in the extent of its doctrinal content: it has demanded assent to a series of speculative propositions. It requires that propositions which are not apparent to natural reason be held to be certainly true. From the Reformation onwards it came to be thought that many of these dogmas were not a true and necessary part of Christianity, but an excrescence overlaying and obfuscating the simplicity of the original source. It came to be thought that the mistake had been to mix philosophy with religion, and to turn philosophical opinions into theological creeds, a mistake which largely stemmed from the incorporation of Aristotelian philosophy into Christian theology. This was scholasticism, that "vain philosophy of the schoolmen" which Hobbes never tired of ridiculing. The pure religion of Jerusalem had become contaminated with the metaphysics of Athens.

The Protestant, and especially Lutheran, theological tradition had tended to emphasize the *deus absconditas*, the hidden God. The gap between human reason and the divine is so immense that any attempt at a systematic ontology of the deity is both blasphemous and absurd. Any such attempts were inevitably anthropomorphic; they struggled to depict God and succeeded only in putting a mirror to human ideals; they were unavoidably bounded by the language of particular experience and culture. Religious practice is thus the voice of civil society in respect of its faith in the unknown God; it is culturally variable and subject to civil amendment. That prayers and theologies are not propositional, but signs and symbols denoting common agreement about our hopes and aspirations, has, since Luther's time, paradoxically been a source both for profound theologies – of a pietistic or fideistic or existential kind[5] – and for profound secular embarrassment and anti-Christian ridicule. Modern theology and modern secularism both began with the claim that that which is being said of God is in reality being said of humankind.

[5] Most notably Pascal, Bayle, Hegel, Schleiermacher, Kierkegaard, and Tillich. On Pascal see Goldmann (1964); on Schleiermacher see Niebuhr (1965).

Proper science and proper piety must both begin with human experience, and not with vain philosophizing.

This frame of reference was peculiarly intense in Francis Bacon, writing in the early 1600s. His concept of the "idols" which obstruct human understanding is often referred to as a source for the modern concept of ideology, and he has often been made a hero of secular consciousness.[6] In searching out the contingencies of ignorance and prejudice, it was scholastic Aristotelianism which he unrelentingly attacked. Aristotle, he said, is to philosophy what his pupil Alexander the Great was to the ancient political world: they were the respective usurpers of the intellectual and political *res publicae*. Aristotle reduced humankind to "mental slavery"; his followers manufacture empty errors which modern academies, churches, and states sanctify. Aristotle is the philosophical Antichrist, "the prince of imposture". The Aristotelian impediments to knowledge have been embodied in social and especially religious institutions. Liberation lies with a return to "true religion." Bacon constructed an epistemology of natural knowledge, but it is predicated upon what he takes to be the task of Reformers, to do what the Bible commands, and first to rescue from distortion what it is that the Bible requires. The evangelical religion has been corrupted by metaphysical religion: Christianity must be restored to its true self.

The mistake of metaphysical religion (Bacon continues) was to try to understand God's essence, instead of devoting itself to natural knowledge of the world. Most of theology is inevitably a series of anthropomorphic fantasies; we cannot describe Him other than "in shadow and trope." To attempt to know anything of Him other than that He is, is as hopeless as it is impious; it is parochial aspiration masquerading as transcendental philosophy. This fideistic and skeptical strain in Protestant theology is crucial in the generation of theories of ideology: that which we assert of God unavoidably reveals only that which we value in our human selves. That our character of God is modeled on man is an assertion co-extensive with the Reformers' onslaught on scholastic metaphysics: it will reach its most complete expression in nineteenth-century German theology, which gave immediate birth to the notion of ideology in Marx.

For Bacon, God has left us to our own epistemic devices, but He

[6] For what follows see Rossi (1968) and Farrington (1964). Bacon's most important works in this connection are *The Masculine Birth of Time*; *The Advancement of Learning*; *De sapientia veterum* (1603–9).

has promised His epiphany in the restoration of natural knowledge; it is Natural Philosophy which is the "handmaid of religion." In Eden, Adam had pure, natural enlightenment, but lost it with the Fall. Our mind became severed from our world, and so became an "enchanted glass, full of superstition and imposture," so that it is now scarcely possible for the "genuine natural light of things" to fall on "the mirror of the mind." Those nearest to the epistemic catastrophe of the Fall were plunged into deepest darkness; they may be said to be in "the childhood of the world," inhabiting "the darkness of antiquity." They groped as best they could towards reason, and they expressed their knowledge of themselves and their world in "fables," "parables," and "hieroglyphics." Their mythologies were their instruments of knowledge, expressing truths but dimly understood. Yet mythologies reveal as well as veil. The "idols" which stalk the path to knowledge are as much the fumblings after knowledge in pre-modern peoples, as they are culpable perversions by the enemies of truth.

Our task is to restore a union between the mind and the natural world, a "chaste, holy, and legal wedlock with things themselves." Bacon prays that God will permit "the unlocking of the paths . . . of a greater light," that the intellect may be "made clean and pure from all vain fancies." The fruit of the epistemic marriage of Mind and Nature will be immense for humanity. Instead of "monsters of the imagination" there will come forth "a race of heroes to subdue and extinguish such monsters . . . to war against our human necessities and, so as far as may be, to bring relief therefrom." Taking on the mantle of a prophet, Bacon urges: "take heart, then, my son, and give yourself to me so that I may restore you to yourself." This phrase is redolent of what lies at the heart of the secular apocalyptic: the sense that mankind is self-alienated and that a redemptive and restorative task in this world lies before it. A promise is held out of being restored and made whole again, of being at one with nature and society. George Herbert called Bacon the "only priest of nature and men's souls." It is not surprising that the Augustinian enemies of the theory of ideology should find in Bacon the archetype of that dangerous and Promethean urge to overcome the epistemic Fall and give to humanity the tools of perfect knowledge (White 1968). Certainly he offers a secular apocalyptic, but for him it was no other than the promise made in the most devout of Protestant theology.

The seventeenth-century endeavor to construct an epistemology which held a mirror to nature was to hold in its thrall the classical doctrine of ideology, for ideology was to be defined as that which was false and fabulous when tested by the canons of natural knowledge. Scholasticism was the archetype of the false and fabulous, and by the end of the century the term "priestcraft" had come to denote its perpetrators. John Locke holds hardly a lesser place than Bacon in the canonical genealogy of the concept of ideology. Although he was no millenarian, his epistemology does have the same location within a sense of the history of true religion. At the end of his life he described his enterprise as the "propagation of the true religion," the "maintenance of the Reformation," and the vindication of all "those great and pious men, who were instrumental to bring us out of Roman darkness and bondage." His *Essay Concerning Human Understanding* has the appearance of providing timeless tools for thinking, but if Locke did his best to abstract it from its contextual moorings, his advisors and enemies speedily re-anchored it. Locke's early readers had no doubt that the *Essay*'s chief effect was to undermine radically those truths of the church which sustained the authority of priests. Locke's friend Molyneux said the *Essay* will "abridge the empire of darkness." The Quaker Benjamin Furly said he was "fully assured that priestcraft will fall, and cannot stand long against the light" of Locke's books. "True and reasonable religion," wrote another, has been rescued from "the great trade of priestcraft in fashion in every church." When churchmen began to attack the book as heretical, Locke detected a conspiracy against him by "the cassocked tribe of theologians." It was natural for contemporaries to see his book as an assault upon "philosophical popery." It sketches a sociology of the sources of wrong opinions and dogmas, and his readers could infer a conventional Protestant history of them. Epistemology was one battle front in an historic struggle to liberate humankind from popery.[7]

In undertaking a revolution in philosophy, seventeenth-century intellectuals were self-consciously acting as Christian Reformers. Their anti-popery was not an incidental, still less a quaint sidelight on the epistemic task; on the contrary, the latter was subordinate to the central drama of modern history as they saw it, the restoration of true godliness. In place of the Augustinian sense of the inevitable

[7] For reactions of Locke's friends to the *Essay* see Locke (1979–82). Locke was a Socinian (a unitarian) and in his time the controversies about Socinianism provided the most palpable meeting-place of the Reformation and the epistemological projects. In 1690 the French Calvinist Jurieu complained: "Socinianism has created a religion unlike all the other religions in the world; a religion without mysteries, without obscurity and without shadow, a completely solid-footed religion, a religion in which nothing is believed because everything is seen; a religion in which reason alone dominates and faith has no place" (quoted by Sullivan [1982: 89]). See also Jolley (1984).

alienation of humankind in the world, an intellectual and existential incompleteness intrinsic to the human predicament, the Reformation was apt to produce a sense that that alienation was historically contingent, and hence reformable. The Christian philosopher was a therapist who would show the way to restore humanity to itself, by the path of knowledge and by the dissolution of the ignorance of the Romish centuries.

Popery was not just the name of a set of false theological dogmas; it was the systematic usurpation of public and intellectual life by the priests. The Reformers saw medieval religion as an alienation, a theft, by priests of the common religion of a Christian people. They saw the priests as malignly engrossing the means of salvation, as fabricating speculative theologies. In a whole series of ways the priests corralled the holy, made it their monopoly. For instance, instead of teaching the duties which all Christian peoples had in respect of their property, the priests had engrossed property in the institutions of the church. Instead of permitting freedom of intellectual speculation, they had monopolized learning not only to the clergy, but to the tendentious metaphysics of Aristotelianism. Instead of preaching the priesthood of all believers, they constructed an independent class of priests. Religion thus became progressively self-alienated. The task of Reformers was to dissolve these false oppositions. In a whole series of intellectual projects, directed as often against Protestant as Roman establishments, the Reformist intellect sought to demonstrate that this or that practice was not of divine right, but a perverse historical contingency. The *locus classicus* was the doctrine of purgatory: it was a false doctrine, but one which both therapeutically answered to human anxieties, and which financially served the clergy by way of fees for indulgences and masses for the dead (Le Goff 1984). The invention of purgatory; the successful defining of testamentary law, and of marriage and legitimacy laws, as being "spiritual" matters for the church; the defining of ecclesiastical property and tithes as belonging to the church *de iure divino*; all this belonged to the edifice by which the material interests of the clergy were legitimated by the fabrication of eternal verities. Conversely, the secularizing of property, of marriage, of the intellect, became the holy task of Protestants. Thus John Selden unmasked tithes – they were *iure humano* not *iure divino* – in a book widely regarded in the seventeenth century as the most serious intellectual blow to the economic foundations of the Anglican establishment. Thus the Venetian anti-papalist Paulo Sarpi exposed papal supremacy, offering a ruthlessly secular account of the historical origins of the papal primacy.[8] They were, like Bacon, Hobbes, and Locke, intellectuals who have easily become heroes in the progressivist histories of human self-knowledge, heroes of the mind who threw off the shackles of ideological mystification, who showed beliefs and institutions to be rooted in contingency when, by perversity and credulity, they had blossomed as eternal verities.

By finding fault as much in the contingencies of the medieval church as in the perennial nature of fallen humanity, the Reformers were apt to demand secular solutions to exigent religious problems. The priests had inverted true religion, and the religious world must be brought right side up. The priests had set up oppositions where none should be, between the holy object of the Eucharist and the profanity of other material objects, between the holy property of the church and profane lay commerce, between the holy office of priesthood and the profane laity. In undoing medieval theology, practical secular tasks were entailed. Secularization began as a project of Reformist Christians. It was not a rebellion against the religious life, or an indifference to it; on the contrary, it set about fulfilling religious ideals in the *saeculum*. It proposed the priesthood of all believers and the sanctity of secular callings. It was a progressive repudiation of the ways in which the medieval church had systematically monopolized religion in the practices, the property, and the priests of the church.

The Enlightenment, for all its own claims, was not radically disjunctive from the Protestant critique of popery. The concept of ideology seems coterminous with the secular rejection of religion. It is not so, for the language of unmasking is rooted in the intellectual culture of the Protestant revolt. It is a habit of mind which became omnivorous and devoured its own children. The Protestant who is firm in his Reformed doctrines, for instance the Trinity, holds purgatory to be a popish superstition. But the unitarian of the eighteenth century throws the Trinity overboard as well. The ship of belief foundered gradually, springing leaks on the reefs of skepticism; the crew, the ship's philosophers, threw overboard first the cargo, then the bulkheads and cabins. Out went purgatory and transubstantiation; later went the Trinity, the divinity of Christ, miracles; then Scripture; and finally the deity Himself. With every one of these issues, from the sixteenth to the nineteenth century, European intellectual culture became utterly preoccupied. The cognitive crew, washed up on desert islands like so many Crusoes,

[8] Selden, *History of Tithes* (1618); Sarpi, *History of the Council of Trent* (1620).

saw themselves as building anew on the foundation of natural knowledge. The propaedeutic tasks of cognition done, the end of ideology achieved, civilization would start over again, unencumbered by the mental lumber of the past. At first the lumber was designated "popery," then "priestcraft," then "religion" and "metaphysics" *tout court*, then "ideology."

VI

In his *Philosophy of History* Hegel re-stated, in his own redaction, the conventional historical self-understanding of the Protestant Reformer. He argued that historically Christianity had passed through three stages: opposition to the world, in the early church of the Apostles, of Augustine, and the Fathers; tutelage to the world, in medieval popery; and realization of the world, in the modern state. The modern world was the "German" world because it was Luther's world. "In the Middle Ages the embodying of the divine in actual life was lacking"; it was a "contradictory and self-alienated phase," because religion was but an "externality." It was an externality in three ways: firstly, transubstantiation was an idolatry, "bodying God in a particular material object"; secondly, "knowledge was the exclusive possession of a class," the priests; and thirdly, the clergy's "acquisition of outward property" made the church an economic externality. These were all calamities, for true religion, for individual selfhood, and for the civil community. The Reformation consists in the annulling of all of this, the "building up of the edifice of secular relations." True religion consists in flooding the secular with sanctity. In place of the separation of priest and laity, monastery and the world, sacred and secular, theology and science, the Reformers infused spirituality into the lay life. The rightful beneficiary of Reformation was the secular commonwealth. Under priestcraft church and state are unnaturally torn asunder; in the modern state the unity of piety and patriotism is to be restored. Religion, in its historical forms, has been a panoply of unfulfilled dreams, in opposition against inadequate commonwealths. True religion achieves its end by its own supersession in the practical life of the community: in future, religion will be immanent in social life. Thus the new religion is a religion of humanity and of the secular state. "Religion, properly understood, contains the same truths as the state expresses in reality."[9]

[9] Hegel (1952, §§ 259–60, 270, 272 Addn.); Hegel (1956: 343–4, 422–4, 435, 378–81).

Across a host of movements in Western Europe in the early nineteenth century, whether in Germany, France, or England, the intellectual mood was apocalyptic. The new socialisms and scientisms were religions of humanity, with their own priests of a new order. Christianity had been superseded, transcended, fulfilled in the religions of humanity. The language of Robert Owen, Comte, Feuerbach, St. Simon, Lamennais, and Fourier was saturated in a secular theology, a secular millennium, in talk of new priesthoods. Cognitive translucency was both the means and the reward in the impending end of the misty ages.

Amongst the secular high priests was Feuerbach, whose influence on Marx was profound, and who came to social theory by way of theology, imbibing the insights of Hegel and Schleiermacher in the 1820s. His work remained deeply embedded within Protestant conceptions of the theological transformations of the human and intellectual worlds.[10] This is especially clear in his early studies of Bacon and Bayle in the 1830s. His "anthropology" of human belief is the foundation-stone of modern conceptions of ideology; it was proposed in 1841 in *The Essence of Christianity*, which took the intellectual world by storm. Earlier, in *Bayle*, he distinguished the "true" religion of humanity from the "positive" religion of the churches. "Positive," historical Christianity he described in Hegelian terms, as the religion which sunders us from our completeness, a religion which binds up the spiritual in clerical hierarchy, and in metaphysics. "Bifurcation is the essence of church Christianity." The Popish religion is *par excellence* the obverse of true religion. Romanism alienates flesh from spirit, in its sanctification of self-denial, chastity, and poverty. The contradiction between Catholicism and the essence of humanity was the historical root and cause of Protestantism. "Protestantism resolved the false opposition . . . it led man from the church graveyard of Catholicism back to his civic and human life."

The Catholic age sundered humanity from holiness; the modern age restores holiness to humanity. True religion is to be brought out from this deadweight of deception, mythology, and "oriental ostentation." A second Reformation was needed, and Feuerbach half-ironically styles himself "the second Luther." He celebrates Bacon and Bayle as the chief liberators of philosophy from theology. He notes the importance in Bayle of a fideistic view of our anthropomorphism: the more devout the sense of the mysteriousness of God, the more profound the disgust at metaphysical flummery

[10] For what follows see Wartofsky (1977). The quotations are at pp. 118, 120, 133, 165, 199, 202, 276, 298.

about God, the more radical the insight into the cultural and political production of ideas about the Godhead. For Feuerbach, as for his heroes Bayle, Bacon, and Spinoza, "all religious speculation is vanity and falsehood": the truly religious task of philosophy is not to address God, but humanity. Yet theology is not merely false, for it contains truths in an inverted and contradictory form; it expresses in esoteric form humanity's true needs and hopes. "God is what man is not." God is the anthropomorphic reflection of human hopes. Once we grasp this, our dreamlike theological mentality will dissolve; there will be an end of ideology. With Luther theology had begun to be "anthropological": it had turned away from dissecting God's nature, and instead addressed what God is for man. Hegel had offered a magnificent stage forward, but remained in the mists of metaphysics: he is the philosophical Pope who must also be overthrown.

Feuerbach remained uneasily indebted both to the positivist, empirical tradition of the English and French schools – he adopts sensationalist and psychologistic accounts of knowledge – and also to the speculative, German tradition in philosophical theology, which is apt to find the Godlike instantiated in man. But both streams can produce the anti-metaphysical conviction that pellucid self-knowledge will shortly dissolve the mystifications which plague humanity. The coming to knowledge of humanity proceeds by stages: for Feuerbach there is a series of historic reductions, from religion to philosophy, to psychology, to anthropology. "Religion is the childlike condition of humanity." Theology is the essence of intellectual alienation, and the critique of all ideology begins in the critique of religion. The *Essence of Christianity* is both post- and anti-Christian; it offers a "true religion," but is also self-consciously an historical legacy of Reformist Christianity.

VII

Hence it is that Marx came to intellectual maturity amidst a Germany intoxicated with theology. He himself remarked that in the 1840s "heroes of the mind overthrew each other with unheard of rapidity" (Marx and Engels 1974: 39). Philosophical and political speculation was captivated by the prospect that humanity could achieve full self-consciousness, and a fulfilled civic life through the critical supersession of Christianity. Feuerbach had the greatest impact; but there were also works like Strauss's *Life of Jesus*. Schelling lectured on the evolution of the divine in history: Engels, Kierkegaard and Bakunin were amongst his audience. In the early 1840s Marx and Bruno Bauer proposed a journal called *Atheistic Archives*, and in 1842 Moses Hess saw in Marx the towering philosopher of the coming generation who would finally "give medieval religion and politics their *coup de grâce*." In 1841, in his doctoral dissertation, Marx arraigned religion at the bar of philosophy. The "babbling" of Plutarch on behalf of the gods he countered with the insights of Epicurus and Prometheus. The latter, he proclaims, is "the foremost saint and martyr in the philosophical calendar," for he began the rescue of humanity from self-enslavement in religion. In the *Theses on Feuerbach* Marx wrote, "Feuerbach starts out from the fact of religious self-alienation, the duplication of the world into a religious, imaginary world and a real one. His work consists in the dissolution of the religious world into its secular basis." But once that is achieved, the chief task is yet to be done: the secular foundation must itself be criticized and revolutionized (Marx 1977: 11–13, 157; McLellan 1980: 127, 71).

The most crucial passage, however, is the powerful opening of the *Contribution to the Critique of Hegel's Philosophy of Right* of 1844. It reveals once again the sense of the centrality of the critique of religion and of theological anthropomorphism, in the historical task of the cognitive unburdening of humanity, the epoch-making role of the Protestant Reformation in that process, and the further need, now Luther's work is done, for another reformation. The passage is worth extensive quotation: it encapsulates the rootedness of the concept of ideology in the Christian Reformist project, and marks the moment at which the concept begins to cut adrift from that root.

> As far as Germany is concerned, the criticism of religion is in the main complete, and criticism of religion is the presupposition of all criticism.
>
> The profane existence of error is compromised as soon as its heavenly *oratio pro aris et focis* [prayer for hearth and home] is refuted. Man has found in the imaginary reality of heaven where he looked for a superman only the reflection of his own self. He will therefore no longer be inclined to find only the appearance of himself, the non-man where he seeks and must seek his true reality.
>
> The foundation of irreligious criticism is this: man makes religion, religion does not make man. Religion is indeed the self-consciousness and self-awareness of man who either has not yet attained to himself or has already lost himself again. But man is no abstract being squatting outside the world. Man is the world of man, the state, society. This state, this society, produced religion's inverted attitude to the world,

because they are an inverted world themselves. Religion is the general theory of this world, its encyclopedic compendium . . . It is the imaginary realization of the human essence, because the human essence possesses no true reality. Thus, the struggle against religion is indirectly the struggle against the other world whose spiritual aroma is religion.

Religious suffering is at the same time an expression of real suffering and a protest against real suffering. Religion is the sigh of the oppressed creature, the feeling of a heartless world, and the soul of soulless circumstances. It is the opium of the people.

The abolition of religion as the illusory happiness of the people is the demand for their real happiness. The demand to give up the illusions about their condition is the demand to give up a condition which requires illusions. The criticism of religion is therefore the germ of the criticism of the valley of tears whose halo is religion . . .

The criticism of religion disillusions man to make him think, act and fashion his reality as a disillusioned man come to his senses; so that he may revolve around himself as his real sun. Religion is only the illusory sun which revolves around man as long as he does not revolve around himself.

It is therefore the task of history, now the truth is no longer in the beyond, to establish the truth of the here and now. The first task of philosophy, which is in the service of history, once the holy form of human self-alienation has been discovered, is to discover self-alienation in its unholy forms. The criticism of religion is thus transformed into the criticism of earth, the criticism of theology into the criticism of politics . . .

Even historically, theoretical emancipation has specifically practical significance for Germany. For Germany's revolutionary past is theoretical, it is the Reformation. Once it was the monk's brain [Luther's] in which the revolution began, now it is in the philosopher's.

Certainly, Luther removed the servitude of devotion by replacing it by the servitude of conviction . . . He turned priests into laymen by turning laymen into priests. He liberated man from exterior religiosity by making man's inner conscience religious. He emancipated the body from chains by enchaining the heart.

But even though Protestantism was not the true solution, it formulated the problem rightly. The question was now no longer the battle of the laymen with the exterior priest, it was the battle with his own interior priest, his priestly nature. Protestantism by turning laymen into priests emancipated the lay popes, the princes, together with their clergy, the privileged and the philistines. Similarly philosophy, by turning priestly Germans into men, will emancipate the people. But just as emancipation did not stop with the princes, so it will not stop with the secularization of goods involved in the spoliation of the church . . .

Marx 1977: 63–4, 69

For Marx, as for any nineteenth-century social theorist, the rhetoric of anti-clericalism came naturally. His prose is often rich in it. But as this forceful passage reveals, these are not merely metaphors. He sees his own theoretical task as being the godchild of the German criticism of religion. There is an historical unfolding in which Luther unmasks the external hegemony of priestliness, and Marx exposes its internal dominion. The first Reformation is complete. The criticism of popery has its natural endpoint in the criticism of religion itself, but German intellectual life has become arrested at this point. Marx's task is a new Reformation, for criticism of religion is the "germ" of his new criticism. Now that "holy self-alienation" has been unmasked, the task turns to its "unholy," material forms. The Reformers made every person a priest, but now the priestliness within the soul must be overthrown. The inner priestliness of modernity turns out to be the fetishism of commodities under capitalism, for, Marx writes in *Capital*, capitalism re-enacts "at the level of material production . . . the same situation that we find in religion at the ideological level, namely the inversion of subject into object." Protestantism disgorged itself into the commerce of the world, spiritualizing it. It liberated the goods of the church, it replaced vows of poverty by vows of prosperity. It renounced the corralling of spirituality into monks and monasteries; it instead tonsured the artisan and the tradesman, and infused divinity into secular callings. Protestantism is bourgeois Christianity. It is the religion of a class, masquerading as true religion. Political economy is the practical theology of Protestants, the holy science of secular priestliness. *Capital* will unmask it, in the name of the truest religion.

Marx's and Engels's *German Ideology* of 1846 is a *locus classicus* of the modern theory of ideology. It is a manifesto of new Reformation, of the dissolution of falsehood by the disclosure of the material and economic foundations of existing belief systems.

> Hitherto men have constantly made up for themselves false conceptions about themselves . . . They have arranged their relationships according to their ideas of God, of normal men, etc. The phantoms of their brain have got out of their hands. They, the creators, have bowed down before their creations. Let us liberate them from the chimeras, the ideas, dogmas, imaginary beings under the yoke of which they are pining away.

Any philosophy which imagines an autonomy for the realm of ideas is puerile. "Philosophy and the study of the actual world have the same relation to one another as masturbation and sexual love." Philosophy is doomed: "when reality is depicted, philosophy as an independent branch of knowledge lost its medium of existence." "Morality, religion, metaphysics, all the rest of ideology . . . no longer retain the semblance of independence"; "where speculation ends . . . there real, positive science begins." The ruling philosophy of any age is the ideas of its ruling class, the ideal expression of material forms, the "illusion of the epoch."[11] In these phrases, the history of the understanding of human delusion has passed from theology to class.

VIII

The preoccupation of European intellectuals with the phenomenology of religious belief might be thought to have been finally disposed of by Marx and by the growth of widespread religious indifference. We are apt to think of the steady decline of religion as proceeding apace in the nineteenth century. Yet, on the contrary, its later decades offered every visible sign of vigorous religious renewal, especially in Catholic politics. Catholic movements flourished in Parnell's Ireland, in Cardinal Manning's England, in Third-Republic France, in Germany and Italy. The 1870s in Germany saw the Kulturkampf, and Marx's successors pondered the continued force of religion. In France there was intense warfare between republican anti-clericalism and Catholic conservatism. In England, J.S. Mill's intellectual heirs, who saw in him a secular saint, now found it hard to discern an ineluctable mental progress beyond the toils of religious belief. Liberalism, perhaps even Protestantism itself, was on the defensive. It is no accident that these years also saw an extraordinary flowering of social theory, intensely interested in the causal structures of human belief, and strongly tending to the bleak and irrationalist conclusion that ideological thinking was an unavoidable characteristic of most of humanity. The Enlightenment hope of ushering in an epistemic epiphany was waning. There was a renewed concern with the causes of religious belief, coupled almost invariably with a deep hostility to it.

That most famous of case studies of ideology, Max Weber's *The Protestant Ethic and the Spirit of Capitalism*, appeared in 1904–5. It argued that in early modern Europe there was some broad alignment between Protestant theological values and the growth of economic

[11] Marx and Engels (1974). Quotations at pp. 37, 47, 48, 60, 103. See also Seliger (1977).

individualism. It was written against a background in which, on the one hand, it simply was the case that German Catholics were less prosperous, less urbanized, and less well educated than Protestants, and in which, on the other, the new Catholic Centre Party was an energetic force in the Reichstag. Weber remarked bitterly on the "virtuoso *Maschinerie* of Mother Church." A man of his liberal Protestant background had every reason to think of Catholicism as hostile to free enquiry and open education, and as the party of rural backwardness. Yet Catholic belief was no less tenacious for being the religion of backwardness. Much of Weber's work hence became the exploration of the religious modifications of Marxian class theory (Stone 1984).

Freud's psychoanalytic project is also recognizably within the mold of historically-minded secularism. He believed the psychoanalyst to be the heir of the priest and the physician, armed with scientific conceptions which his predecessors only dimly grasped. "I wish to protect analysis . . . from the priests. I should like to hand it over to a profession of lay curers of souls." True science revealed that the "real" causal landscape of the human world lay within the family and its relationships: all other modes of relations and of values were projections of father–child and mother–child relationships. God was a projection of fatherhood; our conception of God was (once again) anthropomorphic, and only in grasping this fact do we come to self-understanding about our humanity. Faith – mental dependence on God – stemmed from fears and anxieties; it could be exorcised like other neurotic symptoms. Freud called his book on religion *The Future of an Illusion* (1927); religion is ideology, a mystery to be dissolved. Freud was an atheist Jew amidst the anti-semitic Catholic clericalism of early-twentieth-century Vienna. The Catholic Church, he wrote, "has hitherto been the relentless enemy of freedom of thought and of progress towards knowledge of the truth." Catholicism and Protestantism were stages in the progress of humanity towards its maturity, just as the fear of God lodged in the minds of small children but was later outgrown. Freud was apt to equate modernity with adulthood, with disenchanted rationality, with sanity; and conversely, the primitive with the pre-industrial, the childlike, the neurotic, the religious, the mystified (Pace 1982).

Durkheim's *Elementary Forms of the Religious Life* (1912) is probably the most profound modern account of religious belief as ideology. But he does not share the sense that the discovery of religion's social functionality is a prelude to its dissolution. On the contrary, society without religion is hardly conceivable, for religion is no other than society representing itself by its symbols; the sense of the sacred is the sense of social values. "Sacred things . . . are only collective forces hypostatised." Religion is necessarily a social affair, a thing of ritual and practice, not a matter of private conviction about doctrinal propositions; it is the collective representation of those aspects of a society which lie beyond its existence as a biological organism and hence they are representations which acquire a life of their own; they are not merely reducible to psychological or biological need. Although a skeptical Jew with a background in Catholic France, his outlook is closer to that of the theological tradition of skeptical Christian Reformers, for whom a grasp of the fact of the cultural production of religious values need not be a cause for intellectual embarrassment. He is in a sense splendidly liberated from the relentless epistemic sense that religion is primarily about improbable propositions, and that rites and rituals are merely the superfluous corollaries of those propositions. Durkheim accordingly is today congenial to those committed Christian historians and anthropologists who wish to disengage insight into the cultural rootedness of religious belief from militant secularism (e.g. Bossy 1985). Durkheim himself, however, was a devout and militant republican secularist. His insights were intended as a prelude to the supersession of French Catholicism by a civil religion for modern citizens, a religion in which man is, at the same time, both "believer and God" (Lukes 1973: 338–41 and *passim*).

In England, meanwhile, social theorists were absorbed by the anthropology of religion. An astonishing flood of histories of religion appeared between the 1880s and 1910s. The most famous is Frazer's vast *Golden Bough*. Robertson Smith's *The Religion of the Semites* (1889) influenced Durkheim and Freud. Sir Edward Tylor's *Primitive Culture* appeared in 1871; F.B. Jevons's *Introduction to the History of Religion* in 1896. Their theoretical emphases varied, some were grounded in psychological explanations, others in social structural ideas. Most retained a strong element of evolutionism. Primitive religion is childlike; the savage inhabits a world of fears, mysteries, and superstitions, is busily occupied in placating the ubiquitous supernatural. Monotheism, Judaism, and Christianity represent progressive stages of sophistication. They are part of a uniform path from totemism and magic; priests are stages on the path from the juju man. These anthropologists could not but see themselves as forging intellectual tools for the progressive intellectual emancipation of humankind from its enchanted infancy (Evans-Prichard 1965).

Yet few had much confidence that progress towards the end of ideology was ineluctable. This sense of the inevitability of non-rational beliefs is probably strongest in Karl Mannheim's *Ideology and Utopia* (1929). The epistemic hopes of the Enlightenment project, the hope for a universal class of thinking, is crowded out by the overwhelming sense of the conditioned nature of all thinking and knowing. Nonetheless, Mannheim sets out to construct an academic science of ideology, a "sociology of knowledge," which can become a keystone within sociology. In sketching the origins of that science, he drew attention to the importance of the tradition of skeptical theology, from "Pascal and Montaigne down to Kierkegaard." That tradition of theology, he noted, was psychological and not metaphysical; it situated religion in human predicaments, not in speculative propositions. Mannheim rightly detected the marriage between it and the epistemological project which transformed philosophy in the seventeenth century. This was the "soil" of modern social science. For "the sociology of knowledge is . . . the systematization of the doubt" inherent in the post-Reformation preoccupation with the "knowing personality."[12]

[12] Mannheim (1960: 15, 31, 45). The literature which I have found especially helpful in exploring the theme of this essay includes: Berger (1969); Cunningham (1973): Geertz (1964); Gellner (1959; 1964; 1974); Lichtheim (1965); Minogue (1985); Plamenatz (1970); and Rorty (1980). I am grateful to Sylvana Tomaselli for helpful criticism.

REFERENCES

Acton, H.B. 1955. *The Illusion of the Epoch*. London: Routledge and Kegan Paul.

1966. "The Philosophy of Language in Revolutionary France." In Findlay 1966: 143–67.

Aron, Raymond. 1957. *The Opium of the Intellectuals*. London: Secker and Warburg.

Benda, Julien. 1969. *The Treason of the Intellectuals*, translated by R. Aldington. New York: W.W. Norton. (Original title: *La Trahison des clercs*. 1928.)

Berger, Peter. 1969. *A Rumour of Angels*. Harmondsworth: Penguin.

Bossy, John. 1985. *Christianity in the West 1400–1700*. Oxford: Oxford University Press.

Condorcet, Antoine-Nicolas de. 1955 [1795]. *Sketch for a Historical Picture of the Progress of the Human Mind*, edited by Stuart Hampshire. London.

Cunningham, Adrian. 1973. "Reflections on Projections: The Range of Ideology." In Robert Benewick, R.N. Berki and Bhikhu Parekh (eds.), *Knowledge and Belief in Politics: the Problem of Ideology.* London: George Allen and Unwin, pp. 36–56.

Evans-Prichard, E.E. 1965. *Theories of Primitive Religion*. Oxford: Oxford University Press.

Farrington, Benjamin. 1964. *The Philosophy of Francis Bacon*. Liverpool: Liverpool University Press.

Findlay, J.N. (ed.). 1966. *Studies in Philosophy: British Academy Lectures*. Oxford: Oxford University Press.

Geertz, Clifford. 1964. "Ideology as a Cultural System." In David Apter (ed.), *Ideology and Discontent*. New York: Free Press of Glencoe, pp. 47–76.

Gellner, Ernest. 1959. *Words and Things*. London: Routledge and Kegan Paul.

1964. *Thought and Change*. London: Weidenfeld and Nicolson.

1974. *Legitimation of Belief*. Cambridge: Cambridge University Press.

Goldmann, Lucien. 1964. *The Hidden God*, translated by P. Thody. London: Humanities Press.

Hegel, G.W.F. 1952. *The Philosophy of Right*, edited by T.M. Knox. Oxford: Clarendon.

1956. *The Philosophy of History*, translated by J. Sibree and edited by C.J. Friedrich. New York: Dover.

Jolley, Nicholas. 1984. *Leibniz and Locke*. Oxford: Clarendon.

Lane, Robert. 1966. "The Decline of Politics and Ideology in a Knowledgeable Society." *American Sociological Review* 31: 649–69.

Le Goff, Jacques. 1984. *The Birth of Purgatory*, translated by A. Goldhammer. Chicago, IL: University of Chicago Press.

Lichtheim, George. 1965. "The Concept of Ideology." *History and Theory* 4: 164–95.

Locke, John. 1979–82. *The Correspondence of John Locke*, edited by E.S. deBeer, vols. V–VII. Oxford: Clarendon.

Lukes, Steven. 1973. *Emile Durkheim: His Life and Work*. London: Allen Lane.

McLellan, David. 1980. *Marx before Marxism*. London: Macmillan.

Mannheim, Karl. 1960. *Ideology and Utopia*. London: Routledge and Kegan Paul. (Originally published 1929–31.)

Marx, Karl. 1977. *Karl Marx: Selected Writings*, edited by David McLellan. Oxford: Oxford University Press.

Marx, Karl, and Friedrich Engels. 1974. *The German Ideology*, edited by C.J. Arthur. London: Lawrence and Wishart.

Minogue, Kenneth. 1985. *Alien Powers. The Pure Theory of Ideology*. London: Weidenfeld.

Niebuhr, Richard. 1965. *Schleiermacher on Christ and Religion*. London: SCM Press.

Pace, David. 1982. "Freud contra Ecclesiam." In W.W. Wagar (ed.), *The Secular Mind*. New York: Holmes and Meier, pp. 126–41.

Plamenatz, John. 1970. *Ideology*. London: Macmillan.

Popper, Karl. 1966. "On the Sources of Knowledge and of Ignorance." In Findlay 1966: 169–212.

Rorty, Richard. 1980. *Philosophy and the Mirror of Nature*. Oxford: Blackwell.

Rossi, Paulo. 1968. *Francis Bacon: from Magic to Science*. London: Routledge and Kegan Paul.

Seliger, Martin. 1977. *The Marxist Conception of Ideology*. Cambridge: Cambridge University Press.

Shklar, Judith. 1957. *After Utopia*. Princeton, NJ: Princeton University Press.

Stone, Norman. 1984. "The Religious Background to Max Weber." In W.J. Sheils (ed.), *Persecution and Toleration* (*Studies in Church History*, vol. XXII). Oxford: Blackwell, pp. 393–407.

Sullivan, Robert.1982. *John Toland and the Deist Controversy*. Cambridge MA: Harvard University Press.

Tucker, Robert. 1961. *Philosophy and Myth in Karl Marx*. Cambridge: Cambridge University Press.

Wartofsky, Marx. 1977. *Feuerbach*. Cambridge: Cambridge University Press.

White, Howard B. 1968. *Peace among the Willows: The Political Philosophy of Francis Bacon*. The Hague: Nijhoff.

14

Rights

RICHARD DAGGER

We live, even more thoroughly than did our eighteenth-century ancestors, in an age of rights. This is evident in domestic affairs, where women's rights, children's rights, "gay" rights, and animal rights all have their advocates, as do the rights of the unborn, which the "right to life" movement defends against those who proclaim the pregnant woman's "right to choose" to have an abortion. In international relations, "human rights" has become the watchword of private groups, governments, and supranational organizations, to the point where suspect regimes are occasionally warned that they must improve their "human rights record" if they hope to continue to receive foreign aid. And at the philosophical level, an imposing array of treatises – Dworkin's *Taking Rights Seriously*, Gewirth's *Reason and Morality*, Nozick's *Anarchy, State, and Utopia*, and Melden's *Rights and Persons* among them – testifies to the power of the concept of rights in moral and political philosophy, at least among theorists in the Anglo-American tradition.

Nor is this preoccupation with rights confined to the West, as it was in the eighteenth century. In the Soviet Union, the Preamble to the 1977 Constitution proclaims "a society of genuine democracy, whose political system ensures . . . the combination of real citizens' rights and liberties with their duties and responsibilities to society." Elsewhere, scholars who have claimed to discover the concept of human rights in traditional Islamic, African, Hindu, and Confucian thought have gone on to argue for syncretic conceptions of human rights – conceptions that would temper the "excessive individualism" of the Western notion by wedding it to the communitarian notions prevailing in one or another of these traditions. These mixed

I am grateful to Jack Donnelly, who may not agree with everything I say here, for unusually helpful comments on an earlier draft of this essay.

conceptions face problems of their own, like other "mixed marriages," but they speak clearly nonetheless for the significance of the concept of rights in political discourse throughout the world.[1]

This, of course, has not always been the case. Indeed, there are those who believe that the concept of rights was politically insignificant even in the West until the seventeenth century or, at the earliest, the late middle ages. Whether this is true will depend, as we shall see, on what we take the concept of rights to be. Words are often easier to trace than concepts, however, so I shall begin this brief history of the concept of rights with a glimpse at the etymology of the English word 'right.'

I

In English, 'right' is used in a number of ways to mean a number of things. We may turn to the *right*, for instance, even when that is not the *right* way to turn; the Pythagorean theorem deals with *right*-angled triangles; governments sometimes shift to the *right*; straightforward people come *right* to the point when they seek to *right* matters; and we occasionally find that what someone is doing is not *right*, morally speaking, even though she *has the right* to do it. 'Right' in this last sense – 'right' as a kind of property we can hold, stand on, or act within; as something we can exercise if we choose, perhaps by asserting it against others – is our concern here, for this is the sense that conveys the concept of rights.

Like its cognates in German (*recht*) and the other Teutonic languages, 'right' evolved from the Latin word *rectus* (straight).[2] In much the same way, its counterparts in French (*droit*), Italian (*diritto*), and Spanish (*derecho*) are corruptions of the low Latin *directum* (Miller 1980 [1903]: 48). *Rectus*, in turn, has been traced through the Greek *orektos* (stretched out, upright) to the Sanskrit *rju* or *riju* (straight or upright), which has been connected to *raja* (shining, radiant, a king) and the Latin *rex* (Miller 1980 [1903]: 40). The pattern, then, is for the notion of straightness to be extended from the physical realm to the moral – from *rectus* to rectitude, as it were. Something similar seems to have happened with 'wrong' and 'tort,' which derive respectively from the Old Norwegian word for curved or bent,

[1] For an insightful account and criticism of these arguments, and of the Soviet conception of rights, see Donnelly (1982, esp. pp. 306–13).

[2] The sources for this etymology of 'right' are: Miller (1980 [1903]: 35–48); Salmond (1907: 463–73); Skeat (1978: 519); and *Webster's* (1950).

wrangr, and the Latin word for twisted, *tortus* (Salmond 1907: 465). The moral use of these notions is old enough, in fact, for Hesiod to have called on rulers who "twist the courses of justice aslant" to "straighten" their decisions (1968: 250–64).[3]

But this still leaves us short of an account of how 'right' came to be used to mean a kind of personal possession, something one can "have." In this case the answer lies in an extension of the term from one moral sense to another – from *objective* to *subjective* right, to use the distinction familiar to Continental jurists. By analogy with the physical sense, the primary moral sense of 'right' was a standard or measure for conduct. Something was right – morally straight or true – if it met the standard of rectitude, or rightness. The conjunction of 'right' with a preposition in Old English underscores this point.[4] If something was done "with right," "by right," or even "in right," then it was rightfully done, or done in accordance with the standard of right conduct. From here, the next step was to recognize that actions taken "with right" or "by right" are taken *as a matter of right*. The transition is from the belief that I may do something because it *is right*, in other words, to the belief that I may do something because I *have a right* to do it. Once this transition is achieved, 'right' can mean not only a standard, but also a justifiable claim to act in a certain way – a claim that becomes a kind of standard itself. Thus the concept of *rights* joins the concept of *the right*.

But when and where and why did this happen? When, that is, did subjective right emerge as a concept distinct from objective right? To answer these questions, we shall have to look beyond the English 'right' to its conceptual antecedents.

II

There are two schools of thought, loosely speaking, on the origins of the concept of rights. One view, perhaps the dominant one, holds that the concern for rights is characteristic of political and legal thought only in the modern era, so the concept itself must be either modern or, at the earliest, late medieval in origin. As John Finnis puts it (1980: 206–7), there is a "watershed" in the history of 'right' and its classical antecedent *ius*, a watershed that occurs somewhere between Thomas Aquinas in the thirteenth century and Francisco

[3] Jones (1956: 125) describes Hesiod's views in this way: "It [*dike*] is straight or right as opposed to what is wrested, wrung, or wrong . . . It is set up against any perverse twisting . . . of something essentially plain, direct, and simple. Personified, this 'straightness' is placed among the gods as the daughter of Zeus and Themis."

[4] See the examples under 'right,' definition 7, in the *Oxford English Dictionary*.

Suarez in the early years of the seventeenth.[5] For Aquinas, Finnis notes, *ius* "primarily means 'the fair' or 'the what's fair' "; but for Suarez (*De legibus*, I, ii, 5), *ius* is "a kind of moral power [*facultas*] which every man has, either over his own property or with respect to that which is due to him." In *De jure belli ac pacis* (I, I, iv; 1925: 35), furthermore, Hugo Grotius defines *ius* much as Suarez did, thus strengthening the impression that *ius* was somehow transformed in the late medieval or early modern period from a standard or law defining just or right relationships to a faculty or power belonging to the beneficiary of the relationship – to the one who "has" the right.

Finnis is fairly cautious here, for some 340 years separate Aquinas and Suarez. Michel Villey is bolder. Villey (1969) argues forcefully that *le droit subjectif* – "une qualité du sujet, une de ses facultés, plus précisément une franchise, une liberté, une possibilité d'agir" (p. 146) – is the work of William of Ockham. Although he does not insist that Ockham was the first to use *ius* in the subjective sense, Villey does claim that Ockham provided the first clear and complete definition of the new concept in his *Opus nonaginta dierum* (*c.* 1330), where he deployed it on behalf of his fellow Franciscans in their controversy with Pope John XXII.

Boldness comes at a price, however, and others have disputed Villey's claims for Ockham.[6] Richard Tuck maintains, for instance, that the concept emerged not with Ockham, but in the century before him as the result of an assimilation of *ius* and *dominium* by the later Glossators, particularly Accursius and his followers. According to Tuck, "already by the fourteenth century it was possible to argue that to have a right was to be the lord or *dominus* of one's relevant moral world, to possess *dominium*, that is to say *property*" (1979: 3; Tuck's emphasis). In fact, Tuck says (ibid.: 22–3), even Ockham's opponent, John XXII, employed *ius* in this sense in his bull *Quia vir reprobus* (1329) – the very work that Ockham sought to refute.

Tuck (1979: 13–15) detects intimations of this conception of a right among the twelfth-century Glossators as well; but because they thought of rights as passive rather than active claims, he argues, they could not conceive of rights as a kind of property. As Brian Tierney sees it (1983: 435), though, Tuck is doubly wrong here: wrong, firstly, because he mistakes active rights for passive ones; and wrong,

[5] For a similar view, see Golding (1978: 46–9).

[6] Perhaps I should say Villey's claim *against* Ockham, for Villey seems to deplore the results of this "moment copernicien de l'histoire de la science du droit . . ." (1969: 177).

secondly, because the active–passive distinction makes no difference in this context anyhow. This being so, it seems that references to rights – "either as rights to do something or as rights to enforce claims against others – are commonly encountered in twelfth century juridical works." What seems a watershed to Finnis is, for Tierney, no more than a gentle slope – a slope that begins *before* Aquinas, not after him.

Despite their differences, all these scholars, save perhaps Tierney, believe that the concept of rights is not to be found before the high or the late middle ages, not even in Roman law. But there is another school of thought on the matter, one represented most recently by Alan Gewirth. Gewirth acknowledges that there is little in the way of direct appeals to the concept of rights or of substantial attempts to analyze it before the modern period, but this means only that it is "important to distinguish between having or using a concept and the clear or explicit recognition and elucidation of it . . . Thus persons might have and use the concept of a right without explicitly having a single word for it" (1978: 99). With this in mind, Gewirth proceeds to uncover the concept of rights in feudal thought, Roman law, Greek philosophy, the Old Testament, and even primitive societies. The word may not be present, in his view, but the concept surely is.

This is in many ways a plausible view. It does seem, after all, that wherever there are rules recognizing and governing the private ownership of property, as there were as long ago as the Code of Hammurabi, the concept of rights must also be present. To talk of "mine" and "thine," that is, is to talk of rights, even if only implicitly. In other contexts, too, it seems that the Greeks and Romans, who certainly lacked a specific word for rights, still found ways to talk about them.[7] The Roman law of persons, with its attempt to delineate the ways in which a person could move from one status level to another, seems to reflect a concern for what we now call legal and political rights, for instance.[8] Thus the Roman citizen enjoyed not only an opportunity to participate in politics

[7] See the entries under *dikaios* in Liddell and Scott (1968), for instance, and those under *ius*, especially definitions 10–13, in the *Oxford Latin Dictionary*. Note especially Liddell and Scott's reference to Aristotle's *Politics* (1287b12), *o spoudaios archein dikaios* – a phrase Sinclair and Saunders (1981: 227) translate "if . . . a sound man has a right to rule," and Barker (1971: 147) renders "If the good man has a just title to authority."

[8] According to Nicholas (1962: 60–1), the Roman law of persons was "concerned with the different categories of 'status' – in the modern sense of a condition in which a man's rights and duties differ from the normal, that difference not having been created simply, or at all, by his own consent."

that was denied to others, but a legal standing superior to others as well – to freedman, to resident alien, and especially to slave, who had no legal standing at all.[9] Among the citizenry, furthermore, other distinctions denoted differences in what we regard as rights. Thus the only person who was legally in his own power (*sui iuris*) was the head of the family, the *paterfamilias*; everyone else was, in the eyes of the law, *alieni iuris*, in the power of another (Nicholas 1962: 68). And even the *paterfamilias* could suffer *capitis deminutio*, deterioration of status, whether it be *capitis deminutio minima* – loss of family rights; *capitis deminutio media* – loss of citizenship and family rights; or *capitis deminutio maxima* – loss of liberty, citizenship, and family rights: i.e., enslavement (Nicholas 1962: 96).

Which of these positions regarding the origin of the concept of rights is correct? I doubt that straightforward etymological or conceptual digging will answer this question once and for all, for the answer ultimately depends upon what we are willing to count as "having" a particular concept. If one is willing to look primarily for the idea or the notion, however it may be expressed, then one can confidently say that the concept of rights is virtually as old as civilization itself. The concept may have been embedded in or scattered among a variety of words – in *auctoritas*, *potestas*, *dominium*, *iurisdictio*, *proprietas*, and *libertas* as well as *ius*, to take the Roman example – but it was there all the same.[10]

If one insists that the form of expression is crucial, however, so that a concept cannot be said to exist unless there is a word or phrase that distinguishes it from other concepts, then one would have to say that the concept of rights has its origin in the middle ages. Certainly the Romans could use *auctoritas*, *potestas*, *libertas*, and other words in circumstances where we now use 'rights,' but that itself tells *against* the claim, on this view, that they possessed the concept of rights. They had a number of related concepts, that is, but they were not

[9] "At Rome and with regard to Romans," Wirszubski (1960: 4) says,

> full *libertas* is coterminous with *civitas*. A Roman's *libertas* and his *civitas* both denote the same thing, only that each does it from a different point of view and with emphasis on a different aspect: *libertas* signifies in the first place the status of an individual as such, whereas *civitas* denotes primarily the status of an individual in relation to the community. Only a Roman citizen enjoys all the rights, personal and political, that constitute libertas.

[10] On the relation of these words, and others, to the concept of rights, see Miller (1980 [1903]: 58–131), who defines a legal right as "a claim, a power, a faculty, a liberty, an authority, a privilege, a prerogative, a capacity to act or to possess dominion, empire, power, authority, immunity, status, or some interest put forward actively if necessary in the form of a case or action at law, and recognized by the State in accordance with right, law, and justice" (p. 131). On *libertas* in particular, see Wirszubski (1960, *passim*).

able to distinguish, as we are, the concept of rights from these others. Even the words with the greatest claim – *dikaios* for the Greeks and *ius* for the Romans – betray the absence of the concept because in the classical period both words mean right primarily in the objective sense. Where we say, "I have a right to this book," for instance, they usually said, "It is right that I have this book" – related notions, to be sure, but more than merely a difference in the order of the words. As long as there was no way of distinguishing the subjective sense of right from the objective, then, the concept of rights could not truly be said to exist.

This, I think, is the sounder of the two positions on the origin of the concept. We can say that intimations, anticipations, or glimpses of the concept are as old as legal and political thinking, certainly, but we must acknowledge that these are *our* glimpses; for what seems to anticipate or intimate the concept of rights can seem so only to those who already have the concept. Other concepts, narrower concepts – older members of the same family, so to speak – are easy to find in ancient thought, but the concept of rights itself is not fully present until sometime in the later middle ages. After that, emphasis shifts from the notion of *right* as a standard for conduct to the notion of *rights* as possessions, a kind of personal property. By the seventeenth century, Grotius could begin *De jure belli ac pacis* by distinguishing *ius* as "a moral quality of a person, making it possible to have or to do something lawfully" (I, I, iv) from *ius* "as nothing else than what is just" (I, I, iii; 1925: 34–5). And by the middle of that century, Hobbes could, and characteristically did, go even further (*Leviathan*, chapter 14):

> For though they that speak of this subject, use to confound *ius*, and *lex*, *right* and *law*: yet they ought to be distinguished; because RIGHT, consisteth in liberty to do, or to forbear: whereas LAW determineth, and bindeth to one of them: so that law, and right, differ as much, as obligation, and liberty; which in one and the same matter are inconsistent.

III

Here, with Hobbes, we have the subjective sense of right distinguished so sharply from the objective that they are actually opposed to one another. We also have the concept of rights at the center of political theory for the first time, not only with Grotius and Hobbes, but with Suarez, Spinoza, and, at the end of the century, Locke. It is, moreover, *natural* rights that play so prominent a part in the political thought of the seventeenth and eighteenth centuries. It almost had to be.

If the concept of rights did not emerge fully fledged in the classical period or the early middle ages, it is probably because concepts rooted in status considerations of one sort or another informed thought in those periods. To say *then* that one was a citizen or a lord was to say, in our terms, that one held certain rights (and was subject to certain obligations) by virtue of one's position or role in society. But because the status concepts were fully effective – because they did the work the concept of rights now does – they precluded any appeal to rights as such. To say, in these circumstances, "I am a citizen, therefore I have rights," would have been as pointless as it now is to say, "I am a carpenter, therefore I have tools."

For the concept of rights to appear and gain purchase, the status concepts had to lose their grip; and in order for this to happen, the idea that human beings are fundamentally alike had to displace the belief that differences in nationality, culture, or rank were rooted in natural differences between people. This idea of human equality is an old one – one historian traces it to "the Hebrew account which describes Adam, whose name means 'humanity,' as being created in the 'image of God'" (Pagels 1979: 4) – and there were occasional breakthroughs, such as the "startling" change from "Aristotle's view of the natural inequality of human nature" to the "theory of the natural equality of human nature" in Cicero and Seneca (Carlyle and Carlyle 1950: 8). The idea also found powerful expression in a cosmopolitan philosophy, Stoicism, and a religion, Christianity, that emphasized both the individual and the universal. Yet the idea of natural equality played relatively little part in social and political thought until the later middle ages, perhaps because neither Stoicism nor Christianity invested life on earth with much significance.[11] When it did come into prominence, however, the concept of rights came with it.

What happened, briefly, is that the growing conviction of the

[11] According to Lewis (1974, vol. I: 196), "These two sets of ideas, the Christian and the Stoic, were to become the chief bases of that sense of human dignity in which every individualistic trend in Western political thought is finally rooted." But she also observes that

> ecclesiastical thought also conveyed ideas which may seem to us incompatible with its profound ideas of the equality and freedom of human souls. The early church had made peace with Roman absolutism and with the great inequalities and injustices of Roman society; it was prepared to accept the stratification of the feudal age and the irresponsibility of medieval kings. For Christ's kingdom was not of this world. Ibid.

natural equality of mankind undermined the stratification of society and the status concepts that helped to justify it. Various forms of status were subordinated, at least in theory, to only one, humanity, and in this shift from the particular to the universal the erosion of status concepts gradually made room for the concept of rights.[12] Indeed, once all supposedly superficial differences were stripped away, as they were in *Leviathan*, it was easy – natural, as it were – to move from the notion that all men are naturally equal to the notion that all men have natural rights. As rank and hierarchy fade from the objective order, the objective order itself becomes subjective, at least to the point where the equality ordained by the perceived order of things bestows rights upon everyone. It then seems more straightforward to say "I have a right to this" than "it is right that I have this."

This is how Locke can draw natural rights out of natural law. For we are by nature free and equal, as he says in the *Second Treatise*, "there being nothing more evident, than that Creatures of the same species and rank promiscuously born to all the same advantages of Nature, and the use of the same faculties, should also be equal one amongst another without Subordination or Subjection" (1965, vol. II, § 4: 309). We are free and equal, furthermore, because God, whose property we are, has made us so, and "there cannot be supposed any such *Subordination* among us, that may Authorize us to destroy one another, as if we were made for one anothers uses, as the inferior ranks of Creatures are for ours" (vol. II, § 5: 311; Locke's emphasis). In order, therefore, "that all men may be restrained from invading others Rights . . . and the Law of Nature be observed, . . . the *Execution* of the Law of Nature is in that State [of nature], put into every Mans hands, whereby every one has a right to punish the transgressors of that Law to such a Degree, as may hinder its Violation" (vol. II, § 7: 312; Locke's emphasis).

Reasoning of this sort was neither original with Locke nor confined to works of high abstraction. As Alasdair MacIntyre points out (1973: 153, 158), a Leveller polemicist, Richard Overton, advanced a similar argument in 1646 in *An Arrow Against All Tyrants*. Overton's words, indeed, speak even more plainly than Locke's to

[12] According to Ritchie (1952: 6), the Protestant Reformation was the leading factor in this shift: "The theory of natural rights is simply the logical outgrowth of the Protestant revolt against the authority of tradition, the logical outgrowth of the Protestant appeal to private judgment, *i.e.*, to the reason and conscience of the individual." Others, of course, would award the praise or blame to social and economic factors.

the relationship between rights and the "principles of nature" (Aylmer 1975: 68–9):

> To every Individuall in nature, is given an individuall property by nature, not to be invaded or usurped by any: for every one as he is himselfe, so he hath a self propriety, else could he not be himselfe, and on this no second may presume to deprive any of, without manifest violation and affront to the very principles of nature, and of the Rules of equity and justice between man and man: mine and thine cannot be, except this be: No man hath power over my rights and liberties, and I over no mans . . . For by naturall birth, all men are equally and alike borne to like propriety, liberty and freedome, and as we are delivered of God by the hand of nature into this world, every one with a naturall, innate freedome and propriety . . . even so are we to live, every one equally and alike to enjoy his birthright and priviledge: even all whereof God by nature hath made him free.

The product of this way of thinking is the Age of Rights, exemplified most dramatically in the United States' *Declaration of Independence* (1776) and the French *Declaration of the Rights of Man and of Citizens* (1789). Man, the individual, shorn of status, role, and often cultural identity, becomes the center of the moral and political world, and the chief task of government, in the eyes of many in the West, is to secure his inalienable rights. It was, as Thomas Paine wrote in 1792, the dawn of a new and glorious era: "Government founded on a *moral theory, on a system of universal peace, on the indefeasible hereditary Rights of Man*, is now revolving from west to east by a stronger impulse than the government of the sword revolved from east to west. It interests not particular individuals, but nations in its progress, and promises a new era to the human race" (1967: 404; Paine's emphasis).

IV

By the beginning of the nineteenth century the concept of rights was firmly entrenched in Western legal and political thought. Since then, there have been few attempts to displace, reconceive, or abandon it, but a number of attempts to redefine the role it plays in political life and thought – attempts that were themselves under way as Paine wrote *Rights of Man*.

Two of the early critics of rights theories, Burke and Bentham, started from much the same point – condemnation of the French revolutionaries' appeal to natural rights. For both, the danger of the natural rights approach was its tendency to substitute abstract rhetoric for sensible, practical thinking. "*Natural rights* is simple nonsense," according to Bentham's judgement on the French *Declaration of Rights*, and "natural and imprescriptible rights, rhetorical nonsense, – nonsense upon stilts" (1970: 32; Bentham's emphasis). Rights are conventional, not natural, on Bentham's view, and if we enjoy them at all it is only because we are subject to a legal system; for to have a right is merely to be the beneficiary of a relationship sanctioned by law. Because there are no rights without law and government, law and government cannot possibly be justified by an appeal to rights. Instead, we should look directly to utility, understood most simply in terms of the "two sovereign masters" under which nature has placed us: pain and pleasure (Bentham 1961: 1).

For Burke, the French appeal to natural rights was dangerous not because it was nonsensical but because it was blind to circumstance and tradition. There *are* natural rights, he acknowledges, abstract rights that do not depend for their existence on government: "but their abstract perfection is their practical defect" (1979: 150). To his mind, the French were elevating a fiction, Man, to the status of a god, and proclaiming a new religion, the Rights of Man, in his name. What they and their sympathizers in other countries should be concerned with, Burke argues, is men as they are, in all their variety and particularity, whether they be French, English, or Chinese, peasants, merchants, or craftsmen, nobles or commoners, masters or apprentices. For "I may assume that the awful Author of our being is the Author of our place in the order of existence, – and that, having disposed and marshalled us by a divine tactic . . . He has in and by that disposition virtually subjected us to act the part which belongs to the place assigned us" ("Appeal from the New to the Old Whigs," 1967: 54). We have rights, then, and they are a kind of property, but the kind that attaches to whatever station in life we may happen to occupy. Those who set the individual against others – those who talk of rights *against* society and government – understand neither rights nor the order of things.

This tendency of the natural rights theorists to abstract man from his social and historical context is a common ground of criticism in the nineteenth century, one that unites writers as different from Burke, and each other, as Hegel, Marx, and T.H. Green. For Marx,

> None of these so-called rights of man goes beyond the egoistic man, beyond man as a member of civil society, as man separated from life in the community and withdrawn into himself, into his private interest and his private arbitrary will. These rights are far from conceiving man

> as a species-being. They see, rather, the life of the species itself, society, as a frame external to individuals, as a limitation of their original independence. "On the Jewish Question," 1983: 109

Rather than retreat with Burke toward status concepts and a notion of an objective order, however, Marx looked forward, late in his life, to the transcendence of the rights of man in "a higher phase of communist society," for "only then can the narrow horizon of bourgeois right be crossed in its entirety and society inscribe on its banners: From each according to his ability, to each according to his needs!" ("Critique of the Gotha Programme," 1983: 541). Once that horizon is crossed, presumably, human potential will flower forth and the concept of rights, now rendered useless, will wither and die.[13]

For Green, the liberal, the criticism of the asocial and ahistorical views of the natural rights theorists leads to an attempt at accommodation. Rights are not valuable in themselves, he says, but only insofar as they serve to promote the "moral vocation" or "moral personality" of the individual. As it happens, Green believes that rights are necessary to the pursuit of this vocation, much as Mill believes that liberty is necessary to the well-being of the individual, so rights prove to be very valuable indeed. "There ought to be rights," in short, "because the moral personality, – the capacity on the part of an individual for making a common good his own – ought to be developed; and it is developed through these rights; i.e. *through the recognition by members of a society* of powers in each other contributory to a common good, and the regulation of those powers through that recognition" (1967: 45; emphasis added).

Green's attempt at accommodation, then, is an attempt to tie the rights of the individual to the good of the society to which he belongs. On this view, our rights are not merely rights *against* others; they are also rights *to* the positive aid of others, aid we need in order to develop our powers so that we may contribute to the common good. This is a long way, in less than a century, from Paine's notion of "the indefeasible hereditary Rights of Man," but it was a journey many made in the nineteenth century. In theory, at least, the abstract Man of the Age of Rights had become, once again, a social creature. As D.G. Ritchie (1952: 102) put it in 1894, "The person with rights and duties is the product of a society, and the rights of the individual must therefore be judged from the point of view of a society as a whole, and not the society from the point of view of the individual."

[13] On Marx's views on rights, see Dunn (1979: 38) and Donnelly (1985: 41–43).

V

Where do we stand now, one hundred years after Green and Ritchie, with regard to the concept of rights? It is so widespread and so firmly rooted in our habits of thought that it is all but impossible to conceive of doing without it.[14] Yet it is also difficult to conceive of what we are going to do with it. Almost everyone invokes the concept, but its place in political thought is every bit as much a matter of contention as it was in the last century. Nor is there significant agreement on how rights are to be grounded – in utility? in fundamental rights? in the necessary requirements of rational action? in human needs? – or whether they can be grounded at all. In these respects, we seem still to be stuck in the nineteenth century.

There are, however, two developments worthy of note in the twentieth century. First, philosophers and legal scholars have devoted considerable attention to the analysis of the concept itself, one result of which is an abundance, perhaps a superabundance, of often disputed distinctions: active and passive rights, positive and negative rights, welfare and option rights, special and general rights, etc. By general consent, the most impressive of these was set out in 1919 in Wesley Hohfeld's *Fundamental Legal Conceptions*. As a legal scholar, Hohfeld's concern was that rights and their correlative concept, duties, were too broadly and indiscriminately construed. According to his analysis, this masks four distinct and fundamental relations under law: *rights* (i.e., *rights in the strict sense*) and their correlative, *duties*; *privileges* and *no-rights*; *powers* and *liabilities*; and *immunities* and *disabilities* (1964: 36).

From the standpoint of social and political philosophy, the principal value of Hohfeld's categories seems to lie in the distinction between *rights* – also called *claims* or *claim-rights* – and *privileges* – now better known as *liberties* or *liberty-rights*.[15] On Hohfeld's distinction, claim-rights entail a correlative duty on the part of at least one other person, but liberty-rights do not. The difference may be brought out by a pair of familiar examples. If Jones borrows $10 from Smith, Smith then has a *claim-right* to the return of the money, and Jones has a duty to repay her; but if Jones and Smith see a $10 bill in the street with no one but the two of them in sight, then each has a *liberty-right* to the money even though neither has a duty, *ceteris paribus*, to let the

[14] Feinberg's (1980) "thought experiment" is instructive in this regard.

[15] For helpful discussions of Hohfeld and other developments in the analysis of rights, see Feinberg (1973, chap. 4) and the introduction to Waldron (1984).

other have it. By distinguishing rights from liberties in this way, Hohfeld stresses the relational aspect of rights. Where the rights theorists of the seventeenth and eighteenth centuries tended to regard a right as a faculty or possession, that is, Hohfeld encourages us to conceive of a right as a kind of standing, a relationship between one person, the right-holder, and others. It may not have been his intention, but in this sense Hohfeld's analysis of rights reinforces the efforts of the nineteeth-century writers who sought to endow rights with a social dimension.

Much the same could be said for the second notable development this century in the concept of rights – the popularity of the notion of *human rights* among philosophers, political figures, and common people throughout much of the world. *Human rights* is the direct descendant of *natural rights*, of course, and not, therefore, an entirely new notion. But the shift from "natural" to "human" rights betokens a significant change of emphasis. As the passages quoted earlier from Locke and Overton suggest, arguments from natural rights typically proceeded from the idea of self-possession, from a property in oneself that must be defended against others; with *human rights*, however, arguments usually rest on some conception of a human or (perhaps more precisely) a person as a being with needs and interests that must be met if he or she is to live a fully human life. Thus the *rights against* others of the natural rights theorists tend to become the *claims upon* others of the human rights theorists.

This different emphasis is manifest in the *Universal Declaration of Human Rights*, adopted by the United Nations in 1948. There, alongside such familiar proclamations as Article Three – "Everyone has the right to life, liberty, and security of person" – we find such novel assertions as the right to marry and found a family, the right to rest and leisure, the right to an adequate standard of living, and the right to participate in the cultural life of the community (Melden 1970: 143–9). Whether these really are or ought to be regarded as rights, human or otherwise, is open to dispute; but the important point here is that these putative rights are put forward as important elements or vital ingredients in a fully realized human life. In that sense, the popularity of the appeal to human rights reveals a concern, not for what we are, but for what we can and presumably should be.

This concern is displayed also in the efforts to secure rights for more specific groups of human beings – women's rights, "gay" rights, the rights of national or cultural minorities, etc. In each of these cases, the core argument is that the members of the relevant group suffer because they are neither accorded the same respect nor afforded the same opportunities as other persons. They are prevented from realizing their capacities, in other words, and denied the consideration to which human beings are entitled – to be treated with full respect for their dignity as persons.

Perhaps this is why we live, once again, in an age of rights. No other concept at present captures so well the idea that every person, regardless of his or her place in society, is worthy of respect as a person. Certainly the concept of human dignity, despite the power of *dignitas* as a status concept in ancient Rome (Wirszubski 1960: 12–13), now lacks the conceptual force of an appeal to rights. With the field left to rights, it begins to seem, as Joel Feinberg (1980: 151) puts it, that "respect for persons . . . may simply be respect for their rights, so there cannot be the one without the other; and what is called 'human dignity' may simply be the recognizable capacity to assert claims. To respect a person, then, or to think of him as possessed of human dignity, simply *is* to think of him as a potential maker of claims."

Concepts are like human beings in this respect: they flourish when they have work to do. So long as we continue to think of men and women as "potential makers of claims," then, the concept of rights will not lack for employment; and the more work we find for the concept of rights to do, the more likely we are to think of men and women as "potential makers of claims" who are worthy of respect as persons.

REFERENCES

Aylmer, G.E. (ed.). 1975. *The Levellers and the English Revolution*. Ithaca, NY: Cornell University Press.

Barker, Ernest. (ed. and trans.). 1971. *The Politics of Aristotle*. Oxford: Oxford University Press.

Bentham, Jeremy. 1961. *An Introduction to the Principles of Morals and Legislation*. New York: Hafner.

1970. "Anarchical Fallacies." In Melden 1970: 28–39.

Burke, Edmund. 1967. *The Philosophy of Edmund Burke: A Selection from His Speeches and Writings*, edited by Louis Brevold and Ralph Ross. Ann Arbor, MI: University of Michigan Press.

1979. *Reflections on the Revolution in France*. Harmondsworth: Penguin.

Carlyle, R.W. and A.J. Carlyle. 1950. *A History of Medieval Political Theory in the West*. Edinburgh and London: Blackwood and Sons.

Donnelly, Jack. 1982. "Human Rights and Human Dignity: An Analytic

Critique of Non-Western Conceptions of Human Rights." *American Political Science Review* 76: 303–16.

1985. *The Concept of Human Rights*. New York: St. Martin's Press.

Dunn, John. 1979. *Western Political Theory in the Face of the Future*. Cambridge: Cambridge University Press.

Dworkin, Ronald. 1977. *Taking Rights Seriously*. Cambridge, MA: Harvard University Press.

Feinberg, Joel. 1973. *Social Philosophy*. Englewood Cliffs, NJ: Prentice-Hall.

1980. "The Nature and Value of Rights." In *Rights, Justice and the Bounds of Liberty*. Princeton, NJ: Princeton University Press, pp. 143–58.

Finnis, John. 1980. *Natural Law and Natural Rights*. Oxford: Clarendon.

Gewirth, Alan. 1978. *Reason and Morality*. Chicago, IL: University of Chicago Press.

Golding, Martin P. 1978. "The Concept of Rights: A Historical Sketch." In Bertram and Elsie Bandman (eds.), *Bioethics and Human Rights*. Boston: Little, Brown, pp. 44–50.

Green, T.H. 1967. *Lectures on the Principles of Political Obligation*. Ann Arbor, MI: University of Michigan Press.

Grotius, Hugo. 1925 [1625] *De jure belli ac pacis*, translated by Francis W. Kelsey. Oxford: Clarendon.

Hesiod. 1968. *The Works and Days*, *Theogony*, *The Shield of Herakles*, translated by Richmond Lattimore. Ann Arbor, MI: University of Michigan Press.

Hohfeld, Wesley. 1964. *Fundamental Legal Conceptions*. New Haven, CT, and London: Yale University Press.

Jones, J. Walter. 1956. *The Law and Legal Theory of the Greeks*. Oxford: Clarendon.

Lewis, Ewart. 1974. *Medieval Political Ideas*. New York: Cooper Square.

Liddell, Henry George and Robert Scott. 1968. *A Greek–English Lexicon*. Oxford: Clarendon.

Locke, John. 1965. *Two Treatises of Government*. New York and Toronto: The New American Library.

MacIntyre, Alasdair. 1973. *A Short History of Ethics*. New York: Macmillan.

Marx, Karl. 1983. *The Portable Karl Marx*, edited by Eugene Kamenka. Harmondsworth: Penguin.

Melden, A.I. (ed.). 1970. *Human Rights*. Belmont, CA: Wadsworth.

1977. *Rights and Persons*. Berkeley, CA: University of California Press.

Miller, William Galbraith. 1980 [1903]. *The Data of Jurisprudence*. Littleton, CO: Fred B. Rothman and Co.

Nicholas, Barry. 1962. *An Introduction to Roman Law*. Oxford: Clarendon.

Nozick, Robert. 1974. *Anarchy, State, and Utopia*. New York: Basic Books.

Pagels, Elaine. 1979. "The Roots and Origins of Human Rights." In Alice Henkin (ed.), *Human Dignity*. Dobbs Ferry, NY: Oceana Publications, pp. 1–8.

Paine, Thomas. 1967. *Rights of Man*. In Moncure D. Conway (ed.), *The Writings of Thomas Paine*, vol. II. New York: AMS Press.

Ritchie, David G. 1952. *Natural Rights*. London: George Allen and Unwin.

Salmond, John W. 1907. *Jurisprudence*, 2nd edn. London: Stevens and Haynes.

Sinclair, T.A. and T.J. Saunders. (eds. and trans.). 1981. *Aristotle: the Politics*, revised edn. Harmondsworth: Penguin.

Skeat, Revd. Walter W. 1978. *An Etymological Dictionary of the English Language*. Oxford: Clarendon.

Tierney, Brian. 1983. "Tuck on Rights: Some Medieval Problems." *History of Political Thought* 4 (1983): 429–41.

Tuck, Richard. 1979. *Natural Rights Theories: Their Origins and Development*. Cambridge: Cambridge University Press.

Villey, Michel. 1969. "La genèse du droit subjectif chez Guillame d'Occam." In *Seize essais de philosophie du droit*. Paris: Dalloz, pp. 140–78.

Waldron, Jeremy (ed.). 1984. *Theories of Rights*. Oxford: Oxford University Press.

Webster's New International Dictionary of the English Language. 1950. 2nd edn., unabridged. Springfield, MA: G. and C. Merriam.

Wirszubski, Ch. 1960. *Libertas as a Political Idea at Rome during the Late Republic and Early Principate*. Cambridge: Cambridge University Press.

15

Property

ALAN RYAN

Talk of "the history of concepts" can induce a kind of intellectual cramp. Concepts – as opposed to the men and women who employ them, the institutions which embody them, and the understanding they facilitate or hamper – may well seem to be timeless entities and not natural subjects for a history; unlike chairs and tables, traditions and practices, all of which may remain the same for hundreds of years, in the course of which every part of them is replaced, concepts seem incapable of the identity in change which makes it possible to be a historical subject. The existence-criteria of concepts may be obscure, but they surely do not come into existence only when what it is that they are concepts of comes into existence; nor do they cease to exist when it does. Yet it is quite as compelling to think of them historically; we may distinguish the Greek concept of property from the Roman, the liberal concept from the socialist, we may talk of the concept of property narrowing or expanding – narrowing when work relationships are wholly dealt with by the law of contract and an action for enticement will no longer lie against someone who has persuaded your valet to work for him rather than you, expanding when mortgaging one's property becomes properly defined and regulated, so that the law of property will handle interests previously outside its scope (Lawson 1958: 153ff.).

Does it matter that we are driven to think of concepts in both a Platonic and a naturalistic fashion? The concerns of this essay are so limited that it ought not to do so; but there are certainly contexts in which it does. There are at least two ways of writing the history of law, politics, and social institutions which rely on the reification of concepts for their effect, even if what is worthwhile in these approaches can be captured without giving hostages to metaphysics. The first is Hegelian. Here, the ground of the intelligibility of history is that history is the development of the concept of freedom; by extension it is a condition of the intelligibility of institutions such as ownership that they are increasingly adequate to their concept; that is, that they realize true freedom. To say that Hegel relies on a Platonic conception of the nature of concepts would be silly; but in the absence of some independent standing for the concept, the distinctively Idealist history offered by Hegel would lose its identity and its intellectual interest. Hegel does not quite present a world in which concepts search for adequate embodiment – but he sometimes comes exceedingly close (Hegel 1975: 25).

The other reifying view is less exciting than Hegel's. It is to be found in any number of different writers, and especially in writers who are genuinely intent on writing a modest and metaphysically discreet history. Here, the temptation is to represent legal and political history as progress towards clarity; as institutions respond to the pressures upon them and new distinctions are drawn, so mankind learn to distinguish one concept from another. They distinguish real property from personal property, or the law of things from the law of persons. They get clearer about the nature of negligence, say, or clearer about what the concept of equity will and will not cover. The effect of the philosophical movement self-described as "conceptual analysis" was to suggest that philosophical progress consisted in distinguishing one concept from another – in getting clear that poverty was not a loss of liberty, to take one familiar example. It all quite inadvertently suggested that we had attained a degree of clarity and self-consciousness about what we were up to which no former age possessed. On this view, it is possible to analyze "the concept of property," by seeing where locutions of the form "he or she owns x" are properly employed. I do not wish to suggest that nothing interesting can come out of such analyses. C.B. Macpherson's claim that the twentieth century needs an "inclusive" concept of property to replace the older, "exclusive" concept, for instance, is just the sort of muddled thought which "conceptual analysis" can tidy up (Macpherson 1973). The strength of "conceptual analysis" however does not lie in the dubious proposition that the concepts which need analyzing are a timeless part of the furniture of the universe, but in the sociological and prescriptive exercise which it masked – that of asking why we draw some distinctions rather than others, why we should assimilate some sorts of behavior to each other and sharply distinguish them from others, and so on. For such purposes, an unreflective reification of concepts (or strenuous attempts to disarm the accusation of reification) is merely a distraction.

These disclaimers lead to my positive program in what follows. I begin by distinguishing two contexts in which property has been discussed, the first political, the second moral. Within these broad categories, I shall say something about three connected but distinguishable political concerns and two connected but distinguishable moral concerns. I treat the notions of the conflict of private and public interests, the ideas of virtue and corruption, and the problem of class war, as political topics; I then turn to two problems in the moral justification of ownership – the conflict of justice and utility on the one hand, and theories of liberty and oppression on the other. Having done that, I return briefly to concepts, in order to defend the positivist approach to discussions of property against the essentialist. Finally, I try to show why some sense of this variety of concerns and approaches is necessary by saying something about "republican" political theory on the one hand, and about Marx's conception of a propertyless world on the other.

The distinction between "political" and "moral" approaches to property is not novel. It has been well made by Kenneth Minogue, but it is implicit in much previous discussion (Minogue 1980). Broadly, the political discussion of property is not concerned to ask for the *justification* of private property, either in general, or in individual cases, so much as to enquire into the political consequences of given kinds of property. What makes it "political" is that it is not concerned to answer such familiar questions as whether existing holders of property hold it justly, or whether the distribution of wealth is morally acceptable or utilitarianly optimal; nor is it concerned to answer such questions as whether our common human nature means that we "ought" to live communistically or whatever. Rather, it focuses on the political effects of forms of ownership, not on the acceptability of those forms in the light of a moral theory. To be sure, the political consequences of a system of property rights are relevant to any justification of it, but the contrast is at any rate heuristically useful – it is, for instance, reasonable to describe chapter 5 of Locke's *Second Treatise* as answering the problem of moral justification, even though Locke then goes on to show the political consequences of his account of the grounds of individual private property, and doubtless wrote the *Second Treatise* with those consequences in mind (Locke 1967, vol. II, §§ 25–131). By the same token it is resonable to describe Harrington's *Oceana* as answering the question of political consequence independently of issues of moral justification – even though he no doubt thought that the political ill effects of some systems of property would (morally) justify any government which chose to suppress them (Harrington 1977: 208ff.).

At all events, it is plausible to begin with Plato's attempt in the *Republic* – reversed in the *Laws* though it was – to answer the question of how we can ensure that rulers do not turn the state to their private ends. Plato's answer was quick and brief; we must deprive them of the private ownership of anything whatever. Plato asked the obvious question, of how we can ensure that the Guardians do not tyrannize over the rest of the population, seeing that they have complete power over them, and anwered by saying that they must receive no more than the necessities of life "in the quantities required by men of temperance and courage who are in training for war"; these will merely be "the wages of their guardianship fixed so that there shall be just enough for the year with nothing left over." Were they to have farms and land of their own, they would give up their Guardians' duties and attend to their property; the austerity of their lives and the lack of such property will free them from temptation. Together with the abolition of the family, proposed a little later in the discussion, this will lead them to think of all the polis and all its resources as "ours" and of no single member or resource as "mine" (Plato 1941: 106ff.).

Adeimantus – like Aristotle after him – wonders why anyone would be prepared to live so austere an existence; Plato's answer is not terribly persuasive. The point is not to make part of the polis happy, but to make the whole happy; the aim is not to make the Guardians as happy as possible, but to make the state happy by ensuring that the Guardians do their job. He bolsters this rather bleak reply by pointing out that the Guardians have gold and silver within their souls, so that they have no need to acquire gold and silver in the way oligarchies usually do. But evidently, nothing will really answer the case save the whole Platonic view of the world, in which men and women are fulfilled by doing the job to which nature has called them; the Guardians must, whatever the austerity of their existence, be the most fulfilled because they are performing the most important functions (Plato 1941: 107–8).

That this is not a wholesale moral indictment of ownership as such is evident from the casual way Plato assumes that the rest of the inhabitants of the polis may continue to buy and sell and work in the way they have always done. What matters to him is that the cobbler shall not have a say in the determining of the government of the polis; what the cobbler does otherwise hardly concerns him. It seems that ordinary economic life will go on – subject to the controls which are needed to ensure that the republic's wealth does not make it the object of predatory attention from its neighbors or induce predatory enthusiasms among its own rulers. The ordinary man's ordinary economic concerns are harmless enough, so long as the structure of political control is intact.

In the *Laws*, Plato moves away from the ideals of the *Republic*, by accepting that communism is impracticable; if men could hold everything in common, that would be the best of all societies, but they cannot. What he offers as a second-best is not unlike Aristotle's recipe in his *Politics*; the citizens are to be small farmers, who both farm, and fight and govern. The specialization of the *Republic* is abandoned in favor of a society where rough equality of property is preserved, and public spirit is maintained, not by requiring it of one small group only, but by instilling it in all citizens by law and education (Plato 1926, Bk. V; Aristotle 1946: 377ff.).

The thought that the one and only way to prevent rulers sacrificing the public interest to their private interests is by preventing the ruling elite from having any property of their own is one with a long subsequent history; it extends down to Marx's casualness about the ways in which the administrators of the communist society of the future would behave – with no private property, there would be no temptation for them to act in a non-public-spirited way. However, it received its most damaging rebuttal almost as soon as it was written, delivered by Aristotle in the *Politics*. Like Plato, he thought that a major problem of political organization was to ensure that individuals did not sacrifice the good of the polis to their own economic interests – though his greater fear was class warfare. Unlike Plato, he thought the cure offered in the *Republic* was worse than the disease. The attention which men paid to property was not detachable from its being private property; if individuals had no private property, they would not think of themselves as the common owners of everything in the state, just as their children would not feel themselves to be the offspring of *all* the adults they knew, simply because the nuclear family had been abolished. Rather, children would feel they had no parents, and most people would feel that it was nobody's business rather than everybody's business to look after common property. The remedy must be something other than primitive communism, especially when the austerity depicted by Plato was instrinsically unattractive into the bargain (Aristotle 1946: 66–7).

Aristotle's solution is familiar. He relies on education, law, and public opinion to constrain citizens into public-spirited behavior. He also relies on the restriction of economic activity to agricultural pursuits and a very limited amount of trade. Though Aristotle's metaphysics are less colorfully in evidence in the *Politics* than Plato's in the *Republic*, he too relies on the thought that persons properly attached to their social roles will be happy in them, and that citizenship can be relied on to bring its own rewards if people practice it properly. None the less, to be fit to do so they must not engage in mere money-making activities – they are unnatural, and encourage a boundless acquisitiveness in those who practice them. Farmers are politically sound, because they know that the object of production is consumption, that economics is about maintaining life in a natural way. Such men will be able to subordinate their private interests to the interest of the polis when necessary; and will not be tempted to regard their fellows as sheep for the shearing.

The ingredients offered by Plato and Aristotle became the common coin of any discussion of the problem so posed. This is not to say that there is no other way of handling the issue of private interest and public interest; the end of the eighteenth century saw genuine inventiveness in the discussion – Adam Smith's invisible hand is a mechanism which disposes of the problem by showing how the pursuit of private interest can achieve a public good without making many demands upon the individual. Hegel's treatment of "civil society" in his *Philosophy of Right* borrowed from Smith and Aristotle in equal measure. The modern economy made every man his neighbor's benefactor as well as his competitor through the invisible mechanisms of the market, but this was not enough. We had to be socialized into becoming citizens who could subordinate *all* our interests to the demands of the state; it was largely through war and the lesson taught by the "shining sabres of the hussars" that individuals learned that their private interests were by no means the most important thing in the world. Still, without trying simply to deny the existence of other ways of handling the conflict, we can say that even as late as the 1750s Rousseau's argument in his *Economie politique* and *Contrat social* is still so indebted to the arguments of Plato and Aristotle, that he doesn't so much break new conceptual ground as add to the discussion a psychological and historical pathos that had been absent before. Nor is this surprising; once the argument had been set out as they set it out, there was rather little room for maneuver – either private property made public spirit impossible or it did not; if it did not make it impossible, we required a story about the conditions under which it did not (Rousseau 1912: 192, 250).

The debate over the prospects of "virtue" and "corruption" can plausibly be seen as an extended debate about the kinds of property which encourage public spirit. Before we turn to it, we ought to notice how little Plato and Aristotle do to justify Hannah Arendt's account of the "privacy" of private property (Arendt 1953: 58–72). Arguing that the modern world had become de-politicized, she thought she could distinguish a "classical" concept of property according to which one's property simultaneously launched one into the public arena as a citizen and provided a shelter from the public world. The modern conception of property was simply a concept of wealth – an economic rather than a political concept. This view, interesting though it is in calling attention to the decline of what I have called the political conception of property, is not plausible as an account of what Plato or Aristotle were concerned with. To put it simply, they were concerned with the question of whether the ownership of land (or anything else) would make men too self-interested to govern disinterestedly. The idea that men needed a private shelter from the public world seems entirely at odds with the cast of mind of both of them. Pericles praised the Athenians for a cheerful tolerance of diversity – but even he, the defender of a libertarian social order disapproved of by both Plato and Aristotle, never suggested that people needed a respite from the public realm (Plato 1941: 273–80; Thucydides 1916, bk. II: 35–45).

Nor is it true that Plato and Aristotle's political concept of property was concerned with launching the citizen onto the public stage. Both were exceedingly defensive writers, concerned to limit what might go wrong – Plato's *Republic* is a utopia in which there is no political life; Aristotle's *Politics* describes a polity in which rather little politics takes place. It is true that Aristotle says that politics is a form of rule involving debate and argument among competing conceptions of justice, and he seems to leave room for a good deal of ordinary political activity. But even this is at odds with his insistence that laws rather than men should govern. What he is concerned with is less that men should be launched into active citizenship than that those who are to be citizens should have the sort of property which – along with good breeding and good education – will secure them from the temptations of self-interest, and will give them sufficient leisure and independence to render them invulnerable to mob orators, and unconcerned about sharing in the loot which political adventurers might bring to the polis.

This, then, brings us to the anxieties about virtue and corruption which – as Professor Pocock has so elegantly and so instructively shown – provided the framework of the republican tradition of thought from Machiavelli to the last despairing agrarian radicals of our own day (Pocock 1975). In Plato and Aristotle, the theme appears in two ways. It appears in the context of the discussion of selfishness, and it appears in the context of the avoidance of class war. In the *Laws* Plato is concerned with virtue almost throughout; but virtue is not very specifically political, nor is it very tightly connected with property. As ever, the connection is that the wrong sort of property will result in a loss of virtue – but this amounts to little more than the thought that a man who has too much wealth, or whose wealth is in too mobile a form, will be inclined to consult his own economic interests and will neglect the needs of the state. To this nothing can be opposed except good education and good law. Aristotle thinks in a similar way; the virtues – which, instructively, are plural and a question of character, rather than unitary and political – are inculcated by good education, assisted by good breeding. Property is relevant in that the practice of the virtues requires a leisured life, sufficiently rich in the good things to allow a man to enjoy liberality and friendship, and to spare him from mechanical and degrading tasks. Corruption does come into the argument in one way, and that is in the claim that men acquire characters appropriate to their situation; the moderately well-off head of a farming household will be consistent, resourceful, moderate, and temperate, but not ground down by manual labor (which falls to the household slaves). People engaged in mere money-making are more likely to become greedy and immoderate. Similarly, excessive wealth, quite apart from its impact on social stability in general via the existence of an oligarchy, will have the same effect on individual character; immoderate wealth, assisted no doubt by class pride, will generate immoderate appetites (Aristotle 1946: 238).

All this is rather different from the Machiavellian perspective that informs what has become known as "classical republicanism." Here the notions of virtue and corruption are thoroughly politicized. Indeed, as innumerable commentators have observed, Machiavelli's concept of *virtù* is so thoroughly politicized that it has practically no moral connotations at all. Think what Machiavelli includes in *virtù* – he tells us that cruelty was part of Hannibal's *virtù*, and is puzzled that Scipio was successful without it; *The Prince* is replete with examples of cunning, deceit and brutality – all said to be part of *virtù*. Just what the quality is to which Machiavelli refers has exercised many commentators; it is displayed most clearly in war or in conflict of one sort and another, yet it is not confined to qualities needed for war; Quentin Skinner claims that it is the quality which will achieve glory for its possessor, but that seems to underplay the fact that it is political success which yields the glory, and that *virtù* is that constellation of abilities and qualities which achieves it. Even this way of looking at it neglects the fact that success is not a sufficient condition for achieving glory – Agathocles held power in Syracuse without challenge, but was so vicious that he could not be called glorious (Skinner 1981: 53–5; Machiavelli 1970: 464).

The discussion of virtue and corruption is for our purposes interesting when it occurs in the context of the popular republic. For here Machiavelli's reflections on the success of the Romans allows us to see something quite different from the concerns of Plato and Aristotle. Machiavelli is concerned with the *virtù* of two sorts of people in the rebublic – the ordinary people and the active elite. And what is assumed throughout is that two sorts of economic condition are detrimental to *virtù*. In the first place, the ordinary people must not be reduced to economic servitude and dependency on their superiors; if they are, then they will be recruited for the factions of ambitious men, and will not be loyal to the republic. In the second place, prosperity must not be allowed to subvert the martial spirit of the ordinary man, nor must it be allowed to turn the elite into greedy and factional self-seekers. It is worth noting how little Machiavelli relies on creating what one might call deeply virtuous characters; what he relies on is the ability of the state to offer inducements and issue threats which will make the path of *virtù* attractive to men who are, as he repeatedly says, by nature evil. The Platonic and Aristotelian emphasis on education is absent; everything rests on the construction of political incentives and social mores of a public sort. So, Machiavelli advises us to keep the state rich and individuals poor in order that there is more profit in serving the state than in trying to carve out one's own selfish path (Machiavelli 1970: 201).

The pathos in this story – for even in Machiavelli's brisk pages there is a streak of pathos – lies in the dialectic of virtue and corruption. Virtue creates success; success creates prosperity; prosperity softens the martial spirit and allows the rich to corrupt their fellows. Thus the virtuous republic is doomed by its own success. Later writers followed Machiavelli's analysis to a large extent, though they took off in different directions from his resigned acceptance of the thought that a republic for increase might achieve glory only at the expense of eventual corruption. Harrington, for instance, relies less on the social pressures Machiavelli employs and more on the idea of a balance of social forces, and in accordance with that sees no reason why the commonwealth should not be immortal (Harrington 1977: 209). Conversely, the Machiavellian strain in Rousseau – in the last part of *Contrat social* for instance – is balanced by a Platonic insistence that the austere republic should engage in no foreign trade, and should present no temptations to invasion. Like Machiavelli, he thinks economic independence the foundation of political virtue and sees no way of combining wealth and non-corruption. But, it is clear to him that the sort of property which this requires is agrarian, that property ought not to be mobile, and individuals ought to think of it as a trust for their families, not as their own to do with as they like. "Easy come, easy go" would be fatal (Rousseau 1912: 255ff.).

As Pocock has emphasized, this view of the world has an obvious target in the growth of credit and commerce (Pocock 1985: 235ff.). The world in which property ceases to mean a particular place and comes to mean "assets" simply is very much a world of easy come and easy go; indeed, it has to be such, since the whole point of an elaborate credit system is to enable people to transfer ownership quickly, to enable them to invent new kinds of assets, and to transform the world and social relationships alike. In the English context, the fact that the growth of central banking and the creation of a national debt was the result of the continuous European conflicts of the reigns of William III and Queen Anne allowed the argument to pick up the other great theme which the argument over virtue and corruption embraced, that of the potential of a standing army as an instrument of tyranny. Machiavelli, Harrington, Rousseau, and most other "classical republicans" took it for granted that the only safe form of self-protection was a citizen militia. The private armies of *gentiluomini* struck Machiavelli as pestilential nuisances. When it came to public defense, mercenaries would not fight for you in real danger and would be tempted to take over power themselves in the event of success; the only thing to rely on was your own militia. The Machiavellian hostility to mercenaries and to private armies readily turns into a hostility to a standing army under the command of the monarch – or of the Lord Protector, come to that. With a standing army behind him, any ruler could contemplate reducing his people to servitude; hostility to the very idea was a feature of arguments under the Interregnum, flared up throughout the eighteenth century, and died out only in the nineteenth. This is one source of the image of the armed farmer which has played such a large and strange part in the ideological history of the United States. The implications for property are obvious enough; the preservation of the freeholding farmer is the foundation of good policy; bankers, monopolists, stockjobbers, and the like are not to be trusted. There is little point in tracing pedigrees here, when longer and more careful accounts of all this are so readily to hand; but one thing worth noticing perhaps is the way in which even so strenuously modern and unnostalgic a writer as Hegel relies upon the landed *Stand* or estate to preserve stability and public spirit in the modern state and sees the "reflective" or commercial classes as a threat to peace and constitutionality (Hegel 1941: 130–4).

The final strain of "political" thinking which we ought to notice is wholly familiar from twentieth-century thinking, and is the theme with the longest (if discontinuous) history of all. This is the concern with property as the basis of class conflict. Once again, we find the defensive view of politics put forward by Plato and Aristotle yielding – especially in the latter – the view that class conflict is likely to lead to *stasis*, a term whose flavor is perhaps best captured by the thought of political life coming to a grinding halt, with a good chance of civil war following. Plato and Aristotle did not think of class conflict as economic conflict – it was not the struggle identified by de Ste Croix, namely the continuous pressure of the exploiting class to increase the size of the surplus product of which they disposed and the continuous resistance of the class who produced that surplus. Rather, Aristotle thought of the conflict as a political one, with its roots in the difference between the propertied and the unpropertied, but its driving force in the moral aspirations of the contending classes. Oligarchies were prone to *stasis* because the rich concluded from their superiority of wealth that they were entitled to a monopoly of power; conversely, the poor in a democracy concluded that their possession of political authority gave them a right to demand a share of the other good things of life and therefore a share of the possessions of the rich. Aristotle traced the mechanisms of class conflict through what we might call class conceptions of justice; the rich conclude that superiority in wealth entitles them to superiority in everything, the poor that equality in political authority entitles them to equality in everything (Aristotle 1946: 238).

This is light years away from Machiavelli's endorsement of class conflict as an aid to political liberty. For him, the conflict between the plebs and the patricians showed the usefulness of conflict; the plebs' secession had proved to the patricians that there was no possibility of governing without the consent of the plebian classes, but Machiavelli never supposed that the plebeians felt any inclination to govern the state themselves. Ordinary people, he thought, were generally cowardly, or at any rate unambitious, and more than willing to follow leaders. The struggle with the patricians taught the plebs to stand up for themselves. Curiously, there are streaks of this view to be found even in Burke; though he defends the view that property must have its influence in government and that a ruling class based on landed property is indispensable to a moderate constitutional liberty, Burke acknowledges that class arrogance must be kept in check, and that rulers need an incentive to govern constitutionally rather than tyrannically. Accordingly, he accepts that a lower class sensitive of its position and eager to insist on its rights will be a valuable aid to enforcing a sort of political virtue on the governing class.

The crucial point about such a political picture is that it creates a distance between what we might call the political and the economic dimensions of class conflict. In later writers, most notably Marx, the claim that all previous history is the history of class struggle demands an equivocation both on the idea of history – so that no changes in savage or barbaric societies count as "historical" – and on the idea of class conflict: where there is no visible political struggle, we may count the standing conflict of interest between the propertied and the propertiless as a "struggle," and where there is a visible political struggle we may count it as a success for the materialist conception of history. But less abbreviated histories than that offered in the *Communist Manifesto* have plausibly maintained that much of the driving force of politics comes from the struggle of propertied and propertyless, or from the struggle of the differently propertied. The Scottish historians of the later eighteenth century – Smith, Millar, Ferguson, and Robertson, for instance – not only isolate the creation of property as the crucial step in the establishment of civilization; nor do they only concentrate on such epic passages as the reduction of the Roman free farmer to an urban proletarian; they also insist on the importance of different forms of property in creating different systems of social rank, different political systems, different political cultures. It is taken for granted that conflict is not all that is created; there will be deference and a sense of mutual obligation as well. For all that, it is a tradition notably unsentimental about the inevitable tensions created by differentiated property, and notably ambivalent about the consequences. If politeness and constitutional liberty are one outcome of commercial society where a class balance is achieved, despotism, rule by standing army, proletarianization, and a modern version of the last days of the Roman republic are always possible (Pocock 1985: 235ff.).

It would be pointless to say much in criticism of views so lightly sketched. In any event, the aim is not to award marks for percipience or deduct them for its absence, but rather to set out some of the ways in which property featured in political argument before the establishment of economics as *the* social science of wealth and income, and before the sharpening of political debate into an argument between Marxists and their opponents. The tradition was anyway faltering by 1800. By the nineteenth century several thinkers had taken the point that if we approved of landed property because it anchored men to a particular locality and a settled livelihood, we must approve of any other tie with the same effect, such as marriage – and in a country such as the United States with much free land to be settled, age and marriage would be more reliable anchors than proprietorship. Such simple points do something to explain the evaporation of a tradition. So too do much more complex factors, such as the growth of an industrial society in which the conflict between labor and capital took over from earlier conflicts, and in which the image of agrarian virtue and the political moderation of the landed classes became hopelessly old-fashioned.

We may now turn, even more briefly, to two strands of moral argument about property. I shall not repeat my earlier remarks about the flimsiness of boundaries between political and moral arguments, but will move directly to two cruxes in familiar arguments. The first familiar crux will strike readers of H.L.A. Hart's famous essay on punishment as perhaps excessively familiar – but so it should, since Hart's distinction between the general justifying aim of the institution of punishment and the principles on which punishments are applied to particular offenders was avowedly borrowed from the discussion of ownership in the first place (Hart 1959–60). That is, perhaps the easiest justification of the existence of private property at all – its general justifying aim – is a utilitarian one. Mankind is surrounded by usable objects, and prompted by innumerable wants; but it is impossible to make proper use of what nature has supplied, or of what nature and ingenuity together can supply, unless we are secure in our possession of the necessary resources. It follows that a system of property would be an enormous contribution to the general well-being. We may add further twists to this elementary account. Most people become eager to hold on to what they possess, so security of possession by gratifying that desire contributes to happiness in addition to the way it contributes to our ability to make use of the world and our own abilities. Equally, most people desire security in their own persons, and this tells very directly against allowing property in other people, and in favor of allowing something like property in one's own efforts and abilities.

The elaboration of this argument would suggest – as readers of Bentham will know well enough – that many of the usual legal provisions about acquisition, transfer, and bequest can be justified by utilitarian considerations. We now have a picture of property rights as defined by legal provisions securing to one individual a control over things and rights over things which are denied to others in respect of those particular things or those particular rights. For me to own a copyright, for instance, is for me to benefit from the power to dispose of that copyright in a way nobody else can – joint ownership, of course, can be dealt with similarly. Now we arrive at the familiar crux. We may suppose that in general there is a presumption, let us say, in favor of allowing a man to bequeath his goods to his children – arguments of incentive suggest the institution, as do arguments from making use of natural affection. But suppose the case to arise where we could promote utility much more effectively by depriving the heir and handing out the proceeds to others – here we have the familiar case of the general justifying aim of the institution at odds with the rules it generates. More often, this will emerge as a conflict between utility and justice.

The same conflict may arise if we do not begin with a straightforwardly utilitarian account of the general justifying aim. Two factors often move us at once, one a notion of desert which suggests that people who have labored to produce something ought to have at least the first claim upon it – a Lockean intuition – and the other a utilitarian intuition that productivity and general well-being ought to be encouraged. We might take the idea that the incomes and property of workers and owners should reflect the deserts of the workers and owners in question as the general justifying aim of the institution. But the desire to permeate the entire institution with desert may run into conflict with the utilitarian pressure to employ raw materials and human abilities efficiently, in order that there will be plenty to give the deserving. A capitalist economy, as its most sophisticated defenders insist, may be a very good device for generating wealth but it is not impressive in rewarding desert. The Beatles struck lucky, but were no more deserving than a thousand pop groups who sank without trace. The same goes for Henry Ford and most successful entrepreneurs; capitalism is a glorified system of gambling, and justified *as a system* by the prosperity it creates. It may be right to allow people to earn whatever the market will bear, but it cannot be because that reflects their deserts. It is a tribute to the need we feel to believe that justice and increasing general welfare are wholly compatible that so many thinkers try to tell entirely unpersuasive stories about the deservingness of the successful, and that so many others resist the idea that any attempt to give each person only what he or she deserves would reduce the general welfare quite drastically. Even Nozick and von Hayek, otherwise admirably clear about the fact that what determines success and failure in a pure market is nothing more nor less than *luck*, cannot resist observing that there will generally be some sort of equation between returns and marginal productivity, an observation with more than a hint that the successful are also the deserving (Nozick 1974: 156–8, 187–8).

We can pursue this argument in a variety of ways. I have suggested that it reveals a tension between utility and justice, or between the utilitarian justification of a practice and the utilitarian condemnation of some applications of the practice. Another way of putting the same point is to contrast the approach which appeals to a general justifying aim with an approach which works in terms of individual rights alone. Thus, the Lockean or Kantian account of property tends to push the general justifying aim into the background – or, on some readings, to eschew any such aim altogether. The only question about title is a question of pedigree; does a person's claim to ownership rest either on the initial acquisition of something unowned, or on a chain of lawful transfers with its origin in an act of initial appropriation? If it does, it is legitimate, if not, not. The utilitarian has every reason to approve of property as an institution largely embodying these considerations, but not as *ultimate* considerations; the Kantian seems on the face of it to make them ultimate. (I say "on the face of it" to take note of the fact that Kant, and perhaps Locke too, softens the argument once property rights are secured under a constitutionally legitimate government; governments may regulate property, create new forms of ownership and abolish old ones governed only by the thought that *salus populi suprema lex est* and the requirement not to violate individual rights.) But as against the enthusiast for pedigree the utilitarian will think inquiries into pedigree should be pursued for no more than a few generations; to inquire what might have happened to a piece of land if it had not been unlawfully acquired in 1500 will look like a waste of time. The idea that there *must* be a rightful owner to be found will strike him as silly (Paton 1972: 501ff.).

The argument is familiar enough; its ramifications are variations on the theme of utilitarianism's difficulties in explaining and justifying individual rights, and the difficulties of "absolute" right-based theories in the face of utilitarian considerations with powerful attractions of their own. Less familiar, though not wholly unrelated, is the second moral tension, the conflict between defenses of property as an ally of liberty and attacks upon it as a form of oppression. The connection is that one defense of ownership starts from the fact that all individual acquisition limits the freedom of everyone else to deal with what is acquired. Until this patch of ground became yours, I could walk on it, plant crops in it, dig for coal in it, or whatever; now I cannot. My freedom is reduced. For Sidgwick, the justification of this reduction of liberty had to be utilitarian, that I gain such an increase in welfare from the institution of property that my loss of freedom is neither here nor there. But, it does not take much wit to see that someone who set particular store by *freedom* might refuse to accept the answer (Sidgwick 1891: 142–68).

Quite what follows if we abandon utility for liberty is difficult to say. One route would be to consider what system of property rights maximized individual liberty – a question which masks a large number of desperately difficult and contentious issues. Another might be to rebut Sidgwick's opening assumption. Locke, followed by Nozick, disarms the thought that our freedom is restricted when an unowned object is acquired; we are no less free if we cannot pick *that* apple, so long as there are plenty of others to pick; it is an argument which works neatly enough for goods which are either abundant naturally or readily increased by effort – but which has devastating consequences for land ownership. Even in Holland, it is highly implausible to tell someone that he can readily find more land or produce it himself. But, the thought that the "haves" have restricted the freedom of the "have nots" is perhaps the most powerful objection to private property in the radical lexicon. It gains in strength from further considerations of a political, sociological, and moral kind. For instance, as we have seen already, there is a well-founded tradition of supposing that those who acquire great quantities of property will try to deprive their fellows of their political liberty too. There is, in addition, an economic argument to the effect that in a competitive society, those without property have less freedom than those with property, simply in the sense that they have fewer eligible choices available to them – to work at the nearest, badly paid job or starve is the limit of their choices (Nozick 1974: 262ff.).

These arguments are, on my analysis, moral arguments about the justifiability of the institution of private property. Like all such arguments, criticism and defense gains in power if we feel that there are (or certainly are not) acceptable alternatives to the existence of private property. Since I shall end this essay with a brief account of two interpretations of Marx's aspirations for socialism, I will leave this topic in this unfinished condition. One last point which I ought to make about these arguments, however, is that there is a sense in which they rely on a somewhat different conception of property from that relied on by the "political" arguments discussed before. The arguments over property which I described as "political" were not concerned, save indirectly, with such questions as the extent of the rights over things which property rights gave, nor with the question whether collective property was property in the same sense as private property and so on. Rather, the political interest lay in whether individual wealth must cause its owner to prefer private interests to the public interest, whether wealth subverted the martial spirit, whether land was a more steady basis for politics than was mobile property. By contrast, the moral interest in property is primarily an interest in the basis of certain sorts of rights, and only indirectly an interest in what the implications of that inquiry might be for different sorts of property. And in this context it is interesting to notice that land seems very *obviously* the least morally defensible and the most politically attractive form of property – at any rate from the fourth century BC to the nineteenth century AD.

Before turning to the two interpretations of Marx's hostility to property which will provide my last illustrations of what can be done with both the moral and the political arguments about it, I ought to say something about the analysis of property rights. I shall be brief and evasive, since my aim is to induce skepticism about the possibility of doing anything very useful in this field – or, rather, to induce some skepticism about the chances of being both very ambitious and very useful. Professor Honoré's well-known discussion of the "liberal" conception of ownership is exceedingly useful precisely because it is so carefully attached to a particular context and is not intended to provide the basis for an entire "philosophy of property rights" (Honoré 1962: 108ff.; Grey 1980: 80–6).

There are legal codes which define property; the French code begins with the observation that the right of property is the right of disposing of things in the most absolute manner allowed by the law. This has its attractions as a brisk definition, since it does not imply that, say, a man who owns something he cannot bequeath does not really own it – if the law restricts the rights of bequest, so be it, but the owner owns whatever it might be so long as he can dispose of the property in the most absolute fashion the law does allow. De Ste Croix unearthed situations in the late Roman empire where the owners of heavily taxed land were often driven to abandon it since they would have been beaten, tormented, and beggared if they had not run away from it. Nonetheless, it would be wrong to say they did not own their land even if it was a curse. All the rights over land that anyone did possess, they possessed; they were entitled to say who did and did not enter upon it, they were the targets of the usual network of rights which bound owners to their neighbors in Roman Law. They were chased for payment just because land was not unowned and these unfortunates remained its owners (de Ste Croix 1981: 497ff.).

The French definition has its attractions, too, in taking up our intuition that the law may very well restrict what we may *do* with a piece of property, without restricting our *ownership* of it; thus, to use an example familiar from Robert Nozick, it is not a restriction of my rights as an owner that the law forbids me to plunge my knife in your chest. The law forbids me to plunge anyone's knife in your chest. Nonetheless, it is fair to say that if the law placed too many restrictions on us, we should in the end become unsure whether the law recognized ownership at all. We may swallow peculiar cases if the other incidents of ownership are intact . . . but suppose the owner always had to obtain permission from a certain authority before using the property, before making contracts for its use or sale, or for getting an income from it – would we not eventually decide that there was no such thing as private property in that system?

But what of the state of affairs which according to writers such as Djilas obtains in the USSR, where industrial plant and almost all enterprises are "publicly owned" and yet can be used for the benefit of what Djilas described as a "new class"? Are we to say that the new class which – let us say – can dispose of as large a share of the surplus generated in these enterprises as can Western capitalists is really the "owner" of Soviet industry and business? We are pulled in two directions. The legal positivist in us is bound to say that the new class cannot really be said to own what they make a nice living from, since there is a legal system which assigns ownership to state corporations; should we not strictly say that the new class does not own anything, but occupies a position of power which allows it to secure financial privilege for itself (Trotsky 1964: 216ff.)?

On this occasion, the legal positivist and the essentialist may go together or part company; for the essentialist may seize on one of two different elements as "the essence" of proprietorship. If he thinks that the power of disposal is the core of property right, he too will deny that the new class owns the enterprises it exploits – though he will no doubt think that if it could be shown that, regardless of the letter of Soviet law, the people picked out by the label of "the new class" could make sure that their wishes always prevailed over those of the formal owners, he would have to reconsider. If on the other hand the essentialist thought that the essence of ownership was control, he would be more amenable to the idea that really successful usurpation of control amounted to ownership. Suppose, for the sake of the example, that members of the new class could secure that their own children occupied exactly the same favored position as they; suppose they could determine who worked in Soviet enterprises, what was produced and so endlessly on – might he not then be right to say that denying their ownership would be on a par with insisting that in feudal England only the king owned anything because everyone else notionally held property indirectly of him? It seems to me that if matters did indeed get to this condition we would, perhaps, agree that they were the owners of what they exploited. We might resist even so, for the other thing which moves us is the thought that before they can really "own" the means of production, others must regard their control as a matter of right. If someone else retained an admitted right, even if they did not attempt to recover the control thus usurped, our inclination would be to say that those with the right remained the owners.

Here then is one situation in which the temptation to seek for *the* concept of property is strong, where we are more than usually tempted to think that there is an essence to property – and that what various writers offer as "new" property rights just aren't property rights at all, though they are as one might say "functionally equivalent" to them. I think that in these situations this is the right response, but it is the case for positivism which leads me to say so, not because there is an essence of ownership in which these purported cases do not partake but in which others, equally unrecognized by law, might do. The argument against looking for an essence of ownership is as much heuristic as logical, but it is derived, to take one aspect of it, from such considerations as the futility of arguing over whether the common law before 1925 and the registration of title recognized *ownership* of land. The old doctrine of estates did not follow Roman Law in presuming that someone must be *the* owner of a given piece of land and that all claims must somehow spring from that ownership – but only in the light of highly contentious views of what the relation was between persons and things did it ever make sense to suppose that Roman Law somehow revealed the essence of that relationship in the way common law did not (Lawson 1958: 87–9).

Finally, then, to two issues which point up the moral and illustrate the sort of tactics which I think are needed when we write about the history of thinking about property. I earlier said a little about the republican tradition of thinking about property rights, and emphasized the connection between this and a specifically political conception of freedom. Stated swiftly, the connection is not with the freedom of contract admired by *laissez faire* thinkers, but with the independence of the polity from other states, and the freedom from domination by tyrants or tyrannical aristocrats and adventurers which Machiavelli thought was the great achievement of the Romans. In this tradition, the loss of military vigor and the growth of the *amor dominandi* were the things to avoid. Now, it is easy to see – rather, it has become easy to see, now that writers like Pocock and Hirschman have pointed it out to us – that this habit of thought began to look old-fashioned and primitive as the eighteenth century wore on. Other sorts of liberty became more attractive, as the costs of this republican form of freedom rose – and they rose because what had to be given up in giving up commercial society became more and more daunting (Pocock 1985: 230ff.; Hirschman 1976: 75ff.).

But, as the French Revolution shows, the appeal of old ideas about citizenship could not be brushed aside so easily. The question was whether they could be reinterpreted. One might say that Hegel's *Philosophy of Right* attempts such a reinterpretation, although in characteristically Hegelian fashion what we achieve is not a specifically *political* liberty, but a form of freedom which has aspects of citizenship about it – we are integrated, patriotic and content with our station and its duties – but which also incorporates an element of the new freedom – we may choose our own occupations, and civil society presupposes a market economy – and which transforms both the notion of property and citizenship in showing us a world in which we attain rational freedom under the law.

Now here we might say that there had been a shift in the conceptualization of property: where an old tradition had thought of it as land or money, approving the first and not the second, Hegel so to speak stretched the concept, so that it reflected both man's mastery of nature and society's integration of the individual by way of a whole network of social roles with their attendant rights and duties (Hegel 1941: 153). More dramatically yet, Marx took this reconceptualization of the problem and gave it yet another twist. He simultaneously defended the ancient conception of citizenship repudiated by Hegel *and* claimed that private property in its very nature was hostile to it. Marx's aspirations for citizenship within a true democracy went beyond social integration of the sort offered by Hegel, and went beyond the distinctively political conception of freedom aspired to by Machiavelli and (sometimes) Rousseau. Because the habit of distinguishing the moral from the political and the economic seemed to him just one more aspect of alienation, "true democracy" was not to be understood as either a political or an economic state of affairs. In a manner of speaking Marx subverts the political in the name of the economic, for he builds on the thought that our economic interactions have already given us a common existence, and that our decision-making ought to reflect this, and claims that private property breaks it up into the accidental outcome of a sort of civil war. But Marx also subverts the economic in the name of the political, because the whole point is to create a world in which the assertion of individual, private rights against the needs of the whole society will make no sense. He harks back to the ideal of the fully participant citizen, but looks forward beyond the modern economy which had seemingly rendered that ideal obsolete to a world in which it would be realized (Marx 1975: 331ff.).

But, the second issue to which we must give our attention is Marx's condition for such a world. Most commentators suppose that Marx looks forward to some system of "public ownership"; some are puzzled by the difficulty of discovering what system he envisaged, others irritated by the way he condemns his opponents for drawing up blueprints for utopia but refers himself to nothing more than whatever it is that "freely associated workers" will decide. What, to my mind, makes it more interesting and more difficult than almost anyone admits is that Marx intends to abolish the category of "property" entirely; when the ultimate stage of socialism is reached, public ownership will not be in any serious sense *ownership* at all (Marx 1975: 348, 351).

The difficulty lies in making sense of this thought. It makes sense largely in contrast to Marx's interpretation of the horrors of capitalism; and this interpretation has a peculiar metaphysical force which owes almost everything to its Hegelian background. Marx supposes that under capitalism there are two sorts of oppression at work, rather than one. Capitalists oppress workers, driving them as hard as they can to extract surplus value from them. But this is not because capitalists are individually brutal; they themselves are driven by their capital. The irrationality of a capitalist economy in which production is dictated by the accidents of market interaction is read by Marx as the blind tyranny of capital over its human subjects. The fact that capital is in any case only dead labor leads Marx to tremendous rhetorical flights in which he describes capital as a vampire, renewing its life-in-death by sucking the blood of living laborers. Why Marx sees it thus is no doubt complicated, but one evident influence is Hegel's claim that our possession of the world through a system of property rights manifests – and expedites – the human domination of mere things; according to Hegel, the world becomes humanized in the process as blank and valueless stuff acquires the stamp of human intention. Marx takes this theme and writes his own variation on it. The world records what humanity has done, but what humanity has done is create Frankenstein's monster; so far from the world submitting to human control, it has been set in motion as a blind force tyrannizing over all of us. In terms of their welfare and day-to-day control of their lives, capitalists are much freer than proletarians, but Marx's dramatic story takes the whole human species as its subject, and Marx's claim is that in creating property mankind created something which dominates all of us and turns all of us to its purposes (Marx 1975: 322).

What would a propertyless world be like? It is impossible to say. It may be that it would be our attitudes rather than our institutions which would be so strikingly different from the world we live in. Marx was a rationalist as well as a romantic; he thought that once we really knew what we wanted, the rational organization it demanded was not constraint but liberty. A society in which there was a consensus on what to do would need administrators and would need the habit of doing as they said – not because they possessed authority or the right to command, nor because they owned the means of production, but because that would be the rational way to get done what we all wanted done. Under those conditions, the exact system of rules for allocating jobs and distributing goods would not be a political issue or a moral issue or a legal issue: it would be what Marx referred to as a "practical" issue – and he thought that once social conflict was out of the way it would be obvious to us all what the best solution to practical problems were. If we reached that stage, we should collectively have achieved what Hegel declared was promoted by the institution of property – the rational mastery of the material world by human reason. To do so we should have had to abolish the market and capital's desire for profit. So, on Marx's view, the only conditions under which we succeed in taking possession of the world is when we do it as a rationally organized community, when, that is, private property, indeed property as a legal category, and ownership as a morally significant idea, have been abolished. It is in its way a deeply attractive thought – even if it is no less utopian than anything in his so-called utopian opponents. It is also, in its way, a decidedly alarming thought: for what would be left of such human traits as friendship if there was nothing we could call our own, nothing to give away out of sheer affection for the beneficiary? Not for the only time does Marx seem in danger of throwing out baby and bathwater together in an excess of metaphysical enthusiasm.

REFERENCES

Arendt, Hannah. 1953. *The Human Condition*. Chicago, IL: University of Chicago Press.

Aristotle. 1946. *Politics*, translated and edited by E. Barker. Oxford: Clarendon.

Grey, T.M. 1980. "The Disintegration of Property." In J.C. Chapman and J.W. Pennock (eds.), *Property. Nomos*, vol. XX. New York: Atherton, pp. 69–86.

Harrington, James. 1977. *The Political Works of James Harrington*, edited and introduced by J.G.A. Pocock. Cambridge: Cambridge University Press.

Hart, H.L.A. 1959–60. "Prolegomenon to a Theory of Punishment." *Proceedings of the Aristotelian Society*, new series 60: 6–26.

Hegel, G.W.F. 1941. *The Philosophy of Right*. Oxford: Clarendon.

1975. *Lectures on the Philosophy of World History: Introduction*, edited by Duncan Forbes. Cambridge: Cambridge University Press.

Hirschman, A.O. 1976. *The Passions and the Interests*. Princeton, NJ: Princeton University Press.

Honoré, A.M. 1962. "Ownership." In A.G. Guest (ed.), *Oxford Essays in Jurisprudence*. Oxford: Clarendon, pp. 108–47.

Lawson, F.H. 1958. *The Law of Property*. Oxford: Clarendon.

Locke, John. 1967. *Two Treatises of Government*, edited by Peter Laslett. Cambridge: Cambridge University Press.

Machiavelli, Niccolò. 1961. *The Prince*. Harmondsworth: Penguin.
1970. *Discourses on Livy*. Harmondsworth: Penguin Books.
Macpherson, C.B. 1973. "A Political Theory of Property." In *Democratic Theory*. Oxford: Clarendon, pp. 133–40.
Marx, Karl. 1975. *Early Writings*. Harmondsworth: Penguin.
Minogue, Kenneth. 1980. "The Concept of Property and its Contemporary Significance." In J.C. Chapman and J.W. Pennock (eds.), *Property. Nomos*, vol. XX. New York: Atherton, pp. 3–27.
Nozick, Robert. 1974. *Anarchy, State and Utopia*. Oxford: Blackwell.
Paton, G.W. 1972. *Jurisprudence*. Oxford: Clarendon.
Plato. 1926. *The Laws*, translated and edited by T.R. Goold. London: Heinemann.
1941. *The Republic*, translated and edited by F.M. Cornford. Oxford: Clarendon.
Pocock, J.G.A. 1975. *The Machiavellian Moment*. Princeton, NJ: Princeton University Press.
1985. *Virtue, Commerce and History*. Cambridge: Cambridge University Press.
Rousseau, J.-J. 1912. *Social Contract and Discourses*, edited by G.D.H. Cole. London: Dent.
Ste Croix, G.E.M. de. 1981. *The Class Struggle in the Ancient Greek World*. London: Duckworth.
Sidgwick, Henry. 1891. *The Elements of Politics*. London: Macmillan.
Skinner, Quentin. 1981. *Machiavelli*. Oxford: Oxford University Press.
Thucydides. 1916. *The Peloponnesian War*. London: Dent.
Trotsky, Leon. 1964. *The Basic Writings of Trotsky*, edited by Irving Howe. London: Secker and Warburg.

16

Revolution

JOHN DUNN

The imaginative setting of the concept of revolution was initially provided by the development of theoretical astronomy. But its modern political force has come principally from the massive historical impact of two great political convulsions, the French Revolution of 1789–94 and the second Russian Revolution of 1917, the October Revolution, which founded the modern Soviet state.

The tension between the distanced and plainly supra-human necessitarian frame of its initial meaning and the vividly agonistic political turmoil of its most important modern instances has left the modern conception of revolution in a sorry state. Partly its present analytical debility has been a simple product of the struggle to impose intellectual order through too few ideas upon too vast and heterogeneous a range of experience. But it has also partly derived from the centrality to modern politics of dispute over the character and significance of twentieth-century revolutionary struggles. In addition to this combination of conceptual fatigue and ideological provocation, one further feature of the concept itself renders it even less stable and even more problematic than most other prominent modern categories of political understanding.[1]

In contrast with democracy or justice or equality or liberty, revolution is not in the first place a normative standard which human beings hold up against social and political reality and to which they attempt to induce the latter to conform – to mold it. Rather, revolution is itself in the first place a feature of the real historical world at particular times and places: something which, for example, occurred in France between 1789 and 1794, in Russia between 1917

[1] For the importance of this contrast see Williams (1973: 187–206); and in relation to political understanding see Dunn 1988.

and a date indeterminately much later, in China between 1911 and at least 1949. Even in the case of the concepts of practical reason it is difficult to fashion and sustain clear and rationally shared understandings of politically important and vexed values. But where a concept is standardly employed both to characterize real historical episodes and to express demanding political values there cannot, even in principle, be any decisive intellectual strategy for making and keeping it analytically clear; and there are in addition bound to be overwhelming practical pressures to render those who use it more than a little confused about what they are saying. Modern politics is indeed more than a little confusing, not to say spiritually somewhat dismaying. The concept of revolution epitomizes both its cognitive opacity and its limited human charms. But, since revolution is defined in the first instance by real historical happenings, it also serves handily to remind us that politics is here to stay for just as long as we are. (For most of its past the human species on the whole lived extremely local and culturally segregated lives. But from now on it will pull through as a species – or go under together.)

Modern conceptions of revolution assemble precariously together a variety of distinct ideas: the destruction of old and putatively obsolete political, social, and economic orders; the purposeful political creation of new political, social, and economic orders which are proclaimed by their architects to be decisively superior to their predecessors; a view of modern world history which renders the collapse of the old regimes and the emergence of the new regimes evidently desirable, causally unsurprising and perhaps even causally ineluctable; the existential value and causal importance of human lives lived in the endeavor to speed the collapse of the old and the reconstruction of the new. Except to impressionable readers of Hegel not all these elements are plausibly compatible with one another and every single one of them is open to (and encounters) the most vigorous dispute. No understanding of the historical development of the concept of revolution will (or should) resolve such disputes. What it may do is to help to explain why these elements are now assembled precariously together under the umbrella of a single vaguely specified but highly emotive concept.

It is helpful to begin by asking why the concept of revolution has no clear ancient antecedent, why in a sense it emerges suddenly and fully formed with the collapse of the French *ancien régime*. Before 1789 there was no word in any world language which carries the meaning of the modern word "revolutionary" (the intentional agent of revolution);[2] and the word "revolution" (which figures in a variety of European languages) was in no sense an important instrument of political understanding (Hatto 1949). Yet many of the elements which go to make up the modern conception of revolution were clearly present independently in the political thinking of the ancient world. Major ancient political thinkers, notably Plato and Aristotle, reflected at length on the stability of forms of regime and on the conditions which caused one form of regime to mutate into another. The hectic politics of the Greek polis centered for at least two centuries on the often violent conflict between domestic social groups and the contrasting regime forms (democracy, oligarchy, tyranny) which these favored. Both ideologically and practically the political fate of any one polis was linked intimately with those of many others.[3] With the transition of Greek political theory to Rome (in the person of the hostage Polybius),[4] the intellectual residue of this experience was transposed (in an admittedly not enormously impressive form) into the most influential framework for understanding the triumphant course of Roman military conquest and the more ambiguous trajectory of Rome's domestic politics. It was Polybius's explanation of Rome's majestic recovery from the disaster of Cannae to dominate the Mediterranean world and destroy its rival Carthage, transmitted through the Augustan historian Livy to the Florentine Niccolò Machiavelli, which furnished the most ambitious theory for interpreting the trajectory of modern state

[2] Condorcet (1847, vol. XII: 616–24, at pp. 616–17), "Sur le sens du mot 'révolutionnaire' " (*Journal d'instruction sociale*, June 1, 1793):

> De révolution, nous avons fait révolutionnaire; et ce mot, dans sons sens général, exprime tout ce qui appartient à une révolution.
>
> Mais on l'a créé pour la nôtre, pour celle qui, d'un des États soumis depuis plus longtemps au despotisme, a fait, en peu d'années, la seule république où la liberté ait jamais eu pour base une entière égalité des droits. Ainsi, le mot révolutionnaire ne s'applique qu'aux révolutions qui ont la liberté pour objet.
>
> On dit qu'un homme est révolutionnaire, c'est-à-dire, qu'il est attaché aux principes de la révolution, qu'il agit pour elle, qu'il est disposé à se sacrifier pour la soutenir.
>
> Un esprit révolutionnaire est un esprit propre à produire, à diriger une révolution faite en faveur de la liberté.

[3] Compare the discussions in Plato's *Republic*, Aristotle's *Politics* and Thucydides' *History of the Peloponnesian War* with Finley (1983) and de Ste Croix (1981).

[4] Polybius, *The Histories*, 6. 2–9 (1954, vol. III: 270–89, at p. 288): *politeion anakuklosis*. And see Von Fritz (1954); Walbank (1972, chaps. 1 and 5); Momigliano (1975, chap. 2).

forms in the century and a half that preceded the French Revolution.[5]

The missing element in the ancient understandings of politics which precluded the appearance of the modern conception of revolution was a secular understanding of the history of the world as a single frame of human meaning with a determinate direction of internal development. (This absence, plainly, was not necessarily a deficiency in ancient understandings of politics.) There is good reason to attribute the impact of a linear and unitary conception of world history upon the modern imagination largely to the theoretical structure of the Christian religion and to its extension to virtually the entire population of Europe over many centuries. But although linear Christian conceptions of history did enter powerfully into the making and interpretation of history in major political crises over at least a millennium,[6] it has been a firmly secular descendant of this frame of understanding which features in the modern conception of revolution. And this secular form itself registered not only a complicated array of domestic changes in social and economic relations and in their ideological assessment but also a vision of the remainder of the world from a continent well on the way towards dominating this. By 1789 a linear conception of history did not merely embody an imaginative perspective enforced by centuries of exposure to the idiosyncrasies of the Christian religion, it also captured one decisive and entirely objective feature of the relations between communities across the face of the globe.

Few modern analysts of politics genuinely believe it to be intellectually prudent to rest their understanding of what is occurring politically upon explicitly Christian categories. (Modern Christianity may appraise politics confidently enough; but only in its most uncouth embodiments does it still regard itself as an independent apparatus for comprehending political reality.) Yet no coherent understanding of modern politics is possible which does not put a recognition of global economic and strategic relations at its very centre. Both liberal and Marxist interpreters of modern politics share this emphasis on the overwhelming importance of the world economy and its political armature. But neither, perhaps, any longer has much idea how to disentangle the evident cogency of this viewpoint from the different frame of meaning within which the

[5] For the most expansive presentation of this movement of thought see Pocock (1972, chap. 4; 1975). The key text is Machiavelli's *Discourses on the First Ten Books of Titus Livius*.

[6] Most strikingly, perhaps, in the Great Rebellion in mid-seventeenth-century England.

historical trajectory itself first appeared unambiguously desirable.[7]

The term "revolution" derives from a medieval Latin noun (Hatto 1949; Griewank 1969). Its primary meaning is well caught by the modern English verb "to revolve." Revolution, like the celestial spheres in Ptolemaic astronomy or the earth and the planets in Copernican astronomy, goes round and round. Such a term applied with little effort to ancient conceptions of political experience. But it very obviously does not apply felicitously to major historical convulsions like the French or Russian revolutions.

Speculation about the trajectory of regime forms (sometimes, as with Polybius [1954], centered on the imagery of the revolving wheel) was prominent in the political theory of ancient Greece, as was speculation about the consequences of the conflicting interests of rich and poor, landowners and indebted peasants, and about the stability of political orders. But it was not until the seventeenth-century mechanization of the world picture and the central imaginative role of astronomy in its promotion that the term "revolution" was first applied to major political changes within a framework of any real explanatory ambition. Even then, in the contrasting idioms of thinkers such as Harrington and Locke, it had no very determinate political implication, applying as readily to the restoration of a violated order of natural or historical right[8] as it did to a shift in the social or ethnic basis of political power,[9] and usually in fact signifying little more than a minor political disturbance.

What transformed "revolution" into a central term in the interpretation and practice of modern politics was the combined intellectual and political impact of the French Revolution. Since 1789 it has always been difficult to separate clearly the choice of

[7] Viner (1972). Cf. St. Augustine, *City of God*; Adam Smith, *An Inquiry into the Nature and Causes of the Wealth of Nations*; Marx and Engels (1848).

[8] John Locke, *Two Treatises of Government* (Locke 1967), preface, p. 155: "*sufficient to establish the Throne of our Great Restorer, Our present King William*" (emphasis in original). For the context in Locke's own thinking see Dunn (1984b, chaps. 1 and 2). For the seventeenth-century application of the term see Snow (1962). There is an extensive, if somewhat undisciplined, discussion of seventeenth-century usage in Lasky (1976).

[9] James Harrington, *The Prerogative of Popular Government*, in Harrington (1771: 228):

> Property comes to have a being before empire and government two ways, either by a natural or violent revolution. Natural revolution happens from within, or by commerce, as when a government erected upon one balance, that for example of a nobility or a clergy, thro the decay of their estates comes to alter to another balance; which alteration in the root of property, leaves all to confusion, or produces a new branch of government, according to the kind or nature of the root. Violent revolution happens from without, or by arms, as when upon conquest there follows confiscation.

explanatory and analytical models for interpreting major episodes of violent political conflict within particular societies from political appraisals of their desirability.

Neither the causation of the French Revolution itself nor the reasons for its dynamic impact upon the categories of political understanding are as yet at all well understood. But what is clear is how drastic a rupture it did mark with the prior categories of political interpretation. In this respect it stands in sharp contrast not merely with the English Great Rebellion (first described as the English Revolution in the aftermath of the French Revolution)[10] but also with the Glorious Revolution of 1688 (a self-conscious and ideologically nervous restoration in its eventual political outcome)[11] and even the American Revolution, which appealed to the accepted theoretical premises of British constitutionalism against the practices of British colonial administration (Bailyn 1967). Even the vigorous revival of the European republican tradition (Machiavelli, Harrington, Hume, Montesquieu) in designing a federal constitutional order appropriate for the independent United States did not markedly extend the political imagination of England or Continental Europe.[12]

The classical Marxist vision of the French Revolution as the rising of a vigorously productive and proudly self-conscious bourgeoisie against a parasitic nobility tenaciously fettering the expanding forces of production has been buried irretrievably by the historical scholarship of the last few decades (Taylor 1967; Lucas 1973; Doyle 1980; Furet 1982). But a number of features of the concept of revolution that had taken shape by 1794 were plainly present in the consciousness of some in the course of the half century which preceded its outbreak. The example of the English Great Rebellion, with its devout ideologues, convulsive struggles for popular liberty and memorable climax in the judicial execution of an anointed monarch, had been considered at length by David Hume. Both the episode itself and Hume's skeptical analysis of its causes and consequences received close attention within the highest circles of the *ancien régime* state and amongst the ideologists who mourned its

[10] Guizot (1826, vol. I); and *Collection des mémoires relatifs à la révolution d'Angleterre*, 25 vols. (Paris, 1823–25). For Guizot's own political orientation see now Rosanvallon (1985, esp. pp. 16–25), 'Terminer la révolution'. For the contrasting seventeenth-century application of the term see Hatto (1949, esp. pp. 504–5); Snow (1962) (e.g. Anthony Ascham, *Of the Confusions and Revolutions of Government*).

[11] Compare Kenyon (1977) with the striking account of Locke's own more concrete hopes and purposes in Ashcraft (1986).

[12] Cf. Wood (1969) with the quality of reflection chronicled in Echeverria (1968).

passing and strove to speed its restoration (Bongie 1965, esp. pp. xv, xvi, 59n., 66, 77, 81, 123–4, 126, 159).

Some decades before the revolution there is evidence, both amongst leading royal officials and amongst dissident *philosophes*, of an acute sense of emerging political tension between an isolated and poorly articulated royal government and state structure and an increasingly confident and irritated public opinion.[13] In a few isolated cases there was even some awareness of how far such tensions might in the end lead.[14] In addition, in the sophisticated Scottish reworking of Harrington's political theory by Hume, Smith, and Millar,[15] there was available a conception of the relations between economic and political organization and a vision of the historical trajectory of Europe into which the French Revolution, as this actually occurred, could be fitted with little analytical discomfort.[16]

The revolution began, in the eyes of its protagonists, as a political project to enact the rights of man in the form of a renovated political order of full citizen equality, capable of furnishing a genuine representation of all legitimate national interests.[17] Its political dependence upon the revolutionary *journées*, the insurrectionary crowd action of the Parisian *sansculottes* (Rudé 1959; Soboul 1964 and 1974), and eventually upon the state-administered terror of the Jacobin dictatorship, was a regrettable necessity enforced upon its protagonists by the barbarous obstruction of the partisans of the old regime and by the persistent dissensions and intermittent treacheries within their own ranks. The lesson which partisans of the revolution drew from this conjunction was not that there must be a measure of inadequacy in their understanding of their own goals but, rather, that the self-protecting and self-enforcing power of enlightenment and equality could not hope to operate until the political resistance of the deeply obscurantist and inegalitarian *ancien régime* had been

[13] Baker (1981a; 1978; 1982).

[14] See particularly Baker (1981b) and the remarkable vision of Diderot in the year 1774, cited in Koselleck (1985: 19–20). Chapters 1 and 3 of Koselleck's impressive book are especially instructive on the character of the modern concept of revolution.

[15] See particularly Hont and Ignatieff (1983, chap. 1); also Meek (1976); Winch (1978).

[16] Barnave (1960, chaps. 1 and 2). There remained, however, a distinct degree of political discomfort: see the illuminating discussion in Fontana (1985, chap. 1). For the interpretations of English historians in the nineteenth century see Ben-Israel (1968).

[17] Sieyès (1963). For Sieyès's political thinking see Bastid (1970) and Pasquino (1984a and b); Paine (1915).

crushed utterly.[18] Foes of the revolution naturally drew the very different lesson that the political and social conceptions which inspired the revolutionaries were profoundly incoherent, the motives which impelled them ugly, and the odious means which they had employed a luminous token of their confusion and malignity.[19] The initial explanatory problem raised by the revolution (which was also its principal stimulus to subsequent political action) arose from its apparently unanticipated and uncoordinated political trajectory and its impressive recalcitrance to the shaping political will of its participants,[20] an impact that consorted comfortably enough with the imagery of mechanical determination associated with Newtonian physics, as it did, at least after Thermidor (1794), with an older providentialist theodicy.

The boldest practical lesson drawn from this feature of the revolution was the historical invention of the role of professional revolutionary, synthesizing assurance in the mechanical guarantee of revolution's recurrence with optimism about the opportunities

[18] Sylvain Maréchal, *Manifeste des égaux* (Buonarroti 1957, vol. II: 94–8, at p. 95): "La révolution française n'est que l'avant-courrière d'une autre révolution bien plus grande, bien plus solonnelle, et qui sera la dernière" and the judgment of Buonarroti himself several decades later (Buonarroti 1957, vol. I: 58n.): "Il ne tint, peut-être, qu'à un acte de sévérité de plus, que la cause du genre humain ne remportât en France un triomphe complet et éternel." (See also p. 57n.) Compare Karl Marx, *On the Jewish Question* (1844), in Marx and Engels (1975–82, vol. III: 156).

[19] Burke (1910); Maistre (1890, bk. 2: 148): "L'histoire n'a qu'un cri pour nous apprendre que les révolutions commencées par les hommes les plus sages, sont toujours terminées par les fous; que les auteurs en sont toujours les victimes, et que les efforts des peuples pour créer ou accroitre leur liberté, finissent presque toujours par leur donner des fers. On ne voit qu'abimes de tous côtés"; Bonald (1965).

[20] Maistre (1852, chap. 1, "Des révolutions," esp. pp. 5–8):

> Ce qu'il y a de plus frappant dans la révolution française, c'est cette force entrainante qui courbe tous les obstacles. Son tourbillon emporte comme une paille légère tout ce que la force humaine a su lui opposer: personne n'a contrarié sa marche impunément . . . On a remarqué, avec grande raison, que la révolution française mène les hommes plus que les hommes ne la mènent . . . Les scélérates même qui paraissent conduire la révolution, n'y entrent que comme de simples instruments; et dès qu'ils ont la prétention de la dominer, ils tombent ignoblement. Ceux qui ont établi la république, l'ont fait sans le vouloir, et sans savoir ce qu'ils faisaient; ils y ont été conduits par les événements: un projet antérieur n'aurait pas reussi . . . Le torrent révolutionnaire a pris successivement différentes directions; et les hommes plus marquants dans la révolution n'ont acquis l'espèce de puissance et de célébrité qui pouvait les appartenir, qu'en suivant le cours du moment: dès qu'ils ont voulu le contrarier, ou seulement s'en écarter en s'isolant, en travaillant trop pour eux, ils ont disparu de la scène . . . On ne saurait trop la répéter, ce ne sont point les hommes qui mènent la révolution, c'est la révolution qui emploie les hommes.

Burke (1910, esp. p.7): "liberty, when men act in bodies is *power*."

for personal political contribution which this recurrence might in due course offer to the vigorous, convinced, and politically alert (Rose 1978; Eisenstein 1959; Bernstein 1971; Spitzer 1957). A number of less adventurous lessons were also drawn from the intimate conjunction of violent struggle with the civilizing project of political and social demystification and democratization. In the face of these lessons less intrepid political responses to the revolution divided into three principal groupings. One, which may be helpfully described as utopian, resigned itself austerely to segregating the project of social and political enlightenment from violent competition for political power and authority, restricting itself instead to education and to exemplary social experiments on a modest scale (Locke 1980; Johnson 1974; Taylor 1983; Claeys 1983). A second, epitomized by the Whiggism of early-nineteenth-century Britain, focused determinedly on the imperative to confine political struggle within a constitutional order capable of adapting itself to the practical needs of an expanding commercial society. A third, firmly in the ascendant in Continental Europe after the final defeat of Napoleon, set itself instead to the solemn attempt to extirpate enlightenment as such.[21]

In the century following the restoration of the Bourbons the absolute monarchies which had existed in many parts of Europe in the late eighteenth century were duly modified by the creation of national representative institutions and national markets and by the extension of legal equality throughout their subject populations. Many European countries saw their reigning dynasties overthrown by popular uprisings and in some cases replaced temporarily or permanently by republican governments. These abrupt transitions were universally described as revolutions; and their recurrence helped to sustain the optimism of self-conscious professional revolutionaries from Buonarroti to Auguste Blanqui.[22] But no nineteenth-century revolution was in fact initiated or politically

[21] Jacques Mallet du Pan (1796), quoted in Hampson (1968: 260):

> There has been formed in Europe a league of fools and fanatics who, if they could, would forbid man the faculty to think or see. The sight of a book makes them shudder; because the Enlightenment has been abused they would exterminate all those they suppose enlightened . . . Persuaded that without men of intelligence there would have been no revolution, they hope to reverse it with imbeciles.

Cf. the proposal by Louis de Bonald that the Revolution should be brought to a close by a *Declaration of the Rights of God* which would nullify the *Declaration of the Rights of Man*, in Godechot (1972: 98).

[22] For other mechanisms that assisted the continuity of this tradition of sentiment and action see, in its later stages, Hutton (1981).

controlled for much of its course by self-conscious revolutionaries. None established revolutionary governments with the dynamism and international impact of the Jacobin regime; and almost all in fact terminated in the re-establishment of monarchical institutions.

By the beginning of the twentieth century in western Europe – and despite the rise of mass political parties dedicated to the eventual establishment of socialist or communist republics – the role of professional revolutionary had come to seem something of a romantic anachronism. Only within the more archaic state form and economy of Tsarist Russia was it still genuinely cogent to see the dedicated pursuit of violent political subversion as a clear precondition for civilizing and democratizing an entire society. One principal ground for this shift in political perception was the greatly increased repressive capacity of western European states, with their civil police forces and heavily armed professional soldiery. In Paris in 1830, and in Paris, Berlin, and Vienna in 1848, monarchical government had in effect collapsed almost instantaneously in the face of revolutionary *journées* unleashed by the hungry *menu peuple* of the capital cities. In the aftermath of 1848 the governments of western Europe were naturally at some pains to prevent a repetition of these indignities; and in peace-time conditions they proved themselves for over half a century well able to do so.[23] It was the cataclysm of World War I which brought the direct experience of revolution back to western Europe; and it was its political outcome in Russia which ensured that the category of revolution would remain for the imaginable future at the center of political understanding.

The role of Marxist political theory in inspiring the political leadership of the second Russian Revolution, in October 1917, and the bold explanatory ambitions of Marxism as a system of historical and social analysis, taken in conjunction, render it no longer possible to separate assessments of the character and causation of revolutions from assessments of the political merits and the intellectual coherence and validity of Marxism itself. Liberal and Marxist interpretations of the causes of the collapse of the French *ancien régime* shared an explanatory perspective which inserted

[23] Pinkney (1972); Langer (1966); Tilly (1970); and see Tilly (1975) on the development of the repressive capacities of modern states, along with Engels's Introduction of March 1895 to Marx's *The Class Struggles in France*, in Marx and Engels (1958, vol. II: 118–38, esp. p. 123): "The mode of struggle of 1848 is today obsolete in every respect"; and pp. 130–4 (esp. p. 132 on changing weaponry, scale, and mobility of modern professional armies).

political power firmly into a history of changing social and economic organization, a history which liberal thinkers and statesmen hoped had essentially reached its destination but which the followers of Karl Marx confidently expected would in due course be compelled (mechanically) to move at least one vital stage further.[24] Since the middle of the nineteenth century this fundamental disagreement in explanatory perspective has grounded the two most moralistic and ideologically dynamic understandings of modern politics. (In the course of the present century, dramatically, these two vividly inimical ideologies have come to roost in the two major world powers.)

For liberal thinkers the principal political implication of the French Revolution was the long-term inevitability and the permanent desirability of eliminating arbitrary historical privilege and domination from human social relations. What was to hold modern societies together, following this purgation, was a national and international system of free market exchange and the minimal coercive force required to guarantee the property rights of its participants. For Marxists, by contrast, a market in labor was itself a form of arbitrary domination, as well as a consequence of arbitrary historical privilege and coercion. The indispensable further stage of social evolution, accordingly, was the abolition of private property rights in the means of production and the concomitant organization of production, allocation of labor and distribution of its product on the basis of common ownership. What made this transformation not merely morally imperative but also historically imminent was the ineradicable instability and the growing internal contradictions of market economies organized on the basis of private ownership.[25] Marx himself never succeeded either in working out to his own satisfaction a full analysis of the internal contradictions of the capitalist mode of production or in linking these contradictions convincingly with the instabilities of the trade cycle. Subsequent Marxist economists cannot plausibly be said to have triumphed where he failed. But they have continued to regard the capitalist world economy with skepticism as well as animosity, cultivating a sensitivity to its indisputably erratic movements and inspecting it hopefully for signs of incipient disintegration. Thus far, despite the fearsome destructive-

[24] Marx's own interpretation in fact borrowed heavily from the liberal historians of the revolution: Bruhat (1966).

[25] Karl Marx, *The Class Struggles in France 1848 to 1850*, in Marx and Engels (1975–82, vol. X: 135): "A new revolution is possible only in consequence of a new crisis. It is, however, just as certain as this crisis."

ness of two world wars, these more extreme hopes have been disappointed.

More importantly, however, the instabilities and contradictions of market economies can now be compared in some detail with analogous features in supposedly rationally planned economies organized on the basis of common ownership.[26] Such comparisons, if conducted fairly (Ellman 1979; Pryor 1985; Nove 1983), are not necessarily overwhelmingly flattering to either camp, though each has naturally by now had considerably practice in explaining away their more embarrassing features. No form of modern economy has had marked success over long periods of time in combining such simple desiderata as full employment for its labor force, rising productivity, and increasing provision of goods keenly desired by consumers.[27] Whatever else may be true about it, socialist production has failed as yet to prove itself productively superior to capitalist production; and there is no imminent prospect of its coming to do so. Nor, as yet, has any modern state contrived to combine an entire economy organized on the basis of common ownership with a form of government even minimally responsible to the governed or a range of effectively guaranteed civil rights which remotely matches that of the major capitalist democracies. (None has in fact made the least attempt to do so.) There is, accordingly, no ground whatever for resting an analysis of the modern conception of revolution directly upon the self-understandings of the lineal political heirs of the major twentieth-century revolutions.

How, then, is it now most illuminating to envisage the concept of revolution? To answer this question it is necessary to consider carefully just what we might most urgently require the concept to assist us to understand. One perfectly defensible way of envisaging the concept is to treat it as specified by the full range of historical instances to which it has in practice been intelligibly applied by any human beings at all. This nominalist strategy of understanding has the advantage of simplicity; and, if clearly announced, it could hardly mislead anyone. But it has the massive disadvantage of trivializing the concept beyond hope of recall. Since 1789, and in part because of the impressive historical resonance of the French Revolution, the term "revolution" has been applied with increasing

[26] For the importance of this perspective see Dunn (1984a).

[27] The most impressive exception is provided by the OECD countries during the postwar boom up to 1973, and by the economy of Japan up to the present day. For the insubstantial cognitive foundations of the former see Goldthorpe (1984) and Olson (1982).

abandon to an immense variety of political episodes.[28] Some of these have involved the economic, political, and social transformation of vast societies like Russia and China. Some have involved little more than the unconstitutional exchange of personnel at the summit of existing states. Others have involved a substantial degree of social and economic change orchestrated through an essentially unchanged state apparatus, with drastic consequences for the character of the resulting state.[29] Others still have combined the threat and use of violence from outside the state with a constitutional succession to power and an equally drastic use of the power thus acquired. (The most important example of this pattern was provided by the Nazi regime.) No term used to designate such a huge miscellany of political episodes could hope to serve as an effective instrument of analysis. If revolution is left simply as a term of common speech the extreme promiscuity of its modern usage now precludes its being judged to express a single clear concept.

This would be a matter of no consequence if there were in modern political experience no distinctive and massively important phenomena which the term "revolution" is uniquely equipped to pick out and assist us to understand. But not even their most vituperative foes are reluctant to acknowledge that the communist revolutions of the twentieth century form a distinctive and a prodigiously important type of political happening. The geopolitical and ideological conflicts of the late twentieth century certainly cannot be fully understood simply by an analysis of the nature of the major revolutions of this century. But they cannot even be coherently considered without such an analysis. This fact in itself underlines the most important single consideration about the revolutions of the twentieth century. There are a number of examples in earlier European history (most importantly the Revolt of the Netherlands) in which revolutionary action led to the fission of a dynastic empire and to the establishment of an independent national political unit. But no major social upheaval within a single political unit did in fact produce directly the permanent establishment of a new state form professedly dedicated to consolidating the social purposes of the insurgents. Before the twentieth-century domestic

[28] It has also been applied to an impressive variety of other types of human transformation from the neolithic to the scientific and the industrial. These usages are in every instance posterior to the political impact of the French Revolution and despite their evident metaphorical extension of the initial political image it is the scale and decisiveness of the change in question which they principally underline.

[29] Cf. Trimberger (1978); Halliday and Molyneux (1981); and perhaps the nineteenth-century "revolutions from above" orchestrated by Bismarck and Cavour.

revolutions (revolutions occurring within a single country and directed against their own ruling groups and political orders) invariably terminated in restorations, however dramatic the intervening upheavals and however deeply the restored order was marked by these in its political culture and expectations.

What has been novel about the revolutions of the twentieth century is the proven capacity of revolutionary action not merely to overthrow for a time an *ancien* or a comparatively *parvenu* regime but also to establish a new regime capable of protecting itself effectively and more or less indefinitely. It is this trajectory from collapse to re-creation, for better or worse, which has placed the revolutions of the twentieth century at the center of modern world history. The principal purpose for which a concept of revolution is now required is to focus the character and explain the occurrence of such historical episodes. In facing this task the promiscuity and mental indolence of the term's modern application are not of much assistance.

Since it has been principally the Russian and Chinese Revolutions that have thrust this task of comprehension upon us it may be helpful to lay out the main problems in applying the concept in relation to these. In both countries an ancient (and comparatively economically backward) dynastic empire disintegrated in the early twentieth century; and in each, in due course, an effective new government was established by the military and political efforts of a communist party. In each the collapse of the old order and the establishment of the new were chronologically and politically distinct processes, separated in the Russian case by some eight months and the Chinese case, more strikingly, by almost forty years.[30] In neither case was the initial collapse of the *ancien régime* attributable to the agency of the party which was in due course to construct the new order. (In the Chinese case the party itself did not even come into existence until a full decade after the demise of the imperial state.) It is still extremely unclear how the relations between the collapse of the old and the construction of the new can best be understood. But one important question to press is whether it is in fact appropriate to consider the first and the second in precisely the same terms. It is on the answer given to this question that the basic understanding of revolution as a concept must now depend. (It is important to emphasize that this is a matter of the choice of a cognitive strategy – and perhaps of political identification.

[30] The identification of all these dates is, of course, a trifle arbitrary.

It is not a matter of extra-human necessity – constraint by the laws of logic or even the indefeasible current meaning of a word.)

Each of the two victorious political parties, despite their somewhat heretical status by the canons of international Marxism at the time when they made their decisive bid for power, now possesses a relatively firm frame for understanding the relevant revolution in its entirety. Even the most idiosyncratic of communist parties still profess belief in some interpretation of the framework of historical and political analysis initially devised by Karl Marx. This framework explains the collapse of antique structures of political, economic, and social relations by their productive feebleness in comparison with competing societies and by the political fragility in the face of domestic class forces of their existing state powers. It also explains (with rather more sleight of hand) the establishment of communist political authority in these comparatively retarded economic settings as a particularly dramatic example of the advantages of combining the most advanced understanding of world history and its political implications with the comparatively feeble political resistance afforded by an archaic economy and the state which this supports. (The politics of internal class relations and the world-historical role of the proletariat in revolutionary praxis have to be glossed with rather more circumspection.) This explanatory focus on the advantages of backwardness harks back to Marx's own early political writings, with their emphasis upon the discreditable political torpor of Germany (Marx 1844), and to the leading themes of Russian revolutionary populism in the second half of the nineteenth century (with which Marx himself also flirted for a time in his last years: Walicki 1969; Venturi 1966; Shanin 1983; Knei-Paz 1978: 585–98). In the early twentieth century this stress on the political advantages of backwardness (which in the Russian case after 1917 was essentially an involuntary retrospective accommodation to revolutionary success within a single vast country) was supplemented by Trotsky's insistence upon the "law of uneven and combined development" and the resulting political vulnerability of capitalism, considered as a worldwide system of production and exchange, at its weakest link (Löwy 1981; Althusser 1966: 206–24).

This expansive, if not very tightly coordinated, framework of understanding has the merit of inclusiveness and it does offer a helpful explanatory orientation toward the pattern and timing of the incidence of collapsing *anciens régimes* in the twentieth century.[31]

[31] For a modern (and admirably disinfected) recasting see Theda Skocpol's impressive *States and Social Revolutions* (1979) and see Dunn (1980, chap. 9 and 1985, chap. 6).

How helpful an approach it can offer towards the legitimation of communist regimes even in the longest run is a rather different question and will probably prove to turn principally (barring thermo-nuclear war) on whether or not the Marxist premise of the productive superiority of socialism is in the end vindicated (Dunn 1984a; 1985, chap. 5), a prospect over which even communist regimes at present appear increasingly diffident. But even if a reworked Marxist approach were to succeed in combining an explanation of the collapse of *anciens régimes* with a more convincing legitimation of whatever communist regimes replace these, only those of the most unblinking credulity need conclude that it offers any special assistance in explaining the political establishment of any communist regime that has thus far emerged (Dunn 1980, chap. 9; MacIntyre 1973).

The destruction of an old regime and the construction of a new social and economic order with a state power effectively capable of protecting this is certainly a sufficient condition for a revolution. On any assessment of their present political merits, accordingly, what took place in both Russia and China in this century was appropriately identified as a revolution. If the self-understanding of the political agencies of revolution were comprehensively veridical, or even if there was sufficient reason to see a socialist organization of production as plainly economically and socially superior to a capitalist organization, it would be reasonable to specify the character and seek to explain the causation of revolutions through the categories of Marx's theory of history.[32] As matters now stand, however, it is absurd to accord Marxism any automatic cognitive authority in the explanation of revolutions. And once a Marxist categorization is no longer privileged it is no longer clear how far it is reasonable to expect there to be a unitary causal explanation of revolutions at all.

Both Marx and Engels, in their explanation of the French Revolution and in their anticipation of future revolutions, were at pains to insist that revolutions are a product of profound structural contradictions within a society and not of the political machinations of professional revolutionaries, the "alchemists of revolution" with their exaggeration of the role of human will and calculation and their "police-spy" conceptions of the precipitants of revolution.[33] A

[32] For two spirited attempts to suggest how best to conceive this see Cohen (1978) and Elster (1985).

[33] Marx and Engels, "Reviews of Chenu and de la Hodde," in *Neue Rheinische Zeitung* (1850), in Marx and Engels (1975–82, vol. X: 314, 318); Hunt (1975); Maguire (1978); Draper (1977); Gilbert (1981). For Marx's hostility to "clever politicians" and to the political division of labor see Ashcraft (1984, esp. p. 664).

revolution, Engels observes, "is a pure phenomenon of nature,"[34] echoing the imagery of mechanical determination which the French Revolution had rendered imaginatively so natural. Like other pure phenomena of nature, its future occurrence could be anticipated with as much assurance as any other instance of causal determination.[35] As Wendell Phillips more recently put it: "Revolutions are not made. They come" (cited in Skocpol 1979: 17).

But while the imagery of mechanical causal determination does sometimes fit rather well the political collapse of an *ancien* (or even a *parvenu*) regime, particularly in the face of popular upheavals in city or countryside,[36] it emphatically does not fit the purposeful, strategic, and energetically concerted political agency of a modern revolutionary party in arms, even before the final collapse of the old order. (The Long March was not an avalanche.) Nor, even more clearly, does it at all fit the struggle of a revolutionary party that has once succeeded in taking state power to retain this power and to mold a new society and economy through its exercise. The political prospects for armed insurgency certainly depend upon domestic class relations and the structural strength or weakness of an incumbent state. But the decision to unleash armed insurgency, and the political and military skill with which this is conducted, all play an eminently causal role in determining which states do collapse (Dunn 1982). There is no logical or conceptual relation between the fragility of modern state forms and the competitive prowess of modern revolutionary agencies. Because there is no such necessary link between the two, there cannot be a single and coherently unified modern explanatory theory of even the most important and distinctive form of modern revolution, either in the idiom of mechanical causal determination at the level of a complete society or in the idiom of intentional strategic practice. (There of course can, should, and will be systematic inquiry into the determinants of regime vulnerability and into the destructive and constructive effectiveness of varieties of strategic practice by revolutionaries and by counter-revolutionaries. But these two distinct components must be assembled together in each instance and cannot ever be jointly derived from a single, overarching, analysis.)

[34] "A revolution is a purely natural phenomenon which is subject to physical law rather than to the rules that determine the development of society in ordinary times. Or, rather, in revolution these rules assume a more physical character, the material force of necessity makes itself more strongly felt." Engels to Marx, Feb. 13, 1851, in Marx and Engels (1975–82, vol. XXXVIII: 290). I have taken the translation of the phrase cited in the text from Hunt (1975: 280).

[35] See note 25 above.

[36] Cf., for France in 1789, Lefebvre (1932; 1957); for Russia in February 1917 and the succeeding months, Ferro (1967); for Iran, Dunn (1983).

One important conclusion of the most impressive modern study of the determinants of regime vulnerability, the major impact of inter-state military relations,[37] still further underlines the causal weight of human judgment and strategic calculation. It also calls sharply into question the essentially endogenous and intra-national conception of the nature and causation of revolutions that emerged from the French Revolution (at least as this was perceived from within France itself). Whether or not this has been true in earlier centuries,[38] in the twentieth century it is inappropriate to see the collapse of even the most decrepit and offensive of *anciens régimes*, as Marx (following its liberal historians) saw the French Revolution, simply as the internal overthrow of an increasingly anachronistic and parasitic political order by the vigorous exertions of its thriving and productive subjects. The repressive capacities of almost all modern states depend extensively upon tight and complex linkages with numerous foreign powers; and the revolutionary potency of modern insurgents and the constructive efficacy of modern revolutionary governments likewise depend elaborately upon directly comparable linkages of material aid, upon imported ideas, and upon the modification of strategic expedients pioneered elsewhere.[39] As in any other fiercely competitive political process the causal role of human learning in modern revolution is extremely hard to exaggerate (Dunn 1972 and 1982).

It is not surprising that the concept of revolution should have sagged heavily under these conflicting pressures. Nor should it appear surprising that the same pressures have blighted the intellectual cogency of those social scientific theories of revolution that aspire to the scope and generality of theories in the sciences of nature.[40] Short of a lexically dictatorial world government there is no way of hauling the concept itself back into a neat and definite form. But it is of course open to any user of the concept to establish a precise grip of their own upon the understanding that they will choose to give to it.

In so choosing there are at least two points which it is wise to bear in mind. One is that the most important of twentieth-century revolutions have gained their importance not from the undeniable drama of their commencement but from the scale of their long-term

[37] See Skocpol (1979). It should be clear that the inference drawn here from this emphasis is not one made by Skocpol herself.

[38] Cf. Skocpol's (1979) emphasis on the international elements in the causation of the French Revolution.

[39] This point is forcefully emphasized throughout Skocpol's *oeuvre*.

[40] Compare Davies (1962) and Gurr (1970) with Dunn (1972, Conclusion) and Farr (1982).

consequences. It is the durability and the institutionalized political determinacy of their outcomes which distinguishes modern revolutions so sharply from their predecessors. The key feature of these outcomes in the case of communist revolutions[41] is the union between a particular structure of government (usually under "normal" conditions a ruling revolutionary party on the Leninist model) and the reconstruction of an economy on the basis of public ownership of at least the major means of production. In thinking about revolution it is essential to distinguish sharply between the political decomposition of an existing state form (however spontaneous or externally assisted this decomposition may have been) and the political construction of a new society through a transformed structure of ownership and production. It cannot be appropriate to confine the use of the term "revolution" to instances of this second process, since by this criterion there had never been a revolution until the twentieth century.

The second point to bear in mind is that the key experience which turned the term "revolution" into a central category of modern political discourse was the unexpected collapse of an absolutist political order of some longevity in the face of the angry political energy of its subjects. By that criterion the French Revolution of 1789 has not merely had a considerable array of successors (not all of which have proved in ideological terms its more or less legitimate progeny);[42] it also had fairly clear predecessors, most notably in the English Great Rebellion.[43] The Great Rebellion no more changed the basic system of ownership and production in mid-seventeenth-century England than the French Revolution changed this in late-eighteenth-century France. But in the case of each there was a close relation between the popular insurgency and long drawn-out political struggle and the appearance of drastic doctrines of social and even economic equality.[44] Between the continuing emotional charge of these remarkably exigent ideologies and the more grubby practical consequences of twentieth-century revolutionary state-building the concept of revolution faces uneasily in two very different directions. In doing so it comes close to condensing within a single term the full instability of modern political understanding.

[41] Contrast Iran (Skocpol 1982) and perhaps Mexico (Dunn 1972, chap. 2).
[42] Cf. particularly Iran.
[43] See particularly David Wootton's incisive discussion (1983, esp. pp. 356–7) of Perez Zagorin's two-volume comparative study *Rebels and Rulers* (1982).
[44] For the Great Rebellion see particularly Hill (1972).

I am extremely grateful to the editors and to G.A. Cohen and Quentin Skinner for their helpful comments on the first draft of this essay.

REFERENCES

Althusser, Louis. 1966. *Pour Marx*. Paris: François Maspéro.

Ashcraft, Richard. 1984. "Marx and Political Theory." *Comparative Studies in Society and History* 24 (4): 637–71.

1986. *Revolutionary Politics and Locke's Two Treatises of Government*. Princeton, NJ: Princeton University Press.

Bailyn, Bernard. 1967. *The Ideological Origins of the American Revolution*. Cambridge, MA: Harvard University Press.

Baker, Keith Michael. 1978. "French Political Thought at the Accession of Louis XVI." *Journal of Modern History* 50 (2): 279–303.

1981a. "Enlightenment and Revolution in France: Old Problems, Renewed Approaches." *Journal of Modern History* 53 (2): 281–303.

1981b. "A Script for the French Revolution: The Political Consciousness of the Abbé Mably." *Eighteenth-Century Studies* 14 (3): 235–63.

1982. "On the Problem of the Ideological Origins of the French Revolution." In Dominick LaCapra and Steven L. Kaplan (eds.), *Modern European Intellectual History: Reappraisals and New Perspectives*. Ithaca, NY: Cornell University Press, pp. 197–219.

Barnave, Joseph. 1960 *Introduction à la révolution française*, edited by Fernand Rude. Paris: Armand Colin. (English translation in Emanuel Chill (ed.), *Power, Property and History*. New York: Harper and Row, 1971.)

Bastid, Paul. 1970. *Sieyès et sa pensée*. Paris: Hachette.

Ben-Israel, Hedva. 1968. *English Historians on the French Revolution*. Cambridge: Cambridge University Press.

Bernstein, Samuel. 1971. *Auguste Blanqui and the Art of Insurrection*. London: Lawrence and Wishart.

Bonald, Louis-Ambroise de. 1965. *Théorie du pouvoir politique et religieux dans la société civile*, edited by C. Capitan. Paris: Union Générale d'Editions.

Bongie, Laurence L. 1965. *David Hume: Prophet of the Counter-Revolution*. Oxford: Clarendon.

Bruhat, Jean. 1966. "La Révolution française et la formation de la pensée de Marx." *Annales Historiques de la Révolution Française* 48 (184): 125–70.

Buonarroti, Filippo-Michele. 1957. *Conspiration pour l'égalité dite de Babeuf*, 2 vols. Paris: Editions Sociales.

Burke, Edmund. 1910. *Reflections on the French Revolution*. London: Dent.

Claeys, Gregory. 1983. "Owenism, Democratic Theory and Political Radicalism: An Investigation of the Relationship between Socialism and Politics in Britain 1820–1852." Unpublished Ph.D. Dissertation, Cambridge University.

Cohen, G.A. 1978. *Karl Marx's Theory of History: a Defence*. Oxford: Clarendon.

Condorcet, M.-J.-A.-N., Marquis de. 1847. *Oeuvres*, 12 vols. Paris: Firmin Didot Frères.

Davies, James C. 1962. "Towards a Theory of Revolution." *American Sociological Review* 27 (1): 5–13.

Doyle, William. 1980. *Origins of the French Revolution*. Oxford: Oxford University Press.

Draper, Hal. 1977. *Karl Marx's Theory of Revolution: Part I: State and*

Bureaucracy, 2 vols. New York: Monthly Review Press.

Dunn, John. 1972. *Modern Revolutions: an Introduction to the Analysis of a Political Phenomenon*. Cambridge: Cambridge University Press.

1980. *Political Obligation in its Historical Context*. Cambridge: Cambridge University Press.

1982. "Understanding Revolutions." *Ethics* 92 (2): 299–315.

1983. "Country Risk: Social and Cultural Aspects." In Richard J. Herring (ed.), *Managing International Risk*. Cambridge: Cambridge University Press, pp. 139–68.

1984a. *The Politics of Socialism: An Essay in Political Theory*. Cambridge: Cambridge University Press.

1984b. *Locke*. Oxford: Oxford University Press.

1985. *Rethinking Modern Political Theory*. Cambridge: Cambridge University Press.

1988. "Responsibility without Power: States and the Incoherence of the Modern Conception of the Political Good." In Michael Banks (ed.), *The State in International Relations*. Hassocks, Sussex: Wheatsheaf Books.

Echeverria, Durand. 1968. *Mirage in the West: A History of the French Image of American Society to 1815*, 2nd edn. Princeton, NJ: Princeton University Press.

Eisenstein, Elizabeth L. 1959. *The First Professional Revolutionist: Filippo Michele Buonarroti*. Cambridge, MA: Harvard University Press.

Ellman, Michael. 1979. *Socialist Planning*. Cambridge: Cambridge University Press.

Elster, Jon. 1985. *Making Sense of Marx*. Cambridge: Cambridge University Press.

Ferro, Marc. 1967. *La révolution de 1917; la chute du tsarisme et le origines d'octobre.* Paris: Aubier.

Finley, M.I. 1983. *Politics in the Ancient World*. Cambridge: Cambridge University Press.

Fontana, Biancamaria. 1985. *Rethinking the Politics of Commercial Society: The Edinburgh Review, 1802–1832*. Cambridge: Cambridge University Press.

Furet, François, 1982. *Interpreting the French Revolution*, translated by E. Forster. Cambridge: Cambridge University Press.

Gilbert, Alan. 1981. *Marx's Politics: Communists and Citizens*. Oxford: Martin Robertson.

Godechot, Jacques. 1972. *The Counter-Revolution: Doctrine and Action: 1789–1804*, translated by S. Attanasio. London: Routledge and Kegan Paul.

Goldthorpe, John H. (ed.). 1984. *Order and Conflict in Contemporary Capitalism*. Oxford: Clarendon.

Griewank, Karl. 1969. *Der Neuzeitliche Revolutionsbegriff: Entstehung und Entwicklung*, 2nd edn. Frankfurt am Main: Europäische Verlagsanstalt.

Guizot, François. 1826. *Histoire de la révolution d'Angleterre*. Paris.

Gurr, Ted. R. 1970. *Why Men Rebel*. Princeton, NJ: Princeton University Press.

Halliday, Fred and Maxine Molyneux. 1981. *The Ethiopian Revolution*. London: New Left Books.

Hampson, Norman. 1968. *The Enlightenment*. Harmondsworth: Penguin.
Harrington, James. 1771. *The Oceana and Other Works of James Harrington*, edited by John Toland. London: Becket and Cadell.
Hatto, Arthur. 1949. " 'Revolution': an Enquiry into the Usefulness of an Historical Term." *Mind* new series, 58 (232): 495–517.
Hill, Christopher. 1972. *The World Turned Upside Down*. London: Temple Smith.
Hont, Istvan and Michael Ignatieff (eds.). 1983. *Wealth and Virtue: the Shaping of Political Economy in the Scottish Enlightenment*. Cambridge: Cambridge University Press.
Hunt, Richard N. 1975. *The Political Ideas of Marx and Engels*, vol. I. London: Macmillan.
Hutton, Patrick H. 1981. *The Cult of the Revolutionary Tradition: the Blanquists in French Politics 1864–1893*. Berkeley, CA: University of California Press.
Johnson, Christopher H. 1974. *Utopian Communism in France: Cabet and the Icarians 1839–1851*. Ithaca, NY: Cornell University Press.
Kenyon, John. 1977. *Revolution Principles: The Politics of Party, 1689–1720*. Cambridge University Press.
Knei-Paz, Baruch. 1978. *The Social and Political Thought of Leon Trotsky*. Oxford: Clarendon.
Koselleck, Reinhart. 1985. *Futures Past: On the Semantics of Historical Time*, translated by Keith Tribe. Cambridge, MA: MIT Press.
Langer, William. 1966. "The Pattern of Urban Revolution in 1848." In Evelyn M. Acomb and Marvin L. Brown Jr. (eds.), *French Society and Culture since the Old Regime*. New York: Holt, Rinehart and Winston, pp. 90–118.
Lasky, Melvin J. 1976. *Utopia and Revolution*. London. Macmillan.
Lefebvre, Georges. 1932. *La Grande Peur de 1789*. Paris: Société d'Edition d'Enseignement Supérieur.
1957. *The Coming of the French Revolution*, translated by R.R. Palmer. New York: Vintage Books.
Locke, Don. 1980. *A Fantasy of Reason: The Life and Thought of William Godwin*. London: Routledge and Kegan Paul.
Locke, John. 1967. *Two Treatises of Government*, edited by Peter Laslett, 2nd edn. Cambridge: Cambridge University Press.
Löwy, Michael. 1981. *The Politics of Combined and Uneven Development: The Theory of Permanent Revolution*. London: New Left Books.
Lucas, Colin. 1973. "Nobles, Bourgeois and the Origins of the French Revolution." *Past and Present* 60: 84–126.
MacIntyre, Alasdair. 1973. "Ideology, Social Sciences and Revolution." *Comparative Politics* 5 (3): 321–42.
Maguire, John M. 1978. *Marx's Theory of Politics*. Cambridge: Cambridge University Press.
Maistre, Joseph de. 1852 [1796]. *Considérations sur la France*. Lyons and Paris: J.B. Pélagaud.
1890. *Du Pape*. Lille: Desclée de Brouwer.

Marx, Karl. 1844. *Contribution to the Critique of Hegel's Philosophy of Law: Introduction*. In Marx and Engels 1975–82, vol. III: 175–87.

Marx, Karl and Frederick Engels. 1848. *Manifesto of the Communist Party*. In Marx and Engels 1975–82, vol. VI: 477–519.

1958. *Selected Works*, 2 vols. Moscow: Foreign Languages Publishing House.

1975–82. *Collected Works*. London: Lawrence and Wishart.

Meek, Ronald L. 1976. *Social Science and the Ignoble Savage*. Cambridge: Cambridge University Press.

Momigliano, Arnaldo. 1975. *Alien Wisdom: The Limits of Hellenization*. Cambridge University Press.

Nove, Alec. 1983. *The Economics of Feasible Socialism*. London: George Allen and Unwin.

Olson, Mancur. 1982. *The Rise and Decline of Nations*. New Haven, CT: Yale University Press.

Paine, Thomas. 1915. *The Rights of Man*. London: Dent.

Pasquino, Pasquale. 1984a. "E.J. Sieyès e la rappresentanza politica: progretto per una ricerca." *Quaderni Piacentini* 12.

1984b. "E.J. Sieyès: la 'Politique Constitutionelle' de la 'Commercial Society.'" *King's College, Cambridge Research Centre Paper*. July 1984.

Pinkney, David. H. 1972. *The French Revolution of 1830*. Princeton, NJ: Princeton Unversity Press.

Pocock, J.G.A. 1972. *Politics, Language and Time*. London: Methuen.

1975. *The Machiavellian Moment: Florentine Political Thought and the Atlantic Republican Tradition*. Princeton, NJ: Princeton University Press.

Polybius. 1954. *The Histories*, translated by W.R. Paton, Loeb Classical Library. London: Heinemann.

Pryor, Frederick L. 1985. "Growth and Fluctuations of Production in OECD and East European Countries." *World Politics* 37 (2): 204–37.

Rosanvallon, Pierre. 1985. *Le Moment Guizot*. Paris: Gallimard.

Rose, R.B. 1978. *Gracchus Babeuf: The First Revolutionary Communist*. London: Edward Arnold.

Rudé, George E. 1959. *The Crowd in the French Revolution*. Oxford: Clarendon.

Ste Croix, G.E.M. de. 1981. *The Class Struggle in the Ancient Greek World from the Archaic Age to the Arab Conquests*. London: Duckworth.

Shanin, Teodor (ed.). 1983. *Late Marx and the Russian Road: Marx and the "Peripheries of Capitalism."* London: Routledge and Kegan Paul.

Sieyès, Emmanuel Joseph. 1963. *What is the Third Estate?*, translated by M. Blondel. London: Pall Mall.

Skocpol, Theda. 1979. *States and Social Revolutions*. Cambridge: Cambridge University Press.

1982. "Rentier State and Shi'a Islam in the Iranian Revolution." *Theory and Society* 11 (3): 265–83.

Snow, Vernon F. 1962. "The Concept of Revolution in Seventeenth-century England." *The Historical Journal* 5 (2): 167–74.

Soboul, Albert. 1964. *The Parisian Sans-Culottes and the French Revolution*

1793–4, translated by G. Lewis. Oxford: Clarendon.
1974. "Some Problems of the Revolutionary State 1789–1796." *Past and Present* 65: 52–74.
Spitzer, Alan B. 1957. *The Revolutionary Theories of Louis Auguste Blanqui*. New York: Columbia University Press.
Taylor, Barbara. 1983. *Eve and the New Jerusalem*. London: Virago.
Taylor, George V. 1967. "Non-capitalist Wealth and the Origins of the French Revolution." *American Historical Review* 62 (2): 469–96.
Tilly, Charles. 1970. "The Changing Face of Collective Violence." In Melvin Richter (ed.), *Essays in Theory and History*. Cambridge, MA: Harvard University Press, pp. 139–64.
(ed.). 1975. *The Formation of Nation States in Western Europe*. Princeton, NJ: Princeton University Press.
Trimberger, Ellen Kay. 1978. *Revolution from Above: Military Bureaucrats and Development in Japan, Turkey, Egypt and Peru*. New Brunswick, NJ: Transaction Books.
Venturi, Franco. 1966. *Roots of Revolution*, translated by Francis Haskell. New York: Grosset and Dunlap.
Viner, Jacob. 1972. *The Role of Providence in the Social Order: An Essay in Intellectual History.* Philadephia, PA: American Philosophical Society.
Von Fritz, Kurt. 1954. *The Mixed Constitution in Antiquity*. New York: Columbia University Press.
Walbank, F.W. 1972. *Polybius*. Berkeley, CA: University of California Press.
Walicki, A. 1969. *The Controversy over Capitalism*. Oxford: Clarendon.
Williams, Bernard. 1973. *Problems of the Self*. Cambridge: Cambridge University Press.
Winch, Donald. 1978. *Adam Smith's Politics: an Essay in Historiographic Revision*. Cambridge: Cambridge University Press.
Wood, Gordon. 1969. *The Creation of the American Republic 1776–87*. Chapel Hill, NC: University of North Carolina Press.
Wootton, David. 1983. "Continental Rebellions and the English Revolution." *Dalhousie Review* 63: 349–57.
Zagorin, Perez. 1982. *Rebels and Rulers 1500–1600*, 2 vols. Cambridge: Cambridge University Press.

INDEX